MILLION WINGS

MILLION WINGS

The Wings of Happiness

DR. SURINDER KANSALA

PARTRIDGE

To order additional copies of this book, contact
Partridge India
000 800 10062 62
orders.india@partridgepublishing.com

www.partridgepublishing.com/india

Contents

This book is dedicated to every human being, his feelings and relationships, and related to all, i.e. grandparents to grandchildren. Everyone can read this book by his/her own will anytime or all the time.

Acknowledgements

We cordially thank all of our family members who trusted us all the time, encouraged us, and helped us at every level.

About The Book / Overview

Every best thing in the world which has happened
actually once was a philosophy to start with.

*M*illion Wings wishes that every individual should have a million
wings of happiness, to fly with a smile in the sky of life. Dear friends!
Million Wings: The Wings of Happiness is a worldwide mission of human
happiness expansion, which wants to create an atmosphere of love, peace,
and happiness all around the world. The Million Wings philosophy is
inspired from real life and will be guided forever by that life too. Million
Wings belongs to every human being on the earth, related to all ages and
phases of life. Million Wings feels that every person of the world has the
right to be happy and works on the principle of self-analysis and conceptual
expansion of life. The royal book of happiness writes everything from the
true human heart.

The book is based on the basic fundamental that human happiness lies
in human dreams and desires, and to achieve human happiness, one should
find out realistic human ways to human issues and concerns. The author
has written each and every chapter justifying his following philosophy of
human happiness. The first one is thathappiness is not only a target to touch
but it is actually a range whose one standard side is idealism and the other
side is a realistic human life and anything in between must be taken well
enough to accept them as justified norms of happiness. The second is that
happiness is actually a comfort zone of an individual that is the potential

gap between human freedom and responsibilities which can be widened maximally by raising the freedom to maximum expandable level above which only pain happens and by reducing the responsibilities to lowest level, below which life will not be possible. Million Wings philosophy of happiness works on these basic human instincts of happiness.

This book reflects a whole life and its content is related to common or uncommon day-to-day issues. You can read any topic of your interest, may it be related to personal life, family and relatives, social life, or occupational life or else like dreams and desires, freedom, hope, God, spirituality, meditation, religion, friendships, flirting, sex, love, affairs, marriage, bad habits, politics, education system, society and world laws, parents and children, etc. Million Wings respects your heart feeling, whatever it may be, and supports you morally and assists you to live life by heart so that you can enjoy life to full satisfaction. You must read the *Million Wings* book of new and forever human concepts of human happiness.

Happy you, happy world

Warning in good faith

*M*illion Wings, a royal book of happiness, is not a simple book of idealism; rather it is a royal book of realistic concepts of human happiness. Dear friends! Million Wings agrees that idealism is an utmost standard of living worldwide but we also need a realistic human system of happiness as an option. Human happiness is related to humans' concerns and issues, which must be understood and tackled in human ways only. Million Wings philosophy is a human balance of happiness and fixes a minimum level of social and personal happiness fundamentals towards every aspect of life. Million Wings is not against ideal life and does not give any suggestion to leave idealism but at the same time just suggests, supports, and motivates everyone to live by heart with their own dreams and desires. Million Wings sincerely wishes to create a maximum potential of happiness for every individual and cordially welcomes you to the world of your heartfelt philosophy of happiness.

Explore yourself, expand yourself
Millions of wings of happiness to fly with a smile in the sky of life

Feel the power of freedom
The freedom of thoughts

Happiness starts with the talk of happiness.

Mission

Million Wings is inspired and guided by our daily life. Million Wings' main motto is to make the life of every individual better by working on the thought process, to create an atmosphere of happiness, peace, and love around every human being throughout the world.

Vision

To grow Million Wings as a life-oriented guidance system at the world level, where all aspects of life should be ethically analyzed considering all and maximum possible options and guiding people to achieve the personal satisfaction in *all* aspects of life and directing humanity towards happiness.

Founder's message

Human happiness
Human concerns, human ways

 I always feel that many systems have been working and doing a lot of efforts for human happiness throughout the world but did anyone ask about the real happiness of an individual person, about his real problems, his real thoughts, his real potentials? Everyone knows that the real happinessis in living by heart but no one is actually giving the real opportunities, guidance, and help to fulfil individuals' dreams and desires.

I feel that there must be one common system in the world which should think, understand, and advise like humans do and which can be easily accepted by every human being worldwide too. A system which can also feel the change of time, understands needs, and moves with humans and guides them as well. A system which can tear down unnecessary restrictions and help in increasing freedom, decreasing responsibilities but at the same time keep binding everyone with love, care, and friendship with every passing day. A system which can understand the real feelings, dreams, and desires of humans and which can teach everyone in the world the same lesson openly, widely, and with practical human thoughts of life. A system which can motivate the world to move towards a human balance of happiness. A system which sprinkles hopes of living all around. A system which will give a million wings of happiness to fly in the sky of life and can fully enjoy life and live happily. We all want freedom, and if we have it, let's make it then very graceful.

Balanced freedom, liberty with grace

Live by heart.
Dr Surinder Kansala

Co-founders' messages

Mrs Neelam Jyoti Kansala

Dr Navneet Sidhu

The relationships might be few, but if they are filled with feelings like love, care, and understanding, they are very precious and beautiful gifts. These relationships wipe away all the worries, tension, and sorrow. If we can share our worries and tension with our near and dear ones, surely new ways of peace and happiness will be ours.

Always listen to your heart as no one knows us better than ourselves. Real happiness arises if we live by our own heart, and happiness doubles if we get change to express our feelings and have freedom to fulfil our dreams and desires.

Chapter 1

Human happiness

The real happiness is in living by heart. If we can really live by heart, only then will the real happiness arise; that means if we are happy by heart, we can live happily anywhere, and if our hearts are not happy, we cannot enjoy even the best of the world. If we are able to do whatever we want to and the way we want to, then happiness will be all around us. Although the biggest happiness comes when our sole dream comes true, most importantly our day-to-day happiness depends on satisfaction of our everyday feelings and desires. If our hearts will not be satisfied, then we can't smile or laugh. If we have a better understanding with world about what we do, then happiness will be all around us. We can smile truly only if our hearts feel satisfied and minds are clear. Till the moment questions and doubts in our minds are cleared up and satisfied, we can't be happy.

We, all the humans, have been passing through the same cycle of life and emotional feelings from the beginning. Inspite of lots of differences in race, language, religion, culture and living status throughout the world, every human has the common goal of life, that is, personal happiness. Now, the first thing which comes in mind is, from where to start to achieve every individual's happiness? When we do not know what is the happiness of the person next to us, then what to say him? Where to start?

Million Wings feels that the happiness of every individual may be different and must belong to his own specific interest. Anybody will be interested only in those things in which he himself feels happy. Million Wings concludes that happiness is a person's own dreams and desires, and persons can be happy only if they achieve their dreams and desires, whatever these may be. Any system which will work effectively to support, assist, and help them towards their own interests, will be actually a real system of happiness for them and it's true and right also.

Every individual says, 'My happiness is my dreams and desires, and I would like to join only that system which will help, understand, guide, support, and give me ways to fulfil them at the earliest in a comfortable manner.' This means an effective system must be there which has the capacity to fulfil every individual's dreams and desires. Now the question is how do we favour everyone's dreams and desires? Every individual has different dreams and desires and every individual has his own interest. Million Wings feels that there are as many dreams and desires as there are people on this earth. So it will be very difficult to ask everyone about his dreams and desires at the same time and it is also not possible that every person will able to express his happiness to others. Then how it will be possible to give happiness to all, without knowing every individual's dreams and desires? Where to start? How to start?

Million Wings analysed the whole of the human life from the beginning. Million Wings looked at the different parts of the world, their states of mind, and living standards. Million Wings considered the future life and expectations of humans too. Million Wings thoroughly considered all the dreams and desires (based on human mind and desires) of the people of the universe and reached the conclusion that there are basically two types of factors related to human happiness.

A. Factors beyond human reach
B. Human factors

The first one is the factors which are independent of humans, and the second is in humans' hands. The factors which are beyond human control and reach, cannot be managed by humans but by the superpower, the mastermind, the Creator. For these factors humans can only pray to the Almighty so that all humans may get happy circumstances in their life now and forever.

Hence, Million Wings feels that natural happiness like in-built qualities, like basic nature, congenital habits and manufacturing defects, natural hazards, etc. are not in human hands. The factors which cannot be related directly with human activities, even with the best of human knowledge and experience till the date and time of the events, or the things which cannot be explained by the best of human minds till now are considered natural or beyond humans. Once humans will find out the logic behind them, only at that point intime, would those things no longer be considered as natural hazards. Million Wings feels that till that phase, such natural happenings can be labelled as beyond human reach and can be managed with true and sincere prayer to the Almighty.

Million Wings worked for a prayer for all humans so that they can request to the superpower, the Creator in the very best way for their happiness. Any human being can pray to God anytime, anywhere, in all the situations of life, in their own language and ways. The main logic of the prayer is to convey thanks to God for the chance of moksha given through life and to request the Creator to give the best situation in life (both natural and human circumstances) and the best capacity to select the best decision out of them all the time.

Million Wings feels that the factors of human happiness which directly depend on human beings are actual human factors and can be managed by humans based on the present knowledge, experience, and predictions. Million Wings feels that personal happiness depends upon these human factors. These human factors of personal happiness are as follows:

1. **Personal concepts**
2. **Relationships**
3. **Money and status**
4. **Time freedom**
5. **Entertainment**
6. **Social system and administration**

Most of the time, individual happiness lies in one or a combination of these human factors. Every individual is already doing a lot of efforts within his full capacity, skill, and strength to achieve his happiness. Million

Wings feels that happiness can be expanded more from the point where an individual is right now. Million Wings feels that by further helping, assisting, and supporting, happiness can always be expanded further with better, more comfortable, and faster ways. Million Wings feels that by working on these very important human factors altogether, the happiness of every individual can be further expanded. After thorough analysis of human life and happiness, it is extracted that human happiness revolves around these human factors. Let's understand these basic factors of happiness one by one.

1. Personal concepts: Expansion of concepts, expansion of happiness

Million Wings feels that the most important factor of personal happiness is personal concepts of life. It must be understood that there is some definite age of physical development of the body but there is no age of dreams and desires and there is no limit of thinking but the personal thinking is surely a very, very important deciding aspect of personal happiness. Million Wings feels that personal feelings and thinking are the first most effective guidance to self decisions. If a human is clear for himself, then everything is easy, and if one is not clear for himself, then no one can do anything for him. An individual's happiness may be related with his own thinking and concepts towards life issues. Everyone has different dreams and desires and everyone is working very hard to fulfil them at the earliest. Million Wings feels that it's quite possible that the person may be entangled in his/her own thinking pattern leading to his/her pain and sorrow, and bringing him out of such a confusing thought process will fill him with joy and happiness. And this is what Million Wings concentrates on the most.

2. Relationships: Happiness is finding like-minded people

Million Wings feels that an individual's happiness may be related to his/her relationship world. An individual may be worried about his/her near and dear ones. There may be misunderstanding or misinterpretation of each other's words. There may be lack of communication and lack of self-expression at proper and adequate extent.

The whole world actually survives on relationships of belief, love, and care among people, and nobody can change this truth. Relationships are an easiness of life and no one in this world can remain happy alone for a long time. Happy relationships are the strength of life and the wonderful events of life. Happiness is relationships with harmony, whatever may be the real aim of it. Relationships may be few but when filled with understanding, love, and care are the actual source of long-lasting real happiness. Both short-term and long-term relationships which are based on any mutual benefits will give happiness as long as those in the relationship harmoniously move in the same interest. Heartfelt relationships can/may be temporary or permanent, but are actually happy moments of life. Relationships may be any type, but if minimum respect of feelings is maintained, they will always remain a joyful goodness. Million Wings feels that it is not the total number of relationships one is holding but it is the harmonious coordinated relationship which actually matters.

3. Money and status: Money is valuable

Million Wings feels that financial independence is a very important step toward personal happiness. An individual's happiness may be related with money. He/she may need money to fulfil his/her dreams and desires. Although money is not everything, it is a very important aspect of our life as it is helpful in fulfilling basic needs, resources, and dreams and desires. Million Wings feels that an individual may require money to achieve his happiness. An individual may need any amount of money to fulfil his wishes, maybe thousands to crores. He/she may need money to buy home, car, properties, education, businesses, marriages, or for charity purposes, etc. Earning money is good. More money, more betterment. There is no badness in earning a big amount of money. It's everyone's requirement. More resources of income, much better life. Million Wings feels that every individual is doing hard work to earn money as per his/her talent, skill, and the best of brains. It's good.

4. Time freedom: Time goes where the heart goes

Million Wings feels that an individual's happiness may be related with time freedom. An individual may not be getting any time to fulfil his dreams and desires. A person may have everything in life but may have lack of time. Inspite of all the resources, the person may not able to enjoy his life because of a very busy schedule and job/occupational burdens. The person may need time to spend with his/her family and friends or may need time for self interest or wishes or may need time to serve the community. Million Wings feels that most of the time an individual is busy with his occupation to earn money and the rest of the available time, he/she wants to rest and do some other urgent work and individual responsibilities. Million Wings feels that money is time and time is money. If an individual wants to earn more money, he/she has to spend more time in his work/job/occupation. And if person wants to enjoy more time, he/she has to compromise for money. It's natural that an individual either can earn more money by spending more time or can spend more time by losing money. Million Wings feels that time freedom is a must to enjoy personal resources.

Million Wings feels that both money and time can be achieved together through royalty works. If an individual has skills and qualities which can be a non-stop source of money income, and that too even without work, then it's a double advantage of enjoyment. A person can be free, and at the same time, money generation will also continue; that's a wonderful achievement called royalty income.

5. Entertainment: Happiness is what gives pleasure

Million Wings feels that entertainment is a big source of happiness in our day-to-day life. Entertainment is a chance to get together, sharing enjoyment as per personal interest, mood, and extent. If there are chances, there will be celebrations. Getting together is getting happiness. Creating occasions means creating happiness and then happiness will further create more happiness, e.g. parties, ceremonies, festivals, birthdays, anniversaries, concerts, fairs, marriages, functions, etc. Although every individual has his own taste in entertaining activities, there are some common and sure worldwide acceptable ways of entertainment to all human beings like music and dance, tourism, fun activities and games, technology. Million Wings feels that music and dance events are the beautiful sources of enjoyment and a lovely part of celebrations worldwide. Million Wings feels that tourism is a very interesting good source of entertainment which gives change and refreshment from daily routine life. Visiting new places of tourist interest gives our hearts and minds a new energy and enthusiasm. Just look at the world happily and you will start getting the feasibility of your dreams. Live your enjoyments.

6. Social system and administration: Administrative policies are the root of social happiness

Administrative structure and functional strategies surely affect individual happiness. Million Wings feels that no doubt, an individual's happiness is mainly dependent on his personal vision and concepts of life but it is important to understand that social norms and administrative policies of the state and country play a vital role in happiness at large. Individual can only fulfil his happiness if he is allowed to do so. Rules and regulations of the government must atleast fit into common sense and can be amended from time to time as per social interest of benefit. Everyone should get freedom of expression and opportunities to excel. The best civilization model is where the government and the people can regulate each other in a real-time, accountable, and coordinated manner. If you want to see every citizen smiling, create an atmosphere of happiness in the society. One must remember if the society is in pain, everyone will be affected, and if an individual is in pain, society may not be affected. Genuine policies create a happy atmosphere leading to smiling people. Make the society happy, so that everyone can be happy.

How is Million Wings helpful?

Million Wings basically concentrates on human factors of happiness which are in human hands and can be managed by humans, both individually and collectively as unity. Million Wings' thought process is based on human thinking, which can atleast provide humans some space to stand over. Anyone can adopt Million Wings thoughts and he will really feel himself as a good person. In just a few seconds, he can feel free from tensions and many restrictions. Happiness will be there where a wise, clear, and satisfied mind and heart are, free from many tensions and restrictions, making life as beautiful as one wants it to be. Million Wings gives support for human basic instincts so that every human will feel it as a system which at least understands humans very closely. Million Wings gives easy, effective, and real suggestions on every aspect of life so that every human can enjoy a real, respectable, and balanced life of his own dreams and desires. Million Wings, the wings of happiness, is a philosophy which can change real life into a beautiful inspiring happiness.

Million Wings feels that it is quite possible that an individual may be confused in particular situations of life, which can be disturbing him and stealing his happiness. An individual may be feeling that the rest of the world is responsible for his/her pain and sorrow. An individual may be trying but feels helpless to change the rest of the world for his/her happiness achievement. It may be true but must be only after getting exhaustive, thorough analysis of the situational thinking and finding the best approach to handle that. The most appropriate approach can be extracted by looking into the human's basic capacity, dreams, desires, limitations and shortcomings worldwide. It's important to understand that personal happiness is not only personal concepts of life but also knowing the rest of the world's concepts at the same time. The world means our own family members, our neighbours, our society, and our country and the rest of the people, known and unknown.

Million Wings feels that every person is right at his own place. Every person thinks and reacts as per her/his own circumstance and mental capacities and this is right also. One should always respect a person's own feelings and comfort, and those must be priorities also. Million Wings feels that most of the time, a person is right with his point of view and behaviour but sometimes it may not be absolutely true. Million Wings feels that an individual's personal concepts of a life issue are true but not necessarily complete in themselves, in spite of the possibility that the rest of the world may be having more open, wide, balanced, and practical thinking on the same issue. Sometimes, just understanding the real meaning of something may suddenly bring happiness. Sometimes just knowing more, or another point of view regarding some issue, may change sorrow to happiness. Sometimes the proper definition of some confusing matter may clear the path of happiness.

Anybody can choose his/her own topic as per priority and can read the view of Million Wings on that issue. It is quite possible that an individual may be doing many things as per his/her own thinking but the society and rest of the world may not be accepting or agree to the same. The *Million Wings* royal book will surely help you to refine your fundamentals as human supporter. The *Million Wings* royal book may act as a moral support for you. This royal book may stand by your side to fight with others and validate your actions and words. You can quote the *Million Wings* royal book of happiness in support of your point of view. The royal book may help you in a confusing situation of life where you may be thinking of what to do, what not to do.

Million Wings feels that personal concepts are personal happiness. The more the expansion of concepts, the more happiness will be around. Million Wings works on the principle of expansion of thinking, which will lead to expansion of concepts and hence expansion of individual happiness.

Million Wings feels that everyone is involved in one or another matter of life. A person may be involved in friendship, love, sex, affairs. In this world there are no clear-cut differentiations on these issues. Youth sometimes do not know the exact difference between the friendship, sex, flirting, love relationships. Million Wings feels that people are in relationships but there is a mixture of all the feelings from both the sides. Everyone remains confused about what to do, what not to do. Million Wings feels that if heart and mind will be clear on these topics from the beginning, in a very healthy and logical way, it will become very easy for them to decide better on these important aspects of romance. The royal book of happiness tries to expand concepts on these interests.

Million Wings feels that every individual is related to some profession and may not be fully satisfied or confused with working strategies, norms, regulations, and financial issues. Million Wings tries to explain the common logical ways related with occupational demands and time in an easy manner which may prove effective to resolve professional tensions and worries and bring lots of success soon.

Million Wings feels that on the questions of God, religion, moksha, spirituality, meditation, relaxation, an individual often gets stuck. Million Wings feels that with the understanding of the clear relationship throughout the whole universe, one can easily understand God. The meaning of moksha will be possible only if the ways to achieve it must be as per human capacities. Million Wings' philosophy on God and religion will try to give you an answer to your spiritual queries.

Million Wings feels that an individual may be in pain because of family concerns. Many times, a person is confused on issues related with family, relationship maintenance and may not be clear on how to react and behave with our near and dear ones.

Million Wings feels that parent–children relationshipsand generation gap are the all-time big issues of society. The questions of children's marriages, education, property shares always remain confusing and disturbing issues for families. People find themselves confused regarding love affairs, marriage relations, and divorce decisions. The *Million Wings* royal book of happiness tries its best to settle all these related issues from real hearts in an easy way so that relationships grow at a better pace.

Million Wings feels that there are many factors leading to relationship mismatch which can be settled with a great understanding of human behaviour. Million Wings feels that the main factor for relationship disharmony is the differences in the following factors: age, phases of life, mental levels, self-expression, communication, priorities and aims, experiences and beliefs, comfort zone, circumstances and situations, positions, natural limitations, basic nature and behaviours, etc.

Million Wings feels that no two individuals are equal in all aspects, hence a relationship needs better understanding of both sides and that depends upon knowing each other fully and properly. It's always true that true feelings and intention are the ultimate deciding factor for relationship stability. Many times, people try their best to save their relationships but cannot succeed only because of lack of understanding of each other's true intentions. Each one is the best mediator of his own relationship but still sometimes needs some other caring mediator to save the relationship. Million Wings feels that such genuine mediator is very difficult to find on time who can intervene and help in a friendly way to clarify misunderstandings and convey real feelings and circumstances of both sides to each other.

Million Wings feels that happiness is all about relationship coordination and cooperation between people for fulfilment of mutual interest in comfortable and harmonious ways. The *Million Wings* royal book of happiness tries to clarify many common and uncommon family issues and helps to guide you to deal with such situations in the family and relatives chapter.

The *Million Wings* royal book of happiness is just like a friendly, caring, and genuine mediator for everyone, may it be in parent–child relationship or lovers' bond or husband–wife, siblings' life, friends or relatives and colleagues or rest of the society or world.

Million Wings feels that a relationship is a source of mutual happiness, and by strengthening relationships, happiness can be expanded. The *Million Wings* royal book tries to deliver every individual's state of mind to near and dear ones in a healthy and harmonious way which helps all to understand each other more deeply and truly. The *Million Wings* royal book of happiness is a mediator of relationship building.

The caring mediator understands each and every relationship, may it be parent–child, relatives, friends, lovers, society, and the world. The mediator cares for both sides of the relationship holders and wants to join them in a good sense. The royal book is a mediator which can present individual's circumstances and situations in front of the other side of the relationship. The royal book is just like a harmonic messenger of every individual and his/her near and dear ones with whom they want to be close. The *Million Wings* royal book contains topics in detail on family, relatives, and society.

The book was written on the same issue by considering everyone's state and phase of mind. Each and every topic was written by keeping in mind the interest and comfort of all the related individuals. The *Million Wings* book helps to expand personal concepts and also conveys an individual's realistic feelings to other persons. Sometimes an individual cannot express one's feeling to his near and dear ones, or even sometimes may not be able to express these properly or fully and gets disturbed from relationship harmony. Million Wings feels that, through the royal book, he/she can deliver his feelings to his near and dear ones. An individual can give or gift the book to his/her near and dear ones and refer to a particular chapter or topic to read and understand. The royal book may help as a caring mediator of relationship bonding.

After reading particular view, there is a lovely chance that both sides of the relationship can become close to each other and start understanding each other's true feelings, capacities, and abilities. By such communication of sincere and positive feelings in a healthy and beautiful way, the relationship will start growing in a harmoniousand everlasting mood. Even if someone feels that his/her near and dear ones need some assistance to expand his mind relationship, we can refer to the *Million Wings* royal book of human happiness. The royal book will definitely prove a very effective and feasible, respectful, healthy, and good way to improve an individual, leading to happy and productive life. The *Million Wings* royal book helps in strengthening personal relationships.

Million Wings feels that every human being is now becoming intelligent and organized enough to live in a system of civilization. Every individual needs to understand the basic importance of society, administration, politics, science and technology, and entertainment concepts of human life. Million Wings tries to expand one's approach towards the various aspects of systematic collaborative strategic benefits of civilization, and then the society and world.

Million Wings feels that people are mostly confused between right and wrong things in life. Most of the time, life becomes a mess on such allegations. 'All the bad habits are bad and all the good habits are good' is a norm worldwide. It is right to some extent but not absolutely true. Million Wings feels that nothing is right or wrong. It is a matter of mutual comfort and benefits. If there is harmony in whatever we do, it is good, and if there is no harmony, it is bad. Million Wings feels that people are confused between anger and peace, truth and lie, weakness and politeness, faith and betrayal, and no one is clear on such issues. The *Million Wings* royal book feels that such issues can be solved by the human deep desires and will, and answers to such questions lie in the basic instincts and limitations of the human mind. The royal book of happiness tries to justify the actions on these issues in human ways. The *Million Wings* royal book of happiness will surely help you to extend your concepts on all issues of life and will help to expand your happiness now and forever. You must read the royal book of happiness.

Million Wings is a system which tries its best to work on conceptual thinking at world level. The *Million Wings* royal book of happiness is at the level of humans and tries to save their happiness by their point of interest. It tries its best to make everyone think worldwide and to understand the root cause of everything towards happiness. The first most important step is to balance personal, familial, and social thought processes. Million Wings' point of view is one and the same for all. The *Million Wings* royal book of happiness is not only for one continent but is the same for all parts of the world. The *Million Wings* book belongs to every human being on the earth and gives only one point of view for all the issues of life to everyone, may it be social life, family life, occupational life, or personal life so that everyone can think more openly, widely, and with a realistic approach in every aspect of life and everyone gives equal freedom to each other. One world, one philosophy of happiness is the rule so that every human being learns one and the same harmonious concept of living worldwide, which will lead to fewer contradictions and more friendship among the people around the globe, hence more happiness for one and all.

The *Million Wing* sroyal book will try to guide you to think in a more relaxed, wider, and deep-rooted logical way towards each and every important, relevant issue of life. The royal book tries to open up the lock which is fixed on your heart, will, and desires. The royal book tries to support you to expand your thinking process to the extent of realistic human happiness.

Million Wings philosophy is a natural and comfortable thinking on every aspect of life so that every individual can easily understand, adapt, implement, and execute the same. The book basically is a means to make an individual understand about the basic principle of happiness by self-analysis so that personal skills can be coordinated harmoniously and there will be better and beautiful coordination in personal behaviour skill. The book contains suggestions only after considering every issue/matter of life deeply so that persons will get clear understanding and ways in each and every aspect and can make a better decision in every common and uncommon circumstance. The *Million Wings* royal book provides that kind of plausible planned coordination to family and society where everyone can feel personal freedom and can maintain love, affection, and care too, i.e. balanced freedom, a beautiful and graceful freedom for all. Anyone (grandparents to grandchildren) can read any topic of the *Million Wings* book according to their interest and comfort. Read and understand Million Wings, the philosophy of happiness, yourself and let your near and dear ones also read. Million Wings respects your heart feelings, dreams and desires, whatever it may be, and supportsand motivates everyone to live life according to themselves so that they can enjoy life fully.

Chapter 2
Fundamentals of happiness

As happiness is a common global desire, so the whole world must have at least one major common basic global strategy of living and happiness for all. Humans have been living for thousands of years. If we see the human life cycle, it has been the same for centuries and will remain while life is sustained on this earth. Million Wings feels that humans are living the same cycle from their origin. The basic factors are always the same till now and will always be same in the future. Life is everything from birth to death, from food to sex, from good to evil, from peace to war, from romance to cheating, from violence to hurt, from friend to enemy, from man to woman, from nature to man-made world.

Million Wings feels that living life itself is the best guidance. Humans are passing through thousands of happy and sad moments. Humans have to face sometimes success and sometimes failures and learn from them. This is how life improves just by living life. The human is becoming more and more intelligent day by day and learns from everyday's mistakes and tries to not to repeat the same mistake. By learning from all that, he has reached to this extent that he is moving towards happiness and will keep on doing so.

Million Wings feels that from centuries our religions' preceptors have taught us ways towards happiness. They have given sacred utterances to enlighten the world for centuries. Our religions and preceptors have guided

15

us to live the best of the best life. If a human can follow that, then he can be always happy. Million Wings sometimes is so surprised that even having so much of knowledge, why has the world not yet found the beautiful place, heaven? Is there any deficiency which needs to be filled? Is the human not working to live the best life? Or is it that he doesn't want to do that? A human can't live a 100 per cent appropriate life, is it so? I feel that people are not bad and neither do they want to disturb/worry each other unnecessarily. Everyone wants to live happily, joyfully, and with pleasure. Everyone is doing their best, back-breaking work to live a better life. The whole world wants happiness, peace, and joy. Million Wings thinks that if it is so, then there must be some problem somewhere; because of that, a human is not happy. It may be because there is a lack of something, due to which humans are still confused and disoriented. For centuries, there have been many things which need to be worked out more. Million Wings feels that every human is still stuck in the same tension in which he was years ago and has not overcome that till now. A world may be modernized by technology, fulfilled with facilities, but if the heart is not satisfied emotionally, we can't live happily and will clearly be unhappy, sorrowful everyday and wander insearch of happiness and enlightenment.

Million Wings knows that all though there are many ways towards happiness but they are just not clear. Everyone has their own dreams and desires, so their ways are also different.

If we start thinking from a past era and compare it with today, then we get many such circumstances which are the same and create a problem in our happiness. These are those circumstances only which everyone has gone through in one or another phase of life.

Million Wings feels that personal interest matters and every person will feel relaxed and comfortable if life's rules and regulations will be the same as they need. Every individual wants the solutions of human life, according to the human ways. The book covers the worldwide mentality of people, from highly developed countries to developing countries as well. The royal book contains all the issues of life and suggests the same principle fundamental to each and every individual living in any part of world. Million Wings presents the same words, same definition, same logic, and same strategy for all. Million Wings gives a universal guidance and explanations which hold true for all the people belonging to any country, religion, caste, or race. Million Wings views are not based only on idealism but mainly as per actual human behaviours and thinking and desires. Humans want to live as per their basic nature, capacities, limitations, and desires, and that's a true and right approach too. Let's move together with Million Wings, which will help you in overcoming those situations/circumstances which seem to be fresh from centuries come and free yourself from those problems and fly in the sky of life happily.

Million Wings principles of happiness

Principle: Happiness

Happiness is a satisfied heart. That means a harmonious coordination between what the heart wills and the rest of the world. A harmonious coordination means what we want to do actually happens the way we want, whether dreams and desires may be small or large. Our dreams and desires are our goals of living and we live to fulfil those dreams and desires. Dreams and desires change according to time. When a dream arises in our heart, then our mind thinks to fulfil that. It tells us according to situation, society, and our beliefs, whatever is right, better and feasible for us. If everything is possible, maybe more easily or maybe it's more tough, then our heart and mind make a way out, and with the help of the body, they start working on plans to fulfil dreams. If our soul tells our heart that it is not right according to society, then it depends on our heart how serious it is for its dream; if the heart wants to fulfil its dream by taking some risk, then the mind starts managing its resources, tries to fulfil that thoroughly. It doesn't depend on whether our dream is right or wrong but it rather depends on the harmonious relations between our powers, i.e. heart, mind, soul, and body. Because if we ourselves want to work in one direction, then whatever we are doing is allright, nothing's wrong. We mostly get confused between wrong and right. If we are not killing anyone and not hurting anyone to the extent that he will be permanently handicapped, specially by taking the first step, then everything is all right and we should not be afraid; if the other is willing to do the same as what we want to do, then we have nothing to fear about. We are not wrong. Things may be right or wrong, but if there is mutual understanding, then nothing is wrong. Our dreams and desires need our four powers the most, as where there is a will, there is a way, and like this we reach our goal. If one dream is fulfilled, then will reach the next and the next and so on, and the ones which will arise will be fulfilled one by one.

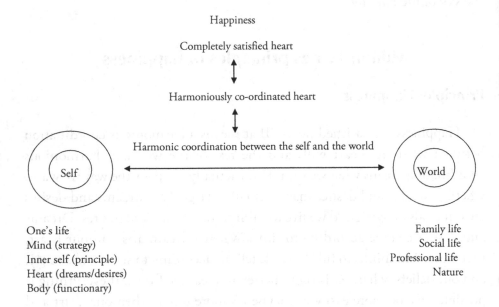

Every individual has the right to live happily and we can get real happiness only if we are satisfied in every field. We can expect probability of satisfaction, if we have freedom to express ourselves freely and have the right to live our lives according to ourselves.

Principle: Dreams and desires, our future

If we don't have some dreams and desires, then for what and why to live? Our dreams and desires are our power, our strength. Our dreams and desires are our future and to fulfil them is happiness. When our dreams are fulfilled, then we move towards our next dream and the next and so on. Million Wings feels that dreams and desires change according to time. Rather these are today's desires or tomorrow. Our dreams and desires today build tomorrow's dreams. Our daily experience gives us moments of happiness and experience too. Our dreams and desires tomorrow are built from today's dreams and desires. More the better way we fulfil today's dreams and desires, we can get more and better knowledge and experience, which will give strength to our dreams and desires tomorrow. Million Wings feels that our life is what we think of and what comes to our mind, and we live according to that. Our dreams and desires change according to time and there is nothing wrong in that. As we live, we want to be better and change done for betterment increases our happiness; every human feels happier with time and this is our ultimate aim.

Principle: Understanding humans

Million Wings feels that every system in the world is trying to make humansunderstand but none is trying to understand humans. Everyone is showing the way toward happiness, but no one is asking for one's own happiness. The dreams and happiness of everyone are not alike. Everyone has different dreams from others. When everyone has different dreams, then why are the same lessons given to everyone? Everyone needs different guidance to fulfil different kinds of dreams. The happiness of everyone is only possible if we ask, listen, and understand one's will, dreams, and desires and then motivate, give freedom and effective guidance to fulfil those dreams.

The humans have basically two cycles of life which are same from the centuries and will remain the same till the life exists. The one is cycle of living and the other is cycle of feelings. Lets see:

1. The human cycle of living

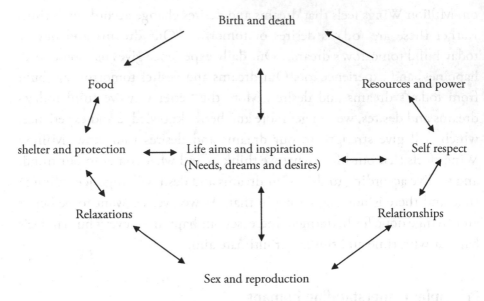

Birth and death

Food

Resources and power

shelter and protection

Life aims and inspirations
(Needs, dreams and desires)

Self respect

Relaxations

Relationships

Sex and reproduction

2. Human Cycle of feelings

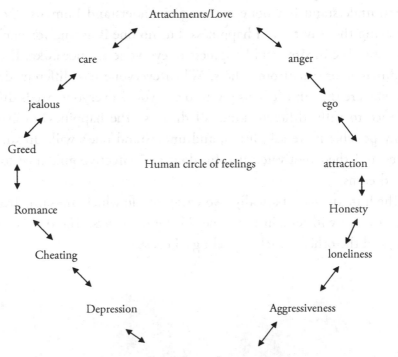

Attachments/Love

care

anger

jealous

ego

Greed

Human circle of feelings

attraction

Romance

Honesty

Cheating

loneliness

Depression

Aggressiveness

Forgiveness and **so on..**

Attachments, care, love, anger, jealous, ego, greed, attraction, romance, honesty, cheating, lonliness, depression, aggressiveness, pitty,

Principle: Everyone is right at his place

Like the cornea and fingerprints, the life circumstances and priorities of every individual are different and unique; so is every individual. Everyone has his/her own attitude/opinions/beliefs towards life which are developed and fixed day to day by the experiences of life, right from birth till the present. No one in the world has perfectly the same circumstances, even in the same family. All are in different phases and stages of life. Hence, everyone thinks and reacts differently even on the same issue. Million Wings feels that one should understand the basic instinct and natural behaviour of humans rather than trying to make them understand. Million Wings feels that the mindset of every person depends upon two factors. The first is his inbuilt basic qualities at birth and second is the circumstances of life. Both inbuilt qualities and life's circumstances are responsible for individual mental growth and fundamentals. Every individual is right at his own place and phase of life. Whatever he/she will see in life will be like that only. Personal happiness depends upon personal approach towards life situations and issues.

Principle: Measuring ultimate idealism

Million Wings feels that humans are measured according to ultimate/best life laws. Different religions have given an ideal way to our society, country and world to live life, and we make persons feel guilty if they can't follow that for any reason. A human has only one best target and that is filled with idealism. But there is no system in the world which can understand the actual problems, capabilities, troubles, and nature of a human and measure humans according to that only. Only if this will happen can happiness not just be a small dot but a great area in which every human will feel secure between the limits of human idealism. The feeling of being wrong and a culprit will vanish. By having a simple human system, there must be those rules which are minimally required and which can be fulfilled by every human easily. It will give them moral support and they will try more to move towards idealism.

Principle: Redemption

Million Wings feels that to get moksha, no one needs to sacrifice their dreams. Neither do they have to move to jungles or hills by leaving home, family, friends, relatives, society. We can get moksha with our dreams too. If we give up feelings of sex, anger, greed, affection, ego, then for what else shall we live? If we don't have any desire, then from where are we going to get motivation to live life? We need not live life as a saint or holyman or live a reclusive life. A person who will live for his dreams will live happily in this world. If he will live happily here, then he will surely get moksha too; that means to get moksha, a person has to live on earth too. Like this a person can live happily in this world and in another world too. To live happily on earth means to live with our own dreams and desires to enjoy life fully. To get moksha, we needn't live spiritually or live a reclusive life. A person can get moksha even in living like a human because God will look for one's intention rather than the work and the way by which work is done.

Principle: Maximum freedom and minimum responsibilities

Million Wings feels that it's human nature that a human wants maximum freedom so that one can do everything that one wants to do. Another part of human nature is one wants minimum responsibilities so that one should be immersed/busy in oneself. I feel that this nature of human can't be changed. The world has been changing for centuries; due to this, human nature is also changing. We have to increase the freedom to that extent above which more freedom will not be possible. That much freedom above which there will be just death and responsibilities, below which life can't be possible. Only this is the way out to increase the happiness to highest point.

Principle: Happiness is comfort/relief

Million Wings feels that what human is doing from centuries? He is changing only. But why? It's because he wants to make his life more comfortable and better and nothing is wrong or bad in that. Whatever a human feels is needed, he tries to fulfil that. He keeps on increasing comfort level and facilities for himself. The moment he gets to know about his imperfections, insufficiencies, he tries to overcome them, and like this, the world keeps on changing. The human is using whatever natural resources he requires that he got that from wherever. He again starts working to find the way out. The time while the world exists, a human keeps on working for a better tomorrow and keeps on moving forward; it's the real truth of the future. This world will keep on moving like this only in search of a better tomorrow.

Principle: Pleasing/plausible coordination

Million Wings feels that happiness doesn't depend on whether what we do is right or wrong, true or false, but depends upon our working attitude, whether it has pleasing coordination with the world or not. God judges us by our intentions and people judge us by our work and working attitude. Million Wings feels that nothing is right or wrong. It's just a comparison point of view. We have to present ourselves to our family, society, and world in such a way that they don't object to us. Whatever may be our dreams, they can't be wrong but sometimes the way to fulfil these might be wrong. Our happiness can be maintained till we have pleasing coordination with the world. Million Wings feels that in real pleasing coordination, a person will feel satisfied and fear-free. When our intentions are not to hurt or harm anyone, then it hardly matters if we are telling the truth or lying. A human should be kind first and may be true afterwards. But yes, if at any phase we realize thisand want to move towards truthfulness, then take the step as early as possible it may be difficult one but will be relaxing one too. It's right that on path of truth coordination links on its own and have no fear about that, but Million Wings thinks that whether it be true or a lie, if a right coordination will be there, then happiness will be all around.

Harmony

It is not only the question of right or wrong but it is a harmonic way of management attitude towards personal problems and situations. Million Wings feels that personal thinking may vary from narrow to wide attitude but happiness is mainly about harmony. Harmony can be achieved by the conceptional growth of personal mind. Million Wings feels that expansion of personal concepts is actually an expansion of happiness: more open, wide, and balanced concepts towards all aspects of life, easier and better harmonious happiness can be achieved in daily life.

Principle: Togetherness is happiness

History itself is witness that no one can be alone. As a human is a social animal so he always needs someone to be with him and it was true and will be true; it might be that a person may have left his family or relatives but still needs someone to live with, to share with. Someone will surely be with him, might be some friend. Maybe you and your own country or abroad. Maybe someone who is our own or maybe a stranger. But someone will be surely with us. Million Wings feels that parents and siblings are there with us since childhood so they know us in a much better way, due to which abond of love is stronger with them. The possibility is this: that they know our nature, habits, and feelings better than anyone else. That's why there is much probability of getting help and encouragement from family. This is very true to some extent; other than blood relations, a human can make other relations by his own choice. Million Wings feels that if a person has company of his choice, then relations can be filled with happiness. There is great joy in having company of same nature, habit, thinking. A person should try to find company of his own kind and not to change another for himself. It will only be possible if the person will present himself as he is, or as he wants to be. Then only that kind of person will stay with us who will be the same. The company which a person wants, he will surely get, but for this, he has to present himself the way he is.

Our feelings can't be good or bad. Everything is all right while we have good intentions and will. The persons who are living alone and away from their families and friends are going through psychological disorders, as to live alone is really embracing the condition, which may be converted to mental illness. Million Wings feels that a human always wants someone to be with him, may it be blood relation, or maybe made by heart. Million Wings feels that real happiness is in relations but that should be that relationship which is accepted by the heart.

Relationships

Relationships are joy. Humans always need friends and caretakers. Relationships are made either by birth or by heart will after birth in life. Happiness increases by the presence of our near and dear ones. It is true that any pain and sorrow or difficult situations can be easily tackled by the support of our family and friends. Our hearts need the people around us whom we like the most. Everyone is interested in a relationship as per personal attitude and nature. Million Wings feels that sooner or later, every human being needs some stable relationship in life. Relationships are required in all ages and phases of life. A relationship survives on heart wishes. Relationships grow in mutual interests. A relationship lasts longer with care. A relationship shines with respect. A relationship excels on love. Everyone needs near and dear ones around to make life easy and happy.

Principle: Who is my mediator? (intermediary)

Million Wings feels that every human should be mediator of himself as every human knows 100 per cent about himself: who he is, what he wants, what his intention is. And every human acts according to that. It is clear that we know ourselves much better than anyone else in the world. So it's natural that whatever we want, we have a say to and do that only. Million Wings feels that whatever a human does himself is his real face and nothing is wrong in it. God judges humans by their intentions, but people judge them by their work and work done. Million Wings feels that it's true that a human may be mediator of himself but still sometimes he can't.

Life itself is the greatest guide. The time we live, we keep on learning and try to improve life with each passing day. Million Wings feels that everyone wants to live according to ourselves and we try to live too. But a genuine guidance can make life better. Million Wings feels that every human has to give that guidance which he needs. Guidance doesn't mean that his direction should be changed but it means one has to give a better way in that direction only in which he is already moving. Million Wings feels that the guidance given according to age, situation, thinking, and need more practical and useful and that will work also.

For better life, guidance is important but only genuine and skilled guidance will make life beautiful. Million Wings feels that to guide one another is the best policy. As life changes according to time, likewise guidance systems should also be changed.

Principle: Manners are bilateral

Million Wings feels that if manners are bilateral, then we can get happiness; otherwise we feeldissatisfied and sorrowful. For how long does a person obey one-sided rules and manners? Even if a person can fulfil that, he can't be happy. There must be sorrow residing inside. If one person obeys rules and is mannerly and the other is just the opposite of that, not obeying rules and is mannerless, then how long can a person be good to another one? Then one day he will also respond the same as another one. Then where is the happiness? Happiness arises from some kind of behaviour from both sides. Million Wings feels that firstly our behaviour should be not mannerly when we meet someone. If the other is not behaving himself, then we can answer him in that way. It means we should talk as mannerless person on first basis and the behaviour afterwards depends on another person's behaviour here; we have to understand that only God can judge humans' intention in the right way but humans judge each other by their action and work done and he reacts on the basis of that only. At any occasion/situation, the way a human reacts, speaks will be taken as his behaviour; no one will see his intention or his feelings about the matter, nor does anyone have so much time to understand another's heart feelings.

Million Wings feels that when any matter goes out of control, the reason behind that is we have not expressed ourselves rightly though we may have expressed ourselves freely. He may not be doing his best to tell his problems, situations, intentions, behaviour, and views to related person so that there should be a good coordination between them. But still sometimes even by doing so much effort, we can't express 100 per cent in the way we want to another person not able to convey the right message. It may be a familial matter, social matter, or professional matter. Many of the times he feels that he is not able to express his 100 per cent and feels helpless at that time and the impact falls on coordination and understanding and in the end we feel sad. At this situation, we need someone who is impartial/neutral, who can judge both and tell them the conditions of one another in a neutral way. This mediator will do the best to increase and bind mutual understanding; it may be you yourself or some third person. These circumstances arise many times when we need a third person or system which has to manage misunderstanding and to create coordination and mutual understanding again so that life will be happy again, filled with happiness.

Principle: individual Change happens itself

Million Wings feels that change is only possible if a person feels himself. Change can't happen just by saying and it also can't happen just by understanding the things. The real change can happen only if a person feels that change has to happen. Whether he can feel it from his situation or from someone else's situations or life has made a person understand that. Forcefully we can change someone only for sometime, but by getting a chance, he again starts doing the same. Million Wings feels that the right time for change is when a person feels himself. Change happens when the right time comes as we have many persons in life who taught us lessons for our well-being and want to change us according to the world. Million Wings feels that we have to live according to our dreams and desires and have to change ourselves according to our dreams and desires. As our dreams and desires change and the moment we feel that change should happen, we can change anyone forcefully neither it works. As we have to remember that to live in today is biggest change. As if we live in today than we can feel and think about change and if we feel it, then change can happen automatically.

Principle: Guidance

Words, talk, and reactions may not able to make another one understand, because of which misunderstandings increase. If well-cultured and mannerly persons ensure that they didn't behave in ill-mannered way then there is no doubt that they are 100 per cent right, and if they want to be strict with the person who misbehaved, then that will be allright. If ill-cultured and ill-mannered persons are able to live easily in the world, then it is not like they are the best but it's because mannerly persons ignore then their misbehaviour and excuse them/forgive them. One-sided good behaviour can just be of great personalities only, who can remain calm against an ill-mannered person, and always remember to save ourselves. One can fight against any power, whether it be physical power, money power, link, or anything else. Million Wings feels that mannerly behaviour should be the first step, and after that, answer the way the other one is answering. Tit for tat.

Principle: Matching concepts is easiness

If an individual has optimistic concepts, he/she will feel the world as a source of happiness and if his life circumstances have given him/her painful concepts, then the world will appear like a hell. Million Wings feels that all through an individual's life means his/her personal situation and circumstance, but it is very important to understand that personal happiness is related to interaction with the rest of the world. It is totally right that an individual's concepts towards life develop by personal situations but it needs to be understood that it is not always necessary as individual concepts must always match with the rest of the world's thinking.

Principle: Happiness is satisfaction and clearance

Million Wings feels that happiness is satisfaction, happiness is a clear mind. Wherever we are, in whatever condition we may be, we can get happiness. If our heart is happy, then wherever we may stay in the world, it hardly matters and we can stay happy in any part of the world. But if we are not happy from the heart, then even in the most beautiful place on earth we can't be happy and we feel suffocated. However, the real happiness is felt when our biggest dream can be fulfilled.

But everyday happiness resides in just little things, feelings and satisfaction of small desires. Million Wings feels that wherever we are, however we are, we have to get happiness there only. We need not move to mountains or jungles for happiness. Infact, we have to find satisfactory answers to all our questions/problems there only, as happiness is a satisfied heart and clear mind.

Principle: Happiness is possible at every place and every moment

Million Wings feels that if we make every small and big decision by our heart and will, then life can be filled with joy. Study, friends, life profession, if all is according to interest and only that number of children who can be brought up easily, support of family and interests of choice, then star happiness will be all aroundand in every moment. I feel that if it seems difficult to do than what, but we have to do all that for happiness, so that it can come true. As it's the only way for a human to live happily 24/7 so that happiness level can be raised to the highest point, to increase happiness to maximum extent, we have to do work on a social level. Let everyone's thinking to reach that extent till it's really required. Million Wings philosophy is a trying for same only, i.e. from grandparents to grandchildren, one nation to international level. Let's increase the practical and balanced thinking of everyone so that everyone in reality can live by heart, with his own dreams and desires.

Principle: Nature is not responsible for unhappiness

Million Wings feels that the things which are not in human hands can't act as obstruction for a human's happiness. We can't judge a human on the basis of things like looks, colour, race, etc., which are not in our hands, so we can't blame each other for that. Every human has the right to select one another according to one's own choice but no one has the right to differentiate on the basis of common/natural or common natural differentiations. We have no right to humiliate one another. The natural things which are related to humans can never be a model for human happiness. A human can be identified on the basis of the things which are in his hands. The identity of a person can be known on the basis of his qualities and talent only.

Principle: Balanced and wide thinking opens gates of happiness

Million Wings feels that the world will appear the same as the ways we look at it and life will seemthe way we think about it. We think in the same way as our surroundings in which we were brought up and it's right too. Every person's thinking depends on atmosphere in which one is brought up and lives in. Everyone is living in a different phase and stage of life. That's why every human thinks differently on same topic and reacts according to that. Situations of everyone are not alike in the world. Even the situation of each member of the same family is different; it can't be alike. That's why everyone is different and unique.

Million Wings feels that as the world will move ahead, our thinking will keep on widening and sorrow and pain will increase for narrow thoughts. Today in the world we can see people with narrowest to widest thinking. But still there are so many controversies. Happiness is not just dependent on thinking or thinking level but also depends on whether there is good coordination or not. Million Wings feels that the wider the thought and thinking level, the happier the heart will be. To increase and widen thinking is a plausible step for society, but on the other hand, it should be balanced for social happiness. It shouldn't be like only one person is happy and another is suffering. Infact it should be like everyone is enjoying life fully.

Million Wings feels that coordination between traditional and modern thought is the right way towards happiness of both sides, i.e. society and individual. Open, wide, and practical thinking will make our lifestyle better and will release undue/unnecessary tensions and worries and doubts. We can understand the world in a better way. Million Wings philosophy reflects this open, wide, and practical thinking on each and every aspect of life so that human happiness can be increased in a fraction of a second. The more open and balanced thinking is, the happier a human will be, and life will be more beautiful. Every human should be judged on basis of open and balanced thinking, and it is the right way to decrease the disagreements. If we think according to an open, practical, and balanced way, it will deplete thousands of worries, issues, doubts which are otherwise just unnecessary. In this way we can have happy heart and clear mind. Narrow and negative thoughts should be washed away as they are the reason for sorrow and sadness.

Principle: Main goal is work proficiency

Million Wings feels that whatever we do, may it be work, thing, strategy, its main motto should be fulfilled. Minimum meaning of work or its project should be fulfilled. If we want to do something more than the desired thing, it's completely one's wish, which is really not compulsion.

Principle: Life will change, not feelings

Million Wings feels that everyone has some dreams and desires for sure. They may be any.

Nothing is right or wrong; it's just a comparison view of life. Life changes with time. Centuries ago, whatever were the thinking and surroundings, these are not same in today's era. The things which were taken as wrong years ago, today are taken as right, and slowly common and social customs and restrictions are decreasing. People are enjoying life freely.

Centuries ago, the trend was something else and now a days something else and maybe something else in future. Million Wings feels that on the basis of feelings and behaviour, we have to make such a logical, practical, and balanced trend that will last while life exits. Million Wings' thoughts for human happiness are based on human feelings, which may have a new birth with time but will always understand humans' feelings, hearts and will always guide them. As life changes, the guidance system also needs to be changed; after all, life changes for betterment only. Changes which have been happening for centuries and which are going to happen in future only aim for human happiness. Human feelings and nature are the same for centuries, but technology and comfort level are increasing. But basic nature feelings and necessities have been the same for centuries and will remain the same in future. How beautiful the world may be with technology feelings of sex, anger, greed, affection, ego are life, it's happiness and will always remain the same. Ways may change but fulfilment of feelings will be happiness.

Principle: Happiness is resources

Million Wings feels that most of the time, dreams, desires, or nature are not wrong. These just need to be fulfilled in the right way so that no one demurs. If dreams and desires will be fulfilled in such a way that no one has a problem with these and if no one will be harmed, then nothing is wrong. Any needs, dreams, or desires can't be fulfilled without resources. Our dreams and desires are not bad or wrong but sometimes the way we opted to fulfil them may be wrong. When our ways of doing work are burdens and ditching or cheating or fraud with someone, that means we are wrong. Million Wings feels that whatsoever be our dreams and desires, we need atleast some basic resources to fulfil them and those resources are good health, helping people, money, and coordination of working strategy. We can get our dreams fulfilled with the help of these resources. If our resources will last longer and hold the field, then our dreams will also last and so happiness will also last longer. The more efficiently we use resources, the more our happiness will last longer. Every human has to collect their own resources and then has to utilize them rightly according to their interest, will, and dreams and it's right also. Million Wings feels that dreams may come after primary needs but however moves along with them. We need to collect resources according to our dreams. Resources determine our dreams, will, and desires. The more the resources there are, the easier to fulfil the dreams. Million Wings feels that a good coordination between our dreams and the resources to fulfil them is real happiness.

Principle: Etiquettes- upto what extent and how long?

Million Wings feels that the human has been learning for centuries and making his life better. From behaviour to comfort, he is trying for betterment of everything. He came out from the jungle to an arranged life. Everyone is living a better life because of this arranged life. Arrangements are increasing day by day in human life. Million Wings feels that somewhere cultured life is increasing slowly, slowly to an extent where we are feeling restricted again. In today's world starting from youngest to eldest, everyone is restricting one another on the basis of cultured life. We all are teaching children in their starting years more than required cultured life; children are scolded on every little thing. We want them to learn everything faster and want that they should be perfect in starting years only and can get a maximum of bookish knowledge. We want to make them perfect and sophisticated so that they will be successful soon. Million Wings feels that it's true that cultured life is important to have a coordinated happy life but it should not be raised to a level that someone feels restricted or suffocated. Culture can be increased to that extent whereone should not feel his deficient of his dreams. Culture means a balanced coordination, not to tie yourself in restriction. In thought following mannerly/cultured behaviour everywhere, we ourselves may not enjoy life. Million Wings feels that being cultured is right till one should not feel restricted, till one should enjoy life in one's own style. Till one shouldn't feel shy in expressing oneself one shouldn't hide their qualities, where one shouldn't smile artificially. Culture is to maintain everybody's self-respect; culture shouldn't obstruct happiness but instead allow us to move ahead for happiness in a coordinated way and that will increase happiness at a social level. Culture is that which allows life to bloom, smile, move ahead. Culture is direction of life; culture is happy behavior in every direction. Culture is behavioral motivation for energetic life.

Principle: Virtue (morality)

Million Wings thinks that life has been moving ahead for centuries but how? In search of better facilities, comfort level will increase. But life is moving ahead on the basis of morality. Somewhere, somehow morality is working; because of that guidance or knowledge, safety stays and culture increases. Someone follows morality and life keeps on moving ahead generation by generation. Million Wings feels that when some social rights are made and protected, that is morality only. Someone from somewhere came out and thinks about the whole world and tries to do something for them to make them happy; that is also morality. Morality is keeping culture alive; morality is keeping everyone bound and takes them towards the future. If morality will not be, their life will stop; life and lives may become extinct if there is no morality. Million Wings feels that it's morality only which provides success to human and other creatures' natural and social level. Morality is guiding life and moving it forward. Million Wings feels that to be moral is not compulsion, or forcefully one can't follow morality; one can't help anyone forcefully. Morality arises by itself in a person and only one can carry it on if he can feel it by heart. Million Wings feels that if someone is busy with himself, that is also all right. It's not necessary that everyone will follow morality. To think about ourselves is not wrong but to have an advantage for ourselves by decimating others is wrong; it's corruption.

Preceptors have been following morality from preceptors for centuries with their own will. Every moral person tries to help others. Morality is guidance, morality is right. Million Wings feels that the dream of some persons is to be moral, the one whose dream is to serve a nation or the world and wants peace in the world. They used to do it according to their wish; it's his happiness, not a boundary. A moral person keeps on doing their work.

Principle: Common sense to specialist

Million Wings feels that management increases personal and social happiness; managing project is management. The thing to understand is this: that management is a basic principle. Million Wings feels that if we want to do anything new in life, we can do it but it should atleast fit into common sense. When we get to know about necessities/things by moving on common sense than we get specialization knowledge in that. Specialization is got by clarifying and giving attention and consideration to common knowledge. Specialization is to check every small and big aspect of a target or thing or project. Specialization can't be away from general knowledge or common sense, and this specialization work becomes management. Management in reality is managed work. Management in reality is alertness so that one can't miss the important aspect of related work and can use resources, time, and mind in a more useful and efficient way. The work and things which are already happening in the world, we already have a lot of knowledge about, so we have not to repeat that mistake. The resources we collected for a project should not be wasted; instead we should get knowledge from the related person and then move ahead in a managed way. For the work which is new or needs to done in a new way, we have to think in a new way and have to do it according to ourselves; our thoughts do whatever we want these to do. Work's success or failure itself will give the way out. Million Wings thought that for success of every work, there is remarkable time, which can be decreased with the help of experienced suggestion but can't be decreased to zero. Managed working strategy is the fastest way towards success.

Principle: Humanism to idealism

Million Wings feels that idealism is a dream; everyone wants to live maximally according to idealism. Instead, idealism is a joint effort from both sides. We can live an ideal and happy life in ideal situations only. A human feels sad at some point in life; this is because everyone is trying to teach idealism to each other and expects idealism from each other. But still idealism is the highest living standard. Every human can't behave as an ideal person, but if someone is doing so, it's respectable. To take a step towards ideal life is always welcomed. But it's not important that everyone has reached there or should reach. Million Wings feels that happiness is not just a point but a huge area whose one limit is idealism and another limit should be that which matches to human nature and capacities, i.e. human thinking (human concern, human ways).

Principle: Freedom is happiness

Million Wings feels that the real energy is a feeling of freedom to be happy. Being restricted, no one can enjoy money or comfort. Everyone, may they be human, animal, bird, whoever it may be, everyone wants freedom; it's right too. Freedom makes life natural. Freedom is success, freedom is health, freedom is encouragement. Million Wings feels that human has been fighting for centuries for freedom and it's right too. Today from children to the elderly, men to women, poor to rich, uneducated to educated, all are becoming aware and asking for their freedom and rights. And this controversy will continue like this while we can't get freedom fully. Freedom is for happiness. Freedom is to express ourselves, freedom is to have our food of choice. Freedom to like, money freedom, freedom to choose relationships, freedom to choose profession, freedom in each aspect of the future. Everyone wants more and secure freedom. But freedom should be in that way that everyone enjoys life, and not being alone and suffering from mental illness. Million Wings feels that freedom should not be only for one person but equal rights, opportunity, and operation so that everyone in society has balanced and secure freedom. The freedom should be that which gives life, freedom should be that which increases happiness. Freedom is that which is secure. Million Wings feels that every human wants balance in life but balanced freedom, not balanced restriction. Balanced freedom, beautiful freedom.

Million Wings feels that freedom starts when we start expressing ourselves. Million Wings feels that controversy of thought is not a crime, to express yourself without fearing that whether you are right, wrong, or bad. Million Wings feels that while feelings are to correct the issues, then it doesn't matter whether we are talking at high volume in anger or repeating same thing again and again. Million Wings feels that we can talk about anything with anyone in mannerly ways. To express ourselves is self-development and is a way to improve self-confidence; may it be success or failure, both express the person. If we can't express ourselves, then no one will understand us. As to understand one's feeling 100 per cent is the toughest job in the world, Million Wings feels that the most personal thing of a person is his feeling, nothing else. Million Wings feels that if we share our feelings with the related person, then it will be more useful. We need not express our feeling to everyone. When one is expressing one's feeling to another, then the person starts to collect his negative points or mistakes and starts to make him understand or makes his secrets public and makes fun of them. But one has to express himself to the related person so that there will be balanced coordination with family, relatives, friends, and colleagues, and everyone's dreams can be fulfilled. If we can't express ourselves, then who else will do this for us? Million Wings feels that the mediator who can tell our feelings to others is very rare. Only we know ourselves better, then only we can express ourselves 100 per cent rightly. The right of self expression never means to insult someone. Most of the genuine peoples donot get angery if someone contradicts them, but the situations worsens only when they start insulting each other. Anything can be expressed to anyone in a decent way.

Principle: Money is a necessity

Million Wings feels that to fulfil basic needs, dreams, and desires, we need money. We can increase our status with the help of money. Money provides us better facilities. Infact, we can't buy everything with the help of money. But money is important to improve the standard of living. Basically money is a unit for workdone, so that every person can afford equal facilities according to their work, which is everyone's right. Money is a source to get facilities inreturn for facilities. Money is the only way to make balance with facilities; hardwork means facilities, facilities mean money, money means facilities, facilities mean betterment, comfort that is dreams and desires. So earning money to fulfil dreams and desires is neither wrong nor bad. Earning money is a good thing. Earn money to the extent you like to earn. So that we can fulfil our needs and desires, Million Wings thinks that if someone wants to work hard to fulfil their dreams, then it's good and right. To have lots of high dreams is not bad and to fulfil them working hard and earning money is also not bad. To have big dreams and desires is not bad. Earning a good amount of money by hardwork is also not bad. Million Wings feels that money freedom is an imposing step towards happiness, as by this we atleast don't depend on others for money. Money freedom is an effective happiness. If everyone is capable of earning money in society, then everyone can atleast fulfil their own dreams by themselves, as the money they earn will be used for themselves only. Million Wings feels that everyone should taught the lesson of being financially independent. Financial independence can help in fulfilling our dreams and desires. Financial independence is a need of human life and a step towards the future.

Principle: Happiness has to be given by society

Million Wings feels that if it's in the hands of one person to make the world happy, then the world would be heaven by now. Then how is it possible to live happily? We can't do anything alone. We all want maximum happiness in our life but by our own way and direction. As everyone wants happiness in their own way, so everywhere there are lots of controversies in thoughts. As thinking doesn't match, controversies keep on increasing and happiness starts moving away. The minimum required coordination in thoughts is a way towards happiness, the start of happiness. Since people by and large can't understand these things till then, we can't make a happy and prosperous world. Human happiness hides in one another and comes from one another. We are dependent on each other. Farmer will provide food, army man will protect, teacher gives us knowledge, doctor provides health, entertainer entertains us, government administrates us, and people support each other. It's happiness, happiness for centuries and will keep on happening in future too. And this general coordination will keep on moving ahead; however, whatever humans do, they do for mutual benefit. Every business in the world is for mutual benefit. If one or another can do it by himself, then he will either suffer from loneliness or undergo mental illness. Every human dream is fulfilled by this world only, then how he can be happy alone, without society, without one another? Habits may be good or bad; all can be fulfilled by togetherness. That's why society is source or key for happiness; someone is society for us, and for someone, we are society so there must be an ideology in society which can provide satisfactory, comfortable, and practical atmosphere, a means to everyone for happy life so that every human can fulfil these dreams freely. There must be primary and minimum required, understanding and facilities in society so that atleast basic needs should be fulfilled, and after that, open, wide, and optimistic thinking so that every human can get the things he desires and his needs can be fulfilled and he can be happy.

Principle: Sex, anger, greed, attachment, ego are not wrong

Million Wings feels that for centuries, humans have been living with feelings like sex, anger, greed, attachment, and ego. Our preceptors, great persons have advised humans to leave these feelings. But still, why are humans not able to leave these feelings and desires? When everyone knows that humans are in pain because of these feelings only, then why are we not able to leave them? Million Wings feels that sex, anger, greed, attachment, and ego give pleasure to humans. These feelings are human happiness. These feelings are an indestructible part of life. That's why humans will live with these feelings wherever they may go in the world. These feelings and sentiments are not wrong. Million Wings thinks that these desires, feelings are made wrong only because the ways to fulfil them are wrong. If humans give up these feelings, then whatelse will be left in life? For what does man live? Million Wings feels that feelings of sex, anger, greed, attachment, ego can be made enjoyable with the right way and policy and rules. Sex can be done with anyone but with mutual understanding, and one can show anger as much one likes to, but no one should die or get permanently handicapped. Be a cupid but don't take anyone's right. Be attached to someone as much you like but don't restrict anyone. Be egoistic but in those things which you have done yourself or in those things which can decrease someone's tensions and can help others. Million Wings feels that feelings and sentiments are life, as while the human lives, these feelings will be alive. The happiness is not in sacrificing them but the happiness is fulfilling these desires in the right way.

Principle: Arranged administration is general happiness

Among all creatures/organisms, only humans are the ones who are working for centuries for better life. As happiness is betterment, happiness in life is more comfort, and the best example of betterment is arrangement and administration humans are getting. And this arrangement taught us to protect self-respect, dreams, and rights of everyone. Learning for centuries, today we have got an arranged society, a society where needs and rights are administrated, by mutual understanding. Today, administration is handling public and general administration only. Administrated administration can give better basic facilities, health, education, food, entertainment, etc. There is law and police force for human rights. Today because of good general administration, this whole world is moving in a good, positive direction. In future they should prove to be more arranged and clear and impartial. Million Wings feels that most people want to live peacefully and happily and be busy in themselves, yes, but still sometimes they fight for theirself-respect and pride and differences in their views. But still everything is managed with the help of family, friends, and administration.

Principle: Police and army are required in the world

Million Wings feels that mostly people want to hang out together and don't want to harm each other. If humans get freedom then take advantage of that and if one restricts them, then they do that by secret ways and means. Sometimes people disturb the peace of society. They are so negative-minded, stubborn that they can't understand, even by trying to make them understand again and again, and they try to fill the world with fear and terror and create unnecessary tension for everyone. These irresponsible and idiotic people can be made to understand by means of forcefulness; in the world, these kinds of people do willy-nilly physical or mental torture to others, or want to kill innocent people. These kinds of people can be surmounted by force only.

These fights can move on. But to do physical attacks or kill someone is wrong. To protect human rights and self-respect is a human need and necessity. Police force is strongly required, which can hold on to peace in the world. For defence of humans radical principle, and freedom, we strongly need a police force. People who do unnecessary willy-nilly, harms self-respect of someone, kills someone should needs to ask them hardly and teach them in solid way. Exploiting someone or killing someone was wrong years ago, now and in future too it will be wrong only. While life exists, it can't be right. Police and army are not needed to kill anyone or to harm someone but are needed for protection of radical principle and human life. Main work of police force and administration and army is to control terrorists and to maintain a peaceful atmosphere in the world. Million Wings feels that if there is no police force, then this world will again be jungle. Terrorists and killers require a police force but on getting a chance, civilized persons start losing their civilization. Million Wings feels that the highest point of civilization is that where a police force will not be required. It needs to be reduced to zero. Rape and murders can be stopped only if there is some fear in world. These negative things and behaviour should be controlled forcefully only. Million Wings feels that there should be full freedom to every human for their needs, desires, and dreams but in arranged manner, and if still someone is harassing another or murdering someone, then he should be clear that he should be killed or have even worse life than death. Million Wings feels that there should not be unnecessary restriction. There should be wide and beautiful freedom in the world but it should be balanced, which needs police and security and strict laws.

Principle: The innocent should be saved

Million Wings feels that duplicitous people can make excuses in every situation and come out of that and enjoy life. But the question is of satisfaction and happiness of those innocents and happiness which is attached to them because of one or another reason and has to stay with them. Million Wings feels that rascalsand corrupt people are taking advantage of etiquette/genuine people. They themselves get enjoyment by disturbing innocents. Million Wings feels that being clever and risky is not bad, as to move along with this world, we need to think by our own mind. It is right too. But on the otherhand, it's also important that innocents' peace of mind should not be disturbed. Innocent and corrupt people are attached to one another by one or another way, like family, relation, relatives, friends, professional relations, or neighbours. Million Wings feels that social happiness is civilization, i.e. the innocent need to praise and cheer up and guide and cooperate with cunning ones and give them a chance to understand and be refined. But still duplicitous bloody-minded people need force to correct them. Million Wings feels that take ease of primary consideration should be given to innocent people's feelings and for their peaceful life; corrupt and duplicitous people keep on finding ways for their own benefits. Corrupt people use innocent people and play with their feelings, make fake promises, aggrieve and threaten them by showing strength/power or blackmailing them. Million Wings feels that no one can be taken as innocent by their age, condition, thoughts, or lack of knowledge, and no one can be corrupt on the basis of misunderstandings, doubts. Million Wings feels that no one is right or wrong on the basis of thought differences but can compare views of both sides. But who is more accurate on basis of balanced thinking, it is difficult to say and hard to judge. Million Wings feels that the decision of who is innocent and corrupt should be made on the basis of common human ideology which is more open, wide, optimistic, and balanced.

Principle: Everyone wants personal benefit/profit, then what's wrong in it?

Million Wings feels that humans want to do everything because of their personal benefit and happiness, and it's right too. A human workshard so that he gets something in return. It's right to think, to do, to want. Why one should do that work which will not give him some benefit and not be beneficial for him? And it's right too. It's his personal will and interest and it's right too. It's not important that every person helps others at anytime without his personal benefit. Million Wings feels that personal deals and products are based on mutual benefit but a human seeks personal benefits too in many other things in life and nothing is wrong in doing so; if a person just wants his own benefit by hurting and harming others, doing work opposite to one's will, racketeering or defrauding others, then it's totally wrong. But yes, if one is getting benefit without harming another, then it's all right. If work is done by mutual understanding, will, and benefit, then it's genuine, right, correct. If someone wants to do something for their ownones or near and dear ones without any benefit or at less benefit, then they can surely do as they wish. It's all personal happiness and will; it's not important that everyone should take interest intrust, in social service, neither is it compulsion. Only those who can do social service, whose will or dream is to help others. Yes, but sometimes to help a needy person is another thing. Million Wings feels that if someone wants to do any work for personal benefit or does any work for benefit without harming others, then it's not wrong; it's clear, it's genuine.

Principle: Try to understand logical principles and rules

Every situation of life can be predicted, neither can be guessed 100 per cent rightly. Million Wings feels that no one can teach whole life. Life itself keeps on teaching/realizing new and old facts. Million Wings feels that infact every good and bad situation of life can't be predicted but still some rules and principles can be accepted so that every situation of life can be handled more carefully from the start. Million Wings' main motto is based on learning from human life experience and knowledge. On the basis of this, humans try to make some important and beneficial principles and rules in every aspect of life which can be used according to time in any condition, and with the help of that, one can get personal benefits, happiness, and satisfaction. Million Wings feels that if we can understand basic, logical principles and rules in every aspect of life, then we can make better decisions in different situations. As life changes according to time, in the same way basic logical principles and rules should also change for betterment, for happy life and right guidance.

Principle: One-sided devotion?

Million Wings feels that everyone has some personal feelings on the basis of one's interest. If one wants to be busy with some work, things feeling and he lost in that he should be lost. It's good and personal happiness too.

Someone is interested in music and another in games. Someone is interested in photography and someone in studies, someone interested in earning money and someone in family. Someone is lost in drugs and someone in sex, someone in gambling and someone in hooliganism, someone in social service and someone in politics and administration. Someone enjoys flirting and someone is lost in love. Million Wings feels that if interest becomes profession, then it's the best thing, as basic needs can also be fulfilled while enjoying interests. Profession gives money, i.e. comfort, resources, happiness. But if interests are different from one's possibility of expenditure of money and one's time is spent in fulfilling one's interest, Million Wings feels that devotion towards one's interest gives personal happiness. Every human wants to live with one's own interest, enjoy one's interest, feel happy with one's interest. Interests are those which can be enjoyed again and again; interests are those for which desire increases day by day. To have devotion for any dream and desire or interest is absolutely right, as that is every human's happiness, that is his nature. Their hobbies might be good or bad but give full pleasure to them, so they will try to arrange time and money for them and they will do these also; it's not wrong to do. Million Wings feels that human hobbies start dominating his mind and soul. These become their happiness. There is nothing wrong in doing so. If a human is collecting resources for themselves, then everything is all right. If person is fulfilling his minimum required responsibilities and is dedicated towards them, along with this he enjoys his hobbies and interests, that is also OK. But he should spend quality time with his family and friends and the rest of the time he can spend according to his interest. If he is arranging money and resources by themselves for his hobby and not misusing any other, then that is absolutely right. If one is fulfilling logical needs, requirement of his family, near and dear ones, then he has full right to fulfil his own interest and hobbies too.

Principle: Mutual understanding, happy relationship

Million Wings feels that romantic relations of humans are their natural will, interest, and hobby and to try to fulfil them is right; nothing's wrong in any romantic relations which may be everlasting permanent relations, may be physical attachment or desires, may be emotional attachment that is it, may be flirt attachment or love; everything is good. Million Wings feels that a person may choose any of the feelings, whatever he wants to choose, but he should be clear to the related person. Nothing is wrong in any feeling but we should be clear to the related person. Being duplicitous is absolutely wrong. Being duplicitous is sneakiness, corruption. A relation may be any but sneakiness is wrong. Million Wings feels that everyone has self-respect and social life that should not be hurt. A boy or girl has to make a relationship with his or her will and understanding, whatever it may be, but being duplicitous and hurting each other is totally wrong and it can't be acceptable.

Principle: Tie relations with freedom

Million Wings feels that freedom is not for one person but it's the right of everyone. If someone is enjoying their life and another is under compulsion, then it's not right. Everyone should have full freedom in life so that everyone can enjoy life. Whether it is child or parent, husband or wife, girl or boy, brother or sister, lovers, our own ones or some another, we ourselves or someone else, everyone needs respect and equal freedom. Freedom is not the right of one person, society, religion, or race but it's an equal right of all people, religions, and races; younger or elder, male or female, everyone needs freedom and the world fights on these issues and they had right to fight on these issues. But it starts from our own homes. Family doesn't oppose freedom but they worry for respect and safety of each other and don't want to hurt them. They don't want their near and dear ones in any problem. But didn't oppose freedom, Million Wings feels one who wants freedom also wants to avoid undue restrictions and boundaries but never wants to fight with family, doesn't want to be apart from them. The one who wants freedom just wants to achieve these goals and happiness, not to disturb or hurt family. We want to have freedom to do something good and to earn a name and fame in society, not to spoil the respect and status of family. Million Wings feels that freedom is in living, not in dying. The freedom which has respect, attraction, security, that is balanced freedom, which everyone wants, i.e. grandparents to grandchildren. Everyone wants to give full freedom to each other, but on the other hand, they also want that freedom should have understanding which can bind relations together, bring them close and not make a person insecure, alone, and sad. Freedom is that which can understand and give love, everyone's logical happiness.

Principle: Loved ones are here so security is here too

Million Wings feels that if loved ones are here in our life then we can think of security; otherwise a feeling of humanity only can save a nation, world, society. Everyone is doing one's best for oneself to be secure, specially parents don't oppose freedom of children but they want it in a secure way. This thinking is absolutely right. Loved ones always care for each other & give suggestions to each other for betterment and success and to do this is correct. Million Wings feels that loved ones have to give maximum freedom till secure boundaries to enjoy life and have to restrict at the point where personal loss is so much that it's difficult to recover or unable to be recovered by any source. One has to care about these feelings of loved ones and suggesting to them regarding every phase and aspect of life. One should not restrict the freedom, security, and love; these should not be reduced. Be tension free. Modern research and technology and the idea of personal freedom will keep on working while it has affection and care for near and dear ones. If every success and research in life will contain affection and care, then only life can be possible here. Else there will be no life anywhere. Million Wings feels how much a human may have freedom, may decrease his responsibilities to minimum level, may discover more and more machines for personal work, but the only logical feelings which keep humans attached are affection and care.

Principle: Affection is everlasting somewhere in one or the other way

Million Wings feels that may the world reach any level, life may be more modern and dependent on machines, humans may be so free, but the feeling of love and care, affection will always reside in their hearts. Every human will always think about their loved ones. Every human will think about their ownones and will pray for them heartily. Everyone always wants security of his relations. A human may argue or fight or stay away from near and dear ones for personal freedom, comfort, rights but from the heart, he will always care for and love them. A human may fulfil his needs with the help of machines or professionals but the feeling of belongingness will always stay in the heart. It's life, it's right, it's true and will be true for every century of the future too.

Principle: Balanced life

Million Wings feels that to live a balanced life is not compulsion but a dream. Everyone expects balanced behaviour from others; they themselves may be living an unbalanced life. Everyone likes their own thinking; that's why they are used to doing things like that. Sometimes, a human may feel that he is not right according to others and sometimes he feels unbalanced. According to him, some habits and desires are like that but still it's hard to change them, to surmount his mind; it's unsteady, transient. It may try hard to understand but again the mind goes in that direction only which the mind wants. Nothing is wrong in doing that or thinking that. And if we can't do what our mind thinks and wants to do, then whatelse shall we do? Million Wings feels that a human's habits and interest are not his compulsion but his happiness. Every human has to fulfil his dreams in such a way that he gets happiness from everywhere, i.e. personal, families, social, and not tensions. If one can fulfil his dreams and interests in an arranged manner, may it be good or bad, then no one will have any problem with that. If one will fulfil his hobbies and interests (good or bad), then no one will have any objection and he himself will also feel happy. In reality, most are living unbalanced life and basically society is a balance of unbalanced people. If one person is unbalanced, then another also becomes unbalanced, and making balance with that person is true and it's right too. In reality, human life is unbalanced life and to make more and more balance is a way of everlasting and permanent happiness for ourselvesand for society too.

Principle: Change for betterment can be done in plausible ways too

Million Wings feels that we can change the world in plausible and friendly ways. We needn't be serious or do a revolt everytime. Million Wings feels that when someone is saying something loudly to make the other ones understand or complaining about each other, their first motto is to explain their side, not to be jealous, nor does it mean to have unfriendliness or enmity. Rather it is sedate or easy. It's not necessary to do with reckoning. Infact we can try to do it with plausible and devoted ways too that will be effective and advantageous, profitable. Million Wings feels that one can easily punish the freak and the corrupt person but can't punish people in one's own family, society, or nation. We have to make our own understand, maybe politely or forcefully.

Million Wings feels that if issues/points are solid, then another has to listen to issues. Million Wings feels that the solid and weighty weapon is conversation of views to make thoughts better is more open, wide, and balanced. The best way to give a good direction to our country is by giving, by discussing the logical and real thoughts. To give satisfactory answersto all questions is a real change. To have clear explanations of all things is a real change. To linkup everything is a real change. Question and answer is a real change. To bring curiosity is a real change. Fights and quarrels are also done to bring change; infact all this is to give a lesson, to slaughter and to defeat. It's true that power is needed to handle corrupt and freaky people. There are very few corrupt people in the world but their narrow, limited, and arrogant thinking becomes a challenge to bringing change. They can't be changed by fights and betrayal, but by understanding them with talks and exchange of thoughts, their kind of people can be changed permanently. The way for happiness should available for every person so that a person can accept that way whenever he wants or feels or needs. Those thoughts which will release their tensions and give them comfort, then everyone will choose them.

Million Wings feels that everyone is already so busy in their lives that they don't want to increase tensions. Change can be brought in a plausible way only. One needs to be devoted, not serious. To increase effective and comfortable thought process at a social level is the real way towards happiness. Everyone already has so many sorrows in their hearts. No one wants to do anything forcefully. Everyone wants to enjoy tension-free life and it's right too. Everyone wants to attach with someone for happiness, not to increase their tensions, problems, and sorrows, and it's right. Everyone wants to share his tension, problems, sorrows atleast to each other and wants to live a tension-free, happy life, wants to laugh, wants to enjoy life. The ones who are living with innocence, let them do so. Living positively, living ideologically—let them. Making a living happily—let them. Making dreams—let them. If you want to give anything, then give security, not seriousness. Alert others, don't make them afraid. Give positive guidance and a more beautiful life filled with hope.

Chapter 3

Dreams and desires

If we don't have any dream or desire, then for what do we live? And why? Our dreams and desires are the biggest sacred word to live for, our motivation to live, our power. Dreams may be few or more. But they should be there. Our dreams are not good or bad according to the world, but the way to fulfil them, according to the relative way, may be wrong. We needn't go in squared planning regarding the right or wrong of our dreams but have to do it in such a way that no one can able to oppose them. If sex, anger, greed, affection, and ego are our primary feelings and nature, then how can a human leave them, then whatelse shall be left? If we leave them, then whatelse shall be done? If these all will be out of life, then what else shall be left? Nothing is wrong in these feelings. These keep our mind and body relaxed and healthy, filling our motivation, keep us busy with ourselves. Sex, anger, greed, affection, and ego are not wrong, but these feelings have to be fulfilled by right policy and channel, then it will be better and enjoyable.

Sex—Romance and sex are a natural will and need. There is no foundation, extortion, or wickedness in that. One can make physical love fully and by mutual understanding.

Anger—Anger is our response. If we don't like something, then we may get annoyed. Then what's wrong in it? To blow up at a situation at the same time will relax our mind; it is much better than to keep it in the heart, better than to scold someone else or be annoyed with someone else. Scolding the same person at same place and time is better. We say many more things being annoyed or fighting or beating them, so what? But yes, someone should not be handicapped or die because of anger. At maximum time, anger is of few seconds and is because of misunderstandings. Remember one thing: while a human is alive and is all right, anything can be corrected at anytime.

Greed—To earn money is a good thing. If someone wants to earn lots and lots of money, then what's wrong with it? If someone is doing hardwork to earn money, then what's wrong with it? Money is our basic requirement comfort, and required to fulfil basic needs. Will to earn lots and lots of money is not wrong. To be selfish is not wrong but while we are giving equal amount of workdone to another, the one who is doing efforts for us should be given his full payment and should do their complete work at the time from whom we are taking money. It depends on his personal interest and needs according to which he will decide what to do with earned money. So do atleast 8 hours work and earn as much money as you want.

Affection—Belongingness in relations can be filled by attachment and care. If we can't care for each other, then we will be alone. Affection increases the relationship bond; we can understand sorrow and celebrate moments of happiness with those whom we feel affectionate. Nothing is there without affection; do affectionate things towards by-birth relations and relations which are made by heart. Be attached to as much attachments as you want to be. There is nothing bad in being attached to someone. There is relaxation in being attached, emotional comfort a strength. Why worry about that thing which can be regenerated and with when stand, as that can be regenerated? But to be attached to a human or living creature special love boundary as it can't be exchanged or compared with anything else. Affection is often one-sided but if another also care for us, then what else will be better than it? Love as much as you can, as you want, but it can't be a restriction, compulsion, or problem for another.

Self-esteem/ego—Be proud of the thing which you have or have earned by hardwork. If a person has earned some status by oneself in one's own society without any guile, then one can say proudly that nothing's wrong in that. It's true that a person works for oneself but if someone can't see that and doesn't appreciate that, then how will he get motivation and happiness? If no one will ask, then a person himself can tell them that he worked like this and then earned a name and fame like this. A human can be proud of anything which is able to decrease the sorrows of someone or helps in giving hope to someone. Be proud of anything which gives moral support and increases faith; it's respectful. To maintain natural beauty, always remember one can't show one's success and start to one's near and dear ones; infact they are the reason to be proud and to maintain that.

Ego and pride are for others, not for one's own. You can be proud of honour and status or success you have gained by your hardwork. If someone helped us, guided or motivated us for being successful, then do mention their more too, then we will be so correct to tell about our status/role. Dreams and desires are our motivation to live. Our dreams are important for us.

We concentrate and collect resources to fulfil our dreams and it has to do. When our one dream is fulfilled, then a new dream and desire arises and we move towards that, to fulfil it. That's how one by one our dreams are fulfilled. To do this is exactly right. If new dreams arise, then what's wrong in that? Dreams may change according to time, then what's wrong in that? Humans are getting wiser day by day. If dreams change or the procedure to fulfil them changes, then what's wrong in that? It's right. For betterment, dreams, desires, or procedure can be changed can be bettered. Arising of new dreams one by one is natural. Nothing's bad in that. Dreams and desires may be any, from little to huge. One, two, three or more. Some seem to be possible and some impossible. After one dream, if a human goes for another dream, then that's absolutely OK. If one dream is not fulfilled and you choose another to fulfil by leaving first, then what's wrong in it? It's also good, it's logical.

If dreams and desires don't grow with time, then will a person succeed and how will he live? Million Wings feels that some dreams are forever, a few keep on changing. Desires of fulfilling both dreams is ethical, right thinking. To fulfil everyday's little dreams and emotions is everyday happiness and satisfaction. Today we are working hard to fulfil tomorrow's big dreams. It's true that the happiest day is when our biggest dream is fulfilled. But everyday's emotions and feelings are also part of that. Our today is our future. Afternoon for morning, evening for afternoon is the future; that is our dream only. It's not important that we have some big dreams or desires. We can't decide forcefully about our dream. The dream which comes randomly into our heart and mind is a true dream; that is our life.

The things, the behaviours, the talks, the style of the world and others with which we become impressed are the reasons which randomly change us. We try to find the things which we really need or want to have, those sayings, direction, guidance, and knowledge which take us towards our dreams. And it's right also. We can't make goals suggested by others as our dreams. Only those things and suggestions impress us which can assure us and we realize that we need to change and only then will we change. To change is a better option, we realize. Then we needn't change forcefully. Our dreams and desires change according to time. We needn't worry about that; when the right timecomes, then that will come itself in our life. It needs to be understood that today's dreams and desires are part of tomorrow's dreams and desires. When the right time will come, then that thing itself can appear in our life as our dream or desire. So if we live moments then today's will be helpful tomorrow in giving direction to our dreams and desires.

The real motto of our life is to fulfil our dreams and desires. Dreams and desires are not good or bad, small or big, most important or least important, but it's a relative comparison. If we are not hurting anyone knowingly, then there is no wickedness.

Whatever our dreams or desires may be, all are right. Our feelings are related with emotions like sex, anger, greed, affection, ego, money, status, revenge, then what's wrong in this and whatelse will our desires be? The human has been living in his emotions and feelings for centuries. All our preceptors for centuries have been giving suggestions to leave these feelings. Then why is a human is not able to attain that? The thing is so simple; these feelings are primary feelings of a human. If a human sacrifices his primary emotions/feelings, then how will he live? These feelings are not wrong but sometimes the ways chosen to fulfil them might be wrong as the time when a human forces someone or ditch someone to fulfil his own feelings, then that's absolutely wrong. Yeah, but if another agrees and joins with his own will, then that's not wrong. To kill or to handicap someone in the first place, is only sin. All others are just based on comparison. We needn't find dreams or desires. The things which arise by themselves in our minds are our dreams or desires.

All the conditions are favourable. It's according to our dreams and desires, it's rare. No one has everything at the sametime. It's the reality of everyone's dreams. Some have something more and another thing less. Someone has a great idea but lack of money. Money is here but with lack of time. Time is here but with lack of ideas; some have everything but no partner or right guidance.

Million Wings feels that one who has positive thinking can do anything and can fulfil dreams in any condition. That one can surely arrange something for his dreams and can fulfil his dreams one by one. Live your dreams. Respect your dreams. Never let anyone steal them, never let your dreams weaken. Make arrangements for your dreams, make a strategy, give direction, manage them. Regulate them, make them compatible, search for a way according to the amount of money you have. Leave less important things for the time being. Tell your dreams and demands to your family and ask for help from them to have company of alike people, talk to related persons.

As all or improve off some company. If you are fulfilling your minimum required responsibility, then do whatever you like to do. Let that happen. If you can't collect/arrange everything at the same time, then do it in parts. If you can't do it in one chance, then do it slowly. If one is not able to fulfil his dreams by every any effort, then why worry? As to do your 100 per cent is real happiness or satisfaction. So, friends, whatever anyone is doing or wants to do, let them do it. Give positive guidance to each other in the right direction; whenever something good is somewhat realized by someone, one can change oneself. Then one's dreams and desires will automatically change. Dreams and desires change according to age and conditions. So whatever suits or is lovable to our heart to get, that is our motive, may that be small desires or big dreams. The desires which arise by themselves are real/true, and that is real happiness.

Do whatever you want to do and fulfil your dreams but never at the cost of life or irreparable major loss. You must remember that you might not be requiring someone to assist you but your near and dear ones are dependent on you, like your spouse and children will be alone without you. Just donot die or get so sick to collapse into darkness. Extract maximum knowledge from the world and find out your safest way of happiness.

If we want to enjoy the maximum, then we should search more to fulfil our dreams and desires. We should try to collect the maximum and latest information at global levels, so that we can utilize our energy, time, money, and efforts to get maximum benefits out of them. We should not waste our resources on futile strategies. If we are confused with a few options, we should start a trial with the cheapest and easiest feasible options. Happiness is finding real good ways to our dreams. So one should talk with concerned people more, search more on the Internet, collect people's experiences. Talk more, discuss more, and you will get better ways to your happiness.

Chapter 4

God

While we can't understand God, the welfare of whole world is not possible. Unless we understand the life cycle, how can we live life? What is life and what is living? From where did we come? Where we are going? Unless we know all this, then what will be the meaning of our goals and work? Who created this world? Who is he? What is his motive? Why are organisms born? Why do they die? Why is this happening? What's all this? Unless a human understands these secrets, then how can the human move towards a beautiful and happy life?

Nothing happens without reason. It's another thing that a human may not be aware of, that reason, or understand that reason or may not want to understand. I think this huge world can't be established without reason. There must be some reason. Earth and the universe can't be created by itself. Someone has surely made it. Someone is here who is managing all this. Then who is that mastermind? What will be his name? Maybe no one knows that or maybe everyone knows that which we call God, Lord, Allah, Bhagwan, Waheguru, Rab; everyone says his name in one's own language. That spirit has created all this, that great spirit which we call param-atma, i.e. God.

According to time, our colossal preceptors, gurus tried their best to give us the best way to live life. No one has seen God yet. No one knows what he looks like. But God is not imaginary/fictitious, he is very intelligent and his religion is natural. God is powerful, everywhere, and the best strategy maker.

God is one and he looks like us. Religions are different; there are different preceptors who made religions that are not alike. But God is one and no one has seen him till now. One day God himself will come to earth and when he comes, he will look alike to everyone. Whatever he says, all the people in world will listen to that in their own languages. God has ultimate power. He has the ultimate, the best scientific eligibility; everything, anything can be possible for him but still he is neutral and the best strategy maker. God is provident. He is a mastermind, one can understand him and can lean on him but can't break any of one's organs for him.

If there is any profit for God in creating this universe, then only he knows that, not we. But yes, every creature can get the best advantage of moksha by getting this life. We humans and creatures and souls must be in some big problem, and that supernatural power (God) is trying to draw us from those problems. He is helping us, and giving us the opportunity to be out from those problems by giving life. God has given the opportunity of mokshato every life by creating this universe. By making a cycle of life and death, he provided a way for moksha. God has created life and the life cycle, and every creature which has a heart is alive, has life. Actually when some life has been born, that regulates the heart. Actually the soul has been born to regulate the heart. The soul is a power of life to move heart/carry on heart. Every creature is alive in which a heart beats. Feelings, emotions, dreams, and desires all are born in hearts and give direction and motivation to life. Emotions are life. The soul keeps the heart alive, the heart stops as the soul leaves it, and if the heart stops, then life ends in death.

When God makes a creature, he uses a strategy of random selection. First importance is of heart. Firstly he randomly chooses the heart then he randomly choosesthe mind and then that heart and mind can get anybody, which is determined by randomly chosen mother and father. On a birth, God gives his part soul to the heart, which then becomes alive and startsone's living in this universe created by God. God, on the basis of randomly chosen heart/mind/body, gives some basic inbuilt qualities to every life, every creature, which make the creature special. Since birth, one can't change the basic nature or presentation of anyone. So when life is born, that is not in a creature's hands what kind of heart, mind, body, soul, basic inbuilt qualities one will get. When life is born, that is basically a feeling which has been born and that may get any kind of heart/mind that may be human or animal. Soul is basic of life. If creatures are here, then it's all because of feelings. Feelings, emotions, nature are one's identity. If emotions and dreams are here, then life will go on. Fulfilment of feelings and desires is happiness. There is nothing without feelings and desires. If there is no soul, then from where do feelings and desires arise? Everything is here because of feelings.

Creatures are divided on the basis of body type. But in reality, every creature is alike; the heart is in every creature. Every heart has equal importance. Feelings/emotions arise from the heart which are the motivation of every creature's dreams and desires. God gives life to a creature through its birth. Life is a collection of different circumstances in which happiness and sorrow both can be there. Circumstances/situation of life of creatures starts from pregnancy only. Mother, father, living standard, thinking, looks, all these are primary conditions of every creature to start life, which decide physical, mental, and emotional conditions. Family, society, world are circumstances for a creature. The kind of atmosphere a creature gets, his behaviour, nature, thinking all develop like that only. When life is born, every creature is helpless. Creature/organism needs food, security, and protection for sometime. How will all this be possible? How well can move life ahead? If a creature and life both will move ahead, then only the creature will get moksha.

God is a mastermind. God had made such a strategy where life can get food, shelter, and protection for sure for sometime. That feeling is of affection. Every creature is born through a mother and the mother ensures a secure life.

God has made a mother's affection so strong that father or family or society may leave that child but a mother can't leave a child God develops affection since pregnancy. The real cause of development of a mother's milk is this only that creature will atleast start understanding, eating, drinking, walking and at that time, if the mother also gets apart from the child because of any reason, then the child can atleast become independent to try to move his life ahead and life starts moving. Life will never stop till it reaches its highest level.

The universe will surely move to that extent where God wants it to go. God has made such a system/arrangement that atleast life will move on its own. God is the best strategy maker.

God planned with such a great thinking and made such rules and possibilities that the whole life and universe can move on by themselves. God is tension free. God is peaceful, God knows everything, God is moksha, God made sequence, God has freedom, God made emotions so that everything moves on its own. God has made the emotions happiness, sadness, dreams, desires, love, anger, ditch, affection, sex, ego, greed, etc. as he knows that if something can help in moving this universe ahead, then those are various emotions only; otherwise, life is meaningless without emotions.

If there will be no meaning in living, then why should life move on? Where should it move towards? How long till it moves on? Emotions are a motivation of life. If the heart is here, then emotions will be here. There is nothing without heart. In other words, the most important organ is the heart and its emotions in every creature.

God is not temporary or imaginary. God moves ahead along with everyone. He is impartial, everywhere, the most powerful and best strategy power. God is a great scientist, God is the best soul, which everyone wants to lean against. God is great power and happiness. God made life to enlighten us. God made the universe for moksha of creatures. God gave life for moksha. God loves each and every creature. All creatures are part of God which got differentiated by doing some mistakes or innocent mistakes. That integral part, that soul wants to develop power, peace, and happiness as God develops its own. That silly part and souls comes to know that love, peace, power, happiness, belongingness which God has is nowhere else. Then they again want to unite with God. Now God has given so many options to his silly souls to be devoured in itself. God had a strategy for moksha of those silly souls. God made the universe to give various options, so that every soul passes through a life cycle and gets moksha. The silly soul which passes this life cycle by a balanced way will get moksha, and those which will not able to do that will again have to go through this life cycle till they will get moksha.

Before a soul is born, God has brainwashed every soul so that the soul doesn't remember anything, doesn't know for what he has been born. What is the motive for his birth? Every creature has to get moksha for themselves, has to become enlightenedon their own. Everyone will get moksha their own generosity, fate. Every organism has to learn on its own, has to find its own way, has to make its own strategy, has to live for itself, has to do everything on its own. Every creature can live the way he wants to live, can do anything, can make any strategy, policy. God himself has made every situation of life. He has made many ways, possibilities, turns which depend on their strategy, fate, and behaviour. God grants birth to every soul in an arranged manner to every organism, and death depends on their work done, strategy of life, and decisions of life. A creature gets life to get moksha. When any creature is born on the basis of random selection, any soul can get any circumstances to live in, any kind of looks and body shape.

An innocent soul can get moksha in its first life also. It may get any kind of appearance or form. If it can't get moksha in first life then the soul can be born again and new birth again starts from blanks, from zero, and conditions change everytime. The life in which soul gets moksha is not born again and it gets free from the circle of life and death and merges into God and gets peace and happiness forever.

On the basis of random selection, life comes into this universe, so a soul can get human life again and again. It may be one can't get human life ever, i.e. for moksha it's not necessary to have particular life or form. Every creature/organism has the same freedom, opportunities, and rights to get moksha, i.e. one can get moksha in any form; an innocent and silly soul has so many opportunities to get moksha. The earlier that one getsmoksha, the earlier that will get ultimate happiness, love, peace forever.

God is everywhere in this universe so that he can closely watch every organism/creature. God always sees one's intention, act, or strategy, which may be any. God gives moksha to creatures on the basis of their intentions. That's why God is in every organism/creature, so that he knows 100 per cent truth and is sure of every organism's intentions. As, if one creature kills another for moksha, then what's wrong for God? It's just nothing as no one can kill God. God is immortal, God has made every condition on the basis of being neutral. Nothing is sure that anorganism/creature will get which condition. God is the best/ultimate scientist. Everything which happens is directly or indirectly related with each other. The whole universe is science.

Whatever the thing is, there is science behind everything and God is the best scientist in the whole universe; nature is technology.

This huge/immense universe has so many mysteries. As the organism/creature will understand that, the more they will get close to God. Today, organisms and life are moving in a direction and one day every creature will surely get, find out God and that moment will be the best moment for the whole universe. Every soul was given many possibilities for moksha emotions; the one which doesn't have emotion is lifeless/soulless. The human is the best and brainiest of creatures created by God till now. Why is it so? How has the human overtaken all creatures? What have humans done that they have become unique in this universe? It may be because the human has done one thing different from other organisms/creatures. Only the human is that organism which is not just living but also learning and extracting something from that and passing that information to his new generations so that all can make better decisions in their lives and can improve life day by day. Whatever a human is learning, watching, seeing, and understanding, he keeps on telling to his new generation for betterment, and the human has become so intelligent and civilized that he starts solving the mysteries. That's why we can say that being human is the best option to get moksha, and all others are left behind as they just live their life and can't transfer their experience to new generations.

We humans are civilized, we are the best so we will talk about the rest of everything by taking human as main as we are leading a life with a collection of different situations. Every organism/creature wants redemption by living their life. Every organism/creature has full freedom to move on according to its own will and mind; where and in which condition organism/creature can be born is not in anyone's hands but death is based on redemption, intuitions, work and work done strategy.

Every organism/creature has its own life and they themselves have to choose it; fate is surely in everyone's own hands. We do work according to our own thinking in every situation and we ourselves are responsible for that. Our conditions/situations are not because of work done in last birth and neither will today's decide the next birth. Our next birth condition/situations will arise in the next birth only, which starts from our birth and is coordinated with lots of possibilities. Which moves on the strategy of today's work done by us. Natural disasters and diseases are not faults of our last birth and neither of this birth. These all are part of situations of this life. Fate and situations are directly related to work done in the present birth.

God has randomly attached some surprising and unknown things/ situations in life. These life situations are made to let an organism/creature think in different directions. So the organism/creature can come to know/ understand about the unique riddle and mystery, God has mixed all kinds of emotions; life has everything, pleasure, grief, jolt.

Actually pleasure is having favourable conditions in life. Happiness can be achieved not only in favourable conditions, as happiness in reality is an emotional stage which can be fulfilled by arranged satisfaction in every condition.

Nothing is right or wrong; it's just a comparison point of view. While the intentions are not to hurt anyone knowingly, then nothing wrong can happen, everything is OK, whatever a human does while not forcing anyone for one's own benefits. Everything is OK, nothing is wrong if anything is done by mutual understanding.

God has given the best opportunity to everyone to get redemption. Humans' intention is to get redemption for humans' cycle. People see, judge by acts/doings but God judges by intentions. What does a human have to do to get redemption?

How we get redemption? What is redemption? If a human can understand redemption, then he will get that also. Redemption is to lean soul in ultimate happiness and peace, to exit from the circle of birth-death and merge into God permanently. That is redemption, is happiness, harmonic relationship, i.e. happiness doesn't just mean a smile or laugh but it means satisfaction of heart and a clear mind.

Redemption can be got by arranged emotional and mental satisfaction, and to do this is human nature. A human wants this only: that he should clear and satisfy everyday. A human wants that his desires and dreams should be fulfilled without hurting anyone. In reality this is secret, for a human lives for himself and his dreams and desires and has attained that level in doing and fate and should have harmonious relations with others. It's the secret of redemption. Anything in life should be done of our own will, and if we have to do with others, then do bother for their agreement too.

God has given one goal to every organism/creature. Anyone can get redemption by fulfilling those goals, and along with that, others also get way, very beautifully God has interconnected those goals with our life. Which can be easily understood by every organism/creature and human tries to fulfil those goals with love, affection, and effort. We all know those goals very well. Then what are those goals which God has given to us? Did we really know our goals? Yes, it's really truth that everyone knows their goals, knows for centuries, infact, knows very well. God has given those goals in the form of dreams and desires to everyone. Yes! There are our goals of life. Everyone's dreams and desires are their happiness and to fulfil them is motivation and goal. God has determined our daily dreams and desires as tomorrow's goals. We don't have to go anywhere to find our goals.

Our dreams and desires which arise in our hearts, whether they are good or bad, whatever, these are our goals of life. Our dreams and desires may be big or small, may be easy or difficult, may change, but they are our goals of life. The dreams and desires which arise in our hearts and we too agree with these and want to fulfil these with our own will—that is our life's goal. That's our future, that's our redemption, that's our happiness.

The secret of redemption to be tolerant for others' happiness and benefits or to be rough or hard with someone for their benefit is exactly right. Our doings are related with this life only. Our last birth's doings and our next birth's doings have nothing to do with this life. Our doings give us redemption. If we can't get redemption in this life, then we have to move through another life, to get redemption in that life. We do new efforts; our new birth is totally clean, blank. That's why we don't know anything about our past life/birth. Our soul again demands a new birth from God and then we are born by our will, so that we can get redemption. But where and in which form we will be born is based on random selection only. Like this, one can get redemption in any birth.

To kill or to handicap any innocent is the biggest sin. To betray or mislead or do anything forcibly is absolutely wrong. On knowing—accepting our mistakes after knowing our mistakes and wrong intention is a secret of redemption.

God doesn't need money, solitaire gems, sacrifices, clothes, food, etc. He is happy just by praying with true heart. God can be remembered anywhere, anyplace, in any condition. We can pray to him. God doesn't need temples, gurdwaras, mosques, churches for prayer. God doesn't need any costly donation, food, repository or shrine, etc. These are all requirements of humans.

The many religions in the world, the many preceptors are not God. They all are great proponents, intelligent persons who try to think of a way of happiness to humans. They definitely are identity of religion but not God. As when God himself comes on earth than he will look alike, language, time, motive, everything will be same. Million Wings feels that humans had framed, made religions according to themselves and claim them as God on international level. God is maker of everything, everyone. And a human thinks that as different, different life policies which change according to time.

Million Wings feels that temples, gurdwaras, mosques, churches are human ways to remember God but not the ways of God. Temples, gurdwaras, churches, mosques are there wherever humans remember God. Humans remember God. One can remember God in any clothes, anytime; anyone(who may be good or bad) everyday or anyday can pray to God in difficult situations.

Life is one religion; it has its own way of teaching that God is one but one can remember him by any name with devotion and love. It means there can be as many names of God as there are humans on earth. One religion, one teaching, one God. It hardly matters how many names of God are here; everything is all right, is correct.

If one is not remembering God, then also there is nothing wrong as God granted birth to blank souls, so howcome they remember God? God is research of human, as it's true that life in the universe started from somewhere. And from where it starts, that is the ultimate powerful everywhere best strategy maker, i.e. God, and if we can pray to anyone, that is God only. Everything is a give-and-take relationship. Only God is that from whom we can ask anything for ourselves, our own pleasure, peace, redemption without any tension of giving back. Ask for anything from God as he never demands that back. Ask for anything from God, without any fear, he will not say anything (good or bad). Ask for anything at anytime, maybe day or night; he listens everytime.

God never gets annoyed if one is not remembering him, nor takes revenge for not remembering, never gets hurt if one is not remembering, as we organisms/creatures live here for redemption. In this universe, one can't make God happy by just remembering him by doing worship, as he has attached our life situations with lots of doings and has attached many possibilities in every direction. Whatever a human wants, he does that, and whatever he does, he gets possibilities in that. Persons can pray to God in any condition with devotion and heart so that he can help us in difficult situations and to get more success and favourable conditions. God judges every life by one's intentions, not by work or doings, and after life, one can get redemption according to him. Sometimes, God makes conditions favourable even without praying, and sometimes even after praying, he can make conditions unfavourable. To give redemption to every organism/creature is very important for God; in the same way, to give positive hope to every organism/creature is also important for God. God knows direction filled with life and universe very well in overall view has to move the universe towards positive hope. Real search of God is life and to live, and slowly he will merge us into himself; it's the best policy.

Million Wings feels that humans close gates of temples, gurdwaras, mosques and churches but to remember God is not penurious of any management/law. People have fights at religions' places, for pictures, sculptures, status, sacraments, and want to move beyond everyone else. That is just disbelieving superstition, as God doesn't need to see their faces but does see their minds. God is in heart and soul, not body.

Million Wings feels that there are paid-for religious places which humans made in the name of God. Religion is not God. Religion is collection of various levels of thinking on various parts of earth given by great persons, perceptions for ultimate happiness. Every religion and perception laughs to live life according to like and conditions. According to time, conditions, and demand, one after another religion was born. Million Wings feels that as time changes, thinking level also changes; likewise, religion also keeps on changing. Religion building became more new and beautiful, and religion also became more profitable and comfortable.

Life has been changing for centuries. But religious procedures are still the same in which religions are made. Today, conditions are not the same; religion is made to give more secure and the best way to live life. Today, humans try to merge God with their comfort. Even God has no objection to that, as he has nothing to do with these things. Centuries before, he was in hearts, today also he stays in hearts, and in the coming centuries too, he will reside in hearts only. All others are human policies, are the ways by which God became help by. Million Wings feels that the only secret to pray to God is by having devotion in the heart; without devotion, there is no use in remembering God. Everything like donation, expenditures, travel to religious place for prayer are all in vain without devotion. Everything else except devotion in praying is fake, is not humility, is showing off. But everything can be done by devotion. Devotion can be combined with any other resources.

Million Wings feels that during building of temples, gurdwaras, mosques, churches, someone must be devoted to this. Someone made them or built them with devotion; some people may have wanted and got their own benefits, but someone surely built them with devotion.

Million Wings feels that a religious place creates religious atmosphere, where everyone goes and feels devoted to pray to God. Someone must pray with devotion. Someone must donate with devotion. Some surely pray for one's good or bad conditions to God devotionally for happiness, peace, and satisfaction.

Today in every religion, we remember management of God according to human management. Management of religious place is also same as another management: opens in the morning, is locked during night-time, can be visited earlier. By spending more money, one can get more sacraments and opportunities. Million Wings feels that religion is also managed like other management projects. We can find many people fighting with each other just to move ahead at various religious places. Main religious leaders have given a business form even to religions, where devotion is measured by level of donation. Million Wings feels that to make someone independent is real devotion of money and thoughts. One needn't live and eat at religious places. Only one is also enough to God to pray. He even doesn't demand this also. He didn't demand any flower, donation, sacrament, etc., as God can be remembered at expenditure of zero, without expenditure of a single penny and of something which is invaluable. Also pray to God with clear heart and soul by closing eyes, bending head, and joining hands. One can remember God anywhere at any time, in any language, in any circumstance. To pray has always been a logical best secret from the centuries and for centuries.

Chapter 5

Life and redemption

Redemption means to be free from the circle of birth-death, and to merge permanently into God for ultimate pleasure and peace, i.e. permanent peace for soul, freedom from life circle, ultimate motto of our life. Now the question is this how this all can be possible. What do we have to do? How do we have to live so that we can get redemption? If God has given a way to redemption also.

Our life only gives redemption to us. Our dreams and desires are the goal of our life. We have to fulfil all our dreams one by one. When we live by our own dreams and desires, then we will live happily, and if we live happily in this world, then we will live happily even after death. It means if we live happily on earth then we will surely get redemption. God has given life to be lived. We needn't move to jungles or mountains to get redemption. We needn't sacrifice our dreams and desires to get redemption. We needn't be renunciate, devotee, saint, or sage to get redemption. We needn't leave sex, anger, greed, affection, ego to get redemption; it's not necessary to not to get married or to not give birth to a child. We have just to live with our dreams and desires to get redemption. We needn't force ourselves to do anything; we can do whatever comes to our minds. That is the way towards redemption. That's the only gate, the only way to our happiness. We have to work for our dreams and desires. One by one, new dreams can arise in our hearts and we live to fulfil them and will get real happiness itself. If we live happily in this world, then surely we will get happiness in other world too.

Arising of new dreams and desires in our heartsis a way towards redemption, and work done, doings to fulfil them are a secret of redemption. The secret is to live to fulfil our dreams and desires, to try our best to fulfil them. We just need to try our best; maybe we get success or maybe not. Do everything, anything as your heart says and same rule is implementedfor others too. Don't do anything against least will; this is the secret of redemption. Nothing is absolutely right or wrong. Everything is relative point of view. Everything is all right, whatever we do, while we are not compelling or betraying anyone for our benefits. Whatever is done by mutual understanding is right; this is a secret of redemption. To kill anyone firstly or to make someone handicapped is the biggest sin.

God created this universe to give redemption to innocent souls. God made numerous lives, numerous conditions, numerous situations. God made air, water, fire, soil, light, and shadow. These are the main elements which life is made up of, whose colour, form, work, and motive are numerous.

The universe is efficient science where everything is related with another because of one reason or another. Every living and nonliving thing is correlated with oneanother. God has created the universe in such a way that life moves by itself. Every organism/creature has to live according to its own needs, dreams, and desires. That is the goal of its life. Every organism has to coordinate in a way that every work done and management should be arranged properly. Every organism/creature's intentions, doings, and managements should be in their own hands. God has given numerous possibilities and conditions which depend on an organism/creature, how they select them and move ahead. All are, directly or indirectly, conditions and possibilities for each other.

Everyone has to fulfil their dreams, needs desires from each other. Every organism/creature teaches life to each other, moves ahead. All gives motivation principle to each other to live. God had directly or indirectly attached one organism to another by one or another reason.

It's true that God created this universe but he doesn't interfere. God has given a chance to departed souls to live in this universe, so departed souls are born in one or another form. As the soul is born, it becomes clean, blank, and as it dies, it becomes blank. God the ultimate power gives redemption on the basis of intentions, workdone, and doings. Otherwise soul has to be born again on the basis of random selection. If an innocent soul has lived life according to the secret of redemption, then that will get redemption. Every organism/creature in the universe lives according to their own will and thinking and then they themselves are responsible for everything. The life which has been born got that atmosphere which was made by another organism/creature in society. Organisms/creatures are responsible for the atmosphere which a newborn will get. Whatever will be the atmosphere, but life of every creature affects that lacks of organism/creature and universe in a direction. Atmosphere on earth is made by organisms/creatures themselves. They can move it in the direction they want it to go; it's totally dependent on their will, need, thinking, and intentions. God never interferes in anyone's life. Whatever the organism/creature wants to do, it does that. There is nothing wrong or right according to God's points of view. God makes the decision for redemption on the basis of life, living condition, situations, and possibilities of organism/creature.

At birth, God gave a few inbuilt qualities and emotions to the organism/creature which become the motivation for the creature to live. Every organism/creature in the universe competes for food, sex, affection, security, ego, love, power, and comfort.

Birth and death are also based on one's doings and intentions. An organism can give birth with the help of their sexual organs and can take life for their ego, pride, and need. So indirectly life and death are also the result of one's doings. Every organism/creature on earth can get redemption. Every organism/creature can get redemption of the basis of its intentions. Numerous situations, conditions, possibilities, emotions in universe are made by God only, and whatever is happening is related to them. Whatever is right or wrong can be judged on the basis of the secret of redemption.

The secret of redemption is such a useful policy that it will be rightly effective in every condition and situation, may it be talk of life or death, maybe talk of plant or of animals/organisms to creatures. May it be talk of the largest creature or of the smallest. May it be time of happiness or sad moments, may it be talk of needs or of dreams. May it be talk of male or of females. May it be talk of earth or may be sky. May it be talk of love or of war. May it be talk of truth or lie. May it be talk of past or may of future. May it be talk of great persons or of carpet.

The secret of redemption is that which has answer of every question. The secret of redemption is that which gives happiness. The secret of redemption is that which can give a result for every intention and doing. The secret of redemption is that which can give redemption. The secret of redemption is that which can make God satisfied/happy. The secret of redemption is that which can solve all problems. The secret of redemption is that which can satisfy us at every moment. The secret of redemption is with what life moves on.

The secret of redemption of God for the whole universe and every life is that for personal happiness, everyone has as to move such a start according to his dreams, will, and needs, that he has to make good coordination between his needs, dreams, will, logic, living products, and emotions. God has given the secret of redemption to every organism/creature that is to do everything with their own will to other to with their will.

God made creatures, and life is a collection/group of conditions. Happiness can't be just in a happy moment but can also be felt in bad times too. Pleasure is when conditions are favourable, and sad moments are those when conditions are unfavourable. It's true that possibility of pleasure is more in favourable conditions but one can be happy in bad times too.

Happiness is that emotional stage of mind and heart, which can be there in every managed situation. To handle bad situations in sad times is also happiness. So it may be sorrow or pleasure, satisfaction of heart and mind is real happiness. It's the secret of redemption. Every small happiness is satisfaction of heart. If the mind is satisfied, then only can one enjoy happy situations. If the mind is satisfied, then one can easily handle/tolerate even uncomfortable, unfavourable conditions and will move ahead towards happiness. There will be smiles only when one has a satisfied mind and clear heart. Smiles arise only if we are really satisfied and clear in mind and heart. While we are confused and unhappy at heart, then we can't smile even if we want to. A true smile is real happiness and it can be possible only if we have satisfactory answers to all our questions, doubts, curiosities.

Everyone is related to this play of life since birth. Everyone is playing this game. Every organism/creature has made it like this only, where everyone is playing. Everyone has freedom to move anywhere in any direction. Every life has its own game and he himself has to lead and conclude himself. But no organism/creature is alone since birth; one has the company of mother/father, brother/sister, and relatives to help in making him independent and intelligent. Everyone can choose relationships according to his own will too, as friends, life partners. Every organism/creature is attached to one another by birth or by circumstances. Circumstances of one are directly or indirectly part of others' circumstances.

Fate is surely in one's own hand. We do our doings according to our own will and we ourselves are responsible for that. Doings are not right or wrong. Work done is a response according to situation, time, and thinking; we ourselves are responsible. Whatever may be our situations, what may be our circumstances behind that. God has given unlimited, numerous options on the basis of random selection. There are numerous ways and possibilities which coordinate with each other; one can turn to anyother way anytime. Our doings for this birth are related with this birth only. Neither are last birth's doings related with this birth, nor will this birth's doings be related to the next birth. Our doings didn't get redemption for us. Whatever the doings may be, it hardly matters. But the intentionsbehind our doings do matter for our redemption. We can do anything for our benefits by anyway. If we are not knowingly hurting anyone's feelings, emotions and not harming another, then we are right. This is the secret of redemption. Everything, every workdone by mutual understanding is right. Our doings, our intentions take us towards redemption. If we can't get redemption in the present birth, then we take rebirth and in the new birth (which may be in any form) again start living in numerous circumstances and do new work to get redemption; like this we can get redemption in any life. Maybe we get redemption in one birth, maybe we have to take numerous births. It's not important to have human form to get redemption. We can get redemption in any form. Every creature is equal; everyone's soul is the same, as only a soul keeps the heart alive which is part of God. Every creature has heart, every creature has feeling.

Yes! It's true that humans are the best creature on earth as whatever humans learn from their life, they transfer that knowledge to their new generation so that life will be better day by day, they can make a better decision in any circumstances, and life will be better and better day by day and happy life on earth is point towards redemption. That's right and true that human birth is the best way to merge into God. The things like natural disasters or diseases or mishaps, tragedies are not the faults of our last birth and his work or doings of this birth. These natural tragedies are part of our life play/game, which are based on random selection. Yes, it's true, that.

Our doings today affect our present life. If we will stay happily here, then we will surely get redemption. That is if we want to get redemption, then we have to live happily on this earth too. That is we have two benefits: here happy on earth, redemption is all ours. It may be happy or sad times; we will be happy if our minds are satisfied. We want to get satisfaction of our mind. Our satisfaction at every second, every moment is our goal. Our dreams and desires are our future. We have to work to fulfil them. Whatever we may be doing, our intentions should not be of hurting/harming anyone knowingly. It's a secret of redemption. To live for ourselves is the secret of redemption. To be engaged with yourself is a secret of redemption. Trying to find and give happiness in everything is a secret of redemption. To live with your own dreams and desires is a secret of redemption. God has given a chance to every soul to get redemption. God has given the secret to get redemption individually and collectively to the whole universe too.

God has asked every soul to live a long life on earth happily; the more the creature will live happily, the earlier it will get redemption. The moment every creature starts living happily on earth, that moment will collectively bring redemption to the whole universe. God has made a very huge universe and connected life with humorous situations and conditions so that anyone can move in any direction and can do anything, whatever they feel like.

God has himself created this universe. God is everywhere, every moment. But God grants birth on the basis of random selection to every soul. The souls which want to get redemption want to live happily as early as possible (on earth). Every soul is in such a hurry that they are ready to live in any form. Whatever the circumstances they will get, that will be their luck. Every soul takes birth through mother and father. Every soul is in search of that organism/creature or plant which wants to give birth to a child so that the earlier they take birth, the earlier they will get redemption. During creation of this universe, God started with a very simple lifestyle. Living organisms/creatures and plants and the rest left everything on nature; an organism/creature can take its life in any direction, on any way. That totally depends on their will and thinking.

Organism/creature, plants in the universe are responsible for the atmosphere, conditions, circumstances, situations, thinking of the universe. God has created this whole universe on the basis of the best science. God has created soil, air, water, fire, sky from which every creature can take birth, can develop. These constituents make life and these constituents give success; these take birth, these constituents die, these constituents are food. These are those by means of which anything can be done, everything can be possible. God created life by immersing soul in various plants and organisms and meanwhile accessed the various feelings and intentions and made them work so that life goes smoothly. God is not magic but a great science on earth, which revolves around the sun. Which is that science which is moving at its own pace and organism/creature is moving on its own pace in this universe which is created and managed by God. God has determined everything, since start till end. But it will be decided by the style of doings by organisms/creatures. Then when will the universe achieve the highest level? As future, God has created unlimited circumstances, filled with positivity. God will find the future through these organisms/creatures only. Someone will surely keep on examining life and will move life with new discoveries and research for betterment. If God and discoveries of the world had made life impossible, then what would be the meaning of life? This universe was started by God and its ultimate end is also God. God is slowly giving his recognition to organisms/creatures. What is God? Maybe the best way to let us understand that is the creation of the universe and life.

A soul will get redemption and ultimate knowledge too. This is the secret of great power, great soulGod, and this is a secret of redemption too.

Million Wings feels that among the creatures which God created, the human is such a creature who is civilized and judging every organism/creature. All other organisms/creatures are still uncivilized. Humans are trying to be more advanced and forward day by day to get better life. The human is thinking and trying to get possibilities created by God. Human happiness, dreams, thinking research, curiosities and desires of better future are the research that put humansabove all creatures. Million Wings feels that humans are above all creatures. If humans will be happy in their life, then possibility is they can make the universe happy. If humans will have more coordination by the right way, then they can easily move universe ahead on the right way.

If humans can make a balanced life, then it will give guidance to other organisms/creatures too. Every organism/creature takes birth and lives to get redemption. Happiness together can get redemption forever. If humans can be happy for themselves, then along with getting redemption for themselves, they may get chance to get redemption to the whole of the universe too. Million Wings feels that in the universe, if humans can live happily, then their universe can get benefits too. Million Wings feels that human happiness can be increased more. Million Wings thought process is a way to increase happiness at a higher pace. A group of thoughts which has dreams and desires of understanding and to make understanding is the logical principle.

Chapter 6

Identity and individualism

Every human being is different, particular, and special. Million Wings feels that every human is a wonderful person. It's sure that everyone has some special quality and ability. Someone is beautiful and another is intelligent; someone is good in sports and another has a good voice. Someone's smile makes everyone as their own and some makes gazes with their coquetry; someone is good at talk and someone rules hearts with the way they care and their affection, etc.

Everyone has experience, belief, and thinking about life which depends upon the circumstances that one gets since birth till now. No one's circumstances can be same; some similarities may be there. Everyone is living in different stages, phases, and situations of life. That's why everyone thinks differently on the same issue. As cornea and fingerprints are unique and different, in the sameway, every person is unique and different.

The surroundings, circumstances, atmosphere in which one spends one's time, one starts thinking and behaving like that. Million Wings feels that no one is complete in oneself, someone has same quality and ability but another may be missing. Maybe some bad character is inside but maybe good in another way. So everyone is not complete but has different qualities and abilities, and this makes a person different and unique.

Every person has his own story and vote bank. One can be just average at some place but may be a big gun at some other place. One may not be good in one field but may be highly skilful in some other area.

In today's world there are people, from those who think traditionally to people who think freely; everyone is right at their place. In the world there is every type of person, from kind to cruel, uncivilized to genuine and civilized ones. There are so many poor to rich people in the world. Whatever the kind of atmosphere one gets, one becomes the same and reacts like that. Everyone is right at their place. As the kind of atmosphere one gets, one becomes like that only.

Million Wings feels that every human being is important. Anything, anyone may be so costly, big, powerful, or beautiful but can't replace something or someone.

No one can be compared with another, as comparison can be done there where situations circumstances are exactly the same. Million Wings feels that however the human is, it depends on circumstances only. But how near or far is he from open, wide, and optimistic thinking? It's a logical principle.

Million Wings feels that when human takes birth, then God gives some emotions, feelings, and inbuilt qualities that make him different and unique. These inbuilt qualities which regulate human behaviour and inbuilt qualities can't be changed easily, but it's also not impossible. Inbuilt qualities make the basic psychology of every humanbeing. Since birth, a person (can be of happy mood, sad mood, positive thinking, negative thinking, mediocre, or neutral) has a basic psychology, which gives direction towards life. A person starts his life based on these basic psychological factors and whatever is already present in the world can be chosen according to his nature. A human can choose those things only which are already happening, going on in the world, which can be found in the world. If those things don't exist in the world, then he can't take them or he will try to make them himself, and like this, life goes on. It's different to change basic psychology but not impossible. It's easy to change psychology in childhood, i.e. in starting years, with the help of effective ways. Million Wings feels that since childhood, one has to understand one's basic psychology, and to provide the positive, happy, and real atmosphere is the best and an effective step for the whole of the society and world. Million Wings feels that capable guidance can make feel anyone, anywhere to change to be better, to be successful at anytime.

Good/real guidance is the best happiness, hope, and success of life. It's true that God has made more positive thinking than negative ones; otherwise it would have been just impossible for the world to move on for centuries. Million Wings feels that ultimately goodness overrules wickedness. This will be the policy while life exists. God grants birth to every creature in some initial life situations and gives unlimited possibilities. Situations or circumstances may be any, but it's one's basic psychology and nature that determines how he reacts to that, and like this, life and living goes on, moves on.

God has made life and the universe in its own limits but related with free will, i.e. everyone has freedom to do anything. Everyone is attached to one another because of some reasons; life will carry on living, but the way they want. Whatever is happiness from the possibilities made by God, it depends on the organism/creature itself what to choose or react to and on what they want to do research. Million Wings feels that identity of one depends on inbuilt basic qualities and nature. Change in human identity or individual can be brought by two ways: one way is that society and the world should give that atmosphere and the other is a human himself has to bring the change in the world in the way he wants.

Million Wings feels that everyone (male or female) has their own identity. Since birth till death that identification will be taken as their identity. Everyone has their own identity, and one is known by that identity before knowing him/her. One may be attached to any number of relations, business, or issues. Million Wings feels that it doesn't matter whether someone is married or unmarried, as being married is just one more relation among all other relations but a person is known by his identity, not because of relations. Maybe one's relatives are at high posts or they're well-known personalities. It's nothing to do with one's own identity. Million Wings feels that every person has to be judged by his own identity, not because of relations or status. It's right and true.

One's identity is one's recognition. What is the meaning of identity? How can people get it, know about each other's identity? Firstly humans will see each other's doings and observe them. Whatever they say and do and react to others on, take that as their nature and decide their attitude, and doing this is right too. Nothing's wrong in this. A person is same as he reacts. Million Wings feels that if anyone knows a human 100 per cent, that is the human himself only. Whatever one is, maybe good or wicked, one knows that clearly. What are our dreams and desires and needs? No one knows that better than us. That's everyone makes a policy in their mind to fulfil that and do the same in front of the world so that they can fulfil their dreams and desires. This means that everyone decides their whole behaviour according to themselves and portraysthemselves to world. Now another person will think the same, whatever you are saying, reacting, doing, and to think the same is right.

Million Wings feels that to understand anyone/everyone at right time and 100 per cent is the toughest job in the world. Now if we just think for a while, who has time to judge intentions of others by ignoring or leaving out the behaviour and reactions? To avoid portrayal and to understand one's problems, circumstances, and situation is not possible everytime, and even if it's not necessary, neither is it any compulsion. People just watch and understand doings and then intentions and then another person's intentions also seems the same as the identity or portrayal. To do this is absolutely right.

Possibility is the pace of life will increase in the future. Everyone wants to live faster, and where there is pace, there are only actions. Behaviour can be understandable but not intentions, as sometimes intentions are also not expressed rightly to high pace and then issues start worsening. Million Wings feels that if someone wants to fulfil their dreams, needs, desires faster and more easily, one has to be practical about one's intentions, behaviour, and actions. If one doesn't express one's feelings, dreams, and desires, then how can another get to know about these? If a person wants to express these clearly, then how he will get company, the right people, and chance according to dreams, desires, and needs?

Million Wings feels that self-expression is key to success of every human being. It's not necessary to express ourselves, our dreams, desires, and needs to everyone. But to talk with related person is right and is a good option. Million Wings feels that to express dreams and desires is right and to confess to related person is happiness. The earlier and more one expresses oneself, the earlier, the longer, and the more time happiness starts arising. Don't fear about whether desires are right or wrong, good or bad, as dreams and desires are not right or wrong. It depends on the way, socially and personally, with one we are fulfilling. Our dreams and desires can be fulfilled socially and some need to be fulfilled secretly and personally. But it doesn't mean that dreams are right or wrong, good or bad. Million Wings feels that dreams and desires are not wrong or bad or wicked while one is doing with his own will and agreement and with the will and agreement of the other person too. Any workdone by will and agreement is good, is right. The more the coordination between intentions and dreams, desires, the earlier and the more happiness and enjoyment he will get. It needs to be understood that another person reacts and acts according to our words, talk, and behaviour, not according to our feelings and emotions, and that too depends on how he took or understood these. That may be our meaning or may not. We can't expect that another will understand the way we want too. But can make ourselves clearer to another person, who will think, 'That is his thinking.'

Million Wings feels that everyone has one's own circlefrom identification circle/frame, and that circle is one's happiness, enjoyment, satisfaction. Everyone makes one's circle more and more wide and comfortable according to oneself. Every person has his personal circle; it's his happiness and right too. It doesn't matter if personal circle or frame is bigger or smaller than another's circle or frame. But what's important is of own circle or frame. It's everyone's right to be clear and safe for his own personal circle or frame. Million Wings feels that everyone lives for their own satisfaction and it's right too. A human's own thinking, living, dreams, and desires are priority and they should be. It's the right way to move with one's will and permission to another's circle. Million Wings thinks that personal frame has nothing to do with another's thinking, dreams, and desires. It's one's own wish whom to allow in and who should not enter his circle, and it's right too.

Million Wings feels that everyone has their own personal life and it's everyone's right and it's protection and security, it's one's own need and responsibility. Personal life has nothing to do with good or bad. The thing or work which a human doesn't want to show to others or the world is his personal life, may it be good or bad. Million Wings feels that will be true and clear to a related person, needn't be explained to the whole world.

Million Wings feels that God judges humans by their doings first; that means to get redemption, coordination of intentions is required first, before doings and action. Million Wings feels that if intentions are right or good, then one may get enough time to settle a thing; one may one be lying only if it needs to be good first, may be true secondly. Happiness resides while there is coordination, may that be coordination of truthfulness or a lie. If intention is right, then one can lie for sometime to handle situations, but along with that, to move more and more towards truth will relay one from all lies. Million Wings feels that is more courageous than to accept the betrayal and to say sorry to the related person. When someone feels that he wants to move towards truth, overcoming all the lies, then he is thinking absolutely right, trying to take this courageous step.

Million Wings feels that it's easy to follow truth and idealism from the start but to move towards truth and idealism, by overcoming lies and fraud is not an easy step but not impossible too. Million Wings feels that if someone wants to overcome a wrong path and wants to move on the right and better path, then he should make policy according to related persons. The time person decides to take the step avoids idealism sametime circumstances itself saves them and helps them.

God has created the best of the best and the worst of the worst circumstances for every person for everytime and condition; circumstances seem to be the same as one's intentions are whatever comes to mind is right, comes to mind is one from those conditions which God has created for us, and the result becomes guidance for tomorrow's life. Whatever a human does is his happiness and guidance; for another it may be good or bad. If to be stolen is someone's happiness, then to catch them is happiness. If someone's then another happiness is to protect that, if someone's happiness is to protect that. If someone's happiness is to take drugs, his suffering from that is guidance for another. If someone is wrong, then someone right should also be there. What is the happiness of someone, only he knows. But at times we can meet many people in search of the same happiness.

Million Wings feels that individual's skill is having real identity may that be a natural gift from God or got that by practice or hardwork. Skill gives one's name fame and success. Every one's first identity is and will be their skill and qualities, then later on, one can discuss about their status and family. It's a real truth of identity. Skill may be natural gift (as beauty, sweet/melodious voice) or may be learnt (e.g. doctor, engineer, lawyer); it hardly matters. Million Wings feels that family and society have to give stress, chance, help, guidance, and encouragement to increase inbuilt or earned qualities. If there is any quality in someone, then he can live happily anywhere, can rise again and again, as one's quality can make him independent. No one can steal our skill, and a human is less dependent on anyone else. Independence is happiness, freedom, power, identity, and strength.

Million Wings feels that a human can't be judged on the basis of those things which are not in his hands, e.g. looks, colours, race, etc. A human can be identified only on the basis of his quality and skill.

Million Wings feels that everyone has inbuilt basic quality according to which he choose from available things and thoughts in the world. A human can be good or bad but he must have some principle, if their behaviour, rules, and principles are the same for everyone.

Everyone is right at their place. Whatever one can be, one's decisions should be same for oneself and another, according to these rules and principles. Million Wings feels that there is nothing right or wrong; it's just relevant behaviour. Right or wrong just on the basis of comparison is good. But it's more important how near or far they are from open, wide, optimistic, and balanced thinking, as balanced life is a principle of peace and happiness.

Million Wings feels that personal balance is the first step of coordination with balanced social life. But being unbalanced has been a truth for centuries. The one who doesn't move according to society or the world is unbalanced, but one's personal happiness is to move according to oneself. Everyone's happiness is that in which one is interested, one's dreams, one's desires that may be right or wrong, balanced or unbalanced, genuine or non-genuine according to society or world. That means if someone's happiness is unbalanced life according to society, then he lives happiness with unbalanced life only. As that all is his happiness, then maybe his action, behaviour, thinking are unbalanced for himself also. This hardly matters.

Million Wings feels that idealism is an international policy for balanced society and world. But a human is unable to make this balance. Million

Wings has made new international human policies according to humans: capacities, thinking, desires which are easy for humans to understand and to follow. And humans can easily follow these and can make open, wide, optimistic, and balanced life worldwide. It's a dream that every human should react like humans only, to create balance and to live a peaceful and happy life to get redemption. Million Wings feels that every human is unbalanced. If we need balanced society, then according to everyone, we have to make and follow balanced principles and rules according to everyone. Million Wings feels that balance of maximum rights is the future, where no one can take extra advantage of each other or any innocent, as theinnocent and weak person is not going to tolerate another's unruliness, extortion, and wrongdoings. They will unite and will ask for answers. They will demand equal rights, respect, comfort, and unlawful people will not able to compel them and will be unable to enjoy. Then enjoyment/fun will be possible by mutual understanding and will not by wickedness or by compelling.

Million Wings feels that a person is answerable, responsible for his commitment and promise. But there is no responsibility, or compulsion, of the thing which one has not promised or committed. That may be a personal issue(like making new relations), may be professional. It needs to be understood that if someone is commanding or sad about the command or promise which is not done, then it's due to their narrow thinking or superstition. There is no problem or mistake from our side, and neither are we responsible or answerable for their condition.

Million Wings feels that to ditch or be wicked to someone only for personal benefit firstly is absolutely wrong. To ditch means to promise something and intention is of doing something else. When one makes false promises only for one's benefit, it is called ditching. These kinds of persons have been disliked for centuries. Ditching is to renege from promises, which is dual nature of person. Human may himself be right or wrong but never tolerate ditching by someone else and it's true.

Million Wings feels that there is an age of physical development of body but not of mind or mental development. That is, anyone's mind can develop to any level at any age. A child may have mind and thinking as of elders, and elders may react and think as children. That means the body develops by the age of 17–21 years but the mind can think in better ways even at a young age.

Million Wings feels that no one can forcefully change anyone's thinking. One can do only what one feels like or wants to do. A human can only change when someone feels change by heart. The real change is that which is felt from the heart, and real guidance is that which can make one realize the change in minimum time.

Million Wings feels that we want to do only those things which we really want to do. It's not always like what we want to do is always in loss according to past experience. We have found many better results with guidance. Life goes much better with the help of good guidance. Guidance doesn't stop us from doing anything or change our direction. But the real motto of guidance is whatever we do should be done with much better and secure ways, then we may work in any direction, good or bad. Guidance is that which gives benefits to human and is aware about everything. The things which give loss is to pervert. The truth is that the world is getting much better and moves on with the help of right guidance, which gives positive hope along with personal benefit. Great persons', preceptors', everyone's logical principle is to give a positive hopeful balanced society in every direction. The best guidance is that which can make human realize quickly about the related issues in better ways to fulfil dreams. Million Wings feels that personal dreams or desires are advantageous to the whole world. Personally everyone does maximum effort, and the guidance which one needs, one will listen to that only. A good person always tell everything politely; it's one's own wish to follow that or not.

Every human is an equally important creature. No one can replace anyone or anything. Everyone's life has some logical meaning which works as direction and guidance for the whole of the world. Million Wings feels that although a person may seem to be good or bad, right or wrong, responsible or irresponsible, he is a very important part of the society, country, and world. Every individual has their own individuality which is based on basic inbuilt qualities condition and circumstances he got till now. Everyone may be compared to each other but the life of every individual is equally important. If some are nice and good, then society gets benefits of that and everyone getsclear and happy ways with their help. If someone is bad or wicked, then one harms another and is oneself also encircled with sorrows. By the lives of these kinds of persons, we atleast come to know that these acts and intentions are prejudicial, then we search for better ways and directions. This means a person may be good or bad, he always teaches something to the world. Wicked person harms himself and world learn from them. Good persons motivate, get benefits for themselves and a positive attitude towards life for another too. A person may have any identity, but reality is that he always gives direction to the world.

Million Wings feels that nothing is good or bad. It's just a relative point of view. If everyone gets benefits from each other, then that's always good. And whoever does harm is obviously bad. Million Wings feels that to betray someone or force someone to do anything for our own benefit is absolutely the wrong way, else everything is OK, right. It means whatever we do is right, is good while we are not harming or betraying anyone for personal benefit. That's why just vanish erase the fear of being right or wrong and do everything with mutual benefit, whatever the heart wants.

Million Wings feels that to understand basic nature is to understand humans. As everyone's cornea and fingerprints are different, in the same way, everyone's circumstances are also different; that's the reason that everyone is unique and different. Everyone has their own experience, faith, and thinking about life, which depend on circumstances and conditions since birth till now. No circumstances or conditions are the same in the world. Even in the same family, everyone has different circumstances. Everyone is living in different stages and phases of life. That's why everyone thinks differently on the same issue. Million Wings feels that even having so many differences and different thoughts, everyone has the same motto for which one is living life, and the ultimate goal is about personal happiness. Million Wings feels that the individuality of oneself is one's happiness, self-respect, right, uniqueness. Identity of someone is one's recognition and whatever the person does or says is his identity, whatever the person presents is his identity; it's right and it's truth too. Million Wings feels that another person reacts according to our words, behaviour, and style, not according to our intentions or feelings. This is right too. Whatever one is showing, the world will take one like that only. What meaning someone will make of another's words and behaviour just depends on their mentality and thinking. One will see the world according to those circumstances which one has faced. Million Wings feels that a human himself knows himself better than the world and gives others maximum of times. The way human is clear and sure about anyone else in world. A human can express atleast his feelings according to himself, and it's never sure what another will understand, feel, or guess from that. Most of the time, everyone has good coordination with each other but still sometimes they start guessing about another's acts and feelings and react according to that. Million Wings feels that the main aim of everyone is to be happy by expressing theirselves. But another will think it depends on their thinking, attitude, and intention too.

If another also expresses himself at the sametime, then it's easy to clarify feelings and intentions, and this ultimately increases coordination in relations. Million Wings feels that after expressing ourselves, we have to give a chance to others to speak and to express their views too. By giving them a chance, we will get to know whether they have taken our things the way we wanted to explain or taken them some other way. Million Wings feels that by giving a chance to another to speak, we will be sure to some level that what we wanted another to understand, he understood the same. To give a chance to another to speak is also one of the best secrets of personal happiness.

Million Wings feels that we can't change anyone forcibly. Whatever one is, he will do the same. One can't improve by just knowledge or thinking; it happens only when one feels it at heart. Everyone's identity always affects another person. When someone is impressed by anyone's words, behaviours, or style, then they themselves start following that in their lives, and that is the real change. Everything is changing every second. Even we ourselves are not aware of that. Humans feel the change in the same circumstance or conditions or a big change, but don't see those little changes which occurs in ourselves in our daily life and we even accept these unknowingly. It's true. Million Wings feels that while talking to each other, we have to express our feelings, our thinking, and not fight or argue or force anyone to change. Actually one has to put their personal proposals to others. One who feels impressed will get impressed itself and feels change in their life. To bring permanent change in anyone's life is to talk maximally about logical and beneficial things by effective coordination is real success, not to bring change forcefully.

Million Wings feels that life seems to be the same as we think about it, whatever may be the thinking of a person, but his principles should be same for everyone. A human may have any nature but atleast he should have some principles. Whatever the principlesmay be, theseshould be equal for everyone. Million Wings feels that everyone is becoming more and more intelligent with time. Circumstances and conditions bring change to humans; change is happiness at every moment. Slowly a human himself feels the change and this change is the real change. Today's small changes are part of tomorrow's big changes. The right time to do anywork is when one someone feels it that to be done.

Million Wings feels that a human has to live his today maximally, as tomorrow is derived from today. If we live our today the best we can, then we will understand and enjoy life and our future the most. (Actually our today is that moment of tomorrow which is closest to us.) Million Wings feels that our today is our future. To live today fully is our future; it's true, it's right. If humans' future will be clear, then our today will be more beautiful. Million Wings feels that if one understands the future's goal and is clear about this, then we can make our today better. No one needs to ask anyone about their future dreams. As God has fixed our dreams and desires as our future's goal, the dreams and desires of every human being, their happiness, and to fulfil those dreams are the inspiration of life and goal of life. Everyone's dreams are important for them, may these be small or big.

Million Wings feels that dreams and desires change according to time. Some are fulfilled and some may be forgotten, some can be made better, and some more can be attached along with them. As dreams and desires change, humans also change accordingly. To do this is not wrong. That's all absolutely right, as dreams and desires change according to time and circumstance. It's a mechanism which prepares us naturally to fulfil our dreams and make us capable of them. Change for betterment is always good; one can change numerous times for betterment. After fulfilling one dream, a person tries to fulfil his next dream. This is absolutely right. Dreams and desires are motivation to live, power to live. Million Wings feels that one should know and understand one's own dreams as they are one's future early as the person understands the dreams. The early ways and directions will be cleared and he will enjoy the present along with a bright future. Million Wings feels that one's past is not an obstruction for the present and future but be aware about future problems so that human happiness can increase more and more.

Million Wings feels that every work has some process time to get success by the right means. Mechanism time can be reduced to minimum but can't be reduced to zero, with the help of knowledge and suggestions. Million Wings feels that to understand ourselves is to get wings of happiness. Persons may be right or wrong, good or bad, but being clear to oneself is permanent happiness.

Being clear to ourselves makes the sky of happiness more beautiful, open, and wide. One can surely feel marvellous freedom and self-confidence in life. We can understand our dreams and desires more deeply by self-consciousness. The person starts feeling happy at every moment when he knows himself more clearly, more nearly. Present and future both become more beautiful and enjoyable. Million Wings feels that real intelligence is being independent personally, familiar socially and professionally. If a human is logically fulfilling conditions of these four fields, than he is a really intelligent person.

Million Wings feels that every human has self-respect and he always wants to maintain that. To do this is right and happiness too. Everything like money, status, power, beauty, and force are all in vain in comparison to self-respect. Humans have been fighting for centuries for self-respect, also fighting today, and will fight while life exists, and to do this is right too. Every human has full right to maintain their self-respect.

Million Wings feels that a human has to do maximum efforts by himself only to fulfil his dreams and desires. Why should someone else fulfil a person's dreams as he has his own dreams and desires? The utmost important thing to fulfil our dreams and desires is morale, encouragement, and maximum tries. Another person can only help us to fulfil our dreams and desires, can give chances and motivate us. But the human himself has to try do hardwork with his own will, power, and affection to fulfil them. Actually the regular tries by himself help to fulfil his dreams and desires. Maybe at present we are getting problems and obstructions too but can surely find someway by regular tries, and dreams come true. God supports by providing multiple ways for those who try with full faith and trust; it's true and it's coordinated truth.

Million Wings feels that every human has to make a good decision according to best knowledge, thinking, and circumstances everytime, then the result of decision may be any but human is clear and right at his place. If a decision made with good intentions may not be right, that's nothing to be sad for, as according to logical human working strategy, one has to make the best decision according to time and situation, and along with that, to do maximum efforts with good intention is the right working strategy. And if failed because of any reason, even then there is nothing to worry about as you tried your best. whatever anyone else may say. A human can first try his best, to be successful with natural and human factors too. Million Wings feels that to fulfil the main motto and logical meaning of any work/thing/project is a primary need. Other than professional responsibility, only the needy need to request, appeal, or ask. Million Wings feels that results give the real answer for just saying and doings. One gets to know about the difference in doing. If results are good, then everything is good. But if results are bad or not good, then one has to listen to others and it's the sad/bad part. Million Wings feels that it's a need to see/feel true and devoted tries by each other and then results, motivations, and faith developby saying and doings, then results may be any. Million Wings feels that to have personal life is everyone's right and its protection is one's own responsibility. If anyone gets a chance and tries to look in another's personal life, one may take advantage of that or may not, may make that public or may not. This is the one from main behaviour of humans. One has to keep one's personal life maximally safe and secure as on getting a chance, most people try to get benefitsfrom personal life. One has to be clear with the related person, needn't explain to whole world.

Million Wings feels that to live for our dreams and desires is everyone's goal. Not to harm or give pain knowingly to ourselves and others, to live with delight is the best life. It's not important to live for others as it can only be done by those whose main aim and happiness is this only. The one who is living for the world, humanism, or the universe is their dreams and desires, not under any compulsion, and they are not doing anything forcibly, nothing's wrong in living delightfully. But to fulfil minimum required responsibility is necessary. For every human, minimum required responsibility is to take care of parents and to fulfil those promises which are done wilfully, e.g. marriage, children. If we help our own ones in times of need and stay beside them then there is more possibility of getting help and togetherness in times of need.

Million Wings feels that work may be easy or difficult, may be related with daily life or special; humans have to do it in sincere and happy ways. It's not necessary to do every work seriously, as intense and great work can be done sincerely, happily, and elegantly too. It may be serious work or related with enjoyment. Only sincerity is required, not seriousness. Sincerity and elegance give happiness and increase possibility of success; seriousness gives tensions and reduces concentration. Million Wings feels that a secret of success in every work is to be sincere and one's willpower is necessary. Be sincere but not serious.

Million Wings feels that to understand the heart and will of others 100 per cent rightly at the right time is the highest challenge. To understand the heart feelings and heart, we need to be affectionate and caring regarding the related person, which needs and demands more and more time to understand someone's feelings and nature. We can't judge or guess by just spending time to judge or guess one's action and thought in different situations and circumstances. Then only can one be successful in understanding another's mind.

Million Wings feels that money freedom is one of the effective achievements to be happy and free. One should not depend on another, atleast for money. Money helps in collecting primary basic needs. Infact, money is not everything but is necessary to fulfil primary basic needs and fulfil necessary dreams and desires. Everyone has to make maximum efforts for financial independence. It's logical thinking.

Million Wings feels that everyone can brag about every thing or work which helps in decreasing another's sorrow or fills them with hope. A brag that can increase self-confidence and fill life with happiness is respectable. A person can brag about every thing which he got or took without harming or defrauding anyone or can brag about natural beauty. Bragging can be maintained on the basis of successful results. If someone brags, then nothing's wrong in it. Because success and successful results need to be maintained on the basis of efficiency and effectiveness to brag. And it requires sincere effort to maintain it. God is the same for everyone. God has given dreams and desires to everyone, given them unlimited conditions and unlimited situations and possibilities to fulfil those. But the actions required to fulfil them need to be decided by the human himself.

Million Wings feels that we can brag about the things which we got by hardwork. But to be egotistic is daring. Daring means 'only I can do it'. Everyone wants to do better than another person, and someone's doings motivate another to move towards better results and success. Million Wings feels that most types of work can't be done alone but need a team, i.e. teamwork, where many people workhard to fulfil that. Participation of every individual may be less or more. Many people feel unimportant and robbed because of ego and bragging and are parted from self-respect and pride. Egoistic and proudpersons lose their helpers and trustworthy persons. Bragging and ego is for others, not for our own ones. Because our own are the reason and power of our ego and pride.

Million Wings feels that only those persons can give advice on issues who themselves have passed those kinds of circumstances or are masters in that subject or are elders we can take advice/guidance from, those people who are intelligent enough or have enough knowledge about different issues of life. Visionary persons themselves try for betterment of life everytime. Million Wings feels that common sense and the voice of the heart always give the best satisfaction. Million Wings feels that coordination of personal intention and attitude mainly decide social activities, in starting the view and thinking which we make about each other, according to that. Behaviour depends upon our feelings about others. If someone likes anyone, then one always tries to find some goodness in their badness also. And if someone doesn't like another person, then one always finds wickedness in their goodness also. If someone is good and thinkswell, then it's all right, but if one has false thinking of being wicked, then we have to change it, and the only way is to get out from the circle of jealousy. Try to understand deeply about intentions, nature, feelings, and circumstances. Like this, personal behaviour can be changed. If there is no compulsion to be with another, then you needn't be bound to relations personally. But yes, if relations are familiar or heartily attached, then try to coordinate with them.

Million Wings feels that lazy and careless persons can be part of some work but can't guide that. A careless person can enjoy his life but doesn't or can't do anything in coordinated ways for family, society, and world. Carelessness means one doesn't fulfil promises made by oneself intentionally. If one is not able to fulfil one's promise because of some clear and genuine reason, then that is not carelessness, as to try by devoting 100 per cent is in one's hands and then maybe one can't reach or be able to get success.

Million Wings feels that careless persons only do as much work as minimally required and are not able to survive without doing that minimum necessary work. A careless person gives importance to only those things which he really likes and give him comfort and happiness. Everyone tries to show future to careless person but he is ignoring work for his present needs also. Why should he worry or think about the future?

Million Wings feels that everyone tries to make a careless person responsible by making him afraid about the future, and careless persons live in the present, not the future. The ones who are tense about the slow action of a careless person are only those who are affected. If a careless person is taking anything or facilities from another, then he has to fulfil atleast minimum required responsibilities towards them. Million Wings feels that to stop or cut off the facilities of a careless person is the effective and easy way to reduce carelessness. Million Wings feels that when he faces reality, the more he has real knowledge about the work, the more confident and effective his work will be. Most people have had experience and knowledge about their subject but when talking about each other's subjects, then misunderstanding, debates, or clash may occur. As less, wrong or just guessing about other fields are the main cause of misunderstanding or clash, common sense is the logical principle to talk with any specialist of any latest field. To know or have the latest knowledge about one's field is the best working strategy and way to success.

Million Wings feels that everyone lives their life completely. They may move on with enjoyment, sorrow, or mixed feelings, but one lives one's life completely. Life is long but don't cut short the moments of happiness. Live every moment of happiness fully. Trying to increase moments of happiness more and more is happiness. Enjoy every moment of happiness according to choice and will and then enjoy it fully. Million Wings feels that happiness increases happiness. Happiness arises from happiness. Happiness makes happiness beautiful. The more powerfully and happily we enjoy the moments of happiness, the more chances of happiness we will get to enjoy. Million Wings feels that we live life fully and long but never cut short the moment of happiness.

Million Wings feels that the lightly we take tensions and sad moments, the more lightly they disappear; most tensions are resolved with time, as the solution which we are unable to think of in anger easily comes to mind after being relaxed. Humans' main motto is not to engage in tensions but is to overcome tensions and enjoy life. Million Wings feels that tensions and problems are like that small baby who is crying, and rude and harsh efforts to make him sleep go in vain, as he starts crying more. The more calmly and coolly we try to make the baby sleep, the more easily and the earlier baby sleeps; in the same way, issues, problems are worsened by fights, anger, and unnecessary shouting and these become more tense. The more calmly and peacefully we think about and discuss problems, the more easily these are resolved and the earlier we can get peace of mind, and again we can concentrate on our work and can enjoy life. Our personal happiness is our ultimate aim. If we can get our happiness peacefully and calmly, then why should we waste our brain power, money, peace of mind, relations, and respect to grab that? We can use all of these in someother work of our choice or to fulfil dreams and desires. We need to use all of these powers when reason refuses to understand even after making things clear to someone and still he unnecessarily acts arrogant and stubborn. Million Wings feels that if our matter/thing/talk is weighty, then high volume is not required; even low volume can give long-lasting results. Our voice will automatically reach everyone if our words are weighty. If one's thinking is effective and powerful, then even low volume can reach every corner. Talk and issues are weighty only if our intentions are good and purpose/determination is advantageous, then it hardly matterswhether the voice is high volume or low volume; it will be equally effective. Million Wings feels that high volume is impressive and effective only if that true from our side. Million Wings feels that if one is clear about oneself, then he should speak and the volume may be high or low. Do speak for self-respect whenever required. Words may be less or more but should be truthful, then they will surely be effective.

Million Wings feels that conflict teaches life. Conflict gives understanding and knowledge at personal level. Conflict doesn't mean graze or being frustrated. Rather, conflict is trying to fulfil dreams independently. Conflict doesn't mean to graze for that thing which we already have but it means to get that thing which is future's dreams. Conflict makes a person capable, does not destroy the person. To stop or interrupt the conflict which is required for health or mind is like torturing someone. To give comfort to a child doesn't mean that he can't even standup to take that comfort. If one is getting food, that doesn't mean to eat more than a required quantity and then die by suffering from diseases. The comfort which is easy but makes humans dependent on them day by day and destroys humans with each passing day is not in humans' favour. Allow children to have conflict so that they can live, not so much comfort that they became lazy and dependent. Don't give cooked life but give good ways, to make life. It's the right chance, motivations, direction for them. Conflict can never be gracious, as it is done to fulfil personal needs, dreams and desires. The work done by heart can't be taken as tension.

Million Wings feels that conflict in reality is the name of teaching minimum required capabilities. Conflict should be done in way that you needn't work twice for the samething. The work which is already used by people may be usedas base and then work for another target. If already you have comfort and money, then increase your qualities and ability, as qualities and ability make the real status. A person needs that much conflict that inspite of having comfort, he atleast can manage himself.

Million Wings feels that workdone by heart and will is always easy; may that work be difficult and without willpower, even small work seems to be difficult. Conflict done by heart may be successful or unsuccessful but it can't be tension. Conflict is part of power and guidance. Conflict is personal happiness, conflict is self-respect. Conflict is experience, conflict is self-status. Conflict is satisfaction, conflict is enjoyment, conflict is hope, conflict is a secret of feeling our dreams closely. Conflict is right, conflict is quality, conflict is ability.

🔱 🔱 🔱

Chapter 7

Behaviour and communication skills

Million Wings feels that no one can live happily alone. Every need, dream, and desire of everyone can be fulfilled by living in this world only. Everyone's happiness depends upon what kind of coordination one has with the world. Everyone knows their happiness, but it needs to be fulfilled in the world, by the world. The better the coordination with the world, the earlier we can fulfil our needs, dreams, and desires. If there is harmonious relation, then there will be happiness all around, and if not, then dissatisfaction and grief.

Million Wings feels that the world is a group of situations and circumstances which have a lot of things to fulfil everyone's dreams and desires. Humans just need to search their path and direction to fulfil their dreams, and for that, we need to be coordinated with the world. This is known as a behaviour skill everyone lives and tries to live for happiness in the world. Behaviour skill is the main way towards happiness. Harmonious relation with the world gives happiness every moment. Million Wings feels that a common problem with us is trying to find out someother meaning from our talks, and the best solution for this is behaviour skill.

Million Wings feels that if we can feel happy just by harmonious relationships, then why make tension or force anyone? Everyone needs to understand that whatever we do, we should do that with our own will and in agreement with that and with another too; do anything with anyone but with their will and agreement. Then everything is right and good. To find alike people is happiness; the world is so huge, we can meet lots of people who have the same thinking. So we have to find those people in the world/ society who havethe same thinking and desires, and the best way to know about that is conversation. To search and find alike persons is the first way towards happiness. Coordination between main thoughts is must. Small things can be managed easily.

Million Wings feels that person with alike thoughts can be found only by conversation. While a human won't talk to anyone, won't meet anyone, then how will happiness begin? The people whom we like, then what's wrong in talking to them or being social with them, and neither does it mean that we have some permanent relation with another. Firstly, we can know each other's thinking by conversation only; if there is coordination between thinking and mind, then go for whatever relationship you want to build. To meet the people whom we like or to talk to them is good. It's known as socializing. Million Wings feels that if we can't express ourselves, then how could another understand us? And if another person doesn't understand us, then on the basis of his own thinking level or by just applying a guess, he will react according to that. If we misunderstood anyone, then obviously we may also take him wrong. Million Wings feels that to understand someone's heart rightly at the right time is the toughest job in the world. Someone might guess about us from our acts, good or sad moods, tense or happy atmosphere but it's not important that he will come to know about right cause/reason too. Our feelings are known well by us only, and only we ourselves can express our feelings, interests, dreams, and desires to people whom we are attached. Whoelse will do that? To express ourselves is the way to know thoughts and thinking of another. The more clearly and truly the person expresses himself, the earlier he will get the company of alike people, and the company of alike people means happiness. Million Wings feels that everyone needs to converse first, then if looks, nature also match, then we can move forward towards other relations. Relations itself are destroyed if nature and ourselves freely are the way towards happiness.

It's common that while talking to each other, we may hurt others or didn't seem to be good or may even hurt self-respect. Million Wings feels that if anyone feels like that, then the heart feels unsatisfied and jolted. Talk at the sametime and situation and answer at the sametime. We are right if we are answering at the sametime in which another is talking or saying something. Don't keep anything in the heart, especially that which increases happiness and peace on saying. Million Wings feels that whatever you feel, express that as early as possible. By doing this, we become tension free, with satisfaction of heart and self-respect everytime. It's right. It's happiness. Expressing ourselves freely and answering another is right, as security and protection of self-respect is the right of everyone. If someone is speaking rudely than answer in the same way, and if another is polite, then be polite. Being right is fault-free power.

Million Wings feels that we needn't tell our good or bad habits, thinking, feelings, interests, dreams, and desires to the whole world but firstly we need to be clear and satisfied regarding ourselves and accept the reality to related person by heart. A human himself knows 100 per cent about himself, and he needn't change himself forcefully; instead he needn't tell 100 per cent about himself to the world. Everyone has their personal life too. With one you feel like having a discussion, just discuss with them. Million Wings feels that personally acceptingbetrayalby a related person is a daring/courageous job in the world. It gives permanent satisfaction to heart, mind, and soul. Million Wings feels that no one change anyone's thinking forcibly. Whatever one wants to do, one will do that only, and let one do it also. Million Wings feels that guidance should be given in that he can fulfil his dreams and desires earlier and through the right way. The human can change his thinking only if he feels it from the heart and acceptsit. Real change is the change which is accepted at heart, and right guidance is that which is able to make a person realize it in minimum time. Efficient guidance can fulfil life with happiness. Mistakes can be made by anyone but rare people have courage to accept them. Everyone makes mistakes but rarely support each other and let another understand. The meaning of every guidance is to fulfil life with more and more happiness. Guidance means to give way or direction to fulfil dreams. It needs to be understood that most dreams are not bad but the ways chosen to fulfil them may be wrong. Because of that, one gets refusal and disappointment. To guide the person rightly at the right time with the right way is the best policy. To give the right direction, way, or suggestion once or twice socially or professionally is enough, but advise many times to people who are attached by birth or heart. This means our own ones try to make us understand many times but another stepsback after advising once or twice. The same way life is changing every moment, rules of guidance should also need to change with time.

Million Wings feels that responsibility of an elder is more than the younger, to give good and right way/direction/guidance. To think this is not wrong; the younger have less knowledge. It's also right maximally.

Million Wings feels that being elder means one who can understand the real situation by his experience, with more patience, in more relaxed way and who can make decisions in more accurate ways. Being elder does not only mean more age. If one expects right or knowledgeable things from elders, then it's wrong, and if the younger is less intelligent, then nothing seems to be wrong. The less the age, the more person can be innocent, speedy, versatile, curious, with more dreams and desires, zeal, spirit, and unawareness of truth and problems of life. Being elder doesn't mean being serious; instead it means to fulfil our curiosities, versatility, and desires in more arranged and secure manner. To turn innocence into seriousness is not being elder, but to move on innocence in more secure way is being elder. Reducing destroying/innocence by showing real problems and truth of life and disappointing another is not being elder; instead, motivating them to search for their happiness, dreams, and desires with secure ways is being elder, and having more experience and knowledge about required fields is being elder. Being elder one may have more common sense, but it's not necessary to have equal intelligence in every field. A young doctor is more intelligent in medicine than an old man. A young artist is more intelligent in music than an aged government employee. A housewife is more intelligent in managing home than a great scientist. A photographer is more intelligent in photography than a renowned player. Being elder means having more knowledge and experience in required fields. Knowledge makes humans great. Million Wings feels that knowledge makes persons great and experience makes success.

Million Wings feels that a positive thinker and curious student can be good and can get experience in any condition but a capable teacher or preceptor can make a good student only if one has interest naturally or brought by teacher. Million Wings feels that teacher and student both are in search of each other. Social education is required, is needed but natural curiosity and modern intention are the biggest search of humans, who search for our teachers by ourselves. Circumstances of our own lives are real challenges for us, and a real teacher teaches us how to handle situations efficiently and helps us in achieving goals. Million Wings feels that our dreams and willpower are the most great and powerful teacher, who searches for the path in required direction in any circumstances. It's true, it's history, it's entertainment, it's future, it's happiness, it's enjoyment.

Million Wings feels that everyone is learning life by living and listening. Everyone is understanding and learning life by their own situations and circumstances and it's right too. Humans expect that they learn by watching, listening, or reading about each other. It's not duty to tell about anything or work but it's duty to ask. If elders didn't tell and the younger didn't ask then it's taken that the mistake is of the younger, not duty of elders. Elders can scold the younger only when they have told them atleast twice to make them understand. When you are teaching someone, then it shouldn't feel like fighting or scolding to do anything. To understand means to do work in more arranged and secure ways, not to do work in tension. Everyone learns slowly from elders to the younger, and always/everytime, everyone is in a learning stage process. One can be more intelligent than another in one or another field. But to be perfect requires one to feel and understand numerous circumstances and conditions, with time conditions, circumstance, capability, and priorities also changing. So thinking and decisions may also change. An intelligent person works according to the priorities. If someone will not teach, then how come someone will learn and understand about manners and all related behaviour?

If persons will not teach each other, then how can life become better? Not just teaching, but teaching by right way, i.e. with love and care, is necessary. The teacher may be very intelligent but he can teach only if he will think according to the level of the one whom he is teaching. It's the secret of teaching. Everyone learns and understands according to one's capacity, interest, and mind; some learn fast and some slowly, and it's right too. Person will be alike as his mental status. It's true. Mental status rises in plausible and arranged atmosphere; let them live in innocence who are innocent, who want to live in innocence while they can. Don't show horrible future to innocent people that they become afraid and feel insecure about the future, as by doing so they can even make their today hopeless; instead tell them the related circumstance and possibilities in such a way that they can understand and can live their future and present in plausible ways.

Million Wings feels that genuine praise about someone's good qualities and work done is the best motivation. It's good to tell mistakes, weaknesses, drawbacks. But repeating these again and again is not right. It can fill you with negative thoughts. It's true, it's right and will be. To criticize creates tensions and to praise makes a plausible atmosphere. Million Wings feels that may it be elders or the younger; if one can handle the time with perfect coordination, then issues will be resolved with plausible ways. The major difference between elders and the younger is that elders can force the younger but the younger can't force elders. To talk in the right manner at a required time is behaviour skill so that everyone can be satisfied. Don't waste unnecessary on family, business, or social place but give more happiness and peace if it can be spent for personal happiness.

Million Wings feels that it hardly matters that one is behaving rudely or not using proper words while the intentions are right; intentions are to resolve the matter. The logical self-respect is to express ourselves without taking tension of being right success. Million Wings feels that whether it is truth or lie, the happiness will last while there is coordination. It hardly matterswhether one is telling the truth or lying, while one's intentions are good. Intentions are not to betray someone or harm someone. Reality is that every human lives to fulfil his dreams and desires, and for that, he may take support of some lies also. There is nothing wrong in doing so, as the aim of the person is not to harm or hurt anyone. But the truth is he is managing time for his happiness. It's right to do so. There is nothing wrong/wicked in lying in hard situations or for social benefits and happiness. But one has to try and to move towards truth from lies. Million Wings feels that firstly, intentions of persons should be good, and being truthful is second. If someone wants to overcome lies by accepting the path of truth, then let him come out; infact help him, motivate him, as only truth can give permanent peace to the heart and right decisions to the mind. Lies can accompany truth for some time. But truth can give happiness every moment while moving on truth since start. It's bit different to attach the knitted lie with truth, and maybe challenging; the feelings of others may get hurt while telling the truth, and these chances are more. This fear always configures our minds, and along with all this, we also need more courage and daring to tell the truth.

Million Wings feels that lying unnecessarily and betraying someone for our own benefit is absolutely wrong. But logical meaning of accepting that by heart is effective only when we don't try to repeat that again. Otherwise it's useless to accept again and again by repeating the same mistakes and asking for forgiveness. Million Wings feels that move with arranged steps when moving towards truth from lie, as the real motive of speaking truth is the same as that of telling lies, i.e. to maintain happiness. When a human himself feels that, he has to maintain coordination of lies then make policies according to another's mental conditions so that more and more coordination can be maintained. On realizing a mistake, admit that to the related person. One may get annoyed/sad at that moment, but with time, one will surely forgive. It's our will to come out of lies and follow the way of truth but it depends on the will of another too, whether he will forgive or punish. Million Wings feels that everything is all right while a person is alive. Everything/anything can be managed while the person is alive. Coordination will be maintained itself on choosing the path of truth. And coordination is needed for maintenance while lying; on being truthful, there is no fear of coordination, but during lies, fear of breakage of coordination always worries us.

Million Wings feels that one person can behave like a great person; infact, behaviour needs to be good from both sides. Firstly one should behave properly as initiative and then one can react according to another's behaviour. One person cannot always behave well or nicely, but because of some problem or compulsion, one can do so. Only great person, eminent person can do so, one who initiates with etiquette and he feels secure and powerful. If someone still behaves arrogantly, rudely, forcibly then answer him in the same way. Nothing is wicked/wrong in doing so. It's right to do this in these conditions. Never expect ideal behaviour from everyone, and if someone is doing so, then respect them. Million Wings feels that idealism is the best way to live life. But it's not necessary that everyone has reached that level or will reach there.

Happiness is widely spread and it has huge boundaries. One limit is idealism and another is logical aim/purpose of life, which are related with initial nature and capabilities. Idealism is not the only way but the best way to get redemption and make life successful, but a logical aim, purpose, or way also gives lots of happiness and helps in getting redemption. Humans have to try every time to live ideal lives or to move towards idealism, but if we are not able to do so, then it's not a crime or wrong. In these circumstances, if a human is fulfilling atleast logical principles and policies, then also it's good, it's right. Logical life is a secret of happiness; it means human issues should be understood according to human ways, then human happiness will be maintained, and to think, to understand like this is exactly right, is correct.

Million Wings feels that never helping others in that way, that you yourself get hurt. To help means to decrease sorrows. But to decrease one's happiness and increase another's is not the right way. This is the logical meaning of help by doing so: a human can help to that extent which he can easily afford to do. We needn't grieve ourselves or our own ones to help others, and doing this to our own ones is not fair. Help others according to your own capacity, not by going beyond the limit. Million Wings feels that you should help only at that time when you really feel like it, and do think twice before helping another so that he shouldn't misuse that. Intentions of helper should be of providing food, clothes, or help during disease. That's perfectly right. If another is misusing your help, then it's their fault, not yours. But if a helper has some hint that another will misuse it, then find out some other way to help. As the money earned by hardwork should be used to help the needy, not to give to others just for fun. Help doesn't mean to donate, but it means to help the needy in tough situations and problems. Help can be done by any means, e.g. money, suggestion, mental, emotional, or physical, etc. Help is not a burden but happiness. Say no directly to the person if you are not able to help him. Help done in need is obligation which cannot be weaned off to that level. An obligation can't be compared with another obligation. A help is like that obligation which can be equalized, but to deplete it is difficult or impossible, as at time of need, that help is priceless, precious, through which errors can be corrected.

Million Wings feels that behaviour and chumming up according to age and continue behaviour skills according to presentation of another. If another is elder then it is expected that he will be more sincere, and while initiating talk, he will start in polite and respectful ways. If another seems to be innocent or less sincere, then initiate talk in polite and lovable ways. If another is a contemporary (of same age), then think that he will have the same thinking as you, then initiate talk in friendly ways, and then react the same way as another is reacting, answer in same way, and decide whether to carry on or not. If another is behaving positively, then can be chum up, but if another is giving negative responses and overreacting to things, than chum up will itself give up.

Million Wings feels that everyone has their own way to express themselves and their personal happiness. Some love to be quiet, some want to speak but less, some keeps on talking. Some speak straight forwardly, some on the basis of a guess or may lie too. Some speak in funny ways, a few speak in a serious manner, a few speak with negative attitude, a few speak just for fun, a few seriously don't take an interest in others, a few speak with responsibility, some with carelessness, some speak in ways of criticizing, a few in teasing ways, a few show attitude, a few are down to earth, a few always find faults in another, a few speak for the benefit of others. So in short, everyone has their own way and intentions. Million Wings feels that there are as many thoughts in the world as there are styles and ways to express ourselves, and nothing's wrong/wicked in doing so. Logical meaning of talk is to express ourselves to the other person, who may take it in any sense, anyway; it totally depends on his thinking and intentions. The way a human speaks or talks is taken as his truth. Everyone reacts and answers according to that. The way a human expresses himself is his natural way. Everyone reacts according to the world's tinge and expressions. To understand one's feelings and intentions 100 per cent rightly is not an easy job and it's even not required, as what one is saying is one's truth and should be taken as truth and you should react and behave according to that only.

Million Wings feels that taunting, criticizing, arguing, and commenting are common ways to express ourselves if one feels like answering in the same way and style as the initiator is reacting. Backbiting or gossiping and rumours are light-hearted entertainment. Infact, most rumours/gossip make things complicated, make a thing much bigger than normal, in which there is more imagination than reality. Backbiting means to talk about those things which are just things, and an individual comments according to one's own thinking about some third person who is not present there. When the third person is not there to clarify things, the two can say anything regarding him. It's just a way to pass time, nothing else. While someone doesn't know about the matter which we are talking about, whatever another is saying about it hardly matters. Nothing's wrong. It's non-evident, not important; it's only of social entertainment, in which one spreads more fakeness, less reality to one another. To spend free time like this with friends is not wrong. If we take gossip and rumours in positive ways, then along with entertainment, it is a way of social information. By talking about or discussing the personal life of another, one must learn something from that. If one can keep a good part of gossip or rumours to himself, then nothing's wrong in that. Everything is OK. Million Wings feels that the rumours, suggestions, and comments about the person can be clarified only by talking to the related person. Gossip is just a start for a person or about an issue; one can get its result by talking to the related person or by investigating properly. Million Wings feels that gossip, backbiting, and rumours are just to listen and leave there. But if we are related to that person, then things are related to us also, then clarify that at the sametime only. Million Wings feels that a person has to talk about the issues related to them. If a person is right, not reprehensible, not a culprit, and not responsible for an act, then he has to clarify his side on the spot. If a human is responsible for an act, then he needs to tell the reason behind that. One has to speak for himself. It's true, it's right. The way a human represents himself, others will see, understand, and behave according to that only. If one can't respect oneself, then how could one expect the same from others? If one represents that he is intense, then others will also think the same. Million Wings feels that a person has to live in plausible and elegant ways so that personal happiness and comfort should be maintained. A person needs to be a hardliner only when required.

Million Wings feels that if someone wants to express himself, then motivate him and give him a chance to speak, and along with that, listening and understanding his feelings in elegant ways is a logical behaviour. The real meaning of giving freedom to speak is listening to them in elegant ways and with good intentions. Elders always askthe younger to express their feelings, mistakes, problems, desires, tensions, but when they express themselves, then elders are annoyed and hard to them, start finding their faults and mistakes, and don't listen to the whole matter; infact, elders start scolding and fighting in between only. In these circumstances, theyounger never express themselves and their feelings start accumulating in their hearts. In these conditions, they start searching for the right person who can listen to them, or become sad and depressed and feel hopeless and forlorn and stuck in non-social conflicts. To give a chance to others to express themselves means having the quality of listening to them wisely and elegantly in ourselves; it's behaviour skill. The right procedure is to listen to our own ones wisely and then give suggestions or help them. Million Wings feels that sometimes on getting a chance, one may react unlawfully and inappropriately along with expressing feelings. If a person is elder, experienced, and high status and allows others to express themselves freely then it doesn't mean to misuse the chance or elegance and disrespect the person. The one who is giving the chance can take that back also, because he wants to give happiness and respect to others too and doesn't want grief or disrespect for himself.

A person has to keep his behaviour more free, wide, and plausible but limits should be maintained strongly and well, so that one can't misuse that. Every person knows their limits and no one is allowed to cross that limit/ border. Behaviour may be free and calm but limits should be strong and well maintained.

Million Wings feels that one who's talking about or talking of a third person to another might use the same words but one's tinge/way might differ, and it can create misunderstanding. So one should take care that one should deliver words in the same way the person has said, so that positive intentions remain the same and not seem like negative ones.

Today everyone has shortage of time. If one has notime to relax and talk, then carry that along with your work. Talk while doing light or little work at home. This is the only way to double the time. If we are with people of our own choice, it is the best time, and along with that, a chance to share our feelings and thought is there. We may wait for free time but whenever we get a chance to talk to lovable persons, or personswho are close to our hearts, talk to them. It's right, it's correct, it's happiness.

Million Wings feels that one can talk on any matter, whether it be good or bad. If one can talk about anything with the right way and in a decent manner at the right time, then nothing's wrong in that; there is nothing in the world which can't be expressed. We can talk about the worst thing in the world by using suitable words. Parents can talk to kids regarding their bad habits. Students can ask any question to their teachers. People can question leaders about any social occurrence. Concurrence can arise from any question to religion regarding living.

Million Wings feels that the way a person represents himself to the world, they will take him in the same way. If we present things in an intense way, then others would take these in an intense way. If we present things in a plausible way, then others will take these in the same way. If we took things in a heavy and tense way, then obviously they would appear the same, and if we take them lightly, then those will appear the same. If we do that in friendly way, then we find them friendly. If we do things with aversion, then we seem like enemies. Million Wings feels that a person should represent himself in the same way as he really wants to present himself to the world. If one wants to make friendly/lovable relations with others, then one should represent in the same way. We want to present with love and in friendly ways, then others will feel the same, understand the same, and if others will not feel the same or understand something else, then our feelings will not be taken in the same way, the way we wantto represent.

Million Wings feels that if a human wants success, then he achieves also. There is no proper definition of success if it's measured on personal basis. Everyone has their own level of success. Success is hardwork, success is happiness, success is satisfaction. Everyone is happy on getting success and feels proud of that and wants to share that with their family, relatives, and friends. Every success is respectable. Value of every success is lawful. If someone has purchased a cycle with hardwork, and another has purchased a luxury car, then there is a difference in success level but logical feeling will be the same. Success doesn't mean to have more and costlier things, but to make a better tomorrow than today is real success. The first motto of life is to fulfil logical needs, and then there is no upper limit of passion or success. Million Wings feels that one should not stop others who express their feelings; instead, motivate and guide them to express their feelings in the right way. It will be a logical success to express our feelings, curiosities, problems; it's the best, strongest way for personal success and self-confidence. Everyone has to express freely. It's the first secret for happiness.

Million Wings feels that the worst sad thing is that which humans can't share with anyone, can't make others understand them. Sorrow can be shared, and others can feel that can be decreased by discussion or by finding solutions. But the fear, tensions, confusions, misunderstandings, weaknesses, arguments which can't be expressed and are kept in the heart are the biggest cause of sorrow. Only one way to resolve these sorrows is that one has to share them with a confidant so that their solutions can be found out. Otherwise, these kinds of sorrows need time and make a way and direction according to that only. Million Wings feels that mostly, people try to tell their feelings and intentions to each other, but instead of understanding each other, arguments and misunderstandings keep on increasing. It happens because instead of understanding, they think that they are more right and another is wrong. Sometimes, humans can't express their feelings rightly and are not able to deliver them correctly. In these conditions, a third person(mediator) can clarify those misunderstandings, and deliver the right intentions in more elegant and coordinated ways. A mediator can be one who knows and understands circumstances and mental conditions of both persons very well and whose intention is to make plausible coordination. Million Wings feels that these kinds of mediators are hard to find, who are neutral and know behaviour skills better. But these kinds of mediators are God's gift for happiness to family, society, nation, world. They help in maintaining plausible coordination.

Million Wings feels that a person himself can express his feelings, thoughts, circumstances in a better way than anyone else. If a mediator is required, then also we need to tell our intentions and feelings to that person also. Therefore, self-expression is the best step towards happiness. It's true, it's happiness.

Million Wings feels that to be annoyed and persuaded is a right of coordination for our own ones and loved ones, who fill our lives with lots of colour. All are our own in by-birth relations and those who are attached by heart, and small things like small fights, arguments, annoyance, misunderstandings, expectations often happen. Our loved ones often get annoyed as it's their right and being annoyed is just showing off and the one who is persuading also teases and tries to persuade. Our own may be annoyed to any extent with us but they are never annoyed at heart and we never get apart from each other and then again get the same on persuading. Million Wings feels that sometimes loved ones get so annoyed that even explanations cannot convince them. Then quietly listening to their hard words used to be equal to asking for forgiveness and persuading them. If then also they don't forgive, then just hug them tightly without uttering a word and then see the magic of that hug, which will erase all annoyance and give emotional and mental relaxation. If we don't know what to do and what not, then just relax and hug them. It's the best and a beautiful secret of persuading our own ones. To hug our own ones gives magical comfort. One can be annoyed when someone tries persuading; otherwise, what's the fun in being annoyed? A person may be annoyed lots of times but be persuaded very easily on persuading. To be annoyed or to persuade never ever means to fight or to get apart; infact, life's beautiful moments become more enjoyable. And interestingly, one may get annoyed genuinely or not genuinely but when someone tries to persuade one, then a warm feeling of belongingness, of relations with care and love gives a feeling of warm comfort, which makes relations stronger. There might be negligible misunderstandings or expectations behind intense annoyance.

In these conditions, try to understand that sometimes mistakes may be made unknowingly; even they are not aware of that or may not get to know the right cause of the annoyance. Million Wings feels that oftenthey guess that there might be some problem, but it's not important that they may get to know about the exact cause behind that. If person who is trying to please doesn't know the exact cause, then the person who is annoyed should tell the right cause so that matter can be resolved earlier and fast.

Million Wings feels that expectations are a natural process. When one has done something for another, then he might expect the same inreturn, and to do this is not wrong; it's absolutely right. One can have expectations of relations but only in those relations where promises were made to each other. If a person expects those things which one has never promised, then there is no fault, compulsion, or responsibility of one to do the same. Million Wings feels that comparison makes a person better day by day. A human has to compare himself with himself. He needs to know what he was yesterday and what he is today and what he wants to be. It means comparison with himself is a secret of personal success. Competition and comparison to another helps in getting and speeding success. Comparison with positive attitude helps in maintaining minimum required level. Million Wings feels that one should not be compared on the basis of things which are not at all in humans' hands, e.g. race, colour, looks, parents. Humans should be recognized on the basis of their qualities. The things which humans have made are now disturbing them (e.g. casteism, religious fights, rules and regulations) and can be changed and it's right too. The things which are disturbing at social level should be changed or depleted rather than carrying them. It's right. Million Wings feels that the way a person represents himself, the world will take him in the same way. If representing things in an intense way, then others would take things in an intense way. If presenting with a plausible way, then others will take it the same. If we took things in a heavy and tense way, then they would appear the same, and if we take those lightly, then those will appear the same. If we do that in a friendly way, then we find them friendly. If done with aversion, than we seem like enemies. Million Wings feels that person should represent himself in the same way as he really wants to present himself to the world. If one wants friendly/loving relations with others, then he should represent the same way. We want to present with love and a friendly way, then one should feel the same, understand the same, and if we will not feel the same or understand something else, then our feelings will not be taken in the same way, the way we want to represent.

Million Wings feels that humans want success and do also. There is no proper definition of success measured on personal basis. Everyone has their own level of success. Success is hardwork, success is happiness, success is satisfaction. Everyone is happy on getting success and feels proud of that and wants to share that with their family, relatives, and friends. Every success is respectable. Value of every success is lawful. If someone has purchased a cycle with hardwork and another has purchased a luxury car, then there is difference in success level but logical feeling will be the same.

Success doesn't mean to have more and costlier things, but to make a better tomorrow than today is real success. For life, the first necessity is to fulfil logical needs, and then there is no upper level of passion or success.

Million Wings feels that while the intentions are good, fulfil your own dreams without hurting others and by maintaining plausible coordination, then nothing's wrong in making excuses. Everything is all right. Excuses help in maintaining coordination between two situations. When a person wants to handle situations along with maintaining personal relations then he takes this way, it's not wrong. Million Wings feels that excuses are used to solve problems and tensions, not to create tensions and problems; excuses are a style to tolerate shocks with ease but can't take the place of personal responsibilities. Other persons are also residing in the same world as a human himself, so excuses should not hurt trust. There is nothing wrong in helping others by making excuses cleverly. While intention is good, then one can handle situations by excuses. One can manage tough situations and get time to resolve mistakes and irresponsibilities with the help of excuses. So excuses and lies will get logical clearance and one can make plausible coordination with world.

Million Wings feels that one may be doing anything for another, but the other will be satisfied only if he would get things according to his will and need. Million Wings feels that we have to fulfil minimum needs of our family and loved ones in the right way, and after that, help, motivate, and guide them in fulfilling their dreams and desires. This is the right way. The best way to fulfil dreams of near and dear ones is by spending quality time with them so that you will be able to know and understand their real happiness. To give everykind of comfort is a reminder of care and belongingness according to worldliness, but workdone by understanding dreams and desires is a junction of logical happiness.

Million Wings feels that heartfelt relations are important. Humans give attentions first to near and dear ones, whom they like. It's right, it's correct. Nothing's wrong in this. First importance is relation of one's choice, then one has to see those relations who like them and then start with familiar way to the rest of the world.

Million Wings feels that whatever one's intentions are, one can give only those things to another. One who has happiness will share happiness, who has tensions will share tensions. Whoever has positive attitude will show positive attitude; whoever has negative thoughts will not warn for security but will pull back. Everyone is right at their place. It depends upon the stakes, that is, what he wants to extract and what not. Million Wings feels that a person chooses beneficial things and takes things according to his own will, need, intention. It's true, it's right.

Million Wings feels that being careless doesn't mean being wicked but it means not to give 100 per cent intention to work. Intention of a careless person is not to harm anyone but it means to be away from reality. A person may be careless in one field but it doesn't mean that person is lazy in every field; careless means not to understand the importance value of a thing or talk. If one person is capable in doing one work, then the person may be careless in another. Carelessness means that person is not interested in that work/field, but maybe he is giving more attention to some other work in which he is interested. It's not necessary that careless persons will be balanced; instead they are lost in one direction and goal. Careless to others means that one is not fulfilling even their minimum responsibility, and personal carelessness means that person is not even handling his own handiwork and may get a disadvantage in that thing which can be managed easily.

Million Wings feels that careless persons live in today and in themselves only. Today's happiness matters for careless persons. A careless person just wants to do those things in which he is interested personally. A careless person doesn't live for others' needs but for his own will and dreams. It's not necessary that a careless person is useless. Maybe he has much success in someother field; careless in one may be important in another field. Not being able to fulfil one's hope can also be carelessness. Carelessness is not favourable to age, experience, capacity, work, and circumstances of a person. A wilfully careless person can't be made intelligent and responsible. Relatives and near and dear ones related to a careless person remainaggrieved because of him, as they are worried about the future of the careless person. Careless persons want to live that much more in today, and their near and dear ones try to improve them by showing their future. Million Wings feels that most of the time, a careless person is not useless but his importance and thinking don't suit others. Million Wings feels that a careless person shouldn't be forced, but motivate him for personal management.

Reserved things should be managed. Help them and motivate them to achieve their goals fast so that their importance can change. Advise careless persons to fulfil atleast their minimum responsibility. Praise them for their small efforts. Try to make them understand the logical importance of every work and that too according to their thinking and intelligence. Atleast try to get them. Try to get minimum required things in the compatible circle of a careless person.

Million Wings feels that the best time of every work is when that is required. To wrong least for the future and to live more in the present is everything for careless persons. Million Wings feels that importance of careless persons may be any, but importance of their near and dear ones are they only. If careless persons are not fulfilling their minimum responsibilities, then their near and dear ones fulfil that by themselves only. Careless persons need to understand that their basic needs are fulfilled because of the love and care of their near and dear ones. If careless persons are doing everything on their own, then their near and dear ones are trying to save them from possible dangers and tensions. Million Wings feels that every carelessness can be tolerated and forgiven, if harm because of that carelessness can be rectified and another chance can be given in those conditions. But carelessness due to which lives are harmed and the harm which can't be rectified can't be tolerated. One losing his life because of the carelessness of another is wrong, so one has to pay its penalty. Even this is right too. The carelessness due to which life is lost should have strict punishment but within human boundaries. Unsocial or careless persons have no right/freedom to take any life or to create a tense atmosphere. Professional intense carelessness should be managed strictly. Million Wings wants it understood that a careless person has a right to be careless but has no right or freedom to take life or torture or to create a tense atmosphere. Near and dear ones and society may give security to careless person once, twice, or thrice but it's not necessary that they do so everytime.

Million Wings thinks that to live with carelessness is the only way in which one has more chance of having personal loss, as leaving aside ownones, the rest of the world finds one or another way to fulfil their damage. Small carelessness is part of life. It can be rectified. Mostly this small carelessness happens unintentionally. Million Wings feels that the main causes of carelessness are innocence, lack of knowledge, and lack of experience, which is unawareness of reality, and the second reason is that the issue in which a careless person is stuck doesn't seem to be more important and useful than that in which he shows carelessness and causes tension/grievance. Results of carelessness don't come immediately because every suggestion seems to be useless to a careless person. Million Wings feels that change can only happen when a human himself feels so and he can feel so only when carelessness disturbs his own enjoyment. Million Wings feels that efficient guidance can show the way to a careless person.

Million Wings feels that a person may be a very intelligent specialist or experienced, but to think about unlimited possibilities is far from human capacities to understand at the same time. The issues/work which are totally dependent on a human himself, he can be sure about everything related to that only. But the work/thing in which one has to be more or less dependent on others for success, to give surety for that is not right. Million Wings feels that the real situations, real needs, real thinking, real behaviour policy to understand and make all this understood 100 per cent rightly are too tough. So on behalf of that, the person himself can't decide and declare 100 per cent results.

Million Wings feels that one can feel anything in any situation as that's his personal reaction, and that may not seem to be right according to present situations, knowledge, and experience. But don't reject the reaction of others too, as that may be true also. That may be any possibility in future. Million Wings feels that one can feel anything at anytime to listen and understand that and to relate that with things and it's his right to and is a logical decision and way. One may get 100 per cent result according to workdone, then also it's not necessary that he will be satisfied fully. Someone may be happy even with small efforts. Human reactions are knowledge, understanding, and experience for future. Lakhs and crores of possibilities are attached with everyone. We don't know what can happen next. Someone isn't affected at all, and another may take the same thing so seriously. Million Wings feels that anything can happen. Persons can assure you of personal capabilities and capacities, but don't be obstinate, arrogant, and overconfident about results. A person can devote his 100 per cent but can't give surety if there is on dependency on others too. A person can be sure, confident and arrogant about the right direction and tries, but only results give 100 per cent surety to the possibilities hidden in future.

Million Wings feels that one doesn't want to take risks about one's future. Then the person should not take any risk regarding himself. To try with a real point of view is the power of hope. To take a risk for the work which can give more benefit seems to be good. What and how much he wants or to do in his life, he has to decide himself. One can't give benefit forcibly. If the try to give benefit forcefully fails, then others complain with grievance and it's right as he himself is not willing. As he is already not interested and he got a loss in same, then obviously he will not tolerate that, and it's right. Million Wings feels that one has to take a risk for others only when another is interested; otherwise don't do that. To make someone agree by explaining is right but trying to give him benefit forcefully is wrong. Million Wings feels that you can be arrogant and sure about personal tries only. As success comes by devoting 100 per cent personal efforts filled with positive points of view is that hope of power which ensures success. Million Wings feels that if you want to make others understand something, then try to make them realize so that they agree by their will, and this will happen only if we try to make them understand according to their thinking. It's easier to make a person understand by giving an example according to work, business, living, or dreams and desires of that person. To have knowledge about a thing/work/possibility, it's not enough to accept that; one will accept that only by knowing real needs and benefits, and it's right too. Effective guidance is that which can give better direction and method before time. Everyone learns by themselves from losses that occurred through problems but to explain things in an effective way before time is efficient guidance.

Million Wings feels that everyone is right at their place, but a cause of fights and tensions is when one is not able to understand the thinking of others.

Difference in level of thinking primarily creates misunderstandings. When a boy shakes hands, hugs, or roams about with a girl, it's friendship, and a third person may take it as flirting. One may talk at high volume to clarify things but another may take it as nonsense or fighting. Someone takes another's surety as capacity and capability, and others may take it as ego or bragging; what one may take as devotion, another may take as showing off. Someone takes one's act as innocence and others may take that as cunningness.

Million Wings feels that only personal thinking, understanding, and actions are more important than what he feels, whatever another's means or intentions may be, and it's right too. One can judge people according to themselves and nothing's wrong in doing so.

Million Wings feels that one sees and feels others' actions and movements according to their will and intentions, and it's true too. If you want to continue relations, then would find force/pressure as good and take every wrong thing as good, and if you want to be apart, then label every good job as cunning. If the intention is to clarify things, then find some solutions by positive thinking, and if the intention is to deprave the things, then find negative meaning of every good thing. Will, intention, and thinking of any person depends on his basic nature, and this basic nature is desired coordination.

Million Wings feels that it's true that everyone sees/understands acts and movements according to intentions of others, and to do this is right. As it's right, others may say/do anything, but what the other one will feel from that he would understand and react. If intention of other is right and wants to attach then he should try to show things in a better way. Million Wings feels that what one feels, that is truth for him; another may do or say anything. In these situations which are out of control, only a third person or system who has open, wide, optimistic, and balanced thinking will able to remove misunderstanding and maintain plausible satisfied coordination, or maybe some third friend, relative, or society, or get the help of government or country in serious matters/conditions. Million Wings feels that personal disputes should be clarified on personal basis first. It's right way, right decision, happiness.

Million Wings feels that every human can take suggestions and help of as many people as he wants. To do this is nature and satisfaction of persons, and nothing's wicked in this. If one is satisfied only then will one follow a suggestion and help, and it's right too. One has to give suggestion and help on personal basis but it depends on another how much benefit he wants to extract from that. If one doesn't follow the advice or suggestion, then don't be annoyed or complain, as sometimes one is not able to decide by oneself; he also has to discuss with others and has to make a working strategy. Million Wings feels that if one has to give suggestion according to one's best knowledge, capacity, and experience, it's logical satisfaction and happiness and leaves the rest of the things on others. That's his will, from how many other people he wants to take suggestions, and which suggestion we want to adopt is solely our decision.

Million Wings feels that when one complains about anything, then nature is firstly human starts explaining the matter and finding faults in others and starts telling his compulsions/duress, and to do this is right. No one wants to take blame on oneself. One can make sure about the mistake and carelessness on the basis of proof, as on the basis of guesses, others also answer on the basis of guesses. It's true. Talk can be erased/blown with talk, but clarifying things is security/happiness of self-respect.

Million Wings feels that when someone is delivering talk of one person to another then during delivering that message or talk to another, words may be the same but things/talk and feeling may differ; one may say something in caring way while suggesting to change, it may seems like another is taunting or finding fault. So while conveying message, maintain the tinge and feeling along with words is right justice. If message is conveyed by positive attitude, then also it's good to some extent but if positivity is converted to negativity, then it can create great misunderstandings.

Million Wings feels that when negative things aren't expectedfrom related person, in these conditions, talk directly atleast once regarding the matter before taking some serious step, as sometimes no one's intention is wrong but things get complicated without reason. Instead of believing a third person, believe the one whom you trust more. Listen to the one who is nearer. If someone is giving negative message about them, do talk directly to them atleast once.

Million Wings feels that for things/work which can be done on the phone, a person needn't go there himself. Only for that work where personal presence is necessary, to move there is right. Being in contact through phone can solve many problems, and many situations/problems can be handled. Many matters can be easily resolved on the phone instead of being present there. To attend to the calls of each other is an easy way of management.

People express their feelings through words and the other tries to understand the intentions from them and answer according to that. Our own ones take our intentions behind the words in positive way and others always catch negative words. Talk to own ones in any way, but while talking to others, talk that much which is required and important.

When our own are annoyed and say some hurting words, then those words or anger are not forever; neither do they want that much hard thing to happen instead fight at present condition. Girls used to repeat the same things again and again but didn't mean to fight, and boys show anger on the same things again and again but didn't mean to fight. It's true. It takes a few minutes to a few days to deplete that effect. This often happens.

Million Wings feels that leadership is a challenging job but not difficult or impossible. The real meaning of leadership is to give the right direction to people of different thoughts, thinking, habits simultaneously and successfully motivate them to do the same work. For this, patience, knowledge, and dedication are needed. The biggest and real training to polish these natural qualities is to meet with people in daily life and to listen to their talk, matters, feelings and understand them. Answer their questions rightly and help them in fulfilling dreams. Everyone has own importance and behaviour and own benefit and problems. A person in every condition and a problem person sees his own problem more in those situations and others' benefits in the same situation. Nothing's wrong in doing so. But benefits of our situations may be a dream of some others. Firstly human has to enjoy freely his situation and, in the rest of the time left, fill his lacks/deficiencies; he should resolve lacks, problems. Only those will give personal happiness.

One who used to joke with others takes another's joke in a serious way and takes their taunt, words, and stupidities as joke only. Million Wings feels, joke with them only who can tolerate that and only as much as they can tolerate. One who is joking has to take care of this first: what kind of nature and thinking and tolerance power another has. Don't hurt the self-respect of others. Where self-respect got hurt, that joke turns into wickedness. Don't joke with everyone. One whom you know better, just joke with them only. Don't joke with an unknown person as he may suffer from stress, limited thinking, or mental illness and may over react on just small things. Million Wings feels that more the coordination with neighbours, the better. Neighbours are the real hope of help in emergency conditions. Million Wings feels that if there is no compatibility or there are more fights or disputes or jealousy with neighbours, then to change place is the best option to maintain happiness and peace of daily living. If neighbours or society all react stubbornly, then there is no use reacting in the same manner and living in a tense atmosphere. To shift to a better place is a much better option. To sell the land/house and shift to a new place is a much better option than fighting with the stubborn, stupid, and corrupt. It will be the right decision. Try to do it, as personal happiness is more important than anything else in the world. We start knowing the behaviour/nature of the one whom we live with, and according to that, share yourself with them. If our thinking doesn't match with another's, then there's no meaning in sharing your feelings with them. It's no use talking to the person whose main motto is to find faults, and negatively, in every work. These persons have nothing to give except grief/sorrow. So a better and peaceful decision is to boycott these persons than to fight or be sad everyday. If they are related by birth or are ones from social relations, then just talk as much as much required, and if someone else, then just leave them. Try to search for new and better people. It will be right. It's true, it's happiness. The only way to realize the importance of already present old person in life is to talk to or to meet new people. It's better to meet new people.

Some people are jealous of others. To do this is natural behaviour. It's right. Jealousy mostly gives positive power to persons. But some people are so sick that they use it to spread rumours about others, to defame them at a social level. Most people believe these rumours, as no one has so much time and need to know/understand the real matter. To hide their own negative points and failures, jealous people spread rumours about others. When you listen to something like this about your own ones, then talk to them directly and clarify the matter and then warn the related person or take some other step. Talk can be clarified by talking. Fights seem to be right on the basis of real proof. Being flawless is power.

Chapter 8
Standards of living

Every human wants to live with more comfort. Living standards also change with time and to move with the world gives happiness to humans and it's exactly right. Million Wings feels that atleast basic level is required with time. Million Wings feels that comfort level keeps on increasing but no one fixed a minimum level/standard of living. There is no limit of increasing the standard. But a person should feel like he has maintained atleast a basic living standard which is satisfactory according to time. On reaching a certain level, the race may be finished and to increase that standard will be his passion, not compulsion.

Million Wings fixed some important living standards for every human being which are called as logical living, and the humans who touch that level, their living standard will be taken as logical living. Standard is that category, may it be higher/more, which will be called logical living only. Million Wings feels that usefulness is availability/priority. Logical living is a minimum living standard for every person which gives logical measurement to success. Million Wings fixes these minimum living standards according to time so that every person has self-confidence of same and satisfactory living standards at world/international level. Goals of logical living are not based on cost of anything but its usefulness is common.

Million Wings feels that humans have to decide a minimum level to fulfil needs of daily living as competition of being better doesn't end, i.e.

119

has no limits. Logical living means that humans are able to do all that work of life which may be available at cheapest cost. Million Wings feels that if the main motto of convenience/facility is fulfilled, then that's logical. Then it hardly matters that may be available at cheapest cost. Logical living is necessary; above that, it's all passion may raise the living standard to any level that is one's will. Million Wings feels that usefulness is priority. Usefulness is logical living. Now if we see the motto of costlier and cheapest mobile is the same, that is, to talk. If we compare cheapest AC car with costlier AC car, then motto of both is to travelin a comfortable atmosphere. The meaning of wearing clean clothes is to cover the body, then those may be costly or cheap. Balanced diet and a stomach full of food are necessary, may it be of transport cafe or five-star hotel. Main motto of TV is to listen to national and international news and entertainment, may it be 22-inch TV screen or the world's costlier screen. Million Wings feels, you spend money till that level up to which usefulness of things increases; above that is just a race.

Million Wings feels that the main goal of every person is to achieve a logical goal. The one who is fulfilling logical living can be at any level, will be taken as the same. After that, a human can raise his standard to any level. If a human is earning more money, then that's his wish. He may purchase comfort of any level and can enjoy it, can purchase costlier things. On having more money, one can purchase costlier things, then that will be one's passion.

Million Wings feels that to reach the logical thing is success and, above that, may raise a standard to any level; that will be passion. To have more money means to improve speciality and beauty along with usefulness. Passions are not duress and passion may have any cost or level. Passions are our own and for ourselves, and they need not be goals/aims for everyone else in society. Passions are happiness and dreams and in the same way, everyone has their own passions which are their dream, their aim. If passion of someother, nothing's wrong in tempting us then making that as our own dream, will, passion. If two persons have the same passion, then they can compete to achieve the goal. If there's competition with others, speedup and excel in success. Million Wings feels that if competition or race on same track gives pleasure, happiness, then nothing's wrong in that. Million

Wings feels you live life according to your own will and dream and do compete for that, as that's life. Million Wings understands that people can live anywhere in the world but they have some common needs. If we just have a look at the life cycle of every human then it's clear that everyone needs food, clothes, shelter, education, business, conversation, transport, entertainment, support. Now if we see that, then it's the responsibility of government to make it available at lowest cost. It depends on capacity of every human whether he can afford that or not. Million Wings feels that usefulness is priority, not only brand.

Million Wings feels that one has to stay in his own country; for the chance, facility, or atmosphere which is not in one's country, do visit abroad for some time to fulfil that, for example, education, meetings, conference. One can roam about anywhere in the world. There are so many natural and artificial tourist places in different parts of the world, where humans should visit if they have time, chance, facility, and passion.

Million Wings feels that living according to the atmosphere which a human likes will give happiness. Million Wings feels, be successful in life as much you want, as much as possible, as much as you desire, as much you dream about. In our own countries, there is no shortage of anything from villages to cities, peaceful nature to fashionable human beauty, simple life to modern life. The life and atmosphere which one wants, one can choose places according to that. If one wants to move abroad, then it's much better to live in metro city of own country instead of moving to another country. As issues related to economy management, government, security can be demanded with much more rights.

Million Wings feels that if there is happy and plausible coordination with neighbours, then life will be easy and happy. No one can live alone; more or less, everyone needs one another, especially in emergency. To give social benefit and comforts, police and government takes signature of some neighbors only. Million Wings feel that during construction, marriage parties, jagran, etc., one has to feel sorry for unnecessary disturbance and ask for help and support from neighbours so that life of neighbours shouldn't be disturbed and the program also ends without any fight or complaints.

Million Wings feels that ones with whom you feel happy and good, meet those people. If you meet with jealousy, duress, compulsion, then free yourself from these boundaries. Go there, where you feel like, meet them, may that be for relations, friends, neighbours. Don't go to any function, program, wedding, seminar half-heartedly. Instead of that, enjoy a cup of tea at home; you needn't go to those functions or meet those people, where heart and thinking don't match. Our parents, real brothers/sisters, children, lovers, best friends are our priorities. Rest of the things are imaginary or worldly. If you are not feeling comfortable with someone, then you needn't meet them, needn't be much frank or social but to say hello/hi to everyone is sign of personal goodness and civilization.

Million Wings feels that socializing itself increases at times when required. Instead of maintaining forcefully, it is much better to coordinate at time when one feelsa need. It's right, it's good till someone doesn't need another. Million Wings feels that gratefulness can't be substituted by gratefulness. But there is a one-each gratification on each other. If one is in the condition that one can do something for others, then one should do that, as to do gratification in the first place is a natural chance to show personal capability.

Million Wings feels, don't help others in that way that you yourself get stuck in problems. Help others only when you are capable of helping without much personal problem. Million Wings feels that clearly saying no is also a type of help so that another can't have expectations, and without wasting time, he can try to get help from some other. To give support and motivation on personal basis is also a logical help, which anyone can do anytime.

Million Wings feels that persons of same thinking and age should live together. Being with incompatible people disturbs peace. The thinking difference between traditional living and modern living often creates tense atmosphere at social or living place and people living nearby often fight with each other regarding way of living. Million Wings feels that ways/ styles of living change with time. Wearing less clothes, coming home late night, music enjoyment, dance, meeting of girls and guys are OK according to modern living, but social or traditional ways take it as stupid and nasty. Nowdiscussion/argument regarding who is right and who is wrong may turn into fights. It's clear that everyone thinks that they are right at their place. Then why is there disagreement?

Million Wings feels that coordination is traditional customs and modernization is happiness for both sides.

Million Wings feels that circumstances change, dreams and desires change, living standards change, so thinking also changes. Million Wings feels that it's difficult to pull back the world, but we can make a better future in plausible ways. Million Wings feels, fulfil dreams while the world doesn't change according to us; till then, we have to fulfil our dreams in such a way that no one can object to us, or we have to make them understand at social level or have to make good coordination or have to live life in personal ways or oppose that. All ways are right. Million Wings feels that whatever good or bad we want to do, we can do but in such a way that no one is harmed from that and there should even be no problem at personal level. Million Wings feels that we live according to our own will and either change the thinking of others or change the atmosphere or place or make such a strategy that personal and social coordination should be maintained; the third way may be the best.

Million Wings feels that everyone has personal life and it's one's right too. Security of personal life is one's own responsibility. Personal life is that which a human doesn't want to tell everyone, may it be good or bad. Mostly personal life is that which is not taken as right at social level, those things which the world doesn't give respect to or may be wrong by one or another way. If it will be so, then why are there so many things which are happening? Maybe because everyone wants that, but no one is able to accept that freely in the world's way. We have to find out the way by thinking about them to present them in respectful ways. Every person lives for themselves and it's right too. Everyone needs to think about that, how one can fulfil one's dreams and desires, not take the responsibility to grab happiness for the whole society, and it's right too. If we see and think, then everyone's life is giving one or another direction to the whole world. Everyone's life and living are lessons for the world. Then why does one need to think in another way about the world? So let them do those things which one naturally wants to do. If one is doing something good, then his success is guidance, motivation, lesson for the whole world. If one is doing something and he fails, then the failure of that is a lesson for the whole world. So by realizing the success and failure of others, one improves or finds some other ways.

Million Wings feels that being away from the balanced and wide thinking according to time is the generation gap. Parents and children argue on one and another issue and that is due to their thinking, priorities, will, and ways of doing work, and both think that they are right at their place. Maybe both are wrong. Million Wings feels that the generation gap is not a thinking gap between the two; instead it means away from international standards of wide, open, optimistic, and balanced thinking. Million Wings feels that arguments between the younger and elders, oldies and the modern, or traditionand modernity is that thinking in which both want happiness and success, but parents want it with more security and the younger wants to do it with freedom and by taking risks.

Million Wings feels that everyone wants to spend their time according to their thinking, will, and way, and it is right too. Everyone has their own priorities and will and they spend time and days according to that. They get happiness, feel good by doing so. To spend the day according to ourselves is right and the best way of personal happiness. But it's not necessary that family, society, and others also live and accept that, and even it's right. Million Wings feels that personal happiness and enjoyment is the will and dream of every person, may their routine be balanced or not. Everyone needs to know how to manage the twenty-four hours of the day.

Million Wings feels that life is everything and every work is important in life. Everyone has twenty-four hours in a day, and they are spent in twenty-four hours. Every human needs to work for eight hours and sleep for eight hours or study or play and, in the eight hours left, has to do all other works of life. Own eight hours means two hours for family, two hours for friends and relatives, two hours for lover or life partner, one hour for social service, and one hour for ourselves. It's the circle of balanced life; now if we want, we can arrange these hours of one day according to one week or according to one month.

Million Wings feels that someone himself and his related person need to think about the beautiful moments they had. If one is devoting less time to another, then it means one is spending one's time on some another thing or place. If giving more time to one, then it means spending time of some another thing on them. Now if person makes some another personal routine other than this balanced routine, then he and others should know who is getting what amount of time and where another time has spent. Million Wings feels that one has to fulfil the required time of their near and dear ones in one year. Now spare someone is more busy in their profession for six months and using the time of his family, i.e. 6×30×2hrs=360hrs then he has to manage this 360hrs i.e., 15 days from his work and has to spend it with his family in that year only. in the sameway, if someone is giving more time to their lover, then that means they are managing that from some another thing of daily routine. One has to fulfil the time of everyone in one year maximum, however he can manage. But if not doing so than he is careless and irresponsible familiar or social person. If someone wants more time for themselves from (average eight hours rule) then he has to decrease his responsibilities. Million Wings feels that if one chooses easy work routine according to their will, then happiness moves along with him for all the time.

Million Wings feels that life is everything. Here every work is important, without which it's impossible to move on in life. Life is main chance to get food, rest, sex, dreams and desires, security, comfort, power, and self-respect. It's life cycle which is attached with everyone for centuries and will always remain attached. One needs to finish all of one's important work while living life. Basically life is a group of situations which have a mixture of happiness and sorrow. Happiness means unfavourable conditions. One has to get full satisfaction in every condition and to do this is a secret of redemption.

It's not important that one can get happiness only in favourable conditions but individuals can extract happiness even in unfavourable conditions too, as happiness is that state of feeling mind which arises by satisfaction in every condition. There is always possibility of squashing happiness in every situation of life. It's very easy to understand that. Now just think of a happy occasion (like festival, marriage, function, party, trips); atmosphere is plausible but if someone doesn't talk to us or will not attend us properly then obviously we feel sad. We can't feel happy even at happy occasion. Our hearts will not feel happy. Happiness depends on our satisfaction on happy occasion, not on plausible surrounding or atmosphere. Now if there is some bad time, like accident of some close friend, our try will be to reach him as early as possible and help him. We get good satisfaction on doing so, and he gets medical help in nearby hospital also gives satisfaction. Every work done on time in bad circumstance is one kind of happiness, as everything done at the right time gives satisfaction to heart and mind, and to do a possible try in bad condition is satisfaction and happiness.

Million Wings feels that persons have to eat slowly and chew properly so that we can get energy from every molecule of food. If the body is healthy and energetic, then all the work can be done faster, can do any work faster, but only food has to eaten slowly. As food gives energy and if energy is here, then only all can another work be done.

Million Wings feels that we have to move toward civilization and according to that, human has to eat vegetarian food, milk, and egg only, as we can get important nutrition required for life. To raise an animal or bird just to kill and eat is against civilization and even life too. Even uncivilized animals are not doing so; even they eat natural animals, birds for food, not raise and then eat them. Million Wings feels that only civilization can give redemption to the whole universe and the human is the only animal which can make the whole world move towards civilization.

Million Wings feels that to have possibility and comfort of doing important things is an efficient working strategy. A human can do that work or thing in more effective ways which he can do easily. A person needn't be tense about that work which he can do easily, to subsume that work in easy reach, which is necessary for the person; it's logical capability as priorities are already compulsions. To manage daily routine according to oneself is happiness.

Million Wings feels that every person wants that no one should obstruct or be able to obstruct work unnecessarily which one is doing, and to think this is not wrong, it's logical. If one is interfering unnecessarily in our life, then obviously we will not feel good. We will not tolerate that, want to teach a lesson to those people as early as possible. This is also right. When someone does carelessness or gives a chance to another, then they start interfering and misuse the chance. Everyone has personal life. Everyone has their own responsibility to protect and secure their personal life. One who gets a chance to exploit one's personal life will do so. In these situations, to protect ourselves is a priority and then we can teach a lesson cleverly to that for corrupt and stupid behaviour. Million Wings feels that our security is a priority and another is logical work. Million Wings feels that one has to keep one's personal matter locked and keep it under password so that some corrupt person can't misuse that. Personal life's security is happiness, peace, self-confidence, self-esteem, power. Million Wings feels that modernization brings betterment and convenience to things and thinking. Sometimes old people stick to that old thinking and don't listen, understand, and adopt new things and thinking; not only this, but sometimes they oppose strongly. Million Wings feels that old things and thinking are more reliable and experienced, so to think like this is OK as old persons and elders have spent their whole lives in those things only. They have spent life in less expenditure and more hardwork. Million Wings feels that the younger or those having modern thinking need to tell elders, old persons, or those having traditional thinking, about better results, try to make them understand, and teach easy ways to use the new things. When elders or those having traditional thinking use the new modern things and see their benefits and are able to do work easily and with more capacity, then they will surely adopt these.

Million Wings feels that near and dear ones are the biggest support of life, may life be centuries ago or centuries later or today's life. But the importance of our own ones is always more and will always remain more than economy, money, status, and other facilities. To admonish near and dear ones for those things, the things which can be got back by money, to hold or make secular things is good thing. If those become broken or spoiled, then it's natural to be sad, but not to take that much seriously or grieve. But needn't take much tension for those things which can be created or can be purchased again. Use AC in that way from which the body becomes relaxed, not to take atmosphere in opposite way. Million Wings feels, use AC in such a way that you don't feel hot but not in the way that it starts getting chilly. Set temperature to 24°-26° centigrade in cars and homes.

Million Wings feels that if a human is confused about living, thinking, strategy of lifestyle, then he should see the lifestyle from north-south, east-west and try to understand from that lifestyle.

If one is enjoying social happiness in one part of the world, then why can't one enjoy the same in another part of world? If social freedom, happiness are acceptable in a better way in one part of the world, then one can live according to that in another part of the world too. If thinking and lifestyle of one can bring happiness on a social level, then what's the problem in motivating to accept and increase that? Co-change is better with change of time, and someone has to start that first which becomes lifestyle later on. Live by heart, in such a way that everyone wants to live according to that. Live the way that everyone wants to live according to that. Million Wings feels that it's everyone's right to live their personal life according to themselves, but at social level, it needs to coordinate the thinking and mental level of people, society. It's social freedom and good way of happiness. Others wish by doing revolt persons do whatever their hearts want, but persons always feel tense and unhappy surroundings. Million Wings feels that to get personal happiness, find favourable surroundings, make favourable coordination with society and your thinking.

Million Wings feels that one can feel depressed because of natural deficiencies, intense personal or professional loss or jealousy, doubts, misunderstanding, ditching, failure or compulsions. Being depressed or accused, an individual can't express himself and may feel disgust or hatred and sometimes even harm himself.

Million Wings feels that no one attempts suicide as passion. Infact, depression is a state of intense mental tension. Nothing is worse than being depressed or lonely in these conditions; one can be relieved by company of near and dear ones, their care, their answers, their quality time. In these conditions, listening and guiding them rightly are equally important. The more deeply one can express oneself, the clearer, more practical and satisfactory solutions we can get. It's the secret to come out from darkness of loneliness or depression and to move towards ray of hope; positive expectation can arise to understand and to get back happiness.

Million Wings feels that to be rich or poor is not only reason but to be right matters. The one who has some rules and principles is right; maybe he is rich or poor. It's not necessary that the poor are always good, helpless, sick, hard-working, genuine, honest, and the rich are always bad, healthy, corrupt, miserable. Everyone works hard to get success, status, comfort, and economy. The right, hard-working, honest poor can get success and be rich. It's not necessary that all the rich are corrupt and betray others. First give attention to the rules and principles of the person, not compare only on basis of money and economic status.

Million Wings feels that uniqueness is not to have branded national/ international brands but 100 per cent authenticity of being unique is personal style. No doubt costly things raise the standard at social level but it's not necessary that it will also be unique. Anyone can purchase a costlier car, but to alter that according to ourselves is uniqueness. Two people may have same clothes of same company, but to choose clothes and designs according to ourselves is uniqueness.

Million Wings feels that uniqueness is to alter the already present things according to interest and make something new and this makes the things special. A thing related to a person becomes special only when the person alters and manages that, according to one's style, thought, need, and dream. Personal management and making is uniqueness.

Million Wings feels that the things which are long-lasting shall be purchased from our own city, may it be bit costlier, as their maintenance is easy in our own city. Yes, but the things which change with trends can be purchased from anywhere. The use of making budgets is that important things come in notice, e.g. food, clothes, entertainment, health, education. Million Wings feels that if natural atmosphere is favourable and good, then enjoy it. Before sleeping, make sure that purpose of doors should be done. That is closed for security.

Million Wings feels that obviously there should be good coordination, healthy relations with neighbours. Must take care of the neighbours in four directions. Neighbours often need help from each other. Today, one, and next day another may need to help each other, sometimes for small things of daily need, sometimes in emergency, sometimes for children, at marriage or function time.

Million Wings feels, try to not to disturb these neighbours atleast to possible extent. Warn our neighbours about an upcoming problem. Ask for help and let than feel sorry. By this neighbours feel good and can help happily. For example, during construction of a new home, neighbour was disturbed by building material. Choose that right way for that during renovation of old home, neighbours' home might also get some damage, so work carefully. While watering new home walls, wood, or paint of neighbour may get damage. Think about them. To construct our new home doesn't mean to harm others' home. Million Wings feels that the way neighbour can help sometimes, even our relatives, friends are unable to do that. Near your homes are those neighbours who live in their own homes but, in times of need(happy or sad moments), become part of our own home. Many small problems and things can happen, no use to fight regarding those things, e.g. car parking, water supply, wastage, music and enjoyment on festival.

Million Wings feels that to collect wealth and assets for children is good but it's better to spend by managed way on today's needs and then the rest of the money can be deposited. But to live uncomfortably is stupidity. If one is busy in collecting money, then one is unable to enjoy life properly, and even if children got everything without any hardwork or for free, then they also become lazy. Parents die collecting money and children keep on fighting for that or use that in wrong ways. Million Wings feels that some amount of money should be kept for emergency situations. But it's better to enjoy easily affordable things and comfort which is inreach than to collect everything by ourselves for them. It's logical living.

Million Wings feels that living is management, which practically comes by living life with demands of time. Human makes things for himself and uses those things. As a human lives, he gets to know about problems and deficiencies and he tries to resolve and fill them. When human things are related with life, it's managed way, it's management. Management in reality is a basic principle which arises by awareness. Awareness helps humans to fulfil their priorities according to own their minds, time, and resources, in better ways. Power, time, resources don't get destroyed or wasted by living life in arranged ways. Infact it gives much more benefits. Million Wings feels that basis of management is common sense, and time keeps on improving that.

Million Wings wants that everyone should enjoy their life. Everyone should live, eat, roam about, dance, sing, listen to music, go for movies, make friends, go for parties gossip, play, study, work, get success and status, earn, flirt, love, marry, according to their own dreams and desires. In short, live by heart and enjoy living. It's life, it's happiness.

🎋 🎋 🎋

Chapter 9
Food habits

For centuries, either one creature or organism was eating another creature or organism or plants. At the start of life, there was only hunger, not civilization.

To live life, whatever one gets from nature, one has to eat only that as food. Slowly humansmoved forward and became civilized. As humansbecame intelligent, the knowledge about food also kept on improving. Humans got to know that there is the need of eating only food, but all nutrition value is found in plants, fruits, and vegetables too. Slowly humans took steps towards vegetarian eating habits but were unable to leave the habit/nature of being non-vegetarian, and today also, humans eat both kinds of food, i.e. vegetarian and non-vegetarian.

An organism/creature is that which has feelings. Everything in which a heart beats, or which grows and can move from one place to other itself is called an organism/creature. It's a rule of nature that to live, one organism/creature can eat another. It's the rule of the food chain. Million Wings feels that it seems to be right if an organism/creature is eating another organism/creature in natural conditions/circumstances, but to bring up organisms/creatures just for food is against the natural food chain. Million Wings feels that to bring up organisms/creatures only for food is not right. Plants, trees, flowers also have life, then what will we eat?

131

Million Wings feels that organisms/creatures and plants both have life, feelings. So anyone can eat another organism/creature, can eat plants, and plants can eat organisms/creatures. Organisms/creatures can eat organisms/creatures; it's a rule of nature that to live, one has to eat something. Organisms/creatureshave been eating things for centuries. One organism/creature is food for another organism/creature or plants. Today, humans are more civilized than other organisms/creatures on earth. Today, humans are eating other organisms/creatures and plants too. Now if we think that both have life, both have feelings, plants and organisms/creatures too. If it's not right to kill and eat then what human will eat? If he will not eat anything, then how can he survive? We can't eat other organisms/creatures, then what we will eat?

Million Wings feels that those things whose feelings doesn't match with humans; they are nonliving for humans and so we can eat nonliving things as there are no emotional similarities, so no bad feelings, i.e. no sorrow, no pain, no desires, no rights. If feelings exist, then only life exists. If no feelings, then what's the meaning of life? Million Wings thinks that today humans are cultivating fruits, vegetables, plants by agriculture science, and eating those. Then it's OK, as plants may have life but there are no emotional similarities.

Today humans are the most civilized animals, who are more intelligent than all organisms/creatures on earth and trying to understand the secrets of nature with their thinking, research, and science. So humans came to know that vegetarian food can fulfil all required nutrition which they are getting from non-vegetarian food. So humans have to eat non-vegetarian food, the best according to his knowledge. And if a human wants to eat vegetables, then he has to eat a naturally existing animal, which comes under nature's rule. There is seafood in the sea which incubate naturally, so humans can hunt and eat them. But today if a human is incubating animals just for food, it's hurting them, it's wrong, as they have feelings too along with life. Everything which we get from animals but doesn't have life can be used as food, e.g. milk, eggs (which don't have life).

Million Wings thinks that another species can eat that species which eat their own species. Nothing's wrong in it. If fish can eat fish, and if humans are eating that, then what's wrong in it?

Million Wings feels that anything can be used as food, vegetarian or non-vegetarian both, but either they should be part of natural process or they should be emotionless. Just think if some giant came and ate humans, then nothing's wrong in that, but if he subjugated humans and incubated their children and then ate them as food, we needn't explain that painful feeling of humans. Today, the human is the most civilized, and with the help of science and technology, he can produce everything that is found in the body. So it's human duty to manage civilization and to use that, as the biggest research which can't be used in the right direction is uncivilized.

Million Wings feels that if we are able to understand rules of nature, then everything will be OK. Anyone can eat other ones. It has been a rule of nature for centuries and even it has lasted till today; to live and for a healthy life, food is a basic need of plants and animals. What one will eat depends on the availability around one. How much power does one have, and what is the taste of the organism/creature? Let's understand now organisms/creatures will eat only whatever is available in the surroundings; organisms/creatures can't make food of that thing which is not available. Now it depends whether that organism/creature will eat that which he can handle easily. The more powerful the organism/creature will be, the more organisms he can make his food. The food of every organism/creature is decided on basis of availability, power, and obviously taste.

Today, the human is beyond all organisms/creatures; it's not because he is stronger or more powerful than all other creatures but it's because he is competing quietly with all other organisms. Today, humans are civilized. The human has the power of science and technology, from which he has made things of comfort and security. Today, humans have knowledge. Humans are becoming intelligent, alert, genius with time. Life is civilized and governed. Today, humans eat plants and animals according to choice, cultivate and eat those plants, fruits, vegetables, cereals, pulses which they like. The organism/creature which human life includes kill and eat that. Today at world level, human is vegetarian or non-vegetarian according to his own choice. Today also, in nature many organisms/creatureseat other organisms/creatures alive. Some carnivorous trees are also here. Organisms/creatures also eat plants. It is nature; it has been happiness for centuries, and nothing's wrong in it.

Today, the human is the most civilized, so he starts thinking that to eat animals is not right; they have life, emotions. Is it right to kill, cut, and eat them? If everything has life, then what will humanseat? Today, humans start thinking that killing organisms/creatures is not right. Then what to do now?

Million Wings feels that every creature has mutual benefit from one another. Nature always gives mutual benefit. Everything of nature is directly or indirectly attached with oneanother. All are meant for each other. Something must to eat, to survive, to live. Million Wings feels that plants and animals both can be used as food. There is nothing wrong in eating vegetarian or non-vegetarian food. But to kill organism/creature before eating, then it's OK. When there is no life, then obviously no emotions will remain. If there is no life and emotions, then organisms/creatures or plants are just food, nothing else than food.

Every organism, plant, everything is made up of life in essence/elements. The universe is created by soil, air, water, fire, and sky, and the whole universe will emerge in this only. We can't eat these elements directly. These elements change into organisms/creatures or plants, into which God merges innocent souls and fills them with emotions and feelings and life starts growing. For growth of life, these elements are of utmost importance, and to get these elements, we have to eat food and this food is derived by eating each other. Organisms/creatures, animals, plants which live life naturally eat each other alive. It's painful.

Emotions hurt. But all these organisms/creatures are not civilized. They have nothing to do with each other's feelings. They just need to satisfy their own emotions. Humans are worried about pain and emotions of others too. That's why a human doesn't want to give pain to the feelings and emotions of others too. A human has no emotional similarities with plants. That's why he eats vegetable food without hesitation. Today also, humans eat other creatures. It's also right as this is the rule of nature. If humans went to the jungle alone, then wild animals will kill and eat humans too. So if human is eating other animals, then what's wrong in that?

Fish eat fish, then what's wrong if humans eat fish? Trees eat insects and other creatures, so if human does so, then what's the objection?

Million Wings feels that plants also have life, emotions. Today, humans have not much knowledge then we have to choose vegetables, as plants directly use those four elements and develop. If we understand, then we will see that mostly organisms/creatures live by eating plants, that organisms/creatures may be eaten by organisms/creatures for their living, to fill their hunger. So if we see it this way, then also if we eat plants directly instead of herbivorous animals, then atleast one life will be saved. As a hen lives by eating plants, so if we eat plants instead of hens, then atleast the hen's life will be saved. Million Wings feels that if human wants to eat both vegetarian and non-vegetarian food, then also nothing is wrong in that. One has to eat food to live and both are part of food. Million Wings feels that may human eat vegetarian or non-vegetarian food but before making them food, kill them properly, respectfully, no life, no feelings left behind, which is a need and right like other organisms/creatures.

Million Wings feels that if we need to follow civilization, then it's better to eat plants instead of organisms/creatures. But yes, if we want to reach the peak level of civilization in future than has to made balanced diet directly from these elements(soil, air, water, and fire) or those parts of plants or animals which don't have life, which can be used wilfully by coordination, e.g. egg, milk.

Centuries ago, the human was also like other organisms/creatures, and with time, he became civilized. Today, human is trying to understand the secrets of nature. The human has gathered a lot of information about food by his knowledge and science and technology. For development of the body, food is a must. All plants, animals, organisms are alive, all have life, all have emotions, and all express them in their own way. Million Wings feels that any organism/creature can eat other organisms/creatures for food, and it depends upon the needs, type of food; power of ourselves can be derived from both vegetarian and non-vegetarian food. Then what to eat and what not? It depends upon the personal taste, will, interest, and thinking. Humans can get everything from plants: protein, fat, carbohydrates, vitamin, silver, everything. Vitamin B12 is the only vitamin which is available in animals only. There are bacteria in humans which make this vitamin with cobalt. We can get cobalt mineral from milk and egg. For this we needn't kill animals.

Million Wings feels that if organisms/creatures are killing each other by natural way, then nothing's wrong in that. For centuries, humans also use organisms/creatures as food like other animals. Million Wings feels that according to the rule of nature, if one animal kills/hunts another in natural conditions, then it's all right. Nothing's wrong in this. It's the right of natural organisms/creatures to kill, hunt, or eat each other in natural circumstances; humans came forward from all other organisms/creatures and became civilized. Now the human himself has to think of how to move towards civilization, leaving behind non-civilization.

Civilization basically means to respect every life. Million Wings feels that nature develops due to coordination of the needs of one organism/creature with another organism/creature. Every plant, tree, organism/creature has life, and nature grows due to mutual relation of each other. The species from which humans get benefits became their friends and helped in fulfilling demands of each other, e.g. cow/buffalo gives milk to humans, and humans give them food. Hens provide eggs to humans, and humans provide food to them. Some organisms/creatures are so capable that humans even have no idea of their friendship, e.g. a few bacteria. Million Wings feels that nature made plants for development of nature, as they convert main elements of nature into important developing elements required for development of organism/creature. The whole of nature eats these important developing elements and grows plants, converts carbon, oxygen, nitrogen, hydrogen, and other minerals into proteins, fats, carbohydrates, vitamins, and minerals. Other organisms/creatures eat these plants, convert them according to their needs, and grow. Million Wings feels that plants are stable at one place so that the whole of nature gets food atleast. Their feelings are not compatible with emotions/feelings of other organism/creature. They are always invisible and will always remain invisible. Maybe we get any results by research. Humans and animals can feel each other's feelings (fear, pain, affections, protection, smiles, crying, laughing, etc.) very easily. But the feelings of plants are invisible and will always remain invisible. Million Wings feels that the feelings, emotions which are invisible may persist or not, hardly matter in each other's life. The plants, crops, fruits, vegetables, organisms which humans produce/grow for food and not able to see their feelings, then it's right to do. For centuries, humans have been cultivating, growing cereals, grains, fruits, vegetables and using these as food. It's right to do.

Million Wings feels that to grow, bring up and kill plants just for food may also seem to be against life. To hunt/kill naturally existing life for food is not against life. Plants have life but their feelings/emotions, which are invisible, can't be felt; that is nothing wrong. The problem is growing, bringing up, cutting, and eating them. To eat them selectively as food is good and beneficial too. Fruits, vegetables, and crops give comfortable and plausible satisfaction to demands of living. The emotions of organism/creature, animals, plants can be seen, felt. To incubate and kill those only for food is wrong. It's right for organisms/creatures to kill and eat naturally occurring other organisms/creatures for their living and need in natural conditions, but when we can't get food in abetter way than doing this, it's against civilization.

Humans are the most developed and civilized animal in whole world. Ever since humans came out of jungles and started living with managed and secure ways, since then, humans have been fulfilling demands of the whole human species in coordinated ways. Now human species has started cultivating crops, plants, and incubating animal for need of food. Now, every human can't go to jungles to collect natural flowers, fruits, vegetables, animals, etc. In these conditions, humans have to adopt the easy way to collect food, as human population is increasing. That's why humans want to make more food from other plants and animals by scientific ways, other than natural ways. Million Wings feels that the more the population of the human species, the more will be neededand demanded of food. To make/produce more food, artificial science will also be needed along with natural science. Maybe we can produce artificial science up to any extent, but it can't replace natural science. In future with the help of science and technology, food will be directly produced from soil, air, light, fire, and water and that food should have maximum power. More development with less food is a goal of the future. Million Wings feels that the organisms/creatures which don't have emotional similarities are the best source of food for each other.

Million Wings feels that humans want to do every work fast. Everyone wants speed in life and that is right too. And to bring speed, we need power and energy from food so that body and mind work and think properly. This energy comes from food. Every particle of food is enriched with energy. The more we chew the food, the more energy we will get, as it's easy for intestines to digest and they can get/extract maximum energy from well-chewed food. Million Wings feels that work may be donewith whatever speed but eat food slowly so that body and brain can get maximum energy and you can speedup with world. Million Wings feels that everyone wants both energy and beauty, and these both are available in food. We need proteins, fats, and carbohydrates for energy, which we can get from wheat, rice, pulses, fish, egg, milk, etc. And we can get beauty from minerals and vitamins in green vegetables, water, fruits, and pulses. So if one wants to be beautiful along with powerful then one should eat fruits and vegetables also with main food. Eat seasonal fruits and vegetables. It's not important to eat seasonal food at costlier prices. Eat natural and seasonal food. It's right. It will be OK.

Million Wings feels that humans are getting managed and arranged with time; that's why humans don't eat animals nor go to jungles to hunt. Today, human are used to getting food by comfortable ways. Human grow/incubate crops and animals which are easy to cultivate than to cut/kill and then use them as food, e.g. hens, fish, crops. Human grow crops, fruits, and vegetables and incubate animals and use them as food in arranged manner. Million Wings feels that to get food by mutual understanding is the right way. Humans giving food to cow/buffalo and hen and in return using their milk and eggs as food is not right. Producing hens just to kill and eat them or cultivating crops just for food doesn't seem to be right. Either it would be naturally and killed or hunt or cut naturally or it died or fall naturally can be used as food. Fish can eat fish, so if another organism/creature is eating no one should object to that.

All animals are the same; either you eat any out of fish, chicken, beef, pork, lamb, horse, crabs, meat, etc. It does not make any sense when we fight to save one religious animal and try to eat other animals which are worshiped by others. Million Wings feels that feelings are same for all animals.

Million Wings feels that humans can use milk, egg, fish as food. It's not any crime. And if it's necessary to eat one either plants or plants and animals, then it's right to eat plants as one's life can be preserved by this.

The animal/creature which we eat is developed from plants only. So why can't humans eat plants directly instead of eating animals? We can get all the essential nutrients required for human development from plants, fruits, vegetables. Civilization says not to kill life. So until we can convert essential nutrients directly to food, till then we have to eat something. In the first place humans should eat plants and if necessary or it's a question of survival, then theycan eat other organisms/creatures.

Million Wings feels that all creatures (plants and animals) after death are part of just nutrition. These are converted things of development, which are very beautifully coloured and tasty. To eat them is our need and happiness. If a person eats milk, cheese, egg, then he can eat all those things which he can get from animals. Along with vegetarian food, if one is taking egg, milk, then one will get a complete balanced diet, then what's the need of killing and eating other animals? It's an ultimate step towards civilization. But to incubate animals just to eat them is worse even than uncivilized animals, as even animals eat natural organisms/creatures killed/hunted by natural ways. Now if the human has become civilized and intelligent, he has to use his knowledge and power towards civilization.

Chapter 10

Clothes/dressing

Wear whatever you like to wear, may that be traditional or Western, whatever suits you according to the latest trend and style. Million Wings feels that main motto of clothes is to take care of body from harmful products/things, and if beauty increases along with that, then that's one of the other benefits. At the start of life, humans were also in naked conditions. Then according to time, they started covering their sexual organs with leaves, leather, etc. Then slowly they started thinking to look beautiful along with covering organs, and today, humans are demanding and reach the level of fashion and technology.

Today at world level, everyone is wearing clothes of their choice. In some countries, only some body parts are uncovered, and in some countries, only some body parts are covered. Million Wings feels that if there is first personal thing is here as human is any, then that is the feeling of the heart and the body comes next to it. Vital organs of that part of the body are a source of enjoyment during sexual intercourse. Million Wings feels that genital organs(private parts) are personal life, not public property. Exposing private parts socially can be harmful and may provoke sexually and can be harmful also. Million Wings feels that atleast private parts should be properly covered. Dress may be any. Maybe there are few clothes on the body, but private parts should be covered properly. Above that may wear any number of clothes, any type of clothes according to personal will, maybe traditional or the latest fashion. It doesn't mean that only private parts should be covered and no need to cover body parts, but it means there should be no exposure of private parts at social or public places. A person can live his personal life according to his own will and can wear any kind of clothes; no one has objections to that.

Million Wings feels that clothes/dress suits individuals according to colour, looks heights, personality, etc. Adopt that fashion style which suits you, looks good on you. Million Wings feels that clothes of own choice are comfortable and increase confidence, and self-confidence brings happiness to the face and the mind. Million Wings feels that private parts should be 90 per cent covered atleast at public places, including inner and outer clothes.

A female is adorned to look gracefully attractive and beautiful so that everyone praises her. She never wants that others misbehave to her. Males also want to look attractive and smart. Males always want that they should look smart, powerful, and energetic and want that females give attention to them and like them.

Males and females both have to visit public places around the clock. Males and females have natural attractions. Private parts provoke sexualism. Whether someone exposes these knowingly or unknowingly, these surely attract or get the attention of the opposite sex once at public places. If private parts of a female are visible, then obviously males stare at her. Nothing is wrong in this. Million Wings feels that persons (male or female) can wear anything they like, Western or traditional, more or less, but private parts should be properly covered so that natural urge of sex at social level should be stopped. If the private parts of females are covered properly, then obviously males will be attracted but if still they misbehave or forcefully do something wrong, then they should be answerable for that stupidity.

Million Wings feels that a father with her daughter, a lover with his mate, a boy with a girl often visit public places. Now if we see then these males take care of females also with themselves. Now, private parts are exposed then every second, men will look or stare. It's part of entertainment for people. Now in these conditions it's the responsibility of males along with females, then another males should not misbehave. Million Wings feels that in these conditions, males will remain tense and will not able to enjoy a function, party, or that moment fully.

Million Wings feels that it's not about more and more clothes but about less clothes upto where female should look unique, more beautiful, attractive along with maintaining self-respect. If we argue that less clothes gives more comfort, then whatelse will give more comfort than a bare form? The thing is not about comfort only, but it's also about mental satisfaction, happiness, and personal self-respect and security. Otherwise, modernity is a bare form. If a female is wearing atleast important clothes then she can handle those kinds of nonsense persons with full power and belief and other males will also support her with full power.

Private parts of every male and female are beautiful parts of personal life. Exposing them casually is not the right thing. Sharing our personal life with one whom our mind and thinking matches, with agreement of the other is enjoyable, respectable esteem. Million Wings feels that when we talk about security of private parts, then priority is of females, as women are sexually harassed, even teased and mistreated. So females need to understand that males feel physical attraction. So if private parts of women are visible than most males stare and some express and few can even react with urge of sex and may misbehave also. Now females need to understand that it's OK if males get attracted towards them and give them attention but misbehaviour is wrong. Million Wings feels that now in the world, we can see females wearing less to maximum clothes covering the whole body. Now who is right? Who is more right or who is more wrong? It can be commented on the basis of whether self-respect and grace of a woman is maintained or not. Million Wings feels that the future may reach to any extent, whatever kind of clothes one may wear, but this romantic, sexual attraction and sex will remain between males and females.

Million Wings feels that clothes are invented for safety of humans. Humans feel uncomfortable to walk, sit, stand while exposing private parts, and possibility of getting hurt increases. If humans cover/manage soft and sensitive private parts properly, then private parts are safe and secure and persons feel comfortable. It's good to look attractive at public places but not at the risk of one's security. Those clothes are useless which can't manage private parts, or slips or breaks and motivate urge of sex of corrupt and stupid persons and become cause of misbehaviour. Wear clothes with style so that they look attractive and everyone gives attention towards the individual and wants to talk about but should not make them exposed that person become victim for lust of stupid persons. Million Wings feels that clothes should be so graceful and attractive that another gets attracted towards person, not only towards private parts. Million Wings feels that if today a human is feeling uncomfortable because of more clothes, then nothing's bad in decreasing them but logical clothes are those which will give protection and comfort to private parts. However a person may be living his personal life, their private parts should be atleast 90 per cent covered at public places.

Chapter 11

Education and guidance

Million Wings feels that the motto of education is to make life easier, happy, and comfortable. Education helps in making person better. Million Wings feels that education will be that which will helps in living life. Subjects of education should be related with life. Education means to make everyone capable of living so that everyone enjoys living with confidence. Education is a social right of every human and a need of all the young and elderly, as education of living life makes humans and society more managed and civilized. Million Wings feels that it's a primary responsibility of government to provide minimum education free or at less cost. The rest depends on personal will and interest of individual, whether to get higher education, further specialized studies, professional studies, or not.

Million Wings feels that the first and main motto of education is to learn one language properly so that we can read, write, and understand the views of others, of the world.

Million Wings feels that there should be one official and school language at world level: one world, one language. Million Wings feels that the language should be that which is used in most of the parts of world that language should be learnt so that we can talk to the whole world. Today, English is widely spread in the whole of the world. Million Wings feels that already widely spread languages should be accepted and motivated instead of spreading one more new language at world level.

Million Wings feels that one language can tie the world. So the future's motto is to tie the world together and leave fights/argument on the basis of country. Like this, the tension of conversation on world level will be over too. If there will be one language on state, country, and world level, then atleast 66 per cent of workload can be reduced in office and school. Money and energy both can be saved, and obviously, more relaxation. One knows a mother tongue since childhood, what is the need of learning that? It's easy to understand international English language in mother tongue. It's workload and tension in schools to learn firstly mother tongue, then national language and then international language. It's really time-consuming, tough to learn and understand the same things in three languages and seems useless for future generations. As far as the illiterate people already in the family like grandparents, parents, or common public at present is concerned, they can continue to speak in their mother tongue. One world, one language can connect the world with one thread.

Million Wings feels that the main motto of language is to talk to each other, delivering and receiving views. So there should be one language so that the world can be tied with the same language. Million Wings feels that school should be like that, that life should seem to be more beautiful since starting of school, not tense or broadened. Education is social effort. We keep on learning everything every moment and learn the same which is happening in world and have to learn that only which is famous/happening at the time in society, as that is worldliness. Coordination of life will be better by understanding this worldliness. Firstly a child learns at home then from neighbours then society, then what is the need for school?

Which are the things which can be learnt from school only? Million Wings feels that the real motto of school is to make understand important things of life in managed and arranged way. Million Wings feels that the few starting years in the life of a child, i.e. 1–10 years, make a viewpoint of life. They become the same as the atmosphere or surroundings they get in the first few years of life.

Million Wings feels that if life seems to be beautiful, interesting, and good since childhood, then they will have a positive point of view towards life.

Million Wings feels that there should be only three subjects in school: (1) language, second (2) maths, and (3) life(personal development). Other than those, sports and good light-hearted entertainment should be main attraction for child. School should start between 8 to10 a.m. and should be of 6 hours. By the age of 10 years, children should learn English language so that they can coordinate with the world and express themselves at world level. Children can talk to the whole world, so self-confidence will automatically develop in them. In maths, the mainly required topic is +, -, *, ÷ throughout, as throughout life only this much maths is used. The third is life(personal development), which should include personal care, how to behave, and morality. At home parents should play with and teach personal development to children and schoolwork is to be taught. Language and maths and the rest of the things children learn by themselves, and what is the use of teaching something else/more for personal development to children? Like this, parents will be satisfied, school will be enjoyable. Children will be happy and teachers will also remain tension free; like this, workload will be reduced and everyone will feel relaxed and happy. In today's era, youngsters have media to know about the world, and what else is left to be taught?

Schoolwork is to arrange life with positive attitude. When a child grows to the age of 10 years, then try to understand his interest and try to give direction and choice to his studies, according to his interest. When children grow as youngsters then they themselves start understanding according to worldliness. Then they can study in college, university as per their interest. Million Wings feels that if children choose subjectsand study according to their own will, then education will seem to be interesting instead of hectic. Education increases personal development, fulfils life with self-confidence. Million Wings feels that it's important to understand our subject, 60 per cent marks are enough.

Million Wings feels that life teaches life, and we learn many things just by discussing freely and by actions/reactions of each other. The life-oriented seminars should be a part of school and college education programme. Million Wings feels that different issues of life can be resolved by discussing them. The life-oriented seminars must start healthy discussion on all common and uncommon issues of life to begin a healthy and positive discussion regarding every aspect in everyone's life, family, friends, relatives. There is no need of any preparation for seminar, but we just need to share our experience, excitement, and whatever we feel from our day-to-day life. Everyone can freely express and discuss his views, emotions, and feelings. The main motto of the seminar is that every person should have open, wide, and balanced thinking regarding every aspect of life so that everyone can live tension free and happily. The life seminars are basically the means of discussion of views. An individual will be clearer about his concerns and get unmatched discussion face to face. Everyone has the right chance to discuss. Everyone should participate and discuss maximally in the life seminars.

Million Wings feels that education is the sure and easy way of success. Million Wings feels that subjects of education should be those which move and help in life. Classes based on life should be a must in colleges and schools. Million Wings feels that a good student will be a great learner in any circumstances and can become a scholar. But a good teacher can't make a student a scholar without his interest. Good teachers and good students are always in search of each other. Million Wings feels that the real teacher is life. So education will be that which can be beneficial in routine life. Teaching and learning every subject is obviously not very useful in daily life but taken as tensions. The things which are related to every person in routine life should be part of education. The motto of today's professional studies is to get professional benefits. Students are given education, but when they have to start their business, they are not aware of small things related to that business. In starting one or two years, students repeat same mistakes, and during session of struggle, they are engaged in trying to resolve those problems, and it is hard to comeout from those problems. Million Wings feels that it should also be taught how to educate the world. When any education is given professional form, then they should also teach about legal formalities related to that profession, in the last semester of course. After completing studies, students take steps with full energy in profession but don't know how to fulfil social and legal formalities. It's important to give atleast basic knowledge and information about a related profession and not make an individual specialized in every field so that profession can be started through right channel, and approach to all another things can be learnt slowly with time.

Million Wings feels that education is social effort. When a child is born, family is the biggest support, family will take care of the baby, family will bring up the child, and family will teach life according to worldliness. Family teaches how to speak, walk, eat. Now when the child grows, then he starts meeting relatives, neighbours, and now people other than family members also leave those impacts on child. Obviously family teach their tradition, influence, and refinement to the child, but the child also starts understanding and learning from other people of society. Now when the child grows up a bit more, then he is sent to school so that he can get education and become a better person. Now school starts teaching the child. Now the child is learning from family, society, and school, i.e. three places. It means the child didn't stay at the same place; he is intouch with three different places, i.e. child learns different things from different places, some good and bad manners, some right and wrong things, some truth and lies. Now the child doesn't stay with one person, so it is the responsibility of only persons to teach and make understand the child every time. A child will take the right steps only if family, society, and school all have a good atmosphere only. A family can't improve the child; only a school can't make the child a scholar. A child will become the same as the atmosphere he gets from the surroundings. If the atmosphere of society is plausible, then obviously the child will have a plausible nature. If everyone talks with respect and love, obviously the child will do the same. If child will get a secure atmosphere, obviously he will live tension free. If there are rules and principles in society, obviously then only will the child learn that. Now if we see then it's the responsibility of society what kind of atmosphere they are providing to the child. All people live according to the surroundings, social atmosphere around them. Family teaches a child according to their surroundings. Everyone moves in the direction in which the society, world is moving. Needs, dreams, desires, pace of life, everything changes according to time. So who changes first, society or people/family? If society changes, then obviously people will change. As society changes, i.e. firstly people have to change, then only can society be changed. Million Wings feels that a few people change first, then some more people change, and then slowly the whole society changes. Now who are those people who change first and because of whom society changes? Why do they change? Is the way the world is doing/moving presently right only? The world has been trying to live the best life for centuries. Yesterday also, people were trying to live best, and today also, they are trying the same and will do the same tomorrow. Then what's wrong in it? Everyone is trying for betterment/comfort/success since birth till death. Then they are doing right. There is nothing wrong in it. How can change be brought to society? We are responsible for the kind of atmosphere in society. Are we responsible for every good and bad, right and wrong happening in society? We haven't made society but society has made us. So we will react and do the same, whatever society has taught us. The time we were born, we didn't know what to do. What is society? Whatever parents, society, teachers taught us, we became the same. The time we became so intelligent, when we could think or decide what is right or wrong, till then we grow up to 20–25 years and knowingly, unknowingly, we are also adapted to those ways.

Million Wings feels that there are many schools for children but there are no formal schools of non-academic life-oriented education programmes for the people 25–60 years of age, where people can/should attend at their will and need.

Do we think that our society is responsible for our present circumstances, direction of life since the time we were born till we grow up, our parents, family, relatives, society, school, college? Million Wings feels that the one who comes earlier the world is more responsible for social circumstances, i.e. an elder is more responsible for circumstances of society. When someone feels, society surely changes; when some feel, think about betterment, society surely changes. When we talk about more comfort and facilities, society surely changes. Society changes when one talks about freedom. Society changes when feelings of discomfort and restrictions arise. Society changes when people feel restricted in social customs; society changes when there is danger to life. Society changes when tolerance decreases. When I felt that, there was my family and society behind the development of my thinking. So whatever I am doing today, firstly they are responsible for this who have given this type of atmosphere. So if my parents are responsible for today's circumstance and situation, then they will say they became the type of atmosphere they got and whatever society taught them, and according to that, they were brought up. Bringing up children like this, responsibility will fall on our elders then on their elders and then their elders, and so on. But we are living in today and our elders died years ago. So now they will not come back, and if they came, then obviously they will tell their compulsions. Now if all are forlorn, then who is responsible? If not we, not our parents, not grandparents are responsible, then who is responsible for today? Education means to have right and arranged knowledge about related issues. The subject which a person studies becomes his future's profession. Profession means to give facilities and products to people, and inreturn, a person gets money. If customers get facilities and products on time, then only will a profession be successful, and it will happen if we know about our work rightly and it is possible if we have studied and been taught rightly.

Million Wings feels that people want work, not marks. If one has good marks but doesn't know the work properly, then those marks have no value. If a person knows work rightly but does not have very good marks, then it hardly matters. So education means to give products and facilities in the right manner.

Million Wings feels that if a person learned and had experience in some work then it's OK and he can manage but if he has good knowledge about every step behind that, then his work starts running with a good pace. The possibility of problems and obstructions can be managed earlier, rightly, and in much better ways if we know and study the basic principle. Million Wings feels that by studying rules and principles we make basic knowledge become better, more excellent. Society wants professional work from studies, because it is the logical need. Million Wings feels that everyone should know their work properly after completing studies; marks may be 60 per cent, then also it's OK.

Million Wings feels that if there is no compulsion for further studies, then let a child study more. If child didn't want to study the subject chosen by parents, or wants to study their favourite subject instead of a difficult subject, let them choose, as the child wants to study and learn something instead of doing nothing. Atleast they will remain intouch with studies, and hope of new possibilities will be there. If students fail again and again in exams, they needn't worry and needn't take some wrong step in tension, as only education is not everything. Life is not just about clearing exams. If one is unable to clear an exam, then one needn't worry, again prepare for the next exam attempt. If a child fails, then the child can try once or twice, again with full preparation. But if exams can't be cleared on trying again and again, then it's better to leave it. Do something else. Nothing's bad in doing so. It's not for sure that to do work, and for being successful, only education is the way but one can be successful by his quality and talent, by working hard. Million Wings feels that if a student is not getting results on trying two to four times, then he should leave that and try for another will, interest, and talent, not to be depressed and lose self-confidence or to do stupidity like attempting suicide. There is everything since the child is alive. So what if he is unable to do one thing? Then he can do some another thing. It's better to do something else, whatever he is interested in, than losing life just because of education, e.g. games, music, business, photography, writer, social work. To clear an exam is just not everything, but overall logical satisfaction is the main aim of life.

There are lots of differences in education and real life. If someone doesn't want to study, then let them be educated about one language and maths, i.e. accounts, so that he can't get failure in life. And success can be gained by betterment of talent, efficiency, and capabilities. Just remember that education is the surest and a reliable way of success but not the only way. Study so that one can talk with world with ease and confidence, not to die for study.

Level of written examination should be according to average students so that average student can clear that, as mostly people don't get perfection during work but learn many things during work. If some want to run their own business, then it's enough to get passing marks but it's important to learn work rightly, as people will ask for degrees when work is not done rightly. If someone wants to do a job at some company, then he has to clear the oral or written or practical examination as it is the first way to judge someone, on the basis of which one gets a chance to show one's capabilities and talent.

Million Wings feels that whoever has knowledge about subjects and matters related to work/profession can learn work easier and can understand in better ways. But one who doesn't have written knowledge about subject can be made to understand a bit, but can't make them perfect easily. Common sense is very effective. But to be specialized is a more arranged and effective way of common sense. It's true, it's right. Education means to improve behaviour skill, which helps in providing benefits to others also; otherwise there is no use of education.

Million Wings feels that saints and religion teach us, make us understand. But their guidance mostly gives suggestions towards idealism, not according to our dreams and desires, and our parents, teachers, elders give us suggestions according to worldliness. Now if we see, then everyone is right at their place. That's why religion and saints have given us idealism: so that life can always be managed the best, and elders want that by living according to worldliness and idealism. We as persons can't give much care to our dreams and desires. Personal dreams and desires are one's happiness. To live with that is ultimate happiness.

Million Wings feels that to fulfil dreams and desires according to worldliness is the best success. Now humans have been living for centuries and now we are able to understand and keep on understanding dreams, desires, emotions, feelings, nature, capabilities, discussions, conclusions, and proofs in almost every direction. Humans are going through so many emotions, since birth till death, hunger to sex, love to ditching, care to murder, etc. There have been changes for centuries towards betterment. But emotions are as they are. Human living style and life is changing with time, but feelings of sex, anger, greed, affection, ego are attached as they are, for centuries till now. The world may reach to any level, but human happiness will reside in one's dreams and desires. Every human feels happy when another gives suggestions, help, and motivation in fulfilling dreams. What individual has to do with other ways and direction? And thing is right too. A human's aim is satisfaction of his own emotions. This is life. Guidance should be in that direction which a human wants. Guidance is to fulfil the same dream earlier, faster, and by the right path in which a person is interested. The meaning of guidance is to help in fulfilling dreams and desires with more comfort and the fewest problems. Guidance doesn't mean to change direction or success or failure; infact, the real motto of guidance is to fulfil dreams and desires in better ways.

Guidance doesn't mean to change dreams and desires by excluding mistakes and failure from history; instead, it's solving these the same way, according to learning from the past, needs of today, and view of tomorrow, which can be in reach of human capacities and helps in increasing happiness. Guidance is showing the way according to human circumstances, age, thinking, and interest. To change someone's desires and dreams against their will is not guidance, as guidance is not changing anything forcefully. Guidance is suggestions for better management. Guidance arises by experience, knowledge, or far-sightedness. Main motto of guidance is to fulfil one's dreams and desires without affecting dreams and desires of others. Guidance is fulfilling everyone's dreams and desires altogether. If we want to make life better faster, then it's possible by only capable and right guidance. Guidance can bring happiness in life faster. Right and genuine praise and clearing away weakness and mistakes with positive attitude and ways and right guidance is the best way to fulfil another's mind with self-confidence; infact it is the identity of good students and teachers. To arise and motivate right things in positive way is more than enough as by this weakness, bad habits and fear will diminish themselves. It is the right path of education. It is a secret of success.

Million Wins feels that everyone, every person is working hard and trying hard to fulfil his dreams and desires. Everyone uses his circumstances, capabilities, resources best according to his knowledge. Whatever seems to be right, better, best, persons do that only. Everyone is capable and takes a step according to himself for his happiness, and it is right too. If a human feels that he can get success by that way, then what's wrong in that? If one doesn't feel like taking suggestions from others, than we can't give suggestions forcibly. If he feels like taking suggestions while working, then he will ask himself. So there is nothing much to think about. Whatever seems to be right to a person, he keeps on doing so. Million Wings feels that person seeks guidance when he himself feels so. Otherwise he does the same whatever he wants to do, whatever another may be trying to tell him or trying to make him understand. Million Wings feels that everyone's life is guidance for all. Everyone will do or keep on doing the same, whatever they want to do. So if they become successful, then that becomes guidance for another, and if they fail, then also that becomes a type of guidance to others. So it means everyone's life is guidance for ourselves and others too. Everyone's life is experiment, is exam. People learn from success and failure of oneanother and keep on improving their lives. And it's real guidance. All guide us: parents, siblings, teachers, relatives, colleagues, saints, religions all guide us at every point, every place, every step, every day. All teach us worldliness, sometimes idealism, sometimes with love, sometimes with crossness, sometimes by some hard way and sometimes by emotional blackmail; all are right at their place. All want our happiness. That's why everyone trying to teach us guides us according to their own way. But guidance doesn't mean just telling and making others understand. Guidance will be successful only if another person feels that he has to do that. With time, every person feels that what everyone else was teaching earlier was right. Million Wings feels that real guidance is to teach and make the thing or feeling understood before time so that another will listen and understand and accept. Million Wings feels that still person human is enrolled in the same emotions for centuries which he had understood well. Million Wings feels that the things from which human restrict each other will enjoy that thing, work a lot. It's true that feelings and desires are enjoyable, may these not be plausible in the end. Self-experience is the best personal guidance.

Million Wings feels that people guide each other. Great person shows path to world to live life, and humans adopt and use them according to their nature, thinking, and circumstance. Whatever person understands and feels from his life, gives guidance and suggestions according to their experience, and it's right too. One will suggest the same, whatever he felt, watched, and experienced. Million Wings feels that when someone is commenting regarding any issue, then in reality he is expressing his views. It's not that he is 100 per cent right and perfect. Million Wings feels that a person himself changes on his personal issue maybe earlier, maybe later on, may be impressed by someone's saying, talks, maybe because of problems. A person doesn't need any force or argument to guide others but has to say whatever he feels like. Whoever feels that it's effective will automatically agree.

Conceptual growth is a process of going through the self-experimentation of personal beliefs and ideas. Sometimes inspite of ample information and experienced data availability, one can learn only if he completes his own potential innovative appearing prospects.

🎋 🎋 🎋

Chapter 12
Beauty and attraction

Million Wings feels that beauty is the first reason of attraction; the meaning of beauty is liking. Everyone has their own liking choice. On basis of that, one (male/female) likes another (male/female) and tries to look attractive. Million Wings feels that to be beautiful doesn't mean that everyone will like them but if someone likes others, that doesn't mean everyone else will also like them. If anyone likes another one, that means one is beautiful for them. Beauty means liking. Liking means beauty.

Million Wings feels that it's true that the beauty of males and females attracts each other for romantic relations. So it's good to maintain ourselves and look beautiful. Natural beauty is a great gift. Beauty can't be developed but the natural colour and beauty can be maintained and one can live neat and clean. If someone is beautiful, then obviously others will look at one, what's wrong in it? Others will obviously be attracted towards those who look beautiful.

Humans firstly look at another person; when male and female look at each other, they first become attracted toward each other because of beauty. It's true and it's right too. Physical appearance, beauty attracts each other. Attraction towards opposite sex is natural. Nothing's bad in looking at each other's beauty. But to misbehave is not right. Million Wings feels, look at each other with respect, in plausible ways. Nothing's bad in casting an eye over at each other. Having a glance doesn't cost anything. Everyone will look at beautiful females and smart males. Nothing's bad in this. There are many people in the world; they interact with each other. Males and females roam about at public places. The world is so huge, and crores of people are there. It's not a crime to cast an eye over one whom we like.

Million Wings feels that attraction begins on appearance. One gets to know about nature later on. Infact, nature carries forward the attraction but appearance gives a kick. Person will obviously look at those who look beautiful. One who maintains beauty obviously wants that everyone should have a glance at them. Most people should praise them. They feel good. Million Wings feels that it's good to try to look beautiful. Humans have different race, colour, beauty, height, etc., which can't be developed according to will, but everyone can try then it's good to look beautiful and must has to do. But everyone should keep themselves neat and clean. Everyone can afford to wear atleast neat and clean clothes. They can comb their hair properly and can make a good hairstyle, can remove unwanted hair, can colour their hair, can make hairstyle according to face. They can give fit and shape to dress according to body shape.

Million Wings feels that everyone has a different appearance and shape. Everyone has a different choice. A few like one thing in females and a few like some other thing. Someone likes fair complexions, someone likes dark complexions. Some like long hair, some like short hair. A few like round faces and a few like triangular faces. A few like sharp noses and a few like round. A few like thin girls and a few like healthy. in the same way, females have different choices regarding males. A few like a light complexion and a few like dark. A few like muscular bodies and a few fit or fat. It means everyone has their own choice. So it's not compulsion; if one likes someone, then others will also like them.

Million Wings feels that everyone has their own likes and dislikes. One surely attracts someone. One female may attract someone. One female may attract numerous males, and one male may attract numerous females. Beauty is to watch. The heart feels happy when casting an eye over beautiful/handsome people, by talking to them, by living with them. Million Wings feels that nothing's bad in giving a glance to beauty but misbehaving with that is wrong. If someone is beautiful, no one has the right to misbehave with them. It's OK to be inebriated, but wrong or hurting comments, even teasing, are intolerable. If someone feels good to the heart, beautiful, impressive, then one can talk respectfully to them. By introducing ourselves, we can converse; hi/hello can be done. If another feels liking and is interested, then surely they will talk to us, and if they don't feel good, then obviously they will reject us. Girls and boys need to understand that they have natural attraction because of beauty and want to come close to each other. Nothing's wrong in liking each other and even nothing's wrong in talking to each other. Everything is right which is done by will.

Million Wings feels that beautiful faces and physiques attract each other. But nature has power to convert that attraction into relations. When people meet after attraction, then coordination of their thinking and nature give a permanent form to their relations. Nature can be known and judged obviously by talking to them, by their behaviour and response. But physical attraction arises by just facing one another. Before judging/knowing nature, looks play an important role to talk, to get near, to interact. But if there is a bad nature behind a beautiful face, then anyone can like them for a little time but it's difficult to like them together for a long time.

Nature plays an important role in binding relations and physical appearance plays an important role to begin relations. Million Wings feels that every male or female should always try their best to look smart/beautiful, must wear good dresses, jewellery, make-up according to own capacity. You must adopt the fashion which suits you. The thing which is socially new or the latest should be tried once on ourselves.

Million Wings feels that female means beautiful, female meansmake-up, female means softness, female means emotional, female means self-centred, female means care. Femalesare the main attraction for males. Every man feels good to have a glance on beautiful females. It's true, it's right also. A female with combination of style and beauty has power to make anyone's heart beat faster. A sweet smile and naughtiness of eyes can make anyone crazy. Style and beauty of a female may attract a male to such an extent that he can go under the desire of sex. Million Wings feels that when a female wants to look beautiful and attractive, then she just wants attention and never wants that anyone should misbehave with her, but when female is attracted towards a male, she wants to get his attention. Choice allows two persons to come close and then talk; things, style of each other play another role to get close to each other.

Million Wings feels that attraction of male and female is equivalent to spending an entertaining time. Males and females pass time by looking atand talking to each other, which is the best way of most of males and females. A male is attracted towards one, two, three, or even more females at the same time and tries his best to attract them towards him. But this feeling is just for sometime. Choice and attraction change when atmosphere changes.

Million Wings feels that every male and female has their own choice; they don't keep on trying to attract anyone but they do so according to their choice. If someone doesn't get attracted towards one, that doesn't mean one is not beautiful/smart, or it's not compulsion that the same person will become attracted towards the one who became attracted, as attraction doesn't depend only on beauty but it is a matter of choice also. Everyone likes another one according to their choice, their likes, the beauty of their choice.

Million Wings feels that the meaning of beauty is to live neat and clean, wearing good clothes according to capability, make-up according to capacity along with beautiful face and physique. When personsbecome attracted towards beauty, then they try to come close to each other. If male/female likes the other's nature too, then the bond of attraction becomes stronger. But if behaviour and thinking don't match, then no one wants to come close. Million Wings feels that it's true that beauty plays an important role in the beginning of attraction, but nature also has same importance to carry forward relations, which makes relations stronger. It's true and will always remain.

Million Wings feels that most of the time, attraction is just because of beauty and is not permanent. Male and female have a glance at each other and move on. A few people stop for a bit longer time to cast an eye over beautiful faces and then move on. Male/female watch each other's beauty from a few seconds to hours and as the atmosphere changes, they forget and get busy in their work. The moment they get attracted toward each other, during that wave, they want/try to get attention, and after that, as time changes, that wave also changes. It's right, it's true.

Million Wings feels that to look beautiful and to have a look at beauty both give feelings of fresh energy. Every male/female should try to improve their physical and social beauty more day by day. Always dress up properly, look smart, try to look good, wear clothes or dresses and do make-up according to complexion and looks. The stylesand dresses which are comfortable improve self-confidence, as whoever's heart feels happy and is filled with self-confidence, then the face also looks more beautiful, so the person looks more attractive. A natural smile on the face increases attractiveness by several times.

Million Wings feels that beauty is to be watched. Have a glance on each other, look beautiful, look smart till the level you want; a person may be elder, may be younger, may be married, may be unmarried, may be alone or with someone, may be committed, may be with family, may be with friends. It hardly matters; nothing's wrong in casting an eye over beauty. If males or females don't look at each other, then who else? The reality is nothing's wrong in looking upon or becoming attracted towards each other. But misbehaving is obviously wrong. Enjoy looking upon each other at social places but in sophisticated ways. Don't use bad comments, wrong signals, physical contact, or force others like uncivilized, wild animals, as these things hurt others, create a tense atmosphere along with anger. No male will able to make contact with any female by reaching out like this. Everyone likes those who are well socialized, mannerly, and good-natured, along with beauty/smartness.

Million Wings is not against casting an eye on each other but will not tolerate any kind of misbehaviour at any cost. Everyone has self-respect which gets hurt by stupidities and then obviously they will oppose that, and most should oppose.

Chapter 13

Meeting people

Million Wings feels that humans are a social animal and often meet each other. It's everyone's right to see each other. Whatever one is showing or presenting, another will definitely look, see, and watch that; it's human nature. Nothing's wrong in that. Anyone can look at each other; nothing's wicked in this. Nobody will get any harm just by looking. People take glances at each other and move on. May they be girl or boy, male or female, opposite sexes look at each other, then what's wrong in it? What's evil in this?

Million Wings feels that it's everyone's right to look with respect, love, care in healthy manner and plausible way. But to look with bad intentions and to give wrong signals is absolutely wrong. If one really wants to have a glance, then one should look with respect and in a comfortable way; no one has any objection to that. But no one wants to be disturbed or tense or worried because of a stare. The way which girl/boy don't like is known to be or taken as wrong. It's natural to get attracted towards opposite sex. Males or females often become attracted towards each other. Mainly people get attracted towards beauty, colour, clothes, style, etc. It's not a new thing but it will also not be old. Anyone can like anyone. One will surely look towards that whom one likes or becomes attracted to. It's natural to have romantic attraction of male and female. This attraction is neither taught nor can it be finished. This natural attraction towards opposite sex is everyone's right. If someone becomes attracted towards another, then let them. It's one's nature and right too. Nothing's evil in this. Mostly this attraction is from seconds to some time. Attraction starts from physical appearance or you can say beauty and lasts till another one is infront of the eyes. The moment another appears or our attention is distracted, that attraction disappears.

Million Wings feels that physical attraction is normal action and reaction. Girls and boys often become attracted towards one another and enjoy that to have a glance at each other. Nothing is wrong in doing so; when someone becomes attracted, then romantic feelings also arise. A desire can also arise, have romantic physical relations, and want to talk to the other person. If someone really touches your heart, then you can request in a respectful manner to talk by telling your identity. If some girl or boy wants to talk or share feelings with another boy/girl, then nothing's wrong in this. One can give a chance to speak and say. The other should listen atleast once and then can give an answer according to their own will. If someone talks to another, then it's not a crime to talk. Real intentions and feelings will be clarified by talking to each other. If someone wants to talk respectfully and comfortably with another at a social place then one should give a chance to him and then can take action according to his behaviour and talk. If someone speaks or talks in a manner you didn't like or didn't seem to be right to you, then clearly saying no is good and beneficial. To talk to someone against his/her will is not any compulsion. It's also not compulsion to allow everyone who requests to talk. If you don't like another, then it's your right to reject the proposal to talk. When another is clearly rejecting or refusing to talk, then don't bother or disturb or force another by requesting again and again. It's not anyone's right to pass wrong comments. Forcing, bothering, disturbing, teasing when attracted is absolutely wrong. And this decision is of what another takes as right, and what's wrong?

Million Wings feels that if someone is itching or touching their private parts then others will think that person has either some infectious disease or some problem with private parts and no one wants to go near to them. Million Wings feels that real happiness is, along with liking their beauty, trying to understand each other's thoughts and desires. After being attracted towards one's beauty and whiletalking to him, we get to know about his nature, emotions, rules and regulations of life, principles and by knowing these, we get to know about whether we can have plausible coordination with him or not. If there will be good coordination, then only will there be a happy and good life ahead; otherwise one can't get anything other than problems and tension. Million Wings feels that there is nothing wrong in looking, becoming attracted and talking to each other. But romantic relations can be made only with mutual understanding, will, and desire. Mutual understanding can't be judged by beauty or attraction, but both have to know atleast a little something about each other. And to know each other, we have to talk to each other. Attraction might start with beauty, but it can be carried forward because of nature only. Everyone wants the same nature as oneself along with beauty. Girls and boys want to talk, meet, eat, have enjoyment with like-natured persons but don't want anykind of stupidity or forcefulness. Most of the time, attraction towards beauty breaks when people get to know each other. Million Wings feels that most misunderstandings are clarified by talking to each other and the rest by meetings.

Relations want similarities, physical and emotional similarities. Million Wings feels that worldwide, people meet each other. One should increase togetherness. You may talk to any number of persons. Try to know each other's nature along with beauty and then make relations as the heart says.

Males/females can have any kind of relation with each other but with mutual understanding. Million Wings feels that everything is OK, whether it be flirting, affection, love, or marriage. A person can choose any kind of relation; nothing's wrong in that. If it's love, then it's good, as love can happen anywhere with anyone. Love is natural affection, which can happen with only one person at one time, maybe married to unmarried, maybe unmarried to married. But affection, flirting, and friendship are planned emotions. They're not permanent relationships. Then it hardly matters whether a person is married or unmarried. If both have mutual understanding, both can manage personal security. Then everything is all right, as love is not planned and all other emotions are well planned. But yes, if someone plans to marry, then the unmarried should not make relations with the married, and married with unmarried. When it's about married only, then all these things are considered, whether one is married or unmarried. Otherwise it hardly matters in any other relationswhether one is married, unmarried, divorced, etc.

Now the question is from where we get people of alike thinking, whether someone will find them for us or others will find us. We are a society or the whole world is ours. Many people of many types? And what kind of relations do we want? Only we ourselves know that better. So the best way is, we ourselves have to choose relations of our choice. Everyday we meet new and old persons in our society, family and professional places, e.g. weddings, functions, festivals, market, college, meetings/conferences, travel, tourist places. Whoever touches the heart, talk to them respectfully and ask to talk for a while. Try to know each other and attach with people of alike nature. It's right, it's life, it's happiness.

Chapter 14

Relations by choice

Million Wings feels that mostly, romantic relations are relations of one's own choice which are made on the basis of personal will and attachment. These relations of choice are started by heart will. Affection means not only to be with a person in happy moments. Infact, intentions are to be with them in their sorrows also. Million Wings feels that most human relations are filled with affections, hope, and love. These are carried on till they fulfil the demands of each other. It's good to have human relations filled with hope. Relations are very beautiful if they start with affection from both sides. In relations, if one is neutral and another is attached by love, then also relations move well. If relations are neutral from both sides in starting and then affection takes place, then also it's good. It often happens when girls or boys make romantic relations, they make romantic relations with other boys or girls too and keep on hiding from each other. They lie to each other and make such relations with others too. When another person comes to know about such relations from others, then there is a tense atmosphere and differences take place. Feelings like blaming each other and doubt take place in the mind. Most people try to clarify that it's wrong, and a few totally resist and start fighting. A few try to convince others that their relations are brothers/sisters or friends, and after sometime, relations of choice start breaking from both sides. One who was in an intact relationship got more hurt and shocked too, and one whose intention is to flirt or betray forgets easily and starts searching for new relations or makes new relations.

Million Wings feels that mostly, relations of choice are not love relations but relations of affection which start from attraction. Every girl and boy naturally got attracted towards each other. Girls and boys often meet each other at social places, e.g. school, college, function, market, tourist place. Girls and boys have a natural desire of attraction towards each other. The heart feels to make romantic relations with beautiful girls or boys. That's why this desire becomes stronger as girls and boys growup and use various tips to look smart. Girls want to look beautiful so that everyone likes them and gets attracted towards them. When someone starts liking someone, then obviously he/she tries to attract that person. Girls/boys try to talk to or meet that person, try to convince them by different ways, try to deepen the relationship, request the other to make a relationship. If the otherone agrees, then it's the beginning of a new relationship.

Million Wings feels that when new relations begin, then a girl and boy talk to each other, meet each other, eat together, have enjoyment together, exchange gifts. Like this, relations deepen more and slowly they start enjoying physical relations and sexual relations. From physical touch to sexual relations, girls/boys can go to any extent. Million Wings feels that a true relation is that which remains the same even after sexual relations. Real affection is that which remains the same even after fulfilment of needs. Mostly, boys after making sexual relations get bored of a girl and start searching for a new girl to make physical/sexual relations. Mostly girls also make relations for fulfilment of needs and do romantic talks and touching with other boys too. Girls and boys do so because of their needs and nature.

Million Wings feels that relations like love, friendship, marriage, affection are not told the right way in society. Worldwide, only love and marriage have been given authenticity of being right. Worldwide, every individual wants to spend life with one male/female but along with that feeling of romantic relations, sexual relations move with them. Million Wings feels that when a girl/boy begins relations of choice, they promise to be in love and entangle each other, and after fulfilling needs, they fight, move on their own path, and this cycle moves on. In this fake cycle of choice, a few innocent girls and boys are also entangled and undergo sorrow, loss of self-confidence. Million Wings feels that most girls and boys actually want romantic relations with each other but they mix all the feelings, e.g. friendship, love relations of choice, flirting. Wanting something else and doing something else and saying something else, and when this happens, it doesn't remain just one relation; infact it becomes betrayal.

Million Wings feels that relations of choice are a very beautiful way. There is nothing wrong if girls and boys are affectionate towards each other. It's natural. It's right too. It often starts with beauty. In human love, person do each and everything for each other and hope for the same inreturn. The basis of human love and relations of choice is fulfilment of exchange of hope. When individual does something for another person, he wants that other person to also do something for him. To think or do this is not wrong. In by-choice relations, if one person does something for another, he also hopes for something good from the other. If another person just keeps on demanding for personal benefit and does nothinginreturn, obviously it hurts and problems start appearing in the relations.

Million Wings feels that in human love, both want equal devotion to carry on the relationship. If it fails to happen, then relations can't be maintained for a long time. When a girl/boy does or manages everything with full devotion and affection and the other doesn't do anything, instead criticizes that, then if one makes relations with some other boy/girl, leaving the first, then nothing's wrong in doing so. Every human wants someone to be with, the one with whom he can share and fulfil his desires, feelings, and needs. When a person makes relations with someone, then he chooses the person as per his own choice. Every girl/boy has their own special choice. Firstly, choice is of physical appearance and looks. Every girl/boy doesn't like other boys/girls just to have romantic relations. The reason is not that they are not smart or good-looking but they don't match with their choice. When a girl or boy gets the face of their choice, then they become attracted towards them.

Million Wings feels that in the world there are millions of males/females but everyone doesn't have the same choice. Everyone has their own choices, and according to that, they are attracted towards males/females. When physical choice isfulfilled, then it becomes a matter of mentality and emotions. Then the girl or boy tries to meet the other. By meeting and by talks, they get to know about each other better. If mentality and needs match and are fulfilled, then that romantic relation is carried forward. Like this girl and boy, male and femalechoose their romantic relations. If girl and boy tell truly, rightly, and fully about their main intentions, then romantic relations become stronger and permanent. But if they lie to each other, then romantic relations starts breaking, as relations can be maintained for sometime on the basis of lies, but with time, it becomes difficult to manage and then hopes aren't fulfilled and the relations break.

Million Wings feels that in the beginning of a new relationship, a person tries his best to present himself, tries to make everything better and better so that they can win each other's hearts and can maintain maximum romantic relations. To do this is human nature and right too. Everyone has to do one's best efforts for the person of one's choice. Nothing's wrong in doing so. Million Wings feels that everyone has his own initial thinking and nature, which he can't resist for a longtime. Secondly, every person has his own resources, the presence of which decides his nature. When males/females beginrelations of their own choice, their intention is to give happiness to each other and to banish their own sorrows and problems. Mostly when human relations move forward, they get to know about downsides of each other also and they get to know about the true nature of each other. Million Wings feels that physical attraction begins a relationship and nature and mentality strengthens and carries forward a relationship. Relations by choice depend on how naturally a girl and boy are attached to each other. The more naturally a girl and boy meet each other, the deeper and stronger relations will be. The more the relations are based on lies or betrayal, the earlier and more sorrowfully relations will break. Million Wings feels that when a girl/boy feels natural attraction for someone, then they see it in positive ways and bother about the needs and happiness of each other and take care of each other. And these relations of choice later on tie the knot (marry).

By choice, love relations are made on the basis of choice and desire of the heart, which only looks on beauty and nature of other person, nothing else according to worldliness. Heartfelt relations don't give importance to race, religion, status, living standard, or occupation. There is no space for worldliness in heartfelt relations, which are filled with love and affection. Everything else is needs and rules of worldliness. Heartfelt relations are the most lovable and plausible relations for every person, for which individuals do everything by heart and in caring ways. In heartfelt relations, everything is done for the happiness of other person and the other also hopes for the same and it is a right of a person also that other person also take care of their needs and hopes and tries to fulfil those. When a girl/boy begins a relation of choice, then they promise a lot. Actually they are expressing their feelings and desires. They are expressing feelings of care, affection, and attraction of their own side, and that expression takes the form of promises. These promises fill confidence, trust, and happiness in relations, which increases hope and affection for each other. To do all this is right and natural too. Romantic relations made by own will and heart are not wrong; infact it's awesome and the right feeling.

Million Wings feels that affection is the main bond of relations, and because of affection, romantic relations take permanent form. Relations can't be maintained if there is no affection in relations.

Million Wings feels that a girl or boy may never tolerate romantic relations with other boy or girl infront of them. Million Wings feels that an individual may have multiple romantic relations; it hardly matters. But no one will tolerate having romantic relations with otherswith whom the individual is committed. It's true and it can't be changed. This human nature will remain as it is and it's right too. Neither is there any another opinion. It's the biggest truth of the heart's choices.

Million Wings feels that only a flirting girl and boy can both enjoy romantic relations, touch or sexual relations infront of each other. Worldwide, romantic relations with only one girl or boy is taken as right and only that is called the right affection. Million Wings feels that a person makes romantic relations for his mental and physical satisfaction. If one girl or boy is happy and satisfied with one boy or girl, then they neither want to have romantic relations with another girl or boy, nor do they have any need. If human is not satisfied with chosen relations, then only will he search for someother relations and he makes these also, as it's his need, natural human need, and it's his right too. If a person is satisfied with person and relations of his choice, then it's his nature. To do this is wrong when a person has promised to have romantic relations with one only. Inspite of promising, a girl/boy's still withboys/girls, then this is totally wrong. If person has promised to one person of his choice to not do so, then he shouldn't do so. If he does so, then he is guilty for other person. It's not because to make relations with numerous persons is wrong but it's because commitment is wrong. If one who has made false commitment is wrong then the one who has made true commitment is many times better than the other.

Million Wings feels that when two persons make romantic relations of their choice and fulfil promises which they have made, it's not because they can't make romantic relations or physical relations with others but they control themselves because of love and commitment and fulfil their promises if they have begun their romantic relations. But if a person has romantic relations with one person, and along with that, he has not promised anything or is very clear to the other, then having romantic relations with multiple people is not bad, is not wrong. A person is answerable or responsible for what he has promised to someone. The things which the person has not promised, he is not responsible for; neither is he under compulsion to answer.

Million Wings feels that false promises will not get human validation as it's a betrayal, which gives totally oppositedirection to happiness or scatters happiness. It's true. It's right.

Million Wings feels that individual may have romantic relationwith one or more people but they should be clear to the related persons. But if person is clear to related persons, it's more authenticity towards happiness and person is more right. Always do the commitments which are in your reach, your desire, your nature. It's real happiness and it's permanent enjoyment. It's flawless satisfaction.

Million Wings feels that affection/love can't be generated forcefully or by education. Love/affection is natural and itself arisesin the heart. Million Wings feels that natural love/affection gives power every second; it's not an issue, field, or work. Million Wings feels that natural love is a beautiful feeling which can be felt at any stage or phase of life. Love/affection can't be searched for; infact it comes by itself in life. People who search for love are innocent, as it can be their need, desire, not love. Million Wings feels that when we want to make some relations with others or others want to make relations with us, then often, chances are that person can't understand the real intention while talking to him. Everyone knows what they themselves want, but if a person comes to know the true intention of the other too, then relations will get the right direction from it and it will speedup the relation. Million Wings feels that a person shares his feelings and body in a relationship, which are the most important property of every person. Nothing's wrong in making relationships. Make any relations with any number of people, but real enjoyment is then only if the other person also has the same intentions. The biggest decision is of the heart; that is what the heart feels. But the important thing is to understand the other one also, what he wants, what he desires. Always begin relations in a systematic proposed manner; the other may be so good, nice, well cultured as a person may have personal relations, i.e. his personal life. It's not important that if may have any relation with good or bad according to worldliness. Intentions and desires of both sides are the base of a relationship. Think serial wise about the otherone as given below.

Intention	Time
Attraction/social interaction only	Temporary, a few hours to a few days
Open-minded friendship	Temporary, anytime, any level
Flirting	Short-term impulse
Cheating	Temporary, few hours to few months
Attachment	Permanent, anytime, any level
Love	Permanent, anytime, any level
Marriage	Permanent, lifelong
Possessiveness	Temporary
Obsessivenes	Anytime, any level

Million Wings feels that love is always 100 per cent one-sided and is with one person at one time. It's true and it will remain true. Love is to have romantic feelings for someone, in which happiness of the other person becomes our own desire, dream, and happiness. If the otherone also feels love for the individual, then the other also feels the same, and these people are very lucky who love each other. To love someone is a natural process which can't be controlled by anyone and which can't be resisted by humans. Anyone can fall in love. But when the hearts of two lowers beat for each other, it's an awesome feeling. A person does everything by his will in love, and nothing seems to be difficult or compulsion, may there be any problem. Lovers just listen to their hearts and do everything for the happiness of the other person. In love a person feels happy in the happiness of the other person and tries his best to banish his sorrows. The highest level of affection is love. It's not important that every person will fall in love. Maybe someone can't fall in love in a lifetime. Once a person falls in love, he/she can't even think about romantic relations, sexual relations, or physical relationswith anyone else.

Million Wings feels that the motto of relations is to attach heartily with someone. A real relationship is that which helps in banishing loneliness of person. Relations may be because of any need. But mental and emotional satisfaction is most important. Relations deepen by sharing views, emotions, feelings, dreams, problems, needs, and personal life and a person surely feels he needs true relations at some phase of life. Million Wings feels that a person may be doing anything; maybe he is careless to any extent, maybe enjoying life, maybe flirting, but if he finds someone with whom he feels emotionally satisfied, then he should try his best to get him/her, should take care of him/her. It's true, it's right, it's a need of the heart. Maybe because of any reason, a person meets with any number of people, may make any relations with them, and if he/she falls in love with someone, then it's absolutely right. But yes, if a person wants to convert that relationship into marriage, then it's absolutely right. These are those relations which make life beautiful. It's happiness.

Chapter 15

Flirting

The main motto of flirting is to establish relations for enjoyment and to get happiness. But there is nothing to do with each other's sorrows. When two flirts are together, then it's necessary to take care of each other's security; otherwise there is no relation with personal problems, tensions, or sorrows of each other. It's true, it's right, it's OK.

Million Wings feels that there is nothing wrong in establishing a relationship for beauty, for physical relations, or for sexual relations as it's not a crime to have these kinds of desires. To establish a relationship for fulfilment of feelings like physical attraction, physical relations, sexual relations is right as sex is one of the basic needs of humans. There is nothing wrong if adult males/females want to enjoy sex. Sex is a truth; this was true centuries ago, today, and centuries in future also. Million Wings feels that to establish a relationship for physical satisfaction is not wrong, but wickedness is to establish a relationship keeping each other in darkness. It's natural to have attraction towards the opposite sex. Million Wings feels that males/females feel attracted towards beauty/smartness of each other. Infact mostly females want to have mental satisfaction and men mostly want to have enjoyment physically or sexually, but males and females both are emotionally attached to each other.

Million Wings feels that worldwide, love and marriage are taken as the best relations. When males are attracted physically towards females and females get attracted towards power or economic status of males, both make the intention of love and marriage as a base. Both assure each other that they will be with each other for a lifetime. Being in these emotions, females give their 100 per cent to the males. Males take advantage of this and enjoy physical touch, sexual and physical relations while the female agrees and the enjoyment goes on. When he gets bored or the female reminds him of the promises of marriage, thenliar males make numerous excuses to escape from the female and they get busy in searching for new females and the first female feels guilty emotionally and mentally. Same way if any female is attached to male because of economic need or some other needs. She keeps on engaging males in emotions such as marriage, till her needs of money and other things are fulfilled and enjoyment is carried on. But when a male is unable to fulfil her demands and needs or she finds someone handsomer or richer than the first male or someone who talks and promises about love or marriage, then the mean female leaves by making some excuses and that male becomes sad and hopeless.

Million Wings feels that needs of resources and sex are not bad or wrong. Infact it's true and right too. Males and females needn't attach to each other by lying to each other. Both males and females like romantic and sexual relations. When someone likesor is attracted towards someone, they look at each other, talk to each other, want to come close to each other, then what's wrong in this? If a male and female like each other, and meet and talk to each other by their own will, then it's exactly right. It's good to know each other. It's good to know about each other's nature, principles, and views. If views and emotions match, then relations continue and it's right also. If both male and female want to attach with each other, just enjoy physical relations or sexual relations, then nothing's wrong in this. Enjoy sexual relations with each other's will.

When males/females become attached to each other just for money and they are clear too about this, then why don't they tell each other? Maybe because they think if they talk about real feelings or needs, sex or money at first or second meeting only, then it's natural that the other may avoid them, and relations may not be carried forward or may break and no one wants this. If a male directly says to make sexual relations with a female at first meeting, obviously she will not agree. And if a female says to a male that she is attached to him for financial needs, obviously malewill hesitate to make relations. Million Wings feels that intentions may be any, but everyone wants a good start, good beginning of relationship. Nothing's wrong in doing this. When males or females attract each other for their purposes, then they firstly need to get close to other by their behaviour and nature. When they come to know each other and feel comfortable with each other in a week or two, then it's easy for them to express the true intentions.

Million Wings feels that males/females are answerable only for those things which they have promised to each other and they are not responsible for the things which they have not promised. While a male or female has not promised any permanent relations (love or marriage), they are not responsible for that. If males or females are having sexual relations or spending money without promising anything, it doesn't mean that they will marry or that is love only. If girls/boys have promised marriage or love, then they are responsible and are answerable. This problem arises when a male or female (one from both) is deeply attached by heart and another is living. Million Wings feels that to make relationships for sexual relations or money is not bad and there is no need to betray each other for this. Any adult males/females are physically fit to have sex but if they can understand this mentally too, then there will not be a chance of any mishap. Million Wings feels that for centuries, males have been attracted to sexual relations and females, for their needs. So when a male and female meet, then how willthis feeling be wrong? Flirt as much you want but with those who have the same thinking, then nothing will be wrong. But to hurt any innocent girl/boy by making false promises is no one's right.

Million Wings feels that while a girl and boy don't promise each other love and marriage but make romantic or sexual relations, then they are not responsible or undercompulsion for marriage. That is either girl/boy has to make a promise for permanent relations before having physical or sexual relations, spending money, and if it is not so, then this means they are not interested in any kind of permanent relations and are related to each other just with an intention of fun and enjoyment. To do this is right.

Million Wings feels that a problem arises when either girl or boy is serious for relations and the other is attached just for fun or fake love. True love and fake love (pretending to love) seem to be alike, and sometimes it's really difficult for a girl/boy to judge whether the other is telling the truth or lying. One can't decide between true & fake because the one who truly loves keeps on loving and the one who is lying is taking advantage of this only. Neither loving nor flirting is wrong. But the problem is when the one who is flirting is lying that he also seriously loves the other. And with time when the one who lies diverts himself, then the one who is truthful has to face sadness. This fake love is betrayal, whose motto is just to have personal benefit, e.g. sexual relations, money, emotional blackmail, revenge, fun/enjoyment.

Million Wings feels that it's not so that males only want physical relations and females, only money. But both want mental and emotional comfort and satisfaction too, filled with love, affection, and care. But if motto is just to have physical relations than be clear to the related male/female since the beginning of the relationship. The earlier that one will clarify things, the earlier one will get the person with alike thinking. If the other refuses, then this is also good, as the earlier one will be clear about the other's will and the other's benefit, the earlier one will start searching for another person. When girls/boys want to attach with each other with will, then only they can enjoy tension-free and fear-free relations. Things which can happen by agreement are right. Maybe that is enjoyment, maybe sex. Million Wings feels that adult males and females need to understand the right meaning of different feelings related with mutualrelations. If a girl/boy is not clear or doesn't know or understand these romantic feelings and desires, then obviously they can't make the right decisions.

Million Wings feels that by the age of 16–18 years, education from family or society is needed for teenagers. At 14–16 years, suddenly girls/boysbecome attracted towards romantic and sexual feelings and they can entangle themselves if they don't have any knowledge. That's the responsibility of elders, to provide them the arranged knowledge by the age of 14–18 years.

Million Wings feels that there are people with different thinking in the world. So if searched by right way, then they can be found nearby only. One who wants to flirt needs to search for people of that kind. If the people with the same thinking, intentions, will, desires meet each other, then they have a lot of enjoyment. Million Wings feels that there is nothing wrong in flirting as it's also one of those feelings which have been here for centuries and will remain while life exists, the one who flirts by the right means.

Million Wings feels that the girl/boy who wants to flirt should get happiness by flirting; they shouldn't be stuck in any problem or tension so that the fun/enjoyment of flirting should be maintained. When girlsor boysbecome attracted towards the beauty of another girl or boy at a social place, then they try their own ways to impress them.

If one is also interested or attracted towards another one, then it's all right, it's perfectly OK. The girl and boy who like each other will obviously like to talk to each other. It's nature and behaviour after beauty, which brings the two together. On beginning to flirt, a girl and boy talk to each other, then obviously they want to know about each other. It's good to talk to each other to know about each other. In a few days when girl and boy feel comfortable with each other, then they need to tell their intentions and will clarify to each other so that one should know about the other's intention before increasing the bond of relationship. It's very beneficial to talk clearly to each other. If both are not interested in any kind of permanent relations like love or marriage, then it's easy to flirt. If girls or boys don't promise about any permanent relations, then later on, they are not answerable for that. If girls and boys talk clearly to each other and are interested in relations of fun and enjoyment, then that's OK. If both want to flirt as per each other's will, agreement and with truthfulness then it's clear from talk that another is serious or wants permanent relations, then instead of making relations strong, one should search for another person, as that is not only girl or boy to flirt with.

Million Wings feels that if most flirting girls/boys feel that he/she is the only boy/girl whom she/he likes and she/he has to flirt with or to make sexual relationswith him/her only, then it's just innocence of their thoughts and mind. Million Wings feels that it's easy for girl/boy to make a fake promise and flirt but the real fun and enjoyment is to clarify the real feeling and do everything with agreement of the other. There is no place for feelings of fear or betrayal if a person flirts by making himself or herself clear and both enjoy the life with abandon.

Million Wings feels, flirt in such a way that one needn't regret for one's whole life, not to be entangled with one person. Be clear to the related male/female; you needn't tell the whole world. Feeling of flirtation is a personal feeling, can be told to one, may not be told to another; it's a personal decision. Flirt in such a way that another should not get hurt, specially yourself.

Million Wings feels that when girls/boys flirt then obviously they are attracted towards beauty. If both like each other, then only the relation can be carried forward. External beauty is not enough for flirting. Their mental status, physical fitness are also required to flirt. Flirting is a well-known feeling, that feeling in which there is no space for permanent relations like love or marriage. In these situations, girls and boys should keep each other apart from problems and tensions. It's right too. When two are flirting, then it means they just want enjoyment. They just need happiness from each other. The main aim of flirting is to meet, eat, roam about, have enjoyment. They don't want to be entangled in each other's family problems, tensions, and problems. It's not any natural love or affection which will withstand happy and sad moments. Flirting is to enjoy temporary relations for happiness.

Know about the mental level of a girl/boy before flirting (girl or boy must be adult, above 16–18 years) atleast before starting a conversation. Before that, mind, brain, and body are not properly developed. If we want to flirt, then there will be enjoyment only if the other is adult and can understand the things well. Girl or boy should aware of the difference between flirting /natural love/marriage / friendship. Flirting girls/boys should know about each other's physical fitness, problems, and diseases. When flirting is a well-known feeling of the heart, then flirting by understanding can increase happiness many folds.

One who wants to flirt can flirt as much one wants, but flirt with flirty ones only. Flirt with those who have the same will and thinking, but don't flirt with an innocent or teenaged girl or boy; don't betray anyone. Million Wings feels that girl or boy may be a great flirt, but they don't want that their partner is flirting with someone else. It's true, it's right, and it's genuine too when a girl and boy are related by the relationship of flirting and when both are together then they have to give importance to each other. When two flirts are attached by promising each other that they will not flirt with anyone else while they are together, then obviously they will not like that their partner is flirting or making relations with someone infront of them or when they are along with them; obviously they will get annoyed, may fight and feel bad.

Million Wings feels that when you are with someone, then spend time with them only. If you want to flirt with someone else, then do this in some other time or after discontinuation of relations with first flirt person. If flirt girl/boy flirts with one or more boys/girls, then there is nothing wrong in this, but to flirt with two or more girls/boys by making commitments with them is wrong, as at one time, committed flirts also want to be with each other.

Million Wings feels that girls and boys, everyone flirts with each other, so there are different definitions of flirting. Someone takes flirting as just looking at each other. A few take flirting as sharing romantic talks with each other. A few take flirting as teasing others. A few take flirting as touching another, like holding hands, etc. A few take flirting as touching private parts, and a few take flirting as making sexual relations. Million Wings feels that everything is taken as flirting from looking to making sexual relations while they have not promised any permanent relations to spend time. Girl and boy look at each other, get attracted towards each other's smiles, laugh with each other but don't make any physical relations with each other is fun flirting. When girl or boy makes physical relations too, it's called full flirting. When these two full flirts are totally clear to each other and give importance to each other, it's choice by flirt, i.e. choice flirt. It's not important a fun flirt girl/boy will be a choice flirt or full flirt. But full flirt is always flirt by choice. Million Wings feels that it depends upon will, understanding of girl or boy up to what level they will make physical relations. Million Wings feels that a boy and girl, male and female are attracted by choice to each other. Opposite sexes are also attached by or wants to attach many kinds of relations and emotions, and flirting is one of those feelings. Million Wings feels that to flirt is an art, not betrayal. It's a perfection, not to betray. It's a better understood and acted thing, not an innocent activity. One who wants to flirt can flirt, flirt to any extent, as they want but with person of alike thinking and will. Then there will be enjoyment with beautiful emotion and desires. No commitment, please.

Million Wings feels that it will be better to choose people far away from family and relatives to flirt with. Flirting is wilful, done by choice, in which relations we made just for fun, to have enjoyment, not to increase problems, tensions. The further the relations, more easy and comfortable it is to flirt. The further two flirts are, the less will be the problems, the more comfortable the relation is, as personal management will be easy.

Million Wings feels that friendship is such a relation in which there is no place for betrayal, may it be personal, professional, familiar, or a social-level thing or problem. A friend may not be able to help, it's another thing, but friends never betray. If friends make some relationship with adult relative (brother, sister, daughter, wife, mother) of friend by their will and desires, then it is not betrayal. As everyone except (real brother/sister, mother/father, children) are firstly male and female and if there is any romantic relationship with them with their will, then that's completely their responsibility. But yes, if someone has done this, with non-adult or by wrong ways, making false commitment, then it's completely wrong. It will not be tolerated. They are responsible for this betrayal and one has to pay surely for this.

Praise by any means gives happiness to another. But doing wrong signs or even teasing is not an attractive thing; infact it's a sign of stupidity, as by doing this person is to give invitation to enmity. It's beneficial to know a bit about mental status of male or female, as if another's intention is also of enjoyment, obviously enjoyment will be doubled. If you want fun and enjoyment, then have fun and enjoyment only. To be entangled with each other is disadvantageous and wastage of time only; use that time in finding some compatible flirt. It will be the right thing.

When males/females want to flirt, then they get attracted towards female/male of their own choice, maybe external beauty or nature. Both the reasons are good. Flirting has also been also a type of attachment for sometime. While flirting with males/females, respect them and don't misbehave with each other because of attachment only. The physical relations in which there is no attachment, basically that male or female is not flirting; infact they are selfish. The flirt male/female who maintains a respectful way is a natural flirt. There is nothing wrong in being flirty and neither is it a wrong desire. To flirt is human desire and nature. Males/females who want to do this, it's completely their personal life. Million Wings feels that flirting is not a wrong desire; one needn't tell it to whole of the world. To flirt is social feeling but it may be one's personal life also. But accept the intention of flirt to related person. It gives calmness, tension-free and plausible atmosphere. Flirting is a beautiful art which allows males/females to do something wrong and enjoy romantic moments in plausible and beautiful ways.

Million Wings feels that personswho want to flirt are attracted by beauty and behaviour but have nothing to do with mental tension and problems. Flirts just need to fulfil their desires and don't want to be entangled with their problems and sorrows. To think and want this is not wrong. Million Wings wants this only, that flirts should have enjoyment and not be entangled in problems while flirting. Try to understand/know the mental level of the other too, as if the other also has the same intentions, then it will be more enjoyable. But if the other is busy or entangled in some other thing/issue, then flirting can't be enjoyed. Maybe the other is already attached or in love with someone, maybe the other is entangled with family or personal problems. Maybe stuck with some disease, maybe the other is beautiful but may not understand flirting by heart, mind, and by inner soul. If one has mind along with beauty, then one can have enjoyment. If a person is flirty or wants to attach with multiple persons, it's allright. Nothing's wrong in this. If an individual wants to flirt with multiple persons, then let him flirt. If an individual has attachments with multiple person, then let him. There is nothing wrong in doing so if the related person has no problem and they know and understand each other, then the atmosphere will remain plausible. But if both are not able to express this kind of feeling to each other, then one has to manage their relation in such a way that this should not affect their other relations. It's a secret of logical personal life. Million Wings feels that if everything is clear between girl and boy and they are satisfied and agree with each other, then there can be any type and any number of relations. Everything is all right, correct and it's logical truth.

Million Wings feels that a person may be attached emotionally, may be attached physically, or by both ways with any number of people, but when he is with one, then he has to spend quality time with that person only. To flirt is also a kind of attachment, maybe with someone's beauty, maybe with someone's nature, or maybe with both. To flirt is not wrong. Flirts respect each other, don't misbehave with each other. Flirts are good at heart. They may want to make relations for sometime with each other. But their intention is not of misbehaving or of defaming. Feelings of sex are not wrong. To share our feelings is not wrong. But they each take care of each other's boundaries and limitations. Flirts may be attached physically or emotionally, but they definitely maintain respect of each other.

Those who betray each other, misbehave with each other are not flirts, but they are idiots. To ditch is not right. Ditching means to betray the person just for personal benefits. To do this is wrong, is bad. Ditching persons choose forceful ways to get benefits. These kinds of persons don't respect another person; they have no attachment with another person, they just use innocent persons. They just need a body to fulfil their need. Million Wings feels that flirty persons are good, not evil. Those who are ditch are actually corrupt, as these people didn't desire romance but have nonsense in mind. The mind just desires sex and the heart has no feelings or emotions.

Million Wings feels that there is difference between flirting and having open and wide thinking/mentality. When one has broad thinking and behaviour, that doesn't mean that one wants only physical relations or pastime relations or romantic relations or sexual relations. Million Wings feels that while males/females don't clarify that they want to flirt, just think that they are attached just in friendship or socializing or humanism. Mostly, flirts and people with open thinking just look alike, and misunderstanding and guessing mostly creates problems between male and female.

Million Wings feels that one has to save oneself from ditching and stupid person, not from flirty ones. Million Wings feels that one always feels respectful by talks and touch. Million Wings feels that when girlsand boys meet and they don't like or feel respect in the way another talks or touches, then they should not carry forward the relations.

Million Wings feels, don't ditch but flirt as much you want and enjoy it, stay happy. If some third person tries to enter or enters, then there are chances/possibilities of arguments, fights, and misunderstandings. Million Wings feels that when some third person enters relations of a couple, then initiation is done by one from the couple, not by the third person. If one from the couple is a flirt or is attached with someone else also, then blaming and fighting with the third person is not right. Instead, the couple themselves has to clarify and coordinate with each other, or they have to part from each other and live happily without disturbing each other's life. If the third person is torturing, blackmailing, misbehaving, or creating misunderstandings, then the third person is more wrong. Million Wings feels that persons who create troubles in relations are around only. But always remember to talk freely and regularly with each other, clear up problems, and it's a way to come out from problems. A couple has to talk to each other and teach a lesson to the third person. And if help of friends, family, or police is required, than do take that. It's the right decision.

Million Wings feels that there are a few freak people in world who think of others as their own personal property. Those who take love like this either suffer from mental illness or are entangled that much in misunderstandings that they give mental or physical stress to their lover. Million Wings feels that this type of mental condition is not love, affection, or flirting; infact it's craziness. Most of the time, these people understand polite ways but sometimes one has to be hard with them. Million Wings feels that these kinds of persons can be tackled by their family's interference or may need help of police and administration too. Jealousy in relations is common, especially in relations of the heart. It's difficult for girls/boys to tolerate that their lover care for another boy or girl infront of them and a third person cares for their love or comes close to them. Million Wings feels that two females can love one male or two males can love one female but it's impossible for them to live together. It's true, it's right too. Million Wings feels that may person flirt or be attached with someone but has to not behave in a romantic way infront of the other. The time you are with one has to be spent with care and love with them only. It's right.

Million Wings feels that a person gives or wants to spend quality time with those with whom he feels or wants; one can't demand time forcefully. When one from a couple makes romantic relations with a third person, then it's natural that the first one will feel jealous, maybe himself/herself flirt or have attachments with any number of persons. Jealousy depends, up to which extent, level, way their lover is attached with another. Million Wings feels that it's not wrong to flirt or have romantic relations with numerous persons while they have clear and respectful coordination with each other. But to spend quality time with one whom we like gives ultimate happiness and enjoyment. Every person has the right to live their personal life, but their security is also their responsibility. Million Wings feels that to spend quality time in relations is important, not but what one has to interfere in personal life, as personal life is that which a human wants to keep secret or wants to keep to himself/herself, otherwise not, never. It's true.

🎋 🎋 🎋

Chapter 16
Love relations

Naturally, male and female are made for each other. It's natural to become attracted towards the opposite sex. Nothing's wrong in this. It's true and it's a beautiful truth. Male and female are incomplete without each other, as the relations of male and female are a combination of emotional and physical satisfaction. There is surely bit of natural difference between male and female but both are equally important. Naturally, male and females are different, as if both are alike, then what is the meaning of being two? Dissimilarity of male and female are their specialities and this speciality brings them together. Relations of male and female become stronger by understanding each other. Who is female? What is the reality of female? What is different and unique in females which makes them special? Female means beauty, making love, make-up, emotions, politeness, soft-heartedness, affection, care, beautiful styles. This is female, who is unique and different from males and becomes the remaining part of them. Male means physically strong, emotionally strong, active, secure. This is male, who becomes the remaining half of female. Nature of female is totally different from males. Girl may be simple girl or a president's daughter but firstly she is female. To look beautiful is the first right of the female. Females always want to look beautiful and attractive and want that everyone should look at them in a respectful way. Do make-up and wear jewellery according to your choice. Politeness, softness, and emotions are unbreakable parts of a female. Females don't express themselves sooner and express themselves by different ways. Females keep on saying about the mistakes done once, but also forget them sooner. Female are more emotional and sensitive and forgive easily. Coquetry of femalesis their heart-touching power; combination of beauty with coquetry is female.

Males also want to look smart and attractive. A male may be a simple guy or a great scientist but firstly he is a male. Males are less sensitive. Males symbolize power and strength. It's their automatic feeling to protect and secure females. Million Wings feels that to understand nature, emotions, and feelings of males and females means to understand needs and behaviour in a better way. Males and females feel romantic attraction towards each other. Males/females may be in any profession, level, or atmosphere but they are firstly recognized as male and female. Except profession male and female are opposite sex. Million Wings feels that except the relation of real siblings, parents and children all are firstly male and female, except one relation. Except these romantic relation can be created with anyone. When feelings which are well known and thought, then try that should be out of friend circle and nearby relations so that they can be enjoyed maximally.

Girls' menstruation cycle becomes stable by the age of 16 years. Reproductive and physical structure also grows fully, i.e. naturally, a girl is capable of giving birth to baby by the age of 16 years, and by the age of 16years physically boys also grow that much that they became capable of this. Million Wings feels that when naturally girls and boys grow to the age of 16 years, then for romantic relations, family and society should also teach them about romantic relations and guide them in a managed and arranged way.

Million Wings feels that mostly human relations are good relations. It's good to have human relations, it's right too. Happiness is to have relations of our choice to fulfil our needs. Relations are power. Relations are security. Relations are satisfaction. Relations are a very beautiful human policy. Mostly humans can't live alone, can't be happy alone. Every person needs support or togetherness of someone. Every male and female are attached to each other because of some feelings, emotions. Million Wings feels that relations which are made by mutual understanding, will, coordination, and desire are made between two opposite sexes and there must be some reason, cause, or need. Million Wings feels that the cause in relations hardly matters when two are clear and satisfied with each other. No feeling or emotion is bad while two are attached by will and desire for each other. Both (male and female) want/desire something from each other. There are many types of feelings to have relations, e.g. physical attraction, sexual will, attachment, love, mental/emotional satisfaction, resources, mutual business or social bonds, betrayal, or revenge.

Million Wings feels that there are many causes of relations between male and female. Million Wings feels that mostly males make relations for physical relations and mostly females want to have emotional satisfaction. Relations between male and female depend upon mutual emotional satisfaction and importance. Million Wings feels that every will and desire is good, and the relations made by mutual understanding are all good. If males and females are clear and agree with each other, there is nothing wrong in relations. If male and female can manage everything themselves for their relations at their own level, then that is good, is right. When male and female agree with each other with their own will and are happy with their relations by managing things, then it's right to do, nothing's wrong in this. Million Wings feels that romantic relations between male and female are happiness and power of human life. The strength of relations is feelings and intention behind those relations. Male or female may attach physically or emotionally, for sometime or lifelong with each other but right is only when they are close by mutual understanding, will, and coordination.

Million Wings feels that mostly human relationships are relations only. Betrayal, flirting, love, compromises, all are feelings. When male and female become close to each other, then there are mostly two intentions. One is natural affection which itself arises in the heart, and the other is compromise. The affection which itself arises is love, means a lovely romantic feeling in which a human himself does a lot for another with his will without expecting anything back. But all other relations are give-and-take relations. Whatever persons do, expect/want the same in return too. A feeling of love arises itself; it can't be planned. But there is a hidden motto behind every other relation, person already knows about that. Million Wings feels that betrayal is not acceptable in relations. To betray is not a feeling. Betrayal is a planned project which is chosen to fulfil feelings. It's not wrong to make relations to fulfil physical, emotional, or social feelings; nor are feelings like love, flirting, compromise, needs wrong.

All these feelings are right, are logical. These feelings have been related to humans for centuries, exists today also, and will continue like this only. There is nothing wrong for male/female to establish a relationship to fulfil these feelings. All these feelings are good and genuine too. That's why these feelings are part of the primary nature of humans.

Million Wings feels that worldwide, only love and marriage are taken as right, but feelings of flirting, sexual relations, compromises, needs are taken as wrong and full of flaws. If these feelings are really wrong, then why these are continued for centuries? Why does a human try to fulfil his desires and feelings at personal level even after declaring these feelings as wrong at social level? Million Wings feels that these feelings are not wrong, but the ways adopted to fulfil these can be wrong; that's why these feelings are taken as wrong. Sex and sexual relations are humans' desire and need, then how can they be wrong? But forceful fulfilment of these feelings with whomsoever against their will make it wrong. If male and female establish relations to fulfil social and basic needs, then what's wrong in that? But not fulfilling promises made with each other makes it wrong. If a male and female met each other just for fun but try to assert, that makes it wrong.

Million Wings feels that every feeling behind relations of male female is right if done with will, agreement, or by convincing each other. Million Wings feels that intentions of many girls and boys are to flirt but because of social limitations and non-acceptance at social level, they can't say that directly; that's why they start talkingabout love or marriage so that another will agree, and fear of non-acceptance by telling truth should bother them. Maybe both are flirts only. But they are not able to tell/express truth because of social thinking and limitations. They may be able to fulfil them secretly but in the eyes of social protectors are taken as wrong at social level, and their life can be made hell. Million Wings feels that worldwide there is every type of feelings in abundance. Then why can't they be abroad through the right path in society? Love and marriage is beautiful, lovely, and clean way of managing life, but all other feelings are also not wrong. If feelings like flirting, sex, compromises are also taken in good sense in society, then maybe betrayal and crime can be reduced, minimized, or abolished from society.

Million Wings feels that the feeling of romance, physical relations, or sexual relations is not created by humans. These have been born along with humans only. Humans have not made these feelings; instead they are non-detachable parts of human nature. So the feelings which arise along with birth, how they can be wrong? To have agreement and coordination of these feelings is right. Million Wings feels that relations filled with love and care are plausible and permanent. Being attached with someone by heart and care are relations of love. Either affection is natural or can arise by getting time filled with love and care. The relations arise in which affection is natural are strong relations, the relations which are started by affection from both sides. These emotional, physical, and social needs are also naturally fulfilled. They needn't make any new relations. Million Wings feels that a person wants to fulfil his personal, familiar, and social needs from relations, and this is also cause of making relations. If these demands and needs can be fulfilled by one relation, then why will a person search for new relations or for what? Maybe this is the primary nature of humans and nothing like a wrong feeling. It's true too.

Million Wings feels that if a human's relations are according to his own will, then he would have interest and affection towards relations. This means if relations are according to choice and interest of girls and boys, then love and affection can be created itself. This means it's a good decision to have relations with a male or female of one's own choice. Million Wings feels that either affection is natural or can be developed by living together. A heart filled with care and love can also bring each other close. One's feelings of affection are called love. Here a person feels attached to a level that the emotional and physical bonding which person feels with that person, he can never feel the same with anyone else. On the other side, if we see then, physical relations can be created by the same way or maybe in a better way. A feeling of love can be felt with only one person. But attachment and sexual relations can be felt with more than one. In love, a person feels so much attached with a person that he doesn't want to get any emotional or physical bonding with anyone else at the sametime. Relations made just for physical satisfaction are short-term relations. Neither is this feeling wrong, not relations. Everything done with agreement is right, is logical.

Million Wings feels that emotional attachment is a priorityfor every person. Physical attachment comes afterwards. If something matters more than anything in the world, then that is satisfaction of emotional bonding. If physical needs are filled along with emotional needs, then it's good; otherwise they can be filled by some other relations. That is emotional attachment at a much higher level than physical attachment, and the one who is close emotionally is the priority. Million Wings feels that love relations don't need any name or relations; neither do they need any proof. All other relations are well considered and then made, and the world may also demand proof for those relations. If a relationship is made by will and agreement, then chances of problems decrease. When male and female accepts each other after knowing everything about each other, it's allright.

Romantic relations of every person are his/her personal life. If he wants to keep that secret, then that's his right and will too. To make a relationship, it's enough for a person to clarify for each other; he needn't tell everything to whole world. It's a need and responsibility of the related person to keep secret of their relations. Million Wings feels that possibility of breaking a relationship remains in those relations also which are made by agreement and will. How can the decision be made at social level if relations break or misunderstandings took place? Million Wings feels that marriage can be a good compromise if a girl and boy decide to live together by their choice, will, desire, and agreement. Every kind of relationship is based on mutual understanding and agreement, which can be moved by understanding and coordination. Paper proof and registration is fast and authentic proof so that if any issue arises in a relationship, then that can be handled at social and administered level, as relations might be personal but a few times they might need social, legal, or administrative help also.

Relations of flirtingare meant for enjoyment, sexual relations, physical relations, and collecting resources. There is no natural affection in flirting; infact it's to create a romantic feeling with the person of choice to fulfil one's desires and intentions. When intensions are fulfilled, then affection automatically starts decreasing and new relations begin. Flirting is fun, enjoyment; flirting is not bad while it's is clear that one is flirting and not promising anything. Relations of choice along with affection are beautiful romantic relations where male and female are attached to each other emotionally and mentally too along with physical relations. This type of affection can't be felt with everyone, but this is also not necessarily felt with one only. A male/female has romantic relations with any number of people. But most of the time, affectionate romantic relations can be felt with one person at one time. During affection, everything is done by one's will and desire and hope to get that back also. If needs, desires, will of each other are fulfilled, then relations are continuous; otherwise they break. This type of affection can often be seen in humans and it's right too. A relationship filled with affection can be felt with many persons at one time, and most things are done with mutual understanding. In this romantic relationship, a person devotes his 100 per cent to the person with whom he/she is at one time. There are both physical and emotional attachments in these relations. These kinds of relations are also good, as people spend quality time with the person whom they are with at one time, i.e. dedicated relationship.

When male and female are attached physically or emotionally to each other, it's known as human love. Often, people live affectionately with each other, care for each other, do everything by heart and will and for happiness of each other and also expect the same from the other too. Persons even complain to each other. It's natural to feel jealous and have expectationsof another. Annoyance-persuasiveness is also continuous; in short everything, anything can help. But have romantic relation with one male/female at one time. Meet everyone but have romance, physical and affectionate, with one person. If any misunderstanding or doubt arises, then one should try to clarify them. But still if they are not satisfied with each other, then they get apart. After sometime, they again get in a relationship with some other person and human love again starts and then they totally become attached to new relations and this sequence moves on. It's often seen that in sincere love, a person ties the knot, in marriage. This human love is a good way of romantic love. While male and female are attached to each other, they don't want to get in romantic relations with anyone else. In this love, emotional and physical attachment can develop with the other only after getting apart from a flirt. Both often get married in these relations.

When males/females get emotionally or physically attached to another without expecting back and do everything by own will, it's spiritual love. In this love, one doesn't expect anything in return, believes in just giving.

Nothing feels like a burden or compulsion or showing off. One doesn't feel guilty or bad even on losing everything. This love can't be replaced, can't be taught, can't be changed, can't be destroyed. Spiritual love doesn't need name of any relation. They may get married or not, but the bond of love doesn't get weaker. In these kinds of relations, male or female can't make romantic relations even if they want to. After being in spiritual love, a person neither wants to marry nor wants to have romantic relations with anyone else. Only those can do so whose dream, will, happiness is love only. Spiritual love can happen anytime in a lifetime, maybe before marriage or after marriage. If somehow this happens, then emotionally and physically person feels romantically attached to him/her only. Afterwards, the person doesn't get attached romantically towards anyone else.

This kind of love can happen even after marriage. Romantic, physical, or emotional love can happen to any male or female and then sex with husband/wife can be done only under compulsion or as responsibility. It's known as still love. Human maximally wants to become attached emotionally and physically to that personally only. Maybe he is attached with his wife/husband also. In these relations, often bachelors get married. If because of any reason they didn't get married, then they feel that special emotional and physical attachment with that person only. They may start getting attached to their husband/wife too, but their heart feels the romantic relations with them only. It's called heart feel.

Million Wings feels that behind every relationship, intention or feeling matters. Mostly if we see than work, presentation may look alike, but what matters is the feeling behind that. In any relations, actual meaning can be understood by romantic or non-romantic feeling. To talk with someone is not romance, but to talk in a romantic way is romance. To hold hands or hug is not romance, but to do the same in romantic ways becomes romance. Romance is done in romantic ways, not by presentations.

In love and affection, a person himself has to do work, which can be done at their level so that when they meet, they can do only that work which requires personal presence and which can be done only if both are together. The work which male/female can do alone should be done by him/her so that they can spend quality time when they meet rather than be stuckin unnecessary work and wasting time, i.e. to do daily work by ourselves fills quality in romantic relations. It's true. It's a secret of love too.

Million Wings feels that mostly affection and care are misunderstood. When one male/female cares, then often others may take it as love. Persons can care in non-romantic ways too, e.g. as friends, for social work, humanism, i.e. it's not necessary that care only means romantic relations. Million Wings feels that while male/female doesn't accept or clarify about love, then care should be taken as friendship, socializing, humanism.

But being possible or obsessive can give pain to other. It can be very painful and dangerous. This feeling is totally wrong. Million Wings feels that love is upto a level while another feels comfortable and happy but when it becomes restriction, it turns into disease. Expectation is normal. If one has done something for another, than one can expect the same in return too. It's good to have expectations in relations but only with those who themselves have promised the same by their will. Million Wings feels that a male/female who has multiple emotional or physical relations may be affectionate or care for all or may be more attached with one but doesn't have love with anyone. But yes, they may have heart feel in future. If someone feels love towards this type of person, then it's wastage of time to fight with them to get belongingness and to tie or restrict them moves them away only. But care and affection can bring them back. It's the only way, it's true, it's logical. If there is no affection or love with this kind of person, then getting apart is better rather than to bind each other with these relations.

Chapter 17

Love/affection

Million Wings feels that heart feel is at the highest level in love relations. Heart feel means that person romantically gets so much attached to a person that as per his own will, he spontaneously does everything for that person and never feels bad or uncomfortable or complains about it. Instead, doing this becomes a spontaneous and beautiful part of life. Million Wings feels that heart feel can be natural or human love. Heart feel means to attach by romantic, physical, or emotional way to the extent that one can do anything and never demand anything inreturn, never expect anything back. Heart feel (natural love) happens once in a lifetime and is always natural. Human love is also for one at one time. In human love, one does alot or everything for another and also expects and demandsthe same inreturn. Million Wings feels that love may be natural or human; both are beautiful, both are lovely, both are right, true, and logical.

Million Wings feels that human love can happen any number of times, with one after another, but heart feel remains one and the same for a lifetime, with whom a person lived or is living or wants to live. Heart feel is the priority, may theperson get them or not. A romantic feeling of heart feel is the most different and most natural feeling in the world which always fills the heart with joy. It's not necessary that a person can have permanent relations with heart feel, and it's not necessary that the other person's heartfeel will also be same. A person can have permanent relations. Heart feel is undetectable relations which are above all relations of socializing. Human can feel heartily affectionate towards some other person also, may flirt with someone, may even get married, but heartfeel remains heartfeel, i.e. the same. A person has moreattachment with heart feel than anyone else in the world; all loving personsmay be there but still the heart beats for heart feel. Heart feel is the most natural and loving romantic feeling, may the person be (emotionally or physically) attached to any number of people.

Million Wings feels that heart feel is always one-sided and is with one person in a lifespan. Those are very lucky if the two who naturally loves each other, i.e. if both are heart feel of each other, then that's the luckiest situation.

They are lucky if both are romantically, physically, and emotionally attached to each other by their own will and desires. If the other didn't do anything in return, then also one can't force or compel the other. The one who loves naturally just expressesone's love, sometimes by words, sometimes with love and care, and helping in tough times or at time of need even without being asked for help. One can't force or compel another to love one; one can just express one's own love is natural love. Never ask for anything in return. It's luck that the other also feels the same. One can't hurt another intentionally in natural love. After being in natural love, a person wants to be attached romantically, physically, and emotionally to that person only; even the thought of being attached to another can't come to mind. Everything is done by will and desire in natural love. Whatever male or female do for each other is never taken as compulsion or tension. If a person lost everything, even then he can't regret and even never expresses regret.

Million Wings feels that natural love can happen anytime, anywhere in any phase or stage of life. The unique feeling of affection is known as love. Million Wings feels that natural love can't be searched for, but can happen itself, comes by itself in life if it has to come. It's not necessary that everyone will fall in natural love and even it's not necessary that in return the same person will also fall in love. This natural love can be felt naturally only. One can't generate it intentionally. Natural love can neither be generated nor be taught. Natural love can neither be stolen nor suppressed. The feeling of natural love can neither be increased nor decreased. Being in natural love, a person can do anything for happiness and comfort of another. Natural love is not related with name, fame, status, wealth, colour, race, beauty.

Million Wings feels that in natural love, one only cares for happiness, care, and respect of love and can't hurt, even a little, knowingly. In natural love one can't hinder innocence of another; instead allow that to bloom and protect and secure that innocence. In natural love, a person tries his/her best to help and fulfil dreams, desires, and needs of his/her love. In natural love, a person cares more for happiness and dreams of another than his own. It's not necessary that a natural lover cares more for happiness and dreams of another than his own. It's not necessary that natural lovers will look attractive to the whole world, but their attraction towards each other matters. Once a natural love is felt with any face then his views, emotions, feelings, principles also feel good. Natural love has nothing to do with beauty or mental level or thinking. In natural love, all good and bad habits of each other are accepted as they are. Personal imbalance of another is accepted as it is and person tries to balance that at own level. In natural love, drawbacks are not told directly, but the person tries to deplete them by secret ways and with positive attitude. In love, good qualities of each other are judged and have to be encouraged honestly.

Million Wings feels that every possible effort is done in love to clarify misunderstandings and doubts which were born in love, with soft and clear ways. In love, male and female never leave each other alone. Million Wings feels that every behaviour, nature, and step of each other is firstly taken in positive ways. Firstly his conditions and circumstances are seen, behind every step or natural reaction. Lovers always search for the reason behind tension and worry about their love and try to search for the problems and causes behind that and try to solve them. In love, mistakes and innocence of each other are handled in such a way that the other should not suffer from any problem or get least affected from that.

Million Wings feels that the feeling of natural love always remains with male and female. It hardly matters whether another is near or far away. Natural love always remains love, as another can't create doubt or misunderstandings in natural love. As in natural love persons trust their love more than a third person. Those who naturally love each other have no space for a third person for romantic, physical, or emotional relations.

Million Wings feels that a male and female who feel unconditional, unforgettable affection with each other, care for each other, want to spend maximum possible time, want to talk to each other, want to share own love feelings, want to listen to their feelings and views, want to live with each other forever, want to make romance but can't force or compel or betray each other. Love is not penurious of any relations or boundaries. Persons live and die for each other in love. If the other also feels affectionate towards the person, then feelings of satisfaction and calmness arise. If the other didn't want to get in any relation with one, even then love and affection can't decrease. If the other wants to live as a friend, then the person who loves will live like a friend with him/her. If the other is cool and of plausible nature, then also the person is happy with him/her. If the other flirts with him/her, then also the person remains happy. If the other feels human love for him/her, even then the person feels happy with him/her. If the other may flirt with him/her or feel affectionate towards someone else, even then the person feels same affection, love towards him/her. If the other loves someone else, even then the person's love remains the same for the other. If the other feels spiritual love with him/her, then he/she feels lucky and keeps on loving in the same way. If the other is married or unmarried, till then the person loves him/her the same way. If the other gets married to someone else, still loveremains the same. If the other is wrong, a drug addict, criminal, till then love remains the same. If the other gets in physical relations with someone else, even then love remains the same.

Million Wings feels that if two persons deeply love each other, then they try their best to live together. Only in spiritual love male/female are unable to get married or fail to make romantic relations. In human love and still love, a person may decide to get apart. In love, if lovers can't live together according to socialism, they are still close to each other, always together. They may get married to someone else, have sexual or physical relations, reproduce, but their heart always blooms for natural love. Natural love is always felt with only one male/female, and that same feeling doesn't arise for anyone else. There may be any level of romantic relations with someone else. Million Wings feels that heart feel and love is that type of natural romantic will, desire, and power, then a person himself has not to do anything and everything happens by itself. Nothing feels like management, boundaries, compulsion willy-nilly, or sacrifice. Infact, personal happiness and satisfaction is felt. If a person does anything for his love for which he was given a tag of denouncement, the world may laugh at them, admonish them, reject them, even then he never feels that his loved one had anything wrong and it is logical and right too. The world may say, do, think anything; the person may have to pay high for that, but still doing anything for heart feel gives satisfaction and seems to be logical too. Lost in affection of heart is a style of heart feel, which doesn't seem to be right according to socialism. But personally it gives satisfaction to do everything for heart feel. This all is affection, love and is right and logical too. Million Wings feels that it's not necessary that feelings of the heart feel always touchthe highest level of feeling and emotions. Heart feel can be that feeling of the heart in which humans may be lost for sometime. With time, a person can come out of feelings of heart and can think with the mind too. Humans may think with the mind and make better decisions but still the sweet feeling of the heart, heart feel remains the same. Intelligence can't deplete heart feel; instead taught to do everything for heart feel in much better, arranged, and managed way. Million Wings feels that person may have any number of romantic relations but heart feel remains the same, remains priority. Heart feel is that natural romantic relationship of the heart in which a human didn't think about or think for personal benefit.

Million Wings feels that it's a great and lovely feeling to love someone heartily. To love someone is a unique feeling in the world. It's a plausible satisfaction to love someone and do everything for his/her happiness. It completes us to haunt, to wait, to look, to have a glance, to meet, to talk, to comeclose.

Love is that wonderful feeling, power, strength which can be felt only after being in love. Million Wings feels that the heart always beats for heart feel. Their voice or presence can't be felt by anyone else in world. The world may dislike lovers; lovers just love each other and their stories set an inimitable new definition and examples for the world.

🌾 🌾 🌾

Chapter 18
Marriage

To get married or not has been a question for centuries which is always tough for married and unmarried fellows. What is the benefit or importance of marriage which makes it beautiful and what are those problems which raise a question for marriage? Today, humans are civilized and free too. What is that thing which humans can't get from anywhere except marriage? A person can live on rent, desire of sexual relations can be filled by mutual understanding, child can be adopted, servants can be hiredto take care of parents. In sickness, the person can get treatment from hospitals which take care completely; on death, the body can be sent to a research centre. Friends have nothing to do with marriage. In problems, friends are here to help. Or some government or non-government organization can help. Ourselves can remain free and self-ruling. Earning can be used for ourselves only. We'll do whatever we want to do, enjoy fun without any fear, tension, and worries.

What is that which can't be fulfilled without marriage? Everything can be done to earn fast money and avail of facilities for ourselves. If there is money, there will be facilities, then what's the need for marriage? Million Wings feels that needs of life will remain the same and can be fulfilled too, may a person marry or not. If we consider it seriously, then every requirement is the same; the only difference is it has to be bought. Everything will be available in market; whatever one needs, one can purchase. Science and technology are advancing day by day and providing more and more comfort to humans, and humans also want the same. In future it's just money which needs to be earned; everything else can be purchased: paid sex, paid meal, paid treatment, paid child bank where a baby can be produced by artificial way, shift parents to old-age home. A baby can be admitted to a nurture centre, mechanical servants and things can be around, and life will move on.

Today girls are getting aware and have to be aware. They also need their rights equally to males. They also want to live free, self-ruled, want to be independent so that individuals can live life according to their own ways; it's right too. Move out of home and enjoy life like males. Girls will also want to overcome responsibility or compulsion of marriage and reproduction. That will be the first day of women's full freedom, when a child can be produced mechanically by machines and then scientists, with the help of advanced technology, will prepare an artificial ovary where a male will give his sperm and a female will give her egg and they can produce the best children of their choice. Both girls and boys can live alone in their rooms or houses, can freely build their future, will get success, live their own will, and enjoy life. A child produced by machine will be admitted to some nurture centre and then whoever will get time will go and meet their child. All will be busy in their lives that whenever one will get time, they will go to meet their families. All will live alone and die alone. This will be a future of machine, a mechanical world, but feelings will never die. Somewhere, a feeling of belongingness will also be there. Million Wings feel that if person needs all those things which can be got from marriage, then why purchase them, when he can make all those by himself? Million Wings feels that marriage can be a very beautiful policy if it can be done by good and nice ways. If we will understand the real logic behind marriage, then it will be a very beautiful and beneficial decision for both girl and boy and both families too. Million Wings feels that marriage will be the right tradition, right decision as logical principle of marriage is a future filled with belongingness.

Million Wings feels that marriage is a procedure or policy where the solution of many needs comes out collectively. In reality, every relationship in the world is built and moves on the basis of affection, love, trust, coordination, and mutual understanding. Social functions are just to share our happiness and written proof is for possible circumstance of difference. A marriage certificate is also a social written verification, and a relationship is that only which can be maintained without marriage also. Marriage is a verified social way to establish a relation. Marriage is well thought of and a beneficial social tradition where a person can get love, support, care all together along with fulfilment of needs. Marriage creates romantic relations in girls' and boys' lives, and one's family members also get a supporting friend.

Million Wings feels that anything/everything in life can be done by servants or machines except the feeling of belongingness. Million Wings feels that atleast belongingness is a need of the future. Everything which is one's part or has natural affection is very affectionate and can't be got from anywhere else. It's true and it will remain with belongingness is a hope and happiness of the future. If life keeps on moving, then that is because of relations filled with affection and belongingness, may the relationsbe by-birth relations or heartfelt relations. Atleast this belongingness and affection will remain the same, may everything be made by machines. In future also, one part will give birth, may everyone live alone. When a girl and boy will reproduce their kid, then that will be their one part. A person will definitely feel affectionate towards the child. It's human nature. It can't be changed.

Million Wings feels that marriage will be the right decision if that is chosen by own choice. It may be arranged marriage or love marriage, but it can be done only if both girl and boy like each other, as girl and boy both are most affected by marriage. Firstly they should feel attracted towards each other's beauty and smartness and then their views should also match. Million Wings feels that if girls and boys marry with their own choice and will, then affection and belongingness will be generated automatically. It's important to take care of thinking level of the parents of girls and boy too, as they also have needs and desires. In real marriage, it's not just mutual relation of girl and boy. Instead it's coordination of two families also. If mentality of both families matches, then it will be very happy and effective relations. Million Wings feel that parents should find a partner for their child as per their will as if children are happy, then only power, status, finance can be enjoyed. Children should take care of parents and family and need to understand each other's needs, as if parents are along with children, then obviously it's beneficial for them, especially when girl is pregnant after marriage.

Million Wings feels that children should marry as per their own choice, may they choose themselves or be searched for by parents. To stay happily with parents is more beneficial for children, and it's a logical aim of marriage. Marriage can be done at anytime after achieving adult age. If someone can live alone and can take care of parents then it's not necessary to get married, and not to marry is not a wrong decision too. If someone's dreams and desires are so and he/she is completely lost in that only, then it's not even necessary to get married. Million Wings feel that forced marriage should not be done. If there are some mutual misunderstandings or differences of view then not to marry them is the right decision, May engagement has also done. Million Wings feel that it's easy to break apart the marriage while there is no child. Once the child has been born, then it's difficult for girl and boy to get apart as then both should need to think about the innocent child also. And it's necessary and a responsibility too, as it's better to break relations than fight for a lifetime. Million Wings feels that if there are some problems after marriage, then they shouldn't reproduce and it's better to get divorced.

Million Wings feels that if girl or boy has any problem with marriage, then they have lot of chances to cancel marriage, may both get engaged, married, honeymoon; till this can be cancelled but it's difficult to break the relations after a child's birth, as first responsibility for an innocent baby is of his/her parents only. If they will not think or take care of the child, then why can anyone else do so? But yes, if bringing up of child is well thought out, then there will not be any problem to get divorced.

Million Wings feels that male/female can get married to any female/male, if the person want to marry someone, as after marriage, then firstly they have to give divorce to girl/boy and give them their proper rights and then again they may marry any number of people but it should be one at one time and living within one home. It will be right; it's satisfaction and justice.

Million Wings feels that after marriage, daughter doesn't became a stranger. Infact it will be a new beautiful and important relationship for her and she has to make plausible coordination. Parents need to make sure that if there will be any problem there, then she is not alone. Her parents are always there for her, and they can come to their parents at any time, whenever they feel like. Million Wings feels that small misunderstandings and fights are normal after marriage. But parents should interfere only if the girl really feels depressed or underwent depression, e.g. misbehaviour of husband.

Million Wings feels that to be born and give birth is the best natural management to carry on life in world. Million Wings feels that love, care, affection, belongingness are the best energy, which are always behind as support. Children are part of parents. There are two-sided benefits from birth. Firstly, an innocent soul is born as a child, which wants to be born in the same form. Through a parent, a child gets natural life. If life is born and life will be saved, then only life will move on, then only one will gets redemption. Children are hope of tomorrow filled with belongingness. The main benefit of having children is having someone of one's own as parent-child relation, brother-sister relation so that natural love, belongingness, and strength can be maintained. Parents also get hope of caring and affectionate future. These beautiful feelings of care, affection, belongingness arise by living together. And to live together, it's important that either person is own part or close to heart. All others are professional relation or relations of need, where both can get mutual benefits but natural belongingness is not there.

Million Wings feels that to give birth to a child is human will but to choose the sex of the baby is a natural process. Child is produced after mating of mother and father. In humans, the sex of a child depends on the part of the father (sperm) even if it is also not in the father's hands, as the mother's egg is of one kind only. Sperms are of two types, one creates girls and another creates boys. Whatever type of sperm joins with the mother's egg, that type of baby starts developing in the mother's ovary. Now which kind of sperm will join with mother's egg doesn't depend on mother or father; infact it's nurtured selection. That is, it's true that baby girl or baby boy depends upon the father's sperm but they can't decide it themselves. If we see it naturally, both girl and boy havethe same importance. That's why God made equal possibilities of birth of both. If both are here, then only new birth is possible. If parts of both will unite, then only new birth is possible; otherwise new birth is not possible. Now the question is, girl has to move to another family after marriage and parents remain alone. Then who can take care of them and their needs? So parents will not get those benefits which they want to get from children. What will remain the meaning of this? If there will be a boy, then he will live with his parents, so they will be supported and a feeling of belongingness from them, and parents will live alone if there will be only girls.

Million Wings feels that there are some problems related to girls according to worldliness or socialism. There are dowry, eve-teasing, name of family and girls move to another family after marriage. That's why people want a boy along with a girl. Million Wings feels that dowry system should be stopped. Girls' efficiency and qualities are everything. If girls' are taught in good way about romantic relations, physical relations, and sexual relations, then they will get to know about real intentions of another person and can easily escape from betrayal and exploitation, and being cruel will not able to take advantage of them by compelling or betraying them, and exploitation is not tolerable in any condition. A lesson should be taught to these kinds of people.

Million Wings feels that the only reason/meaning of teaching family is that their name should be known in the world. Million Wings feels that the best way to get name and fame whilethe world lasts is to do such a work that their name shines with pride and the name of their pedigree will itself remain in world. What is the use of giving birth to a baby just for purpose of pedigree? Yes, if you are able to do something special/unique in the world for name and fame of family, it is the best, strongest, most tremendous way of getting name and fame. If parents want to get a name and fame through children, then they have to help and support them to fulfil their dreams. They may do something so special and great that they will give an immortal home to the whole family. Million Wings feels that it hardly matters whether he/she is a boy or girl. Actually it's not the matter of girl or boy but what matters is equal opportunities, motivations, help, trust, faith as the energy, will, and capacity of everyone is the same to do something in life. Million Wings feels that girls and boys should get the same respect, opportunities, and care. There is nothing in the world which only boys can do and not girls. Maybe children and parents can't live together always, but in times of need, they should be there for each other; it is the benefit of being social and personal relations of humans. A question of moving a girl to boy's home after marriage is also recuperating. Girl and boy both will live apart from their parents and both will meet their parents as per will, need, and commitment. Husband and wife both will be professional and both will be independent. It's the future and it's right too.

Million Wings feels that if there is anything in the world which will give moral support, then that is a feeling of belongingness. If there are two children, then they will get/feel moral support of each other. Even after death of parents, children (brother-sister, sister-sister, brother-brother) will get support of each other. Everyone needs someone own and it will remain the same. Million Wings feels that there should be two children atleast. A difference of three years is enough between two children, as children get mixed up with each other. They play with each other, their time will be spent in good ways, and it's easy for parents too. Their bringing up also becomes easier. The earlier the children will go to school, the more the time parents will get and they get ease to fulfil their needs.

Million Wings feels that there are extramarital affairs worldwide, which creates tensions, sorrows, problems in relations of husband and wife. There may be any reason behind extramarital affairs but it's clear that no one will accept anykind of romantic relations with third person. Two females can love one male and two males can love the same female but can't live with each other after knowing truth. It's true. If there is any kind of extramarital affair, then there is dissatisfaction and trouble will arise in the heart and it becomes difficult for them to tolerate all this and they want answers for the same. Million Wings feels that when husband or wife comes to know about extramarital affair, then it will be painful, there is no doubt. But firstly they should confirm that; this should not be any misunderstanding. If it's true, then it needs to know what is the reason behind these types of relations.

Million Wings feels that marriage doesn't mean restriction of a whole life. But if there are differences between husband and wife and they want to get a divorce, if they go to court, then they should get divorced in the first six months after filing a case as court should know that they had come to court after suggestions and tries of clearing up misunderstandings by family, friends, and relations. Trying for their patch-up is wastage of time and a cause of increasing pain. What's important is that both want freedom from the relationship so that both can restart their life in a better way. Property should be divided in such a way that their basic needs like food, clothes, shelter, etc. should be fulfilled. If there are children, then keep them with parents or government organization for their betterment and equal amount should be sent to them for their expenditure.

Million Wings feels that the intention of extramarital affairs decide the decisions. The first thing which comes to mind is betrayal, which is the main cause of pain and anger. Because of this he undergoes wistful depression and may do suicide or harm or kill another in anger and disgust. Both activities are right at their place. But to take someone's life or to give own life is not explainable or right, as if we consider it deeply then there will surely be satisfactory solutions of these problems also.

Million Wings feels that logical principle of selection will be fulfilled while husband and wife are fulfilling each other's physical, mental, and emotional needs. In every relationship, it's important that person has to fulfil atleast logical needs and else another is doing it hardly matters. If husband and wife are giving satisfactory time to each other, fulfilling emotional, mental, and physical needs, then extramarital affairs have nothing to do with their own relations. If husband or wife are not giving satisfactory time and are taking more interest in extramarital affairs, then the innocent suffers and there is a problem for the innocent one. In these conditions only to live together is logical if the innocent husband or wife is attached to married life with love, care, and own will. Because only these husbands and wives can love and understand, tolerate feelings of their wife and husband respectively. When husband or wife has extramarital affairs, then it's clear that they don't have natural love and affection with their partner. Their marriage is just a compromise or just human affection or some compulsion. If someone has an extramarital affair or has natural love with some other male/female or has affectionate relations or love relations, then they can't make lovely relations with their partner even if they want. In these circumstances, the innocent husband or wife can live with his/her partner if they have natural unconditional love for their partner, and in natural love, one wants to live for happiness of the other and wants nothing inreturn and doesn't regret for anything. If the extramarital affair's natural love, then let them go; setting themfree from the bond of marriage is the right decision. These persons can't live together in one home, as in these conditions, self-respect of everyone will be hurt. Doing this knowingly is difficult and painful. It can be possible if both love the same person naturally and unconditionally or have an intention of betrayal or some compulsion. Reason may be any but to separate the innocent (husband or wife) and the third person (lover) should be priority.

Million Wings feels that except for this, it's better to get divorced. If there is no affection and care for each other, then it's tough to live with each other 24/7 and obviously a painful compulsion too. It's impossible to tolerate the extramarital affair of one's husband or wife without natural love. Only in spiritual or natural love can a person tolerate worse conditions and impossible things. Except this, all other conditions to get apart are peaceful, satisfactory, and with security of self-respect. To get apart is priority, and later on, divorce can be taken as priority; administration of country should secure financial needs, bringing up of children. Only that fellow will move out of home for whom it's easy. Only that will take care of children who want to get divorced. Government has to ensure that there should be divorcee homes for the needy husband and wife where they can live during divorce procedure and can live there comfortably and respectfully (till possible solution). If husband and wife both are flirts and both have romantic relations with other males or females, then they have to get divorced only if both don't have mutual coordination. If husbands or wives have extramarital affairs, then they themselves can understand and know whether they are flirting or have affection, but if they don't have human love, thenthey should not get divorced.

Million Wings feels that sometimes parents, siblings are not there or left them alone. Then government of country should surely manage administration for married females, children, and elders so that another person, relatives, in-laws should not take extra advantage of their weakness. Government of the country should be so helpful that anyone can ask for help without any hesitation, and the corrupt should not feel that there is no one for helpless persons and they do whatever they want.

Million Wings feels that logic of husband/wife is of satisfaction, fulfilment of physical and mental emotions. This is of utmost importance for husband and wife, that their partner should fulfil their needs and expect this if they are doing anything else also, then it hardly matters. Husband/wife has to keep their extramarital affairs away from home, as husband or wife will not tolerate that a person living nearby is having any kind of romantic relations with their partner. Every male/female has to keep their extramarital romantic relations away from family members and other related persons specially when these relations are limited to just flirting or affection. Extramarital human love is a natural affection in which relations of husband/wife is personal responsibility. Or another love will be maintained by love only. Those males or females who love by heart never want to hurt their innocent husband/wife intentionally. It's truth and will remain true.

Million Wings feels that the question is not whether to get married or not, but the question is when should a person get married? If we see it superficially or deeply, then in every human's life one time comes when he wants to live with just one person and wants to share his emotions and feelings with him or her only and this feeling can arise at any age or phase of life. A few people want this initial phase of life and a few want this as they live life. Million Wings feels that ahuman may be in permanent relation by the age of 16–35 years. But it's not important that they will feel the same. If a person gets a partner of his/her choice, then to marry him/her will be the right decision, enjoyable relations, may he/she choose her/him himself/herself or maybe advised by parents. It's impossible that male/female will 100 per cent match with each other, but if main thinking, dreams, and desires match, then the logic of relations is fulfilled. Million Wings feels that forthose children who want to get arranged marriages, the parents have to get marriages for their children by the age of 20–35 years. Those children who want to marry their love, they also need to tell this to their family so that parents should start doing efforts and let them marry sooner. Million Wings feels that if children want to get married by their own choice, then parents need to understand their feelings. If the child is genuine and is capable of managing everything, then parents should let them marry and allow them to live as per their will, with their love. They will live happily and will get success, will respect their parents, will take care of them, live by heart. So let them live. Those who are not adult and are not able to fulfil their needs professionally, instead of separating them, let them wait till they become adult and motivate them to be independent and give them time and make them sure about marriage too. If they are really attached to each other with love and care, then they will definitely try to refine their capabilities and qualities. And if they are able to do so, then they have full right to get married. In love marriages, children just want to live together; if they are adolescents, then we can wait, and if professionally they are not capable, then we can wait till they become independent. But to stuck or entangle them in boundaries of society like caste, religion, status make them depressed and sad and possibly they will fight and have conflict for this. According to society, parents figure out for goodwill, benevolence of their children but always remember a person has lifelong attachment to the relations related to heart and affection, but may hide them. If parents marry off their children best according to society, then surely a child gets married for respect and because of affection for parents and tries to live with them affectionately. Affection, choice, and care are those special things which automatically make life bloom. Children who want to marry a partner of their choice definitely take care of the feelings and needs of their parents too, along with their own feelings; happiness of children also matters for those parents who allow their children to marry a partner of their own choice. Those types of parents are absolutely right at their place and want to see their children's maximum independence. To think this is absolutely right and logical. Children also have to respect and care for their sweet parents. Those children who go for love marriage also love and respect their parents; if it is not so, then it's more possible that they may not have quality love; instead they might have misunderstandings of love and affection. Million Wings feels that those who love can never misbehave with loved ones or near and dear ones.

If any girl or boy doesn't want to get marry, then nothing's wrong in this; neither is it the wrong decision. When a girl doesn't want to get into relations of marriage, then it's all right; it's not necessary that they have to get married. If a girl or boy doesn't want to get married, then it's clear that they are so independent that they can manage everything by themselves. They have the guts to manage everything alone. Those girls and boys who don't want to get married then have to be clear that they have to be independent for their living. If their family or parents don't want or allow them to live with them, they have to live alone; there is nothing wrong in doing so. They may purchase their own home or get that professionally or live with friends but they have to manage that. Government of the country should provide proper and secure hostel facilities to these girls/boys so that any girl/boy who needs to move out of home should live respectably and securely. He/she can earn and live.

Million Wings feels that to get married is not such a big deal. But to keep relations good and managed is a nice thought. Million Wings feels that if marriage breaks because of any problem, the hope of girl or boy should be alive; both have equal rights that they can restart their life. There should be government hostels. If parents are not able to give support to their children, Million Wings feels that government and administration of the country just have to ensure respectful management like a family. People should live with their own families. But if someone has to get apart from family then they should atleast have some hope that they have atleast a last hope to live respectably.

There should be every type of government hermitage like old-age home, young hermitage orphanage, widow hermitage, divorcée hermitage, handicap hermitage so that needy persons should have a last hope. These hermitages should be competent in themselves. There should be professional options for those who reside there so that they can do work and can earn their living. It's true, it's the future. It's a logical system.

Million Wings feels that people who love each other and can marry and live with each other, they are very lucky. But if they can't live together because of any reason, then it's not easy for them to forget each other. Million Wings feels that lifelong heart feel remains the same with whom person feels so. Million Wings feels that one needn't try to forget heart feel. Those who try to do this are innocent. Persons can't forget heart feel even if they want to forget; it's just impossible. Heart feel is that happiness which always gives beautiful feelings to the heart. The moments person spends with loved ones are strength and power. Those beautiful moments give peace of mind. Lovers have the strength of precious plausible moments, which give strength for the whole of life. Because of any reason if persons aren't able to get their love, they always allow heart feel to smile in their heart. In these circumstances, family may force/suggest them to marry someone else. Million Wings feels that nothing else can take place of heart feel. A person may feel affectionate towards someone else with time, but heart feel remainsthe same. But relations like flirting, marriage, affection may be with any number of people. There is nothing bad or wrong. If heart feel has affection for someone else, it's allright, it's OK. The meaning of heart feel is to feel maximum affection and attachment with someone. But it never means that a person can't get attached to someone else. Yes, it's another thing that person feels affectionate towards any number of people but with only one can feel at the level of heart feel. Feelings of affection and care can't felt with anyone else. But this beautiful and emotional feeling can be felt with anyone else. One may marry someone else according to worldliness, society to fulfil and satisfy needs. But if both start living together, then obviously they feel care and affection towards each other. New relations can't take the place of heart feel but fulfil emotional and another important needs. Because of all this, lives of humans again start blooming with affection and care.

Chapter 19

Sexual relations and sex

Sexual attraction is a physical enjoyment. It has been part of basic needs of males/females for centuries. A different type of happiness is felt in sexual attraction, sexual relations, and sex, a feeling which can be felt but can't be explained. Sex and sexual relations are romantic physical desire and satisfaction. Million Wings feels that sexual relations and sex are a physical happening which is nothing in itself. It takes the form in which it is done, i.e. with which feeling it is done. It gives happiness when done with will and desire of both male and female, and it is very painful when done forcibly.

Million Wings feels that sex is the feeling which is not created by humans themselves; instead it's attached naturally by birth and becomes a basic need and nature of humans. Sex and sexual relations are not found or discovered by humans; instead these are effective ways of development of the universe. God has attached reproductive organs on males and females and made this undetectable part of humans. God made natural attraction between opposite sexes to move the universe and made sexual relationsa unique, beautiful, lovely temporary enjoyment so that male/female can't deny it and life moves by itself. Birth is the best way for carryingthe world's growth.

If innocent souls will be born, then only they will get the chance of redemption, and slowly, slowly the secret of God can also be solved. Then only the whole of the universe will get redemption, peace, and happiness.

God made reproductive organs and way so attractive, beautiful, and amazing that male and female become attracted towards each other and enjoy feelings of sex and sexual relations and offspring will be born. This is God's plan, power. The real motto of sex is to give birth to offspring. But to make it attractive and enjoyable is God's plan.

Million Wings feels that feelings and pleasure of sex and sexual relations are attached to us since birth, and it's a need and nature of humans too. So this feeling can't be wrong, if God himself made this feeling along with us. It's not wrong to have sex or have physical relations. There is nothing wrong in this. It's not a crime. That's why males/females in the whole world are not able to leave it.

From sex, anger, jealousy, greed, and affection, sex is a feeling which God made an undetectable part of life. That's why this feeling can't be banished till now; neither is it possible.

Million Wings feels that attraction of males/females towards each other and having sex are right. Sex is true, is need and reproductive power, ultimate enjoyment, and pleasure. Arising of feeling of sex in heart is right. There is nothing to worry about and take tension. Just eliminate the fear of sex from mind. Sex is right, need, pleasure for male/female. Sex is not nonsense; neither is it rare. Infact sex is a good and natural feeling. If we understood rightly, then it's not any evil; neither is there is any harm in having sex. To think and have desire for sex is not a crime. Neither there is any loss of respect or health.

Million Wings feels that sex has no shape and form and meaning in itself. Instead it takes the shape of that feeling with which it is done. If done with love, then it takes the form of love. If done with affection, it takes the form of affection. If done with feeling of flirt than it takes form of flirt. If done in compulsion, then it takes the form of compulsion. If done as profession, then it takes the form of profession. If done forcibly, then it takes the form of forcefulness. The intention and desire with which it is done takes the form of that only. It has no form itself. Experience of sex is also felt the same with how it is done. It is very interesting, pleasurable, and enjoyable when done with will and desire. It is very painful when not done with mutual understanding and will. Million Wings feels that sex is a very beautiful way of human love and affection; maybe it's not everything. It's not true that having sex is love. Sex done just for physical satisfaction is just a need, nothing else. Sex done just for need has no value in human relations. Every male/female needs to understand that the meaning of having sex is not always affection or love; neither is sex everything in love. Sex is just a human need and nature. It may be affection, love, enjoyment, responsibility, forcefulness, betrayal, flirting, madness, or profession. Million Wings feels that if someone is having sex with another without his/her will, it's totally wrong. It's not right. If done with mutual understanding, then all feelings are right. Every male/female need is harmed; it's not status or respect to understand that sex is just a physical happening which is related more to the heart than the body. When sex is done forcibly and without the other's will, it's a physical accident. But its effect is seen more on self-respect and mind and heart of a person rather than the body. Because of this, self-respect is harmed, not status or respect etc. In the sameway, if a male/female has sex with multiple people, then respect or status isn't lowered. Infact it's their personal will, life, pleasure, and happiness. Million Wings feels that sex is just a physical play and meeting which is just meant for physical enjoyment, nothing more than that.

Million Wings feels that there is no age of the heart and mind but the body has an age when it develops fully and that age is 16–18 years. Even in adolescent age, the feeling of sexual relations may arise, and an individual may be attracted towards the opposite sex. But if sex is done before the development of the body, then it may worsen instead of growing, which may affect natural growth and capability. Million Wings feels that sex should be done after a proper growth and development of body so that body should not be harmed and till then mental development will also develop to a good level so that girl/boy can understand the feelings and emotions related with sex and sexual relations and can decide for themselves, according to their own will, desire, knowledge, and eagerness. Full development of body, mental preparation for sexual relations, and partner of choice make this feeling enjoyable and complete. Million Wings feels that by the age of 14–18 years, it's necessary/important to give knowledge about issues related with sex and sexual relations. Like this, girls and boys will understand and enjoy these feelings by the right and good way. Crimes like rape and extortion will also be reduced or may vanish from society. Then no one will be afraid of extortion of girls/boys. When girls/boys understand all this by themselves, then the tension of these things will also vanish.

Million Wings feels that if girls/boys, males/females will get freedom of all this in managed ways, then they needn't do it in hidden ways, will do it in tension-free ways and they will enjoy sex and sexual relations in better ways. This is true that at social level, males/females will talk more clearly and openly on these issues. Million Wings feels that in sex and sexual relations with any number of persons with whom choice matches, and whose will, dreams, and desires match and are compatible, there is nothing wrong, no badness, and nothing to be afraid of. The best secret of enjoying sex can be felt only when it is done with will, desire, knowledge, and satisfaction. Million Wings feels that it's also true that a person can't have sex and make sexual relations with everyone. Every male/female has his/her own choice and wants to establish romantic relations with them only with whom they want, who likes each other, who attract each other, with whom they feel comfortable. Physical relations can't be made with everyone/anyone. To have sex without comfort and choice is just wastage. Sex and sexual relations can be enjoyed only if the choice matches, and with will and agreement (selective sex).

Million Wings feels that heartfelt relations are those which remain the same even after making sexual relations; it means affection should remain the same. Love and affection don't decrease by having sex; infact they increase. Infact, it's not important that sex is there in love and affection; instead it's necessary to understand that sexual or physical relations are beautiful ways to express love, but these aren't everything. Infact if affection decreases after having sex, then that is not love. Million Wings feels that real love starts after sex. Physical and sexual relations deepenand strengthen love relations. If affection decreases, then that is not love but just physical attraction; infact relations break after having sexual relations.

Million Wings feels that sex and sexual relations are just a social accident which can happen with anyone, at anytime. Million Wings feels that male/female should get only happiness and enjoyment by sex. Sex and sexual life should remain secure for the body. If there is more security, obviously enjoyment will be more. To avoid sexually transmitted diseases, use condoms. That's why every male/female should have atleast one condom with them.

Million Wings feels that sex and enjoyment of sex are internal feelings which increase by touching sexual parts. Sexual relations and sex are emotional feelings which mostly don't depend on length/width of sexual parts.

But there may be any personal choice; that's another thing. Sexual relations take a start from sweet and romantic ways of male/female and then move to the highest level of enjoyment of sexual relations. Every male/female has their own ways of making physical and sexual relations. Mood and sexual relations may be more or less at different times.

Million Wings feels that sexual relations and sex are efficiency which becomes more competent and enjoyable with time. Satisfaction of physical relations or sexual relations is not always fulfilled by new partner, instead may be fulfilled by need and desire of choice.

Million Wings feels that if persons don't get the partner of their choice, then it's better to move to a prostitute to fulfill a need instead of doing misbehaviour, forcefulness, rape, etc. Million Wings feels that if a hooker is by choice, then no one else should have any problem. It is a professional compromise which helps in fulfilling needs of sexual relation of males/females and gives fixed value in return. Million Wings feels that for satisfaction of sexual needs there should be physical attraction, and along with that, it's enough to satisfy physical and emotional demands of another. It's not necessary that there should be emotional bond for fulfilment of physical needs. To be a prostitute is not a crime; she should just be seen as a professional. Professional sexual relations have nothing to do with self-respect and other feelings. Prostitutes should get authenticated permission and should have proper residential places and should avail all facilities of safe sex.

Million Wings feels that if naturally homosexual wants to enjoy sexual and physical relations with own will and desire than that's their personal will and rights. But to do that forcibly is totally wrong and painful. To have sex with animals and another organism is totally wrong.

Prostitution: sex is a desire and pleasure act. Prostitution is not a bad thing if chosen wilfully as a career. Prostitution should be legal all around the world in a respectful and enjoyable manner. Human beings have varieties of sexual fantasies and desires for having sex with different styles. Prostitution is a contract of sexual services. Everyone must understand that sex is, no doubt, fucking to orgasms but one has to be ready for it. Majority of the people cannot just start intercourse directly. Everyone needs, infact likes, more or less, a little foreplay for erotic moods and better peaks in desires. Sex is not only about being just girl or boy but it's about personal preferences and choices actually. Million Wings feels that all professional sex services should include flexible options of foreplay, touching body, kissing cheeks and neck and below, handjobs, oral sex, anal sex, and intercourse. The minimum time should be at least thirty minutes. Professional sexual charges can be fixed as per personal calibre. Lip kiss is a sign of a little more intimacy and may or may not be a part of prostitution sexual act. This professional approach gives good satisfaction to customers and good money to prostitutes too. Million Wings feels that if there is international sexual prostitution bazaar, then they should know global sexual practices and tastes of the people around the world. Sex is a both physical and mental pleasure that comes from sexual satisfactions and that can be anything from just eye contact to intercourse. Partners need to set a good mood and comfortableness with sexual partners. At international sex bazaars, there should be international sexual options. The charges can be fixed and step up with types of sexual contracts. Safe sexual practices are to everyone's benefit at large. A prostitute must be respected as an individual because if she is there, only then one's night can be happening. If she is comfortable, then someone will get more pleasure out of her.

Million Wings feels that enjoyment of physical or sexual relations doubles if there is emotional attachment too. Emotional bond also has the same or may be more important in sexual relations. That is, sex is also one emotional satisfaction. But for mental and emotional satisfaction, a person needs a lovely relation. The partner can be changed for physical or sexual relations but emotional and mental belongingness and love can't be got from everyone or anyone. Emotional and mental affection and love can be established only if they are spending quality time with will and desire along with making romantic physical relations. So that person can share their personal feelings. If someone is satisfied mentally, emotionally, and physically with one person and enjoying life, then it's a double advantage.

☵ ☵ ☵

Chapter 20

Non-romantic relations

Million Wings feels that most people are good at heart. Their main motto is just to live cool and happy. These types of males/females tease each other, give funny comments to spend time in lovely and funny way. A motto of these person is not to have any emotional or romantic relations. Infact, these types of persons want to live and see others happy. These types of people are very clear and truthful at heart and are good by heart. They take life in positive ways, smile themselves, and make others smile too.

Million Wings feels that these types of people think that the more lightly they take life, the lighter, more comfortable and cool it will appear.

Million Wings feels that cool males/females think that the easier they take life, the easier and more comfortable it will be and will obviously look better. Smiles/laughter give birth to smiles/laughter, i.e. happiness arises from happiness. Small happy and funny moments banish small problems and tensions. Atleast a person can be released from tensions and problems for some time. These types of males/females don't differentiate between own ones and others. They meet or spend time with all. These types of persons look at others in a respectful manner, smile with them, tease or pass funny comments to each other. This makes surroundings plausible and everyone feels comfortable and good. These types of people don't want to hurt or to give pain to anyone, neither do they differentiate as per status, nor do they want fights. They don't interfere in the personal life of anyone or give false comments. They can't make anyone feel low intentionally. Most persons take a liking to these types of persons and they are everyone's favourite; social atmosphere becomes plausible, fresh, and good because of these people.

Million Wings feels that friendship is a non-romantic relation of male and female, which has a cool, open, wide, and comfortable atmosphere. One expresses himself without any fear to friends. Friendship can be done with anyone of any age. But special friends are only those with whom nature matches and has good coordination. One may have any number of friends. Friends and friend circle are the world. There is affection, care, and security in friendship. Friendship is fun and enjoyment. Friends always take care of friends and think for betterment of each other. If they feel any danger in any work, then obviously they warn them. They help in removing weakness, may tease or fight with each other but always help and stay with each other in time of need.

Million Wings feels that there is affection and care in friendship, supporting each other in time of need. Everything is done by will and happiness in friendship. Friendship contains rights support, and care. Take care of friends in problems. Don't leave each other in time of need. Friendship can be done in any relation, and except in romance, every relationship can be friendship. Friends can be of any religion, caste, country, age. Friendship itself has unique style. Friends are attached by heart to each other. Friendship can start from anywhere, e.g. family, relatives, neighbours, professional place, school, college, social places, functions. Friendship can be started in plausible situations or in times of problems. The friends who are special are very close to the heart and it has feeling of belongingness.

Million Wings feels that friendship is hard between male and female, as it's often seen that either person reacts in a forced way because of romantic feeling or expresses his/her romantic feeling again and again. Because of this, male and female can't live as friends with each other and mostly they get apart. If one has romantic affection and another has 0 percent romantic feeling then that relation is just a friendship. If both male and female want to get in any physical relations then that's a romantic relationship, not friendship. If male and female firstly become friends and then get in a romantic relationship with will and desire, then nothing's wrong in this. It's all right.

Million Wings feels that when male and female meet each other, it's not necessary that they have romantic feeling or will for physical touch, physical or sexual relations. If male and female like each other's beauty and nature but don't have any romantic feelings for each other, then they can be friends always. If the male or female has no romantic feeling for the other, then this relationship is just friendship for the other also who has romantic feelings for that person. Million Wings feels that when male and female become friends, then the friendship is very deep and emotional. They meet each other in society without any fear, share their feelings and talks, have enjoyment and roam about, also meet with families. Neither male nor female has any romantic feelings for the other. That is just a clear, true, unforgettable friendship.

Chapter 21

Family and relations

To fulfil our needs comfortably, filled with belongingness, filled with favourable trust, beneficial natural or human relations is family. Since birth we spend most of the time with our family. As family members live together, so they know better about the nature, habits, feelings, qualities, and weakness of each other. Affection increases for each other. Everyone has a possibility of getting more sympathy, help, and motivation from one's family.

Million Wings feels that every individual has family since birth. To understand relations of parents and children is to understand family. To get redemption, every innocent soul wants to be born as a creature in this world. Every soul waits for whether they will get someone of their own who wants to give birth to child, so they will get a chance to be born. Parents combine their parts and a child starts developing in the mother's uterus. Innocent souls get a lucky chance that they can be born as a child in the world. Parents love each other deeply and want a sweet baby from their parts who can be the hope of their tomorrow, filled with belongingness. Like this innocent soul and parents wants each other and the birth of a new soul is possible. God made this procedure on the basis of random selection. But birth takes place only if both are wilful.

A soul has been born, now what next? An innocent soul is with parents in the form of a baby. According to the secret of redemption provided by

God, one has to live maximum time happily on earth. Now if parents leave their child and move, then obviously the life of the child will be finished then again soul has to wait for new birth. Parents also want that they should bring up a child and a hope of the future's belongingness will come true. And at a young age, a child will try to take care of their parents in old age and desire to fill their life with happiness so that they will get redemption. Parents bring upthe child and teach him worldliness, and try to fulfil their needs and hopes. Children also play with their parents. Like this they both love each other, give a healthy and good life to each other so that they can live a happy and plausible life, so that one gets help in redemption. It's true, it's will, it's an emotion which gives importance to family.

Million Wings feels that if responsibility of a person is decreased, then it's clear that it's the duty of person to fulfil them. And it's a natural responsibility of parents and children that they should take care of each other in time of need. Relations which are filled with love, care, affection, trust, and capacity of understanding may be rare but are very beautiful and priceless gifts.

Affection can be there in relations, either if it is own part (egg or sperm) or by-birth relations or heartfelt relations. A relationship of belongingness is either natural affection or arises by living together. Every relationship which has belongingness, either natural or gained. There is nothing/no one which can replace it; neither are these relations alternatives of each other. Every human has his own relations which are his parts, or he himself is part of that relation, i.e. parents and children. First-degree relations are those who are siblings, i.e. brother, sister. Relations are those who are offspring of the same grandparents, uncle/aunty. Relations are those who are offspring of the same great-grandparents. Human parts relations and first-degree relations are non-romantic relations, which have more possibility of affection and care. Million Wings feels that often a family has parents, brother, sister, husband, wife, children; everyone has their own special place, relations, and importance. Family members may be attached to each other by different relations, needs, work but all have plausible and beneficial coordination and that is power. Million Wings feels that relations are happiness of heart, which is emotional affection, help, and motivation. Expect this all other in worldliness and can be fulfilled from anywhere except money, comfort, sexual relations, etc.

Million Wings feels that happiness comes in life by fulfilling needs (food, clothes, shelter, support, affection, and care) and then it needs chances, motivation, and help to fulfil dreams, make mutual coordination between girls and boys which are initiated by parents. If we consider then food, security, and affection as basic needs, everything else can be understood and learnt and can be earned itself from life. Only these things are important, which parents have to provide to their children. All others are extra advantage to children. In the same way, children have to give food, security, and care to their parents. Everything else is extra advantage for parents.

Million Wings feels that arguingand fighting etc. on small issues are just normal things. There is nothing like tying up or break of relations. Circumstances and misunderstandings vanish or are resolved by talking to each other. Annoyance is resolved by asking for forgiveness and by forgiving, and the relationship again gains the same form and strength. Million Wings feels that there may be lack of misunderstandings in heartfelt relations but they never get apart from each other. Maybe they are very annoyed. In relations of affectionand love, intention is just of living together and happily. There are relations that take a stand in time of need and take care of each other. Joy of victory is incomplete without family and friends. Million Wings feels that children are the hope of tomorrow filled with belongingness. The type/kind of atmosphere which children will get in the first six years of life affects their mental level, behaviour, and nature. To fill the child with more and more positive thinking and plausible ways and self-confidence is the first step towards success in life. Million Wings feels that children are not short forms of elders. Children have their own special and lovely world. They learn slowly by listening to and seeing elders. It's necessary to make them understand for their benefit. Million Wings feels that every parent needs to teach their children and not to fight, beat, or bother them.

Million Wings feels that firstly, responsibility is of elders, not the younger. They should give atmosphere filled with positivity and plausible hope. Allow and motivate children to express themselves freely. Allow them to play and have enjoyment according to their will. Parents and family have to make secure boundaries for children, where children can live freely. Allow children to show their capabilities, by motivation and praise. Million Wings feels that thinking capabilities, qualities, and self-confidence of children are their real recognition. Make outdoor games as a passion of children. Make their habit of doing own work so that wherever child may go, he/she can take care of atleast himself/herself. Teach good and minimum required maths and English nicely. Self-confidence is that seed which can be sown since childhood and is care of success and child will have good and comfortable coordination with the world.

Million Wings feels that everything seems to be a toy for children, and whatever is in their reach, they want to play with them. It's not a responsibility of children; instead it's elders' responsibility that they only allow toys to reach child, not other important, precious things. Otherwise, it's not the fault of children. Million Wings feels that only those things should be shown to children which you want to give them.

Million Wings feels that elders are ideals for children. The way elders react and behave with them, they react and behave in the same way. Children learn worldliness from elders. The way elders react, children think that one has to do that only and they do the same. Maybe they are doing right, maybe wrong. It's true. Million Wings feels that the things which elders want to keep away from children, they should not do same infront of children, or shouldn't give that type of atmosphere.

Million Wings feels, give birth to children when you are mentally prepared for their coming, with will and desire for them. Give birth to only that number of babies whose bringing up is possible. It's not play to give birth to children and you needn't do this.

Million Wings feels that there should be atleast two children at a difference of 3 years. Million Wings feels that gives the kind of atmosphere that they should have, positive attitude and affection towards life. If life seems to be interesting, beautiful, and enjoyable in the starting years of life, then only they will see it with positive attitude, hopeful and in plausible ways. Youngsters are a power of family. The human mind has no age, but the body has. Every male/female body is grown by the age of 16 years. Million Wings feels that youngsters should know about those family matters which directly affect them. Youngsters are filled with energy, new hopes, dreams, and desires. It's that time when they can have enjoyment and at the same time have to be perfect in capacities and qualities. Give real and wide knowledge about good and bad facts in society by the age of 16–18 years in comfortable way so that they can be happy in a more secure way. In a family, relations of brother-sister, sister-sister, brother-brother are very sweet and lovely. In a family, brothers/sisters who are of almost same age can understand each other's needs, feelings, and desires nicely. Sometimes if they are unable to share their feelings with parents, then they share these feelings with each other. For happiness of each other, they help each other, give support in tough situations, and help each other to overcome situations. Siblings care for and support each other. Million Wings feels that even siblings have their own recognition and nature, have their own dreams and desires. But their understanding, affection, and coordination are different and more special than the whole world. Siblings have naturally non-romantic relations and they should not get married, as there are many suppressed disorders which run in families; if siblings get married, then those diseases can flare up.

Million Wings feels that even if everyone in a family lives in the same atmosphere and home, still everyone has different feelings and emotions. Everyone in a family, elders, married, unmarried, children, all have different ages, relations, needs, dreams, desires, and mental level. Because of this, everyone has different points of view and emotional feelings. Even in the same circumstances and atmosphere, it gives different influences, effects. Everyone feels as per the phase and circumstances. Everyone reacts according to their thinking and knowledge. Family members may have different opinions on same issues. The head of the family should take care of this and has to make the best decision for the family. Everyone has their needs, dreams, desires, solutions and hopes.

Million Wings feels that elders should choose subjects, education, or profession according to the interest and desire of young girlsand boys (siblings). After primary education, elders should guide and motivate them as per their will and dreams. Family should understand that education becomes profession later on, and profession is a means of living for a whole life. If education and profession are as per interest, then parents should not worry for their future as if they will choose their interest, passion as their education and profession, then obviously they will do everything by themselves. Parents needn't ask or force them everytime to do the same. They will atleast pass in a subject they chose, and by working in their professions of interest, they will atleast earn their living; there are more chances of becoming more successful in the profession. If education or profession of choice are not available, then give them a choice of education and profession which matches their choice so that living can be secured.

Million Wings feels that youngsters should get married when they will take their stand. When parents can ensure that, they will atleast fulfil their basic needs. Million Wings feels that parents and siblings can help in time of need and according to potential; it's good, it's right, it's beneficial and they can think about their marriage. But the youngsters who are unable to fulfil their requirements needn't be bound by the responsibility of marriage and children.

Million Wings feels that capable/deserving children should marry as per their will, thinking, and choice. If children will get married according to their choice, then chances of extramarital affairs and divorce decrease. While searching for partners for girls/boys, they should take care of possible qualities, then family status then beauty/smartness then wealth. Million Wings feels that in an arrange marriage, if the girl and boy feel romantic attraction towards each other, then only there is the benefit of good nature and behaviour. Parents should find family and house of own choice but couples marry only if they like each other, without any pressure and forcefulness. Million Wings feels that there is nothing wrong if a girl/boy choosesa partner of theirown choice. It's not a crime. Qualified and capable children can find partners of their choice.

Million Wings feels that children can marry a partner of their choice only when they are capable of fulfilling their needs and are independent. There is a difference between liking and getting marriage. The earlier they become independent, the earlier they will get a recommendation to get marry. Million Wings feels that a girl/boy should understand that along with attachment of both, they are attached with each other's family too.

Parents have hope from their child's marriage that they should have affection for them and will take care of them at desired time and should maintain plausible coordination with them. Million Wings feels that in love marriage, girls/boys need to understand that it's not just association of girl and boy but also their families. Million Wings feels that may children and parents fight, live separately, both will able to spend/live their lives happily or in sorrow. But it is also true that if children will have love marriage, parents will definitely get benefits from that and the child will also get benefits if parents will live with them.

Million Wings feels that after marriage, the girl is most affected who became part of a new family by leaving behind her family. A girl has to adjust and understand according to culture, needs, thinking, and nature and has to keep them happy. In these circumstances, she needs sometime and help. In the first year of marriage, she gets to know about culture of the family and learns by making small mistakes and tries to make coordination with them. Family members also understand the will, nature, thinking, and working capacity of the girl. Million Wings feels that the first year after marriage is the year of understanding and coordination as in the initial time if there's plausible coordination and understanding in relations, then happiness and affection in the family will keep on increasing.

Million Wings feels that relationship of mother and daughter-in-law is not a relationship of change or of humiliating each other; infact it's a sporting relationship. Mothers and daughters-in-law need to understand that both have their different and special places which can't be replaced.

Mother and daughter-in-law should clearly understand that mother-in-law's son and daughter-in-law's husband is not a thing to divide and share; infact they should give affection and love to him so that the guy can live happily if there is coordination between mother and daughter-in-law, then mother's son and wife's husband will not become tense and worried. Infact he will feel good and will give more love and respect to both. Million Wings feels that there is no competition; neither do they have to prove themselves. Mother and daughter-in-law should clearly understand that there is nolimit of this mutual competition. If mother-in-law wants, then she can denigrate daughter-in-law, and if daughter-in-law wants, then she can claim anything, but there is equal loss of both in these circumstances as anyone may be defeated. But defeat is of the guy only and if the guy is defeated, then it's defeat for both. Often there is dissatisfaction and stress in mother and daughter-in-law regarding household work. Mother-in-law has worked in those circumstances when there were fewer facilities. So it's natural that she had to work hard. Daughter-in-law works in those circumstances where physical work decreased. Million Wings feels that everyone wants to avail of facilities and comfort so that both will finish their work in less time and can avail of more time for themselves so that they can take rest or spend time in fulfilling dreams and desires. Million Wings feels that physical capacities will decrease with time, and brain and technology are the future and time. Million Wings feels that comfort will always keep on increasing with time; mother and daughter-in-law should understand that daughter-in-law should do the work which needs more energy and mother-in-law should do that work which requires less energy.

Mother-in-law should understand and learn new technology and should take benefits of that. If daughter-in-law is a professional and she doesn't do or want to do household work, then she should make sure mother-in-law will do the work which is in her capacity. For hardwork like washing clothes, washing utensils, care of animals, there should be a helper or servant.

Million Wings feels that the relationship of sisters-in-law is very beautiful. They are like friends. Both are in almost same age and phase of life and can better understand each other's feelings. Sister-in-law helps her sister-in-law with mother and brother; sisters-in-law can help in choosing dress, make-up, etc. for each other.

Million Wings feels that a housewife takes care of family by submerging her dreams, desires, profession, and capabilities and qualities. Health and happiness of family, special upbringing of child, and care of elders are possible only because of the housewife. There may be servants to do household work, but no one is able to give belongingness and love as a housewife does. Million Wings feels that specially in taking care of health, more importance is given to professional work than household work in society. Worldwide, a professional lady is given more importance than a housewife. Because of all this, feelings and self-respect of housewives get hurt. When importance is not given to household work, then why will a lady waste time in household work? Every female has self-respect. A lady will want to do that work which is given importance and respect in the family. Today, females can do all that work which males can do. Females have capacity to do all that work which males can do.

The female wants to do that professional work in which she will get respect. She will feel free. This is the only reason which a female has to leave her natural qualities like affection and care and has to work for social recognition and has to choose professional career.

Million Wings feels that this world, nation, family is kept moving because of affection and care of housewives for centuries. Specially upbringing of child is possible only because of the housewife. Million Wings feels that taking care of what's precious, i.e. taking care of family, housewives should get maximum respect. Obviously then she will handle family by will, heart, love, and affection. A housewife should get best recognition in society. If a housewife wants to do some professional work along with household work, then it should be her choice or will, not compulsion. If a housewife does professional work along with household work, then she has a right to get more respect.

Million Wings feels that every family member should be independent. Independence doesn't mean only to earn money, as everyone in a family can't earn money. Let's understand the meaning of independence, e.g. child's duty is to study, and doing light or little household work is independence. Younger members should do professional studies and doing so with this help in household work is independence. Elders should manage relatives then they are independent. Like this, if everyone is independent, then that means the family is independent. Million Wings feels that if there is financial capacity, then everyone should do work in divided parts according to capacity. Maximum free time in a family should be spent in taking care of children, the diseased, or elders.

Million Wings feels that the culture of religion and family is meant to make social and familiar life happy, beautiful, and comfortable. Maybe there is no personal comfort or the like. Million Wings feel that while private parts are properly covered, all clothesare good. While natural beauty is maintained, all make-up is good; while the body is getting nutrition, every food is good and delicious. Those thoughts which will give more freedom, comfort, favourable conditions, security, humans will definitely try/ are trying to accept them in their personal life. And this is the future's truth.

It's right, it's logical, it's happiness. Million Wings feels that it is not about rules and regulations of religions; infact it's about feeling of easiness and use which humans always desire, and nothing is wrong or bad in this. To change with time for betterment is a need of the future. Million Wings feels that family members spend more time with each other; they know each other's nature, behaviour, thinking, etc. in a better way as compared to others. Affection always increases by living together and there are possibilities of getting more help and motivation from family. Million Wings feels that the whole world likes good-naturedness but only family can tolerate bad or strict nature and behaviour. Somehow family toleratesan aggressive, hostile, or violent nature, tries to make one understand, forgive, and listen but outsiders have nothing to do with this. Outsiders never tolerate any abuse, misbehaviour; they neither like or listen or have so much time and patience to understand compulsion and nature. Unknown people respond in the same way at the same time. If we consider, then it's right too. What others have to do with mental and physical circumstances of others, just think how to respond for misbehaviour and how to teach them a lesson. Person need to understand that bad or wrong habits are tolerated by own ones or people who are heartily attached. The rest of the world only tries to teach lesson.

Million Wings feels that there may be arguments, fights, violence on small issues in family. But there is nothing like any breakage or knot in relations. By meeting again in sometime, relation again gains same form and strength by asking for forgiveness and forgiving.

Million Wings feels that family and heartfelt relations are cause of ego. Ego is not for family. Our ego is for others, not for own ones, as they had made us so. May there be any level of argument with family, it's nothing to worry about. If there is any kind of misunderstanding, every issue can be cleared by talking on the related issue. Million Wings feels that a person has to express himself freely to family. Maybe family members, parents are rude and hard-natured but internally they are filled with love, affection, and care for family members.

Million Wings feels, live with family (love/friend) without any fear and doubt as there may be any level of misunderstanding or problems in heartily attached relations but they can't live away from each other. These are those relations who help each other in hard-time problem and take care of each other. These are those relations which may be anywhere but always pray for well-being of own ones. Million Wings feels that relation is happiness of heart, which gives emotional attraction, help, and motivation. Any need of life can be fulfilled from anywhere. Million Wings feels that if someone wants to stay with lover or husband, wife, or ownones and has government or private job at long distance, then leave that job. Leave unnecessary tension and live happily.

Million Wings feels that a real motto of the life of a person is to live and fulfil needs, dreams, and desires. A person fulfils needs in comfortable and compatible way through family. Minimum needs like food, clothes, and security is one of the benefits of having family. But family is also main source of changing mood, and refreshing mood. Otherwise if in twenty-four hours, a person remains busy with his dreams, then he will go mad. His mind will not work with the same pace. To sit along with family and friends sharing talk, fun, enjoyment creates emotional and mental comfort strength, and fresh and again get ready to work for dreams and desires.

Million Wings feels that who have caring mother, talk, desires and enjoyment with friends gives feeling of that happiness and enjoyment, gives strength at every moment.

Million Wings feels that parents should give share of their wealth to a girl also. They have to make the girl independent. After marriage, a girl has to live with her husband at his home and both should live together happily, but if they get divorced because of any reason, then if girl is independent, then main cause of tension will not exist. If parents or relation will be unable to help, then also she can manage herself. Million Wings feels that marriage is a relation between girl and boy filled with romance, affection, and care, not a solution of wealth, property, or financial security. Division of property should be according to time duration.

Maximum percentage should be in situation of having child. Responsibility of child is equal for both (husband and wife). Million Wings feel that if old persons of a home want to do a little work, then let them, as they remain active by doing so and feel importance for themselves. Nothing is bad if elders want to do work, according to their capacity. Health also remains fit, morale feels supported, e.g. feeding child, warping cloths, cutting vegetables, moving out with children to the park. Million Wings feel that while elders are able to do work, let them work. They will feel happy and healthy.

Million Wings feels that when children and elders talk, then sometimes their attitudes don't match. Firstly there should be equal freedom and chance for every family member to express themselves. Secondly the matter/issue, may it be any, should be expressed in friendly ways.

It's not important that elders must be right always or the younger are always wrong. But the thing is, as distinct, wide, and long as the younger can think of knowledge, they are right till that level and they are having wide vision. That is, children think about fewer possibilities, and elders can see more widely on more issues. Children or the youngermight think about only beneficial and good causes, and elders even look at a serious matter regarding the same issue.

Million Wings feels that children or the younger want to do everything faster as per their curiosity and interest. But elders want to do everything in calm and managed way. Children or the younger don't feel bad in fulfilling dreams even by taking risks, and elders want to fulfil dreams and desires of the younger in secure ways. Million Wings feels that well-being and security of the younger matters more, is more precious for elders than their dreams and desires.

Elders want to let the younger have enjoyment in more secure and cool ways for a longer time instead of taking risks for short-term enjoyment. Elders never want to cut short the happiness of the younger. But their motto is to protect younger from every problem and tension. The younger don't want to be stuck in problems knowingly; infact the same work should be done in a better and more secure way. To do so, their family and elders can help them.

If elders listen to the younger, then their intension and feelings can be rightly understand and children will not be afraid of elders; infact they will respect them. Children also need to understand that if elders have given a chance to express themselves freely, that doesn't mean the younger has freedom to misbehave. Misbehaviour should not be accepted at any cost. Million Wings feels that anything/issue in the world can be shared with anyone but in a respectful manner, as if respect is maintained, then the way of talk will be automatically sober and good. Million Wings feels that the younger have freedom to express themselves, not to misbehave with elders. Elders also have a right to make them understand, not to scold them. Use of force is only required when the younger cross maximum fixed limits, i.e. when risk is maximum and profit decreases. Million Wings feels that elders needs to understand and think about desires and ways according to the modern era also along with their era and should help them. Children also need to understand that time may become modernized day by day but elders will always remain attached to them with more affection, love, and care and will for their happiness and success along with health and wealth. It's true, it's affection, it's love, it's happiness.

Million Wings feels that in a family, every family member is condition and lesson; every person has one's style and experience. Someone has a positive attitude and some have negative attitudes towards life. All family members remain attached to each other in each and every condition. Talk on every issue may be in cool and calm style, affectionately, angrily or rudely, etc. Everyone affects another's life, specially the lives of the children. Sometimes family members can't restrict each other freely and, because of this, were annoyed at heart. But still everyone wants to live together. If child do something which causes personal loss, which is hard to fulfil or impossible to fulfil, if parents need to be strict, then nothing is wrong in this. Fights in the first twinkling of an eye, in the second blink, agree with each other, and in the third blink of an eye, everything becomes normal as earlier. In first-degree relations, one may fight but there is nothing like being knotted or misunderstanding. Million Wings feels that maintaining respect of each family member is logical. May fights or get annoyed with each other any number of times. In the home, females may be tense but talking to their husbands in the evening makes them relaxed and tension free. Husbands may remain in any condition or circumstance for a whole day but a warm hug from the wives makes them relaxed, feel tension free and free from problems. Children are equal for all in a family. In arguments, fights, elders might involve children; they may solve their own purpose but they hurt innocent children and knowingly or unknowingly they are filling them with negative thoughts.

Million Wings feels that to allow children to choose ways/directions according to their own choice and interest and qualities is a step towards happiness. Children who take an interest in natural bases, in the same subject, remain busy with them, try to help and motivate them in same direction to get success, e.g. music, dance, study, game, science and technology. The children who are curious get busy with full interest in the same thing and try to understand that. Those children who are filled with curiosity and qualities do something to make family and country full of pride. If childrendo something which becomes personal, which is hard to fulfil or impossible to fulfil. In these conditions if parents needs to be strict than nothing wrong in this.

The children who are lazy and do not do anything, to motivate them is main motto of elders. Ask children to participate in different activities; it will help them, in finding these interests. Those children who don't want to do anything have to atleast take care of themselves and it's a responsibility of elders. Million Wings feels that real happiness for children is to know and improve interests and curiosities. If we see, then these are only children and teenagers who have no knowledge and experience, who need to handle, take care, and to provide security.

Million Wings feels that everyone in a family has their own style, behaviour, and thinking and they react in family. A person has to stop doing unnecessary misbehaviour or stop doing forcefulness. To boycott them is the right decision rather than to use forcefulness on own ones. Million Wings feels that the younger learn from elders. If any member doesn't like the behaviour of another person with children, then they have to tell and have to make the child understand. Million Wings feels that it's personal efforts to make thinking of child open, wide, and balanced. Children and teenagers meet many people daily and may be impressed by them. Persons can be present everywhere with one another, but make sure that they can meet everyone with personal security and can enjoy success. They can teach reasonsfor both positive and negative thinking but will choose a beneficial and beautiful way of life.

Million Wings feels that if anyone sacrifices for some person, then the biggest cause is that they are attached with love and care and affection. To do something for own ones is to bring happiness for them. They may taunt them later on or may have expectations from them. When their own ones talk about their efforts and sacrifice, that means their expectations are not fulfilled. To do or say this is not wrong. It's all right if at anytime own ones have tried their best according to time and thinking by sacrificing their happiness, and if they say something about that later on, then what's wrong in this? Sometimes in anger while arguing or fighting, a person counts his possible efforts, then what's wrong in this? It's all right, it's logical.

Million Wings feels that another also knows the sacrifices of ownones. But repetition of the same again and again makes them feel like unknown persons. It may be possible that someone may start feeling himself as compulsion or headache for his ownones and may argue or fight too or start counting another's lacks. As parents sacrifice alot for be betterment of their children and when child grows up, they also expect parents to behave and react according to new generation. Mutual coordination is disturbed because of difference in thinking, living style, dreams, desires. Because of this, expectations get hurt, so they start telling about their sacrifice. It is natural. It has been happening for centuries and will continue as it is. There is nothing serious may family members fight to any extent but they realize with time that family members always argue or fight for betterment and happiness of each other. If we can't share our feelings with ownones, then whom else can we share with? Million Wings feels that by-birth and heartfelt relations may fight, taunt, argue to any extent, but they never want anything bad or wrong for each other. Million Wings feels that whenever there are different views on the same issue, then firstly listen to suggestion of our own loved ones (by-birth, heartfelt relations), may ownones be careless, worthless, innocent, mischievous, younger, uneducated, or stubborn to any extent. While things or issues are not clarified, take the stand of ownones. Exotic ones may be very intelligent, smart, educated, or elder. It's logical, it's belongingness. If two ownones start fighting, then try to save both and try to find out some satisfactory middle way. It will be the right way. Don't make lifelong decisions fast for transient issues. If own one gets hurt because of your mistake, then first give him/her aid; mistake can be improved later on also.

Million Wings feels that relations are not just for a day but relations are of the time which is spent together. Relations deepen by sharing feelings, emotions; the body may be shared to any extent. The more emotional the relationship is, the stronger it will be. And important physical relations can give transient happiness but not belongingness. Million Wings feels that if there is any mishap, then firstly try to protect own ones you earn sold later on but try to perceive and support them at time. But others/exotic enrol, entangle harm. Children may make mistakes of any level (small or huge); parents may scold, admonish them but their motto is to see child happy always by saving/protecting them from problems. Parents get calmness and peace if children are happy, secure, and successful. It's true and will always remain true.

Family members often try to teach management to each other so that there will be a plausible coordination. Million Wings feels that those who stay together have to face hard and difficult conditions too. Those who stay away like friends, brother, sister relatives have it easy to suggest and move. There who live in tense atmosphere all the time but still tolerate each other's misbehaviour take care of each other and sometimes may get disturbed and it's natural to feel jealousy or hatred. It's true and logical.

Million Wings feels that in family, females often become tense or quarrel or argue on some issues, e.g. between mother and daughter-in-law, sisters-in-law. In family, everyone has to live together and if this quarrel continues for twenty-four hours then everyone will remain tense. It's hard to leave home. In these conditions, give responsibilities to females according to their work and advise them to not to interfere or least interference in each other's work. Don't give them time to spend together; infact give them resources according to their choice and interest so that they can remain busy there. Husband for his wife, son for his mother, brother for his sister have to find satisfactory and respectful solutions according to their issue.

Million Wings feels that after marriage, children make their own home. The longer they stay together, the more the benefits they can avail. But if they keep on creating a tense atmosphere, then quarrels increase, then it's better to get them apart and let them handle their responsibilities on their own. Those children who live away or apart from parents they should send atleast minimum required money and having to take care in serious condition is a logical responsibility for them. Logical meaning of to getting apart doesn't mean fighting or breaking relations; infact it's to be independent, responsible, and to maintain plausible coordination with each other.

Million Wings feels that it's a responsibility of every person to make children independent so that they can independently handle every condition with confidence. Children should be well aware of outer society and family till they reach young age. Girl and boy both are equal. Both should get equal respect, care, love, and opportunities; children should be taught small household work also so that in time of need they can manage themselves well in market, school, college, organization relations so that they can take care of themselves if required urgently. Children should know atleast one vehicle from cycle to car so that they can move themselves.

Million Wings feel that in families, children need much attention. When children reach a young age from childhood, family members should try to make them maximally independent. To do this, the whole family should work in managed ways. Children should brought be up in a way that they will not look appear a burden to anyone. Children should think in such a way that they should feel interested, curious, and affectionate towards life. Give them responsibilities and restrict them according to their age. Give them freedom to express themselves freely. It's necessary to understand freedom doesn't mean to misbehave or to do work in wrong and harmful way, instead to give opportunity as per own way. Restrictions are meant to save child from harm, not as restriction from doing a particular work. Intention of parents/elders is just to make a child understand, not as wide range for child to live life. But strictly warn them to not cross required boundaries.

In juvenile phase, children feel many mental, emotional, and physical changes. It is that age when many new feelings arise in them, e.g. development of reproductive organs, menstrual changes, change of voice, sudden development of body, and more sensitiveness regarding every natural and human feeling. Teenage children get attached to that feeling about which they have little, half, or incomplete knowledge, e.g. romantic attraction, drugs, fights. From 12 to 16 years, a child may feel scared, happy, or enjoyable by feelings. Family itself needs to tell/explain about those issues to them.

Million Wings feels that there is no age of the mind/brain; anyone can think up to any level, any extent in any age. But the body has age. By the age of 16–18 years, the human body has developed fully, so action/

movement which affects the body should be done after full development of body, e.g. physical relations, sex, drugs. In juvenile age, the sensitive mind of a child starts understanding the existing culture and customs of society; a few corrupt people or people with wrong intentions may try to make children or teenagers' family aware so that a child doesn't hesitate or afraid to move out in society; instead they should be able to take deliberate steps for their security and protection rather than making them feel him afraid or anxious. Million Wings feels that perceiving should look like perceiving only; it shouldn't feel like fighting or scaring. To be strict with children didn't mean to restrict them or beat them. Instead limit their boundaries strictly and clearly for their benevolence.

Million Wings feels that there should be a head of the family who can maintain balanced freedom in society. It's very important to maintain management in family, as family is the smallest measuring unit of society and nation. The head should make decisions and work smoothly, softly, and hardly too. Family should motivate for more and more open thinking so that everyone can express themselves freely but should not misbehave. Everyone should do their important work by themselves. Million Wings feels that without a head, it's hard to manage home and family. The head of family should be educated financially free and should understood importance of every relation deeply and widely. The head should discuss every social familiar issue with elders and the younger so that a decision should be made only after viewing every aspect. Issues of marriage should be related to youngsters and elders only; it has nothing to do with children or teenager should be discussed with professional members. On social and relations issues, discuss with elders and take their advice. Intervene in family issue and try to resolve them as early as possible.

Million Wings feels that there should be proper daily schedules for every family. Every person should sleep by maximum 10–11 p.m. and should wakeup by maximum 7-8 am. At home, TV should be switched off by 10 p.m., and in personal rooms, it should be switched off by 11 p.m. TV should be switched on in morning after 6 a.m. Breakfast should be done between 8 and 10 a.m., lunch by 1–3 p.m., and dinner by 8–10 p.m. so that everyone should remain healthy. It's easy for housewives to manage, and everyone will able to do their own work in time. Million Wings feels that by eating food, a person will remain fit and can fight against diseases. Million Wings feels that night is to sleep and day is to work. Night doesn't mean 11 p.m.; instead it naturally start darkening by 6–8 p.m., and in the same way day, start lightning by 6–7 a.m., not by 10–11a.m. If someone sleeps or wakes up late, one has unmanaged lifestyle, then to do this is own will, nature, or compulsion. But schedule of nature can't be changed. It has no alternative. Million Wings feels that person should sleep for 6–8 hours to remain healthy and fit. So if rest and sleep are so important, then persons should use best time to rest, sleep. To sleep, time should must include hours from 11 p.m. to 6 a.m. In a week, a person can work for seven days and can do two professional night duties, or enjoyment; otherwise, sleeping at night is naturally healthy.

Million Wings feels that parents try their best to make their children perfect and intelligent. Give them education according to their interests, professional possibilities so that children can be independent. Parents move children to another cities and countries for higher education. When children become responsible and capable then in search of good opportunities, they move to other cities and countries after education and gaining required knowledge. Children search for new possible opportunities and it's right too. If parents have to keep child with them, then what's wrong with making them so capable? What is the benefit of doing so much hardwork? It's only worth the parents' and children's hardwork when children get success and make life better.

Million Wings feels that parents and children should atleast maintain as much coordination as their minimum needs should be fulfilled in satisfactory ways. Children should try to not to move to another country for the opportunity and education which is available and metropolitan cities of own country than avail them; it's much better than moving to another country alone.

To remove peer and sibling pressures, give rewards to individual as well as collective efforts. If one achieves something, the others who contributed significantly must benefit. Individual and collective rewards develop helping, well-wishing nature, togetherness, and independence altogether.

It's better to move to metropolitan cities to get same education and do the same business than shifting abroad. But yes, for higher education or special technology which is not available in own country, then person can move to another country for sometime. Million Wings feels that it's not fair to move forcibly or with problem to another country for the same things which are easily available in own country. To live in one's country, government, law with one's friends is a plausible level of living securely. If family is financially good and everyone's mental level is also favourable, even then if an individual moves to another country for simple education and business, then it's just wastage of money, time, and relations. Million Wings feels, move to the nearest possible place from parents for study and business so that in time of need (happiness and sadness), persons can avail of each other's help.

One should live in one's country and, if one wants, can roam, look, see the whole world as per will, capability, and opportunities. But to move to another place for few same things can be choice or passion but not good for needs and happiness of family. If children are living away from parents, they should make sure of the needs and security of parents. If children are moving for higher studies and business training for sometime, then it's OK. Children should try to settle in their country; they may settle in big cities or metropolitan cities. If person will settle in own country, then expenditure will be less and more happiness, belongingness, and name and fame will be there, will remain close to own ones and will able to enjoy life more. If children want to go permanently, then they should take their parents along with them as early as possible. Sometimes, child need to struggle more in initial phase or it's difficult for parents to leave their work and to move; sometimes, children do not have that much arrangement or parents don't want to move by leaving their parental place or they aren't able to adjust at new place. In these conditions, it will be difficult for parents and children to live together.

Million Wings feel that maybe parents and children can't live together but feelings of belongingness are more important. Parents and children should maintain minimum contact and should meet each other in time of need or some management. Be in contact with each other by phone, Internet. If children are dependent upon parents and are in own state or country, then it's easy for parents to meet and help children, and if parents are dependent on children, then it will be easier for children to take care.

Atleast required and necessary money should be sent to parents at times. Talk to parents atleast once or twice in a week; if parents talk to children, then they feel happy. Secondly if parents are alone at home, older, or don't remain healthy/fit, then it's important for children to ensure their daily living and needs, and to do this is very easy. Make professional relations with people like electrician, sanitation, rickshaw, transport, milkman, grocery store, medical storein parents' city and give them advance money and contact them via phone whenever required.

Request neighbour or relative, give them responsibility that they should help them in time of need. In extreme emergency, go yourself or ask parents to come to you. Million Wings feels that if parents will be happy then obviously children will enjoy happiness to more extent.

Million Wings feels that financial capacity and thinking affects family atmosphere a lot. If daily/basic needs will be fulfilled rightly, then there is more possibility of happy and plausible atmosphere in family. If everyone is getting food, medicine, education in time, this means logical principles are fulfilled. Home may be our own or rented house; it hardly matters. To fulfil basic/necessary needs of everyone is the main responsibility of parents; comfort, ease, resources, etc. come afterwards. And to fulfil this is neither responsibility nor forcefulness nor compulsion for parents. If parents are capable to fulfil these things easily, than it's OK. But there is no need to work like donkeys to fulfil those demands of children. Parents need to fulfil basic/genuine needs of children but it's not important to fulfil non-genuine needs; also, neither is it the children's right to get these. Parents also have a right to live according to themselves and to be happy. Don't give built-in life to children; instead give them comfort only on the basis of their success. Give ease and comfort to children only if they are doing their work properly and nicely. It's important to grow thinking level of children along with providing them comfort. Parents may provide financial freedom to children, but their own capacities and qualities are their real recognition.

They will get to know about right use of money and property if they can be filled with self-confidence, habit of doing own work, and increasing thinking level. If a family is financially capable, then they should avail of facilities, should enjoy life but not get addicted to this so that money will not ruin child or child ruin money.

Million Wings feels that the logical meaning of heritage property is that children have financial and professional security. Property is not to fulfil needs, to fulfil daily needs child has to work daily. Property and finance is financial security. It can be used in emergency conditions, circumstances. Million Wings feels that property is not meant to fulfil daily needs, instead providing means to fulfil them. Remember, to divide property in children is parents' will, not any forcefulness or compulsion. Parents can give any property to any extent to children but, along with that, give them high balanced thinking also; otherwise, money and children will destroy each other very fast. Million Wings feels that parents needn't collect money/property for children, instead using that money for education, improving qualities, business. It will be better. While a person is alive and mentally fit, he has a right to change his will any number of times.

Million Wings feels that any amount of money is always less for enjoyment and comfort. Million Wings feels that property should always be divided in equal proportion, may financial status of children be equal or different from each other. During division of property (home, property, etc.) other than money, it is difficult to divide in equal proportion. That's why minute difference during division are negligible. Approximately 10 per cent more or less during division is just a normal thing. During division, it's also important to take care of agreement of children too so that they shouldn't fight with each other. Otherwise, division of property on equality basis of random selection is the right way; parents shouldn't give their property while they are alive. The will should be opened after death only. Million Wings feels that to help a child in emergency condition is another issue, is genuine. Parents should genuinely help children to set up business. If parents need to spend property/money of their part on them before division, then they should spend that.

Million Wings feels that if two families unite together, then it becomes a big family. In reality, few like small families and few like big families. Million Wings feels that whole matter is of management, capability, and clarity. If big families should be managed properly, then possibilities of help during emergency conditions or situations and security is more than nuclear or small families. Mainly when two married children start earning, then if the head of the family (father, grandfather) keeps the whole of their earnings with him and does expenditure from that, then it's often seen that they can talk about more or less earning. Those who earn more put in a greater share, obviously want more comfort and ease. And the ones who earn less also avail of the same comfort. In these conditions, tension, fights, arguments are expected more.

Million Wings feels the head should take equal amounts of money from all children for minimum basic expenditure at home and let them use the rest of the money by themselves. One who is capable can afford/avail that much comfort. It's right, it's logical.

Million Wings feels that it's not wrong, bad if children live separately, as to live separately is proof of financial or social capability and success. To be separated never means to fight or argue, instead to meet each other, be with each other in happy and sad moments. Million Wings feels that money is equivalent to workdone by person and he wants to spend and use that according to himself. Exchange of money should be clear. One has to know the amount given to another for helping him. It's another thing if he delays to return or maybe the helper didn't want to take that back. Million Wings feels that if money is limited, then a person has to spend firstly for their children then for themselves then parents and then on siblings, in the end for friends and relatives.

Million Wings feels that in family, the younger and elders often argue on new and old issues. Disagreement on new and old times is generation gap. Million Wings feels that in reality generation gap is not actually difference in thinking level but actually it is being away from balanced and wide thinking according to time. How much difference the younger and elder have depends upon their personal thinking, circumstances, priorities, experience, and technical ways. But mainly it's affected by how far or near a person is from international, balanced, open, and wide thinking. Who is more near to logical, balanced, open thinking is more right, may that be elders or the younger. Million Wings feels that generation gap is that argument in which both want happiness and success but parents want the same with more security and children by taking more risk. Parents/elders need to understand that with time, ways of living also change. So thinking also changes and children needs to understand that times may change but nothing is above personal security. Million Wings feels that whole family should understand that it's impossible to pull back a whole society or universe but can move towards a beautiful future by more plausible, better, and secure ways.

Million Wings feels that festivals are symbol of happiness. They generate atmosphere of families and social togetherness. Main festivals of country or state should be celebrated together, e.g. Diwali, Lohri, Holi. Small festivals can be celebrated anywhere with friends.

Million Wings feels that house may be our own or rented but home should be there, as a house ensures comfort and security. To have a home is logical and to have own home is success. A person can avail of many government facilities if he hasan address of his own, a permanent house address. Permanent house address is trustable proof. Million Wings feels that home may be small, big, comfortable, or not but a person should try to make his own home by the age of forty years.

Million Wings feels that it's natural to have a bit of annoyance, jealousy, arguments, fights, taunts, etc. between sisters-in-law but it's really appreciable if the one having good co-ordination. But if it's not, then there's also nothing to worry about. When femalestalk about each other's faults, lacks or pray for each other, then males often feel like taking some serious action/step but it's female nature to tell about small things and their likes and dislikes to husband or each other; it doesn't mean to create tense atmosphere or fights. When females talk to their husband or children according to themselves, then they feel satisfied. They may repeat things or may complain. They get satisfied by doing this. Females show their anger by talk or speech and males may do physical strike also.

Million Wings feels that males know their mother, wife, or sister well. That's why males can maintain/establish a plausible and comfortable atmosphere. Mother, wife, sister all tell their things, in their own favour, to males. That's why a male has to take a satisfactory step according to their thinking and circumstances.

Million Wings feels that female can tackle mutual fights and arguments themselves. Males only need to interfere only when there is physical strike. Million Wings feels that with relatives, one has to take/give help from each other often in disease or other problems. Neighbours, friends, relatives support each other to do this; it's right too. Small help in time of need create respect and affection.

Million Wings feels that to help each other doesn't mean to move everywhere with oneanother; instead it is right management according to situation, doing most urgent work in time of need, e.g. to make coordination with related person, professional help, financial help. Financial help can be done according to own convenience. Help as per requirement. Even if you are capable of helping more, even then help as per need of others. Million Wings feels that parents' logical responsibility is to make their children capable/efficient. Make them so much talented that they can tackle any problem/situation themselves and are able to manage socially important matters/issues. Now the question is, till what age do parents need to take care of children? At what age do they become smart enough to handle any situation? Sometimes it feels like after marriage, children become wise. Sometimes even for their whole life, parents worry about children. Million Wings feels that when a child is personally and financially independent, then he/she becomes wise. All other things, like socializing, behaviour, living, a child can learn from life.

Million Wings feels that age has nothing to do with wisdom. Infact wisdom of a child depends upon mental, physical circumstances of life. A few children become wise and develop sooner and some develop slowly. Most children are mentally and physically fit and few have low mental level, so they should try to be independent as per physical conditions. To handle physical, mental, financial conditions is being independent. With the help of available different education and medical institutes, try to make children independent so that they can manage even if they are left alone.

Birthday and anniversary are very important occasions in family. To give best wishes on birthday gives a feeling of belongingness and happiness. Million Wings feels that to celebrate birthdays or anniversaries together makes plausible romantic atmosphere. Friends, dear ones, loved ones always remember birthdays and anniversaries and try to give best wishes according to their own different and unique ways. Only few remember birthday of each other, who deeply loves cares for each other. Million Wings feels that the more husband and wife talk to each other, the more it will be beneficial for the whole family, as husband (boy) can well understand any familiar or wife's issue and can make situations more comfortable and can fill relations with more sweetness and coordination.

Million Wings feels that everyone needs age-mates to be along with them in family so that they can freely share their feelings with each other and can also get help to do their work. If a child gets age-mates, then they can play together and will feel happy; children may be of same family or of neighbours but if a child spends time with children, it's better, as it's difficult for parents to be with a child for the whole day and to play with them. If child gets companions then atleast half the tensions of parents vanish and they also get sometime for themselves.

Million Wings feel that everyone may live together in a family, still they need quality time of each other. Children should meet parents with full interest so that they can talk/discuss on every issue/matter in detail and can express their feelings, needs, issues clearly. If a family is spending quality time with each other, then the family will feel happy. They will feel satisfied, and relations filled with affection and coordination will be maintained.

Million Wings feels that if someone is giving proper time to family, then one can use the rest of the time according to oneself; no one should have objections to this. It's important for husband and wife to spend quality time to be satisfied. If husband and wife are giving quality time to each other, then it's right and expected that they have personal, secret, romantic or non-romantic relations, but husband and wife are satisfied with each other. The mutual satisfaction is logic of married life.

Million Wings feels that arguments, fights are often seen in families; there is nothing wrong or bad in this, as everyone has different thinking and circumstances in the same family. Children fight with parents. Parents teach, make them understand, threaten them, frighten them. If someone said anything to each other, they feel as if self-respect was hurt. Some have a strict nature and someone has strict principles. Someone has no schedule and someone is strict about time. One is careless and another is very sensitive; one always remains in a sad mood and another keeps on doing mischievous activities. One is very stylish and another may not even know how to eat; one always supports and another doesn't remain even close to others. One touches success and another remain sleeping; one is a favourite of all, and another has to be taken to a party forcibly. One remains quiet and another has to be made quiet. One always reacts like a specialist and another doesn't even understand a little. Everyone is unique in family and nothing's wrong in being so. It's right and logical too. In family, one always expects ideal behaviour from each other. Sometimes serious arguments may take place. Million Wings feels that ideal behaviour is a dream and not utmost important behaviour. Persons may be of any type/nature but in family every person is their own. Maybe everyone can't live together but they should be together by heart.

Million Wings feels that shopping is enjoyable and alternative work but only if done with loving people. As those persons who know each other's choices and with whom choice matches, they can shop well in enjoyable ways. Otherwise it's just management, not enjoyment. Million Wings feels that everyone has his own choice and has to shop according to that. Everyone has to shop according to ability and capacity. Every person should fix the budget according to capacity and according to the will of family members also, for what they want to purchase and what types of things they want to have.

Sisters-in-law, husband and wife, mother and daughter have good coordination of shopping, and with friends there is always an enjoyable atmosphere. Million Wings feels that females should shop with family; males have nothing to do there. Shopping for small children has to be done by the mother only; the father can also do. Buy comfortable and enduring things for older persons. Males can shop for themselves or females can also move with them.

Million Wings feels that every family member has their own importance, place, and work. Everyone has their own work, and with each other's support and help, they fulfil the needs of each other, as everything can be fulfilled anywhere but chances of getting support from family in problems or in time of need are more. If one family member is careless or reacts carelessly, then the whole system of family is disturbed. If one family member is really sick or helpless, then other family members take care of him/her and support him/her. In family, everyone keeps on teaching each other for benefit of each other. Million Wings feels that a person who needs help, support should always be calm and cool. In family, everyone demands help with a right of belongingness and everyone helps with a feeling of love and affection. In family, no one needs to help by compulsion or forcibly; neither is family the only hope or way. Infact relations filled with belongingness and affection are foundation of support and basic power. To take care and fulfil minimum requirement of parents and relations made by will? Choice like partner and children are important responsibilities.

Million Wings feels that family members should behave with each other as per age, stage, circumstances. Then only one can listen and understand; others' logical intention should be of understanding each other, not to show another down or frighten. Family members can try any number of times to make others understand. Million Wings feels that another needs to understand once or twice but can try any number of times to make family members understand. In actuality it's more important to understand than to be understood. It is very important to know that what are the desires, priorities, thinking, nature, age, behaviour of another. In reality the meaning of 'to make understand' is complete if a person will able to deliver his issue/matter in the right way which he wants, and it will be possible only if things are said according to another person. To understand each other's interest, priorities, desires is understanding each other.

Million Wings feels that every family member should get equal opportunities to express themselves clearly at times. If a family member didn't clarify things at the time or is not able to clarify them, it becomes a cause of mental disturbance, tension, and dissatisfaction. To talk to each other at the same time is happiness. To express ourselves at the same time makes us feel satisfied and light. In family, the younger and elders are known by experience and softness, not just by age. If family members talk respectfully to each other, then annoyance can be resolved. Million Wings feels that by talking at the same time, members don't feel jealous or ashamed; nothing went wrong if there is a bit of annoyance or fights. Many misunderstandingsare resolved by talking and even peace of mind will be maintained. By keeping things in mind, anger and annoyance increase to a level that person may start from starting and tension/fights may increase to higher level. To fight on small things is normal. Arguments are often seen in families. These all are secrets and ways of learning and teaching.

Million Wings feels that being with age-mates gives special satisfaction even if they are all family members who are along with each other. Listen to each other, support, help each other in difficult situations. But still sometimes persons miss coordination of age-mates. Parents and other family members play with children but still children love to play and be with children. Mother-in-law and daughter-in-law share their feelings/emotions with each other. But still both needthe company of age-mate friends. Husband and wife may live like friends but still husband likes the company of males and wife likes the company of other females. If mother-in-law has company of a neighbour age-mate, child has group of neighbour children, daughter-in-law has company of sister-in-law and neighbour friends, males have other male friends, then all feel more emotionally satisfied and peaceful.

Million Wings feels that when a person constructs his own house, may it be small or big, theliving room or veranda should be more spacious, as all members can sit together mainly there and coordination increases. Use light colours on walls (white, off-white), by which a home looks bigger and more comfortable. It's important to have air crossing in home by doors or windows so that air can flow everytime intothe home; possibility of diseases is also reduced. Make home according to comfort and as usedin daily life, as it's just mutual management with friends and relatives.

Million Wings feels, help family members in being independent so that they can take care of themselves. Our responsibilities decrease by doing so, and for us their independence will be plausible freedom. Help family members and relatives in such a way that they can feel maximum support, not in a way that they become careless and worthless or take extra advantage of that help. To help ownones means to help them and motivate them to be independent. You must have a calculation of the amount of money given to help (though you may not want it back) so that others should value your hardwork. Help means to fulfil logical needs, not to give comfort and care to irresponsible relatives.

Million Wings feels that no one is useless/worthless. They just need support of ownones. If a person gets opportunities, help, motivation, guidance as per interest, capacities, desires, he will surely shine sometime. They may need a bit more time but they will surely shine. Yes, it's another thing that he has not expressed yet or maybe isunable to express. Maybehe hadn't got a chance or been given a chance. Maybe he has less personal experience. Million Wings feels that a person may have thousands of lacking points or negative points but just one quality is enough to bring success and fame. Let inbuilt or internal qualities come out, trim them, and put them infront of the world. When people will get benefit, happiness, they will surely like that. Have trust in ownones; it will be their greatest strength.

Million Wings feels that relations filled with belongingness are the biggest security. Belongingness is the biggest moral support of a person. This belongingness can be got from family, friends, and partner of choice. A person may go anywhere in the world, may do any level of work, may be enjoying life to full extent, may be busy in fulfilling desires and dreams. If he has moral support of ownones, then happiness doubles. A person will feel confident to have someone of his own in the world. He will feel secure, confident that he can talk with someone at anytime whenever he needs. If he has confidence that he will talk in time of need, whenever he feel alone, whenever he feels like, whenever he has time, them he will always have positive moral support, he will have a positive attitude. If he has confidence that may everyone left him alone but he can move to ownones without any fear, tension, and insecurity.

A person will be independent and feel happy, if he has confidence that ownones may fight, argue but are attached to him/her and will surely support/help in time of need. If any own had gone far away may be by fighting, by arguing, misunderstanding or in search of dreams and desires, then maybe we didn't ask him/her to stop but never stop when he/she wants to return.

Chapter 22
Relatives

Those who are attached by heart and affection and understand can give feeling of belongingness and satisfaction. Million Wings feels that the relations which are filled with love, affection, care, trust, understanding feelings may be few but are the most beautiful and precious. Every person has by birth relations (family) and heartfelt relations (friends/love), dedicated and concerned relations. These are those relations which are very important, which can't be replaced by anyone, and neither are these relations alternatives of each other.

Million Wings feels that feeling of belongingness is power and this moral support was birthed by care and affection. This can't be sold or purchased; a feeling of belongingness itself took birth is by birth relations and heartfelt relations. A relation can be felt own if it is filled with love and affection. Parents, siblings, children, lovers/partners, relatives, everyone has their own special place. Every relationship has different feelings, love, and care. There is no competition in these relations. Mother can't be replaced by lover, lover can't be replaced by mother. Neither mother nor lover decreases each other's love. Children increase love in brothers or sisters. Siblings can't replace friends; neither are friends alternatives of relations or relatives. Nothing can replace the love and soft touch of grandparents. Trust and support of ownones don't allow nonsense people to cross their boundaries.

Those who take care, support, help or try to take care, support, help in difficult times are our own.

Million Wings feels that when there is love and affection on both sides of relations, then they became ownones for each other. One-sided love gives one-sided relationship not both-sided belongingness. It's important to understand that we are their own, for those to whom we are attached with love and heart; it doesn't mean we also become their own for them also.

Million Wings feels that if a person really wants enjoyment, then he should only invite those fellows to parties and functions with whom he really feels goodness and belongingness. If people will be few, then they can be invited in a better way. And they will not complain if there will be any mismanagement. All will enjoyfully and there will not be any tension on their minds. Million Wings feels that a person needn't attend a function under compulsion or for the sake of socializing; instead he should spend that time in fulfilling dreams and desires. It's better to take a nap than doing some things under compulsion, better to spend time with lovely friends, playing with kids.

Watching a movie, having tea or coffee, eating popcorn or icecream, this time is more beneficial than spending time in compulsion, much better. Manage time for own needs and desires rather than spending time in compulsion.

On meetings, on functions, on weddings, on festivals whenever family and relatives meet, they present some gifts to each other. Million Wings feels that this give and take doesn't feel like gift exchange, instead has become a custom solemnity. Give-and-take relations are becoming that custom in which whatever is given is expected back and if it fails to happen, then it becomes cause of objections and annoyance. Million Wings feels that give-and-take relations is a custom which is a burden on emotional and financial status. At times of weddings and functions, tension/compulsion of give and take worries first. Million Wings feels that in relations, everyone demands satisfaction of self-respect and in realitya person gets happiness from love, affection, and respect of relations, not by exchange of gifts. If a precious and costly thing is given with callousness, it doesn't give satisfaction and happiness. Million Wings feels that give and take should be of love, care, affection, respect and it's just by taking and attending to each other properly, not by exchanging clothes, money. Gifts of love, care, affection have been more important for centuries, then why can't their feelings be given importance/stress than anything else? Every person has his own living style as per his/her capacity, and to do this is his happiness and right too.

Million Wings feels that it's another thing to help each other in time of need. But putting unnecessary tension in a custom of exchanging gifts is totally wrong. Let's abolish this give-and-take custom/tradition. To meet each other with love and affection is real happiness.

Million Wings feels that if someone really loves another, then they should meet, give presents and gifts to each other to express their happiness. Gifts and presents should always be given according to own happiness and capacity, and nothing should be demanded or expected in return; to present a gift is just one way of expressing feelings of love and affection, giving satisfaction to the heart. There is nothing to do with the cost of the gift. It just depends on will and capacity of person who is gifting. Million Wings feel that love and affection don't need any gifts and presents.

When a person is presenting something, then that's his happiness, not compulsion or force and it's according to will and capacity of another, not right of another. Million Wings feels that it's another thing to fulfil needs/desires of another, presenting gifts on happy occasions like birthdays, marriages, functions, according to capacity is a way of expressing love/affection. This can be done by nearby relatives and friends who understand each other.

Million Wings feels that spending time with ownones is a precious gift. Million Wings feels that presenting a flower and chocolate is a beautiful way of expressing love. On national festivals, giving a hug and having sweets together is just like a gift. Meeting each other with love and affection and in a respectful way gives more happiness than a present. Million Wings feels that in society we should stress on meeting more and not on formalities of exchanging presents.

Million Wings feels that social customs and tradition are made to remember important relatives. Today everybody is just engulfed in his personal life and not able to give attention to anyone other than parents and children. Birthday parties, marriage parties, festivals providea good chance to celebrate happiness. That's why important customs are related to marriage, so that persons can meet atleast important relatives. Relations get importance and respect by customs, e.g. sister feeds horse at marriage, uncle used to give bangles to girls and bath to boy. Sister-in-law paints eyes with kajal, brother-in-law helps in getting ready, brother helps during phere (seven rounds of Hindu marriage), etc. Like this, the logical meanings of customs provide ways to meet each other; otherwise sometimes we don't have time to meet each other.

Million Wings feels that relations are happiness of the heart. If person is not willing to meet, then what's the meaning of meeting forcibly? Million Wings feels, always meet each other with heart and will, may relations be far relations, neighbours, or friends. Get free from those relations which are just formalities. You needn't meet anyone under compulsion or jealousy, or forcibly. Relations are also continuous where there is love and affection, and happiness also increases there only. All of the rest are just solemnities, etiquette, and showing off.

Million Wings feels that most relations want to live together but don't want to interfere or to be in problems because of each other. All are busy in their lives, enjoying happiness and fulfilling responsibilities. Million Wings feels that if relatives can meet each other only in time of need, then also it's all right; nothing's wrong in this. Relatives should be attached in a way that they should be there in time of need; otherwise they can remain busy, happy, enjoying their own life. To think this is right, logical.

Chapter 23

Money

Money is a great unit which converts hardwork of person into equivalent facilities. Money provides amount equivalent to work done. Million Wings feels that money is work done. Money comes by giving facilities and goes by taking facilities. Money is facilities. Every person should get facilities according to their hardwork. It's not completely right. Million Wings feels that money is a symbol of efforts, labour, work done. And every person should get fruit of efforts.

Financial independence is the most effective achievement towards freedom in life which can reduce dependency for money on others. Money, though, is not everything but is a very important part of life, required to fulfil our basic needs and dreams. Million Wings understands that money and feelings both have their own importance. Happiness cannot be purchased by money only; neither can money replace feelings. But we can adjust as much money with the feelings as we want. We have to accept it that if there is no money problem, then happiness and peace double. Million Wings practically knows that money is not everything, but it is required to fulfil our daily basic needs.

This world has been moving for centuries because of combined efforts. A single person can't do all the work alone to carry on life. Every person can't cultivate his own wheat, cereals, etc., can't make separate departments of electricity, water, sanitation, etc. Every person can't do everything on his own for himself. A person can manage two or maximum three facilities for himself but can't manage all of them. Every person can't do everything for himself. A person needs to manage everything in combination. One person will do one work, second will do another work, and third will do something else, i.e. different persons will manage work of different departments for each other. One will provide food, another will provide security, another will provide treatment, etc. Like this, everyone will provide services to each other and life will be easy. For centuries, services have been provided in return for services.

Problem starts when one service needs more hardwork than another, so it is very important to equalize the service. So it has one solution: to make a unit for work done / service so that service can be equalized by providing a proper amount for a service. Like this, money was born. Now everyone gets money equalized to service provided. If he needs anything, he gives money and gets the thing he likes. Now a person gets full benefits/service according to himself. Service can't equalize another service. And with the help of money, it becomes easy to manage two different services. Now person has no fear of getting a smaller amount in return for more service.

Work can be of two types: physical and mental. Million Wings feels that mental work is possible if another will do that physically; maybe physical work is of same person, or the mind of one and physical work done by someone else. To do any work completely, both mental and physical work are important. But question is, what will hands make if there is no strategy? Hands require a plan made by the mind. Million Wings feels that to make service available to each other, it's also necessary to understand that plans/ strategies can be successful if hands will give them real shape. If no one will do physical efforts, then how can service facilities be made? Now it's easy to manage the work which requires less mind and more physical efforts. If the mind is here, then it will make thousands of artificial machine (as hands) and can take work from them to provide service and one natural hand starts doing the work of thousands of natural hands. In today's era, humans have made a lot of machine systems which are replacing humans. Million Wings feels that it's not possible to replace natural human handswith machine hands everywhere, everytime. Natural mind and hands are best, will remain best, were best, as where the artificial hands, mind stop working, there natural hands, mind give completion to work.

Million Wings feels that importance of mental and physical work is the same, may price/value vary. Million Wings feels that money is more where risk is more, and where risk is low, money is also low. In the coming era, importance and value of mental and physical work will be the same, i.e. mind used will be equal to physical work done. It's the future.

Earn money as much you want, as much you can. The costlier demands and desires earn the bigger amount of money. Passion has no limit and a person can't be replaced by value.

Million Wings feels that to fulfil logical needs of life is success. Above that is passion, not compulsion. Money can be spent to a limit where logical level starts equalizing. And it depends upon the purpose of related service. Million Wings feels that maximum value of earned money is today. Value of money decreases as time pares.

The amount of money which a person uses to keep for security should earn for today's happiness always. Million Wings feels that if today is here, then only tomorrow will be here, if no today, then no tomorrow. Every human is worried for emergency conditions, situations in future like disease, accident, death, etc. It is right too. If a person becomes forlorntemporarily or permanently, then there will be problems all around. When person grows old, then how he can earn money? Every person should keep some security for disease, old age, and forlornness. A person should get ready for possible circumstances of tomorrow, and money is the great way to avoid these tensions, to make everything allright. Upto some extent, money can provide secure future; then what about today?

A person has to earn food, clothes, facilities, services today and has to fulfil desires and passion too. May it be happy or sorrowful times, money is always required. Now every person has to earn money today for today and for tomorrow also. If we have to just earn for ourselves, then also it's easy but what ifwe have to earn for children, other dependents, ownones also? Now if a person wants to earn a living in a better way, then the person has to start preparing from today onwards. Now if the person will have to do this since today, then he has to work and work always. How will he get comfort and happiness of today?

Million Wings feels that person has to live for today, live in today and has to make proper plans and strategies for tomorrow. Today, humans are civilized and they know well that there are some emergencies, situations, things which can happen with anyone, e.g. disease, accidents, old age. Government/administration of every country has to make social policies for their primary/basic circumstances only.

A person mainly has to live for, work for today only. The future should be so secure that everyone can avail of that. Insurance policies are a solution to these problems. There should be those types of insurance policies which help in emergency conditions, not for collection of money. By doing this, insurance policies can be got with smaller amounts of money. Policies continue in less money, and after a death, the family gets more money; it is more effective. In the same way, there should be health insurance, education insurance which can handle natural and human forlornness, and the rest of the money which a person keeps on collecting, other than insurance, should be used to enjoy today, as today is in our hands and the future will be according to own thinking. It's not sure; no one can say it confidently. But by having managed administration and government, a person can be free from or get relief from many emergency tensions and problem.

Million Wings feels that money is comfort, i.e. easy to earn and can provide comfort. To choose professional work as per interest feels comfortable and to spend money according to will, desires, and need is comfort. By working in a profession, a person can earn a good amount of money. But yes, if a person has multiple resources, that's even better. Do as much work as you want for eight hours a day that will be comfortable.

Million Wings feels that everyone wants to spend less to fulfil his needs and demands. To do this is right, logical too. If a person wants/demands more quality for a smaller amount, then what's wrong in this? Money is a unit for workdone, then why should a person waste it? Obtaining/gaining benefit of every small unit of moneycollected by hardwork is right. A person wants to spend the lowest amount. Maybe he is earning more benefit on spending more? To do and think this is right. Spending little by little again and again is more comfortable. If person wants to spend more at once, that is also right.

An individual works in his/her profession/occupation with full interest and hardwork so that he/she can earn a lot of money, and it's an excellent approach too. Every person should work for himself; he must concentrate to do his job with full sincerity and enthusiasm so that lots of money showers on him. Million Wings feels that every individual is already doing his/her efforts to raise his/her financial status and they must continuethe same, because that's the very effective way to earn day-to-day living. Million Wings feels that other than main occupation and job, if there is more additional extra source of income comes on the way, one should also adopt along with.

An individual may not be able to find enough time for himself and for his/her family and friends because of busy work schedule. Royalty means money without work, i.e. money will come again and again from the same good work done only once in life. Royalty means no tension of earning money. Only a few people around the world gets royalty income, e.g. singers from songs once sang, directors and actors from movies once made, scientists from research once done in life, writers from good books once written in life. The same work gets replicated and will give recurrent money.

It is very important to understand that every person belonging to any profession earns money, maybe less or more, but on the basis of his skill, qualification, and hard work. They will not get money if they do not work. It's totally true and right that if we work, we will get money, and if we do not work, then we will not get money. It does not matter whether a person is a big businessman or highly qualified (e.g. doctors, lawyers, CAs, eng. administrators) or small-scale workers. But no one has permanent income. If they work, only then they will get money, otherwise not. If even the people who have big maternal/paternal properties will not work further, their resources would start reducing and ultimately be finished. Everyone has to work in routine to earn ongoing income. Royalty means the money will keep growing high without active work all the times. Usually one work gives one-time money but any work related with royalty gives money again and again from the same work.

It's an art to earn money. The art has relation to works that fulfil needs of the people. Even the uneducated or less educated can earn as much amount of money as he wants by his qualities and by providing service to people; fulfilling needs, demands of people is earning money, maybe by getting education or by being uneducated. It's true, it's logical.

☗ ☗ ☗

Chapter 24

Profession

Million Wings feels that the identity of every person is his profession. Profession plays a main leading role to fulfil needs, dreams, and desires. Profession is money. Profession is the main source of person.

Million Wings feels that if a person becomes his profession, then there will be success and happiness. If the work of a human will be same as his will and desire, then he will do that heartily with full capacity and strength, will not feel compulsion in work chosen as per interest. The person will do that happily, by which change of success and benefit increases more. Million Wings feels, try to understand the interest, passion, and desire of a child since childhood and give him education. Practice according to that so that it will become profession later on, as he/she wants. When education or profession will be against will and interest, then it will feel like compulsion. In these conditions/circumstances/situations, success is ever far; it's hard to fulfil daily needs.

Million Wings feels that profession is neither big nor small. Its need/demand makes it special. Like a person is known by profession, in the same way, a person can give a different identity to work. Million Wings feels that if we compare work and individual, then it's the individual who is great, not work. If a person will not do anything, then nothing will happen even with great work like being a doctor. And if a person does hardwork, then even a small shopkeeper who is selling food in one corner of the country can open a chain of restaurants in the world.

Every common man should understand that every field is a speciality in itself. And every expert must understand that every speciality basically revolves around common sense. Personal dreams and desires are the driving force, common sense is the starting strategy, and personal satisfaction is the goal. Passion is determined dedication towards one's goal, irrespective of final outcome. Passion is the pathway leading ultimately to personal relaxation, whatever may be the final result, success or failure.

Million Wings feels that work may be any, it depends upon the person how high he can take that. Million Wings feels that importance of a profession is decided according to its need but self-respect of every person doing any work is same. It's his right too. It's the future. Million Wings feels that benefit in any profession should be decided according to labour/work done. They should get the benefit equivalent to their workdone. Hardwork/labour means total expenditure, total mind used, total physical work, total time used. A person should atleast get expenditure equivalent to total work done to provide service to customer.

But, Million Wings feels that to give 100 times benefit is wrong. Benefit policies in the society, country, or world should be same. Million Wings feels that maximum 100 per cent benefit can be given. Now it should be decided by person while choosing profession whether he wants to fewer products but more beneficial products or more products but less beneficial products. Profession and workdone should be usedto earn money, but limits of benefits should be the same. Million Wings feels that price of initial raw material should be decided as per international level; the rest of the things can be decided by itself.

Million Wings feels that a person has to think about which profession he is interested in and capable to do, how much hardwork he can do, and what amount of money he wants to earn. Million Wings feels that in some professions, doing work at night is duty, not compulsion, e.g. health department, police department, army and security department. If workers working in these departments are working at night, then their motto is to maintain peace in the country, not just for money; infact they are working for social responsibility. In same department, workers can work at night too along with day so that people will get more benefit, e.g. transport, media, politician, electricity department. There is no compulsion for these workers, neither is it responsibility. To work even at night is their personal will and benefit or maybe personal compulsion which they have to do; this not any social responsibility.

Just a few corrupt people in one field never means that the whole of the department is corrupt. If a few sick people are doing bad in some field, it does not mean that the base, purpose, and intentions of the same profession are not good. The need is to shout the odds and improving through awareness. Common amendments must be done as early as noted in interest of the people, by the higher authorities.

Million Wings feels that in any work, comparison should be done on common basis, not with the best person, as the extremely hard-working can be cause of motivation or goal. Comparison in profession gives a speed-up to our success. Becoming better and better in one's profession is a secret of success. A person who achieves name and fame and earns more money in his profession shows possible capacity of earning money from work so that every person should have hope and target to achieve professional success.

Million Wings feels that to provide service or product to customers with clear way is priority. Every liquid product should have natural purity and weight and minimum quality and price should be fixed so that comparison can be seen. It's a responsibility of government and administration to fix it. If someone wants to earn more money from the same product, then he should make product better and can sell at a higher price. But having benefit by compromising quality is not acceptable. Million Wings feels that professional success is not to earn money by betraying. Infact providing better and more useful things to more people is success. Million Wings feels that customers should have the right to know, ask any question regarding the product of a company. This awareness is the future.

Million Wings feels that to start a profession, spend money on extremely important things which can give results too. Before starting a profession, do know about need of that profession at that place. Even if there is enough money, then also spend money like a miser. Save the amount as much you can save. Before spending money, think twice. Ask everyone why to spend this much money. Atleast ask two related persons before finalizing a deal. Million Wings feels that the mind can be used again and again but money once spent can't be recovered. New plans and ideas come to mind;

sometimes an idea looks very beneficial and sometimes feels like it will not work. Sometimes when already half the work is done on an idea, again suddenly a new plan or idea arises which gives signs of more possibilities and success. But the amount spent was wasted, and even if it is recovered, then its recovery is worthless price.

Million Wings feels that following the already established systems in the world is not wrong. But yes, if a person wants to do totally new business about which no one knows anything, then it's natural to face problems by changing policies and plans again and again. Money expenditure increases, and when the mind reaches some good, then it got difficult to collect money. Million Wings feels that if intention of providing facilities to customers along with earning more, then obviously business will grow faster. If customers will feel the need for a product and get comfort too, then obviously they will buy that even in a greater quantity. Million Wings feels that history is witness that only those products become famous which give comfort and easiness to life. This will remain policy of the future while life exists.

In each and every professional course, the students must be taught how to deal with the public and about rules and regulations and laws related to that field. Only professional education is not sufficient. It's very important to understand that not only doing work is necessary, but to keep the record of activities and outcomes is also important for the long run or analyses. As long as the professional responsibilities move in the right way, people and administration don't ask anything, but if something unfavourable happens, then everyone starts asking demands written proof and fundamentals and that seems right also. Other people will come to know only from records. In professional dissatisfactions, the emotional points have nothing to do with justice but only authenticated literature and records are a must. Record-keeping proves right evidence. Million Wings feels that record-keeping is peace of mind and security. Written work supports our professional ups and downs. Self record-keeping is a beautiful way of learning and understanding the programs vacations and helps to improve skill and capabilities.

Investment in profession or business must be like that; each penny of money must be utilized in a proper way, must bring benefits in the beginning of any profession or work, always keeps the utility of product or service on the priority basis. One must understand that initially all the glamorous and hi-fi presentation may help to bring a product/service to the notice of people but products and services are always being preferred by the people on the basis of utility only. Million Wings feels that consumer or customer all around the world always consider and choose useful things, and cheaper is better. Main motto of mass media/advertisement is to make people aware of product or service, not to spend more on mass media to make the product costlier. Once people become aware of a product or service and find that useful, then they themselves keep on telling others and add automatically customers. This is a secret of every profession and it's a logical secret, as professional success depends on sales of product.

Price of product depends upon how easy or difficult it is to make and its availability. If product can be prepared easily and raw material for product is also easily available, then its cost can't be too high. If a product is easily available, then why will people purchase the same product at a high price? The meaning of potency remains on cost. Million Wings feels that nationally or internationally, when anyone researches a new product or new policy, then worldwide as people get to know about benefits, they would definitely try to purchase it. If its price suits the common man's pocket, then they purchase it, and if not, then they try to make the samething at a low price and try to get the samething at a low price and try to get the same benefit from that. And doing this is not wrong. It's human nature, which has been here for centuries and it's right too. If anything or policy is beneficial for one person and is beneficial for another person also, then he would try to make things resembling that and would get benefit from that. Million Wings feels that the rule of potency may be there on a thing or policy but everyone takes logical personal benefits, and to do this is right too.

Million Wings feels that if we see, then patents are for innovation and name and fame, not with money. If one has made something new and innovated, then one's name should be registered at national and international level and should get respect. And not to get patents just for business purpose for the innovation, actually which is done for improvement or betterment of humans. Patents don't mean to get more monetary value. If it's not easy to make by common ones, then obviously a person will get more value of it, and if it's easy to make, then the same person will get less value ofcourse. This is a real business policy. It's true and will remain the same.

In any business, marketing strategy is equally important in any business success as the basic product and services are. So 50 per cent of the finances and mind are required for advertisements and assistant employees.

Any profession which is of specialized nature is not easily understandable to the common public, hence a specialist needs to explain the value and utility of the product or service in their respective languages. Explain specialised concepts/things/issues in general, common ways or as per their related professional examples.

Whenever we put our profession-related information for general public, it should be in relative, required important common points of interest and should be in simple and straight forward language and meanings, especially on websites and folders.

In business management, persons at high level should have a written agreement with employees, atleast agreement of minimum time frame, holidays, responsibilities, and pay. Principles and rules should be the same for everyone. In private institutions, firstly work and working strategy need to taught to workers/employees and when they learn, then on getting rise in payscale they move to another place. They feel as it's their right. Every employee takes resignation in their pocket. And on just little misunderstanding, they get ready to resign. It's always important to keep personal and professional life apart from each other. The only real emergencies are medical ones. Everything else can be pre-decided. Amendment of rules and policies can be done for betterment. Million Wings feels that to accept another professional opportunity by leaving first profession is everyone's right, need, and happiness; everyone wants success and it's right. Those who leave their first job after fulfilling commitments, then no one can stop them from doing so. Fulfilling commitment at first professional place is the first step towards success. To leave first job in between, before completion of commitment, just for personal benefit is totally wrong. Million Wings feels that at professional places, behaviour/nature of person is to be kept in mind then work and need. Catch new options only after fulfilment of old commitment. If another has firstly done that, then it's right to do the same with himself. It's a clear decision.

Million Wings feels that profession/business is mutual commitment where customer is given a product or service in value of money. Company or businessman should have to give the right product, at the right time as per commitment, and consumer has to give right amount of money as per commitment. Professional commitment takes place because of mutual needs, and to fulfil that is professional responsibility, not compulsion. If a professional team fails/problem occurs to fulfil demand as per commitment, then they should inform of the same as early as possible to a related person. It's the right of a customer so that the customer can decide as per his needs, and if it's necessary to cancel the commitment, then he can do so and can fulfil his needs or demands from somewhere else. The responsibility of person who breaks commitment is more to pass the right information, and if another doesn't do so, then obviously he will be taken as wrong. Maybe circumstances are natural, maybe artificial, maybe related to himself. May related to other but there is no fault of customer; only product and service of need matter for him. If professional team also informs at right times, gives right information timely then they are also taken as right at their place. If both agree again, then it's all right; otherwise, commitment can be cancelled.

If a customer is not giving full payment according to commitment or is not collecting goods or service on time, then it's completely his responsibility/mistake. In these conditions, a professional team reminds the customer and gives information about expiry time of products and service. In these conditions, the professional team is absolutely right and the whole responsibility is of customer only.

Million Wings feels that real management is to handle circumstances rightly and to maintain good coordination and to fulfil promise and commitment on time. Million Wings feels that management is not just bookish knowledge; instead as a whole person a manager should know the logical aim and havethe ability to deliver his service/product in a responsible and capable way. This professional coordination is personal management. It's a logical meaning of every work, it's responsibility.

The biggest difference in thinking and doing work is that circumstances vary. The more the person is responsible for doing work, the more the possibility of delay. A worker/employee fails to do work on time sometimes because of genuine and sometimes because of non-genuine reasons. And because of this, product is not able to be delivered timely. Million Wings feels that clear strategy speeds up work and responsible employee is strength of work and mutual coordination is success of work. It's true and will remain true.

It's important to fulfil all legal formalities and papers regarding business. Million Wings feels that legal formalities regarding business should be easy so that if any individual wants to attach with any occupation, then easy formalities will work as motivation for him.

Million Wings feels that day is for work and night is for sleeping. This is a law of nature and it's right and logical. That is, every person has a right to work during day and sleep at night. Now if we see department of worldliness, then there are a few departments in which persons have worked in day and night too. To do this is neither their hobby nor responsibility nor moral duty, e.g. health department who have to work even at night for care of patients, police department who have to remain awake at night for security and peace in society. There are a few departments who work at night as moral duty for happiness of society.

Million Wings takes these departments as tougher departments who have to work at night. Those who work in these departments, whose morale duty is to work even at night, should get more facilities; pay of those who work at night should be more than those who work in day. An individual workingat night to fulfil his needs should get more pay as he is providing facilities in night.

Million Wings feels that there is no limit of doing work as per own will and interest. When occupation is chosen as per own will, then a human enjoys doing work and he feels less tired and gets more success and money. But doing work without interest is hard to do and a person feelsvery tired. A person can work day and night according to his interest. But working without interest feels like a burden. Million Wings feels that person can work maximum of eight hours with fresh and energetic mind and body. Working for more than 8 hours doesn't give the expected advantage. It's possible to work for 12–16 hours in a day for a few days. But every time, again and again doing this much work feels difficult and is not in humans' favour. Million Wings feels that if a person works for 12–14 hours then result of that is equivalent to workdone for 8–10 hours. That is, working effectively and efficiently for 8 hours in a day is much better and can give more money and success than working slowly and unwillingly for 12 hours.

Million Wings feels that if person has to maintain his balance, then working for 8 hours a day is the best working strategy. To work for more hours is for sometime. But working for a long time, more than three months in a year, is not in humans' favour. It's difficult for the same person to work always at night. In any occupation, these should not be more than regular night duties. It's 100 per cent true that a person can't relax fully in a day after working at night. In any occupation, person can work for 48–72 hours in a week. The more person works effectively, the more his pay should be. Person should not get work more than 16 hours in a day. Even if the employee agrees, then also he should not be given work more than 12 hours/day/week, as by doing this, the health of the employee can worsen; chances of professional loss are more. More money and time may need to be spent to correct that. If persons work with interest in any field, then they will surely get success. Million Wings feels that if the occupation of a person is the same as his interest, will, and dream, only then he will achieve success and deserve praise. Professional education and practical knowledge regarding work is always useful and become a real cause of success. A person may be interested in work or develops interest in work later on; it's one and the samething, as success is related to interest, not work.

Million Wings feels that profession/occupation can be chosen only after knowing the interest. Curiosity, optimism, and surety arise by doing so, by which persons become more capable and efficient and skilful and able to gain professional heights.

Million Wings feels that education and profession of person should be based on person's interest, will and agreeableness. If there are already occupational options available in society as per personal interest, then it's easy to choose them and be able to live happily. But if occupational options are not available according to interest, then it may be hard to earn money for a living. In these conditions, a person can choose a profession in the related way to his interest. Even if it is also not possible, then the person has not to choose his second interest for his profession, so the person can work a little or as per time on his first interest and can earn a living through his second interest. While choosing education, a person has to take care of both interests and to earn a living. If the first passion can't be profession, then the second interest can be chosen for profession to earn a living.

Today, if passion or interest of person is not related with profession, then maybe he himself can make his interest as profession tomorrow. All occupations available today at international level were once interest or passion or thinking and then with regular tries, they gained this level, e.g. music, games, photography, painting, dance. Future occupations are those interests or passions which give happiness or comfort to people. When these types of interest take the form of occupation, they become hope and motivation for others also who have the same interest. To earn a living, a person has to choose the nearest possible profession related to his interest. If interest or passion can be moved on, then hope of tomorrow increases.

It's often seen in offices workers/employees at higher level behave miserably with employees at lower level. In these situations, employees havethe right to complain to high authority in office. If that higher-level person is also not right, then the employee has the right to complain to police, administration, or media.

If employee is related with well-known organization, company, or educational institution, then they obviously have a minimum of professional knowledge. But it's not necessary, as if the person himself can't show interest in learning, then he can't learn even at the best institutes. So if employee belongs to highly recognized place, even then atleast ask about minimum necessary things before offering a job. Remember that occupation is social responsibility, not carelessness; it's true.

Million Wings feels that an individual can get a job on personal recommendation but his minimum responsibility should be filled by himself only. The one who is recommending is just helping to give a start/chance. But to maintain the job and be successful depends upon the hard work of the person himself.

Million Wings feel that a person can be recommended by someone but the person himself has to prove his talent. It's true, it's logical. If people suffer because of a government employee, then government has to pay for the loss, e.g. clerk fills wrong name, age, address, number on form. In these conditions, a person himself doesthe whole procedure again. Electricity bills which are sent on high price need to be correctedby visiting again and again. People have to keep carbon copies of their legal paperwork so that it should be clear that mistake was on the part of government employee, not of general public. In these conditions employee has to say sorry, correct the work, and pay for that.

Million Wings feels that to give the right suggestion regarding profession is a secret of permanent and long-lasting success. First three years of every profession or person is a most precious time. Mistakes are normal things to happen. In second year, stability tries to take place, and in third year, profession is settled to a suitable level. This is the only year which maintains bonafide as passion. Income may be less because people like the right and timely delivery of service, suggestion, and product. These things are a secret behind success and take it to a high level. If there is no bonafide and trust, then a business can't run for a longtime, as consumers have many other options.

Million Wings feels that mistakes, profit, loss, and success are part of business while there is hope of goodwill, while there is hope of professional success. People surely understand by giving them right and timely information and stand along with them. Atleast trust and goodwill will always be maintained, which is professional security. Professional speciality is a special type of education that learns and understands some issue so that more benefit can be gained. Being specialized means to have special knowledge experience of one's work along with general knowledge to improve issues/matters. Specialized means to give more wide and specialized service to customer or consumer.

Million Wings feels that a specialist is the person who has more knowledge of his field. But to talk and console people is behaviour skill. A specialization means to handle tougher issues. But a specialist has to deliver his views to the common man in general language only.

Million Wings feels that if there are needs, problems, issues in life, then products and services are there. Customers and consumers are here, so specialists and companies are here. In every field, a customer or consumer has many options and he will remain a permanent customer of that company where he will get respect and satisfaction. It's necessary to have more and more behaviour coordination and satisfaction along with doing things right and well. Million Wings feels that these people will be successful who have their own will and interest in doing something. These people have a modern level of thinking in their skill, quality, and knowledge and make better products according to needs and hopes of people. They have to keep an eye on their competitor also, as comparison speeds up professional success. In the real world, comparison is to make ourselves better, to make ourselves better than ourselves, not others, as to be better than othersis to make ourselves better than ourselves. Million Wings feels that people who move forward naturally stay ahead.

Million Wings feels that if someone is doing their work with full responsibility and capability but has rude behaviour with people, then also people don't want to visit him again. Every person, may they be a needy person, has self-respect. They just have a compulsion to rate rudeness, as they get a new chance or option, then obviously they want to move there. Behaviour skill increases success manifold. Million Wings feels that in every field/product/service with more uses, speciality and lower price are the biggest secret of success. By behaviour skill, a person can reach the highest level of success. Million Wings feels that when customers or consumers have to go to a specialist to get suggestion, then they have to go to the person who has a related degree and minimum experience of one year (especially in doctors' field).

Million Wings feels that it's important to answer in every profession. Answering is important in every profession, may it be a small or international company. Doing mixing, betrayal, cheating in product or service are equal crimes. May it be a tea seller, ex-army man, rich or poor, officer or general public, small-scale shopkeeper or large-scale seller, private or government, any profession, if product or service of same value is not delivered, then it's betrayal, then they are irresponsible and are equally guilty. Everyone should be answerable.

Million Wings feels that in the professional field, a high authority (private/government) can misuse his power, position, or quality. In these circumstances if he does physical or mental torture, then do complain against him. Do complain, inform the managing director or government or police department.

Million Wings feels that when someone has some professional dream, then he has to be personally self-dependent, self-managing, and impartial. Try to give equal responsibility management, finance, and strategy to partner so that partner should spend equal amount of money and mind. Then value of each other's qualities will be maintained and less possibility of misunderstanding and false beliefs. Instead of doing partnership, take a loan. Appoint employees in occupations as per need. At every level/place, minimum level and maximum level should be fixed as per percentage of profit.

Million Wings feels that careless, corrupt, and irresponsible employee take unnecessary advantage of the goodness of another employee. Do your own duty and help only upto the same level, don't help so much that another will take unnecessary benefit. Million Wings feels that in a profession, level and pay depends upon work quality and capacity of employee. Profession has nothing to do with personal relations. In every profession, rules and regulations should be the same for everyone. And every employee at a professional place is just professionally attached to each other.

Million Wings feels that whenever an employee is kept in any occupation, then along with his work and responsibilities, he should be aware to talk respectfully with other employees. And first eligibility for success/promotions should be behaviour skill, may it be clerk, security guard, receptionist, helper, or high-authority employee.

Million Wings feels that when individual enters a profession, then it's expected that he should know his work rightly. These employees who are trained first are expected to do their work/responsibility/duty rightly. Occupation/profession is basically combination of many hands and brain. By which all living and basic needs of society are fulfilled. Million Wings feels that in professional studies, both theoretical and practical knowledge is given so that by getting primary introduction, they can handle their responsibilities in a good way.

Million Wings feels that at profession places, it's difficult to teach first and then to take work, as employees move to new places after learning for more benefit. These are the main problem at professional places. It's necessary to understand that according to need and time, employees can be trained but it's not possible to teach everything since starting. Million Wings feels that there are profession colleges and institutes. At professional places, it's necessary to work more and pay is given inreturn for work, not for teaching them.

Million Wings feels that MLM is a very effective and beautiful policy of earning money. Those who follow rules and regulations of MLM rightly can earn unlimited money, name and fame and to do this is not very difficult. MLM has ability to give money and time freedom to all, which is normally impossible to gain in any other profession. MLM can increase friendliness and trust in relations. Money can shower like rain, which we can't even imagine. In MLM, possibility of earning is more than expenditure. Expenditure is low, so obviously risk is low and there is no upper limit of profit.

Million Wings feels that a person has to attach to a graceful MLM profession along with his main profession. MLM is multiple source of income. MLM has real possibility to help in fulfilling dreams and desires of people. If we see all other occupations, they are also related to providing product and service to people, through people to people. In the world, there is no profession/occupation which is possible without network of people. It's good, right, logical. If we see deeply, then every person is attached to networks in daily life, maybe in another form. It's another thing that they don't get financial benefits or are not given these. Million Wings feels that with the help of MLM professional policy of products are distributed, then every person will get more benefit.

Million Wings feels that professional products and services are made for satisfaction of consumers, and employees of company should fulfil needs and desires of consumers. Satisfaction of consumer is a must. Products or service may be costlier or cheaper; if consumer is happy with a little, then don't give him more forcefully. Satisfaction of consumer is a must. It should be the minimum motto. It's more than enough if minimum compulsory level of quality, utility, and standard of product is maintained. Million Wings feels that to fulfil minimum compulsory things related to product/service is professional responsibility, and what level it will attain depends upon personal needs, desires, and passion of consumer. It's a logical marketing principle and will remain so.

Million Wings feels that to help relatives, friends, or links means to help logically. At professional places, professional work is done not to fulfil formalities of relationships or socializing. An employee has to fulfil needs of all people at a professional place. Because of this, he is unable to give more time or service to relatives or known persons. Even for friends or relatives, professional help is important only and by understanding time and compulsion, they also don't want to disturb work of employee. Million Wings feels that in the professional field, managed professional rules and regulations have to be followed, for which already special facilities and rules are made for near and dear ones so that neither employee or another employee has to be tense or worry, nor relatives or near and dear ones be bothered much and other people should not suffer. It's professional happiness.

Million Wings feels that the kind of work expected or needed from employee should be taught same work and gave same work. The work which needs more physical work and less brainwork should be trained according to that. In professions, a degree only is not enough; infact everyone demands perfectness in practical work and it's right too. If by small courses, six-month diplomas, or yearly courses a person can do the same work equivalent to a big degree, then why waste time, money, hard work, comfort?

One can take work advantage of less educated or uneducated people by giving them minimum required training. So by educating people in managed way, the company can give them a profession too and work can also be complicated. By which more people can get work/job and more manpower using less money. It's necessary to give knowledge regarding each and every aspect of work at high level only so that work can be guided properly. Million Wings feels that by doing practical work, persons get closer to perfection and learn work. A person may not have a proper degree regarding same work profession. Actually doing the right work is a logical professional need. While professional work is going well, then nothing else matters. But if there is some mismanagement in the professional field, then everyone questions the degree, papers, and practical experience of a person. To do this is not wrong; it's totally right.

Actually the future is of specialization. Every person wants full authentication and satisfaction in every product and service in every field, and it's their right too and professional adaptability too. Million Wings feels that consumers want maximum benefits in less expenditure, and professional employers also want to have more benefits from their product. Both are right at their place. Problems and failure may happen with a highly educated specialist too because of natural reason, which seems to be OK. But if the same loss happens because of less experience, then it's taken as carelessness, unconsciousness, andinauthenticity. Million Wings feels that taking work from less capable or less educated employee is risky or a compulsion, not right. If there is more work at different professional fields and deficiency of capable and qualified people or financial problem, then government or administration has to see how product/service should reach consumer at genuine price. There is no limit of more education, practical work, and money. But to make rulesand principles according to minimum required needs is social happiness. Million Wings feels that a person of the same professional fields knows well about problems and solutions of the related problems and they have to notify government, administration and high authority of country. Even government and high authority should also consider their suggestions which are directly related to consumers.

Million Wings feels that an individual has to work atleast for one year with his experienced senior so that he can get to know about real work strategies and related problems and should learn from them. Million Wings feels that after education, an individual has to start his personal work only when he feels self-confidence in himself. Atleast one year experience is beneficial for both sides, i.e. personally and socially.

Million Wings feels that occupational responsibilities are social responsibilities. It's OK if there is personal loss because of carelessness, but loss of professional group, consumer, or customer is totally wrong. There is no place for carelessness in professional responsibility; neither should it be tolerated. Million Wings feels that doing own professional work sincerely is real responsibility and delivering that responsibility with calmness and in friendly way to customer is social work. If work is responsibility, then behaviour is social work. Person needn't go separately for social work. Infact delivering product/service to customer in mannerly, cool, and calm way is social work only.

Million Wings feels that personal and professional life affect each other. If an employee is sick, he is unable to concentrate on work. Social, familiar, and personal tensions and issues disturb capability and capacity of professional work. Professional tension and problem also disturbs personal life. If it rarely happens, then everyone can understand and try to cooperate, but if this happens often, then everyone has a problem. Owner and employee both can adjust for sometime, as no one wants personal loss and it's right too. It's true that profession is mutual agreement between owner and employee. Both are responsible in their own way to deliver product/service to consumer on time. But the owner is answerable. Head/owner has responsibility for behaviour of employee too, along with product/service. It's often seen that manual misunderstandings and disagreements cause a tense atmosphere all around, because of which professional work is disturbed. Million Wings feels that if any loss occurs because of personal issues/matter, it has to be payable by employee, and if it falls much more than financial capacities of employee then it's the responsibility of the owner.

Employee and owner have to understand genuine problems, situations of each other. Owner maximally deducts pay of employee or can fire the employee from the job and employee can maximally leave his pay or can resign. But it's necessary to understand that money and manpower are not available freely. Neither does the owner have so much money nor so many employees that work can be handled afterwards. If in a natural problem, owner has to help financially or by giving holiday, then the employee has also to do his best to fulfil financial needs and responsibilities so that work can't be affected in their absence. If employees are giving minimum required information, training, or knowledge to their colleagues, then in hard times professional work can be handled rightly. Owner should have some all-rounder employees. They have to be trained so that they can handle situations for sometime.

Million Wings feels that owner/boss and employee have to sit in different cabins. By maintaining levels at professional places, management is also maintained, specially owner/boss who has to sit apart in a different cabin to do business deals.

Million Wings feels that in every profession there are a few risk and problems. To handle them and solve them is part of professional management. Every risk in making and delivering product isa personal or professional risk. These are not a responsibility of consumers.

Million Wings feels that when a consumer/customer purchases something by paying for them, obviously his intentions are that he should get full benefit of every penny he spent, and to think this is absolutely right. It's not only to start product or strategy/service but real matter is to fulfil promises which are already done.

Million Wings feels that in any occupation/profession, only 10 per cent of people are corrupt. Because of them, the other 90 per cent also has to listen and tolerate. In any professional department, there are very few people who misbehave with consumer/customer. Because of them, self-respect of the whole department is hurt. Million Wings feels that loss incurred because of arrogant or stubborn employee should not be tolerated by ourselves. In these conditions, inform high authority and personally remain clear. Then it's a responsibility of high authority what step they should take. Be clear about your own work boundaries and responsibility. Don't take responsibility for others' work. It's different to help each other sometimes.

Million Wings feels that customers can teach a lesson to these 10 per cent kind of employees. If high authority gets a complaint on some employee again and again, they have to take some strict action against him. If personally you feel uncomfortable with attitude or behaviour or have some loss because of irresponsible behaviour of employee, then one should complain regarding him, as on getting complaints again and again either employee has to improve or placement of another in place of him becomes urgent. Try to give the right direction faithfully and in time of need should be given primary importance. Maybe a person is unable to withstand a test of professional degree, rules and regulations as general and common sense and skill is mostly right. If you have brainsand quality, then sell that and earn money. If you have money, then invest money to earn money. Million Wings feels that work may be small or big but it's beneficial only if money is collecting or has more possibility of collection soon.

People demand effective work, only benefits and that too with more and more authentication. It is possible if a person has complete and new information regarding his profession, as knowledge of all profession-related possibilities gives authenticity and explicitness to words and expertness. Don't behave in romantic manner at professional place in professional time. It's not wrong to be attracted towards the opposite sex but to give minimum required attention to work and others is logical justice. There is no doubt that person can be attracted towards the opposite sex at professional place; there may be nothing wrong in this but behaving romantically or forcefully is surely wrong and obviously this affects goodwill too. If there is any romantic relationship between owner/boss and employee or employee and another employee, that's their will and they can have any behaviour with each other, other than official timing or profession place. For professions (related professions) which are already working in society, a person wants to do same work should definitely get minimum knowledge regarding expenditure, time needed, and manpower needed from experienced persons. Million Wings feels that it is natural to make mistakes in work which is totally new.

Million Wings feels that if there is management in business, then a logical decision is to see the intention of workers, policies, and experience. Their degrees and education may be complete even according to law; during mismanagement, it's necessary to check the expertness and experience of specialist who even hasa full degree. The reason is clear: value is of doing work rightly, not of only collecting degrees. If you need to promote your employee, then try to promote the one who is senior along with intelligent. By doing this, chances of mutual problems of employees decrease. Million Wings feels that while taking help from friends or relatives, minimum expenditure on product should be paid. The decision of responsibility examination and motivation of employee has to be kept in owner/boss's own hands, as leaving this to employees disturbs their mutual relations. Owner/boss and employees are attached to each other for mutual benefits. It's not important that both would have same dreams. Owner/boss wants work on time to fulfil his dreams and employee wants his pay ontime to fulfil his dreams. Meaning is to give/deliver 100 per cent best quality product/service to customer/consumer according to time and personal interest and hard work of individual to get success. Whenever person starts new work, obviously he is worried, tense, and afraid. It happens with everyone; he may be king or bagger. As human works, he learns from mistakes and failures. Slowly person becomes expert and gains full self-confidence. It's the only right procedure and the fastest way of success: don't stop, keep on moving, continue your path. Same is the feeling of Million Wings: that time of one to three years is natural to get confidence, faith, and success.

⣿ ⣿ ⣿

Chapter 25

Leader, government, and administration

We need international leaders who think globally and direct their own country as ambassador of happiness. Moving forward means behaving unitedly more organised and systematic balanced way but remember that inhumane ways are moving back to unorganised worse life. Million Wings feels that managed society is possible only because of good administration. It's impossible to move society without administration and law. Every person has personal thinking. On just one issue, people have thousands of suggestions and millions of disagreements. Everyone has a different point of view. Most people don't have enough knowledge. They discuss on the basis of small knowledge and most by making assumptions on issues and entangling themselves and are not able to find satisfactory solutions. So a leader and administration are needed.

Million Wings feels that a natural leader can bind the society, can take them towards progressive directions. A natural leader is the one whose dream is to serve the nation. A natural leader is the one whose main aim is to make society happy through managed ways. No one can make a natural leader, but his dream is to do social service and morality. This sort of leader can make a splendid administration. This sort of leader makes advantageous policies for residents, along with this, takes society and country towards progress. Million Wings feels that the leader of a country should be educated, atleast graduated so that he can talk confidently at national and international level. Main leaders of every department should be experienced and workers of the same department. People want security and fulfilment of basic needs from government. Government administration has to see how to do this. If government of the country will not do this, then who else will do this? If government of the country feel themselves forlorn, then how will the common man do all this? To make beneficial policies for residents of the country is a responsibility of government only. The leader has to make team of intelligent and experienced people who can make amazing and awesome policies by discussion. The only secret to make a country happy is to make it independent.

Million Wings feels that the leader or government of country may be anyone, but a common man should have right to ask questions regarding responsibilities and policies of government. A leader should be one who has positive thinking and advantageous intention towards the country. It's necessary to have police and army to maintain peace in country and this is also a responsibility of government and administration.

Million Wings feels that the common people may not guide or lead but they make decisions. The common people may not make rules and regulations but always make decisions of right and wrong. First measurement of administration and financial management is to increase happiness and satisfaction of people and financial status of country, and international level comes afterwards. According to need of the country, there should be sources of industry, factory, education, occupation, and entertainment. Only those things should be imported which are not available or availability is less in own country. Try to promote things of own country at international level, not only to give importance and motivation to things of other countries. Those things can be exported which are in excess. The more the country is independent, the more powerful it will be in the world. A leader is that who wants benevolence of the country, whose dream is to work for everyone, whose goal and aim is to work for success and happiness of the country. A leader is that who just thinks about the country in every situation. The best leader is that whose sole intention is towards success as a country, to give direction towards progression of happiness and success in managed and authentic ways. Million Wings feels that a natural leader can guide in a better way, as he/she feels and understands every sorrow or happiness, easy or difficult, natural or artificial situation with more positive, arranged, and social ways, to make balanced, impartial, and socially beneficial decisions. This is a natural quality which improves and strengthens with time. If such a leader got right and good teacher, then he sets an example for everyone. Leaders guide the society and country. Leader makes ways and policies for every class of society. A leader is a country's pride for the people of the country. People want that their leader should be an all-rounder, want to see him capable in every situation and phase. A leader is the faith of people.

A leader should be a great personality. People should feel awesome by leaders' thoughts. People want to see their leader active and strong in every situation. People want to see their leader in both cool and strong ways. For betterment of the country, he should be a supporter and motivator and should handle criminals strictly. That is, a leader should be that who can guide well in every situation.

Million Wings feels that a leader should know politics also. The main motto of every leader is to progress country in every direction. But a few wrong and corrupt people try to put obstacles in way of their work. To create misunderstanding between a leader and the common people, they spread negative waves. They find non-genuine weakness and mistakes from policies and decisions of the leader. They bring forward issues of casteism, religions and create an atmosphere of unnecessary fights and disturbthe peace of the nation. Million Wings feels that politics directly has nothing to do with progress of the country. Instead politics is to hold leader at his position. For development of the country, its need is good politics, not politics. Politics is for people. A good leader should make strict policies for these corrupt people so that they can't harm coordination and trust of people and leader. Million Wings feels that whoever is living in a country(may be of any caste, religion, race) are residents of country and their security is a responsibility of the government of the country. Their population may be less but they are part of the country while they are living in the country; their self-respect and life are a responsibility of the leader. People may fight, argue with each other but to take life can't be tolerated in any condition. It's necessary for every leader to understandthat ammunition or gun power can be used for enemies, but it can't be used for our own people; they just have to understand in every situation, maybe with love, or strictly, but not with ammunition. Neither they should have permission to fight with dangerous weapons nor should this be tolerated. An individual should have the right to say one's opinion either in writing or by speaking.

Million Wings feels that a leader should be clear that whenever people have fights or dangerous fights, thenthe first, primary responsibility of police or army is to control people without thinking who is right and who is wrong or who has started it or who is responsible. Riots of people of the country should be handled seriously. As the more people die, the more the issue will become serious. The leader of a country should understand that matters can be resolved, while the person is alive. A war of caste, religion, race is a war of issues, not of weapons. Weapons are just an option for corrupt people and not for innocent people.

It is government's responsibility to protect their citizens from criminals and terrorists rather than common people should pick guns for their self protection. If people do so, it means the leaders and the governments are not able to maintain peace and justice in the country and having no holds to stop crime. Giving guns to common man for self protection must be the last resort, in fact it indicates the end of the nation because many of the citizens will start misusing them soon. So there should not be any law in any country to give permissions to carry weapons to common people, but at the same time the government must ensure the control of criminals to establish peace and law order in the country.

The people should raise voice against common anti-human activities happening anywhere in the world to any people. The killing of innocent people anywhere is wrong and needs to be checked by the rest of the world collectively, no matter what country and religion. Let's end the war and start fighting crimes unitedly.

When a leader has to guide, then he is just a leader whose main intention is of social work and justice. The leader of a country may belong to any religion but he should give respect to all religions. The leader of a country should understand that religion is a collection of views and casteism is human division. Through which we understand the thinking, faith, and living standard of each other, and an intelligent leader collects together the strength of togetherness and moves that in the right direction and helps in providing happiness and success at the social level. The leader of a country should definitely oppose the negative waves and misunderstandings spread by opposition from time to time so that faith between citizen of country and leader should be maintained. The leader of a country should attach to citizens by social media so that enemies of the country can't take advantage of misunderstanding and wrong communication co-ordination. By the means of political strategies, the leader of the country should teach a lesson to people/enemies who have wrong intentions. The priority is to motivate friendly relations at national and international level. But it should be clear to every native that if they try to disturb peace in the country in any way, it will not be tolerated in any condition. On basis of proof, answers can be given to them. Secret and security agencies of the country should also be given concern and high-tech knowledge also so that answers can be given to unpatriotic people.

Million Wings feels that a heartfelt will of every leader is to make the country successful and to increase friendly relations at international level. Politics is helpful to be in position with positive attitude. Then only can he guide the nation.

Million Wings feels that elections should be done in such a manner that there will be least expenditure and least disturbance in the life of the common man. Leaders of every country should deliver their points of view and issues with the help of TV, radio, etc. to the general public. There should be continued presentations on TV and radio regarding views of different parties one month prior to elections so that people should come to know about the thinking, intentions, and policies of different parties and will be able to choose the right leader. There is no need to disturb the daily life of common people, finance of the country, police/security by collecting rush. A person can vote by presenting there and at one place only.

Citizens of a country just want more facilities at lower prices. To want this is right also. While making a budget, government has to fix prices of products/service in such a way that atleast every citizen can get maximum ease/help in fulfilling logical needs of daily life. There is no upper limit of success, passion, needs, etc. Priorities are food, health, education, and security and will remain priority. Other things like comfort, easiness, international products should be increased in a way that logic of priorities will not be disturbed. Million Wings feels that the value of important primary things should be fixed at a minimum according to expenditure done on products during preparation/production of product till delivery to people. Give this information to citizens too so that they will also come to know that it's genuine and there is not much margin and this extra value is going to add to the account of the country for emergency conditions.

Million Wings feels that logical needs of everyone doing average work should be fulfilled and everyone who is doing hard work should get success and passion should be got by those who are passionate, as value of passion has to be paid, e.g. highly standardize cars, costly clothes, costly product/service, etc.

If there will be peace in the country, then only can people live peacefully in the country. To maintain peace, it's necessary to have police and army force. It's not so that we have to attack other countries but it's to protect our own country from enemies. If there will be security at the border, then corrupt and dangerous people who want to disturb the peace of the country will not able to enter the country. To maintain peace inside the country, those of the same country also fight with each other, by which the internal atmosphere of the country may also become tense and unsafe. If there is no police force, then people also do forcefulness, have fights, try to beat or kill each other and even don't bother or care about each other. People do as per their will and entangle with each other, e.g. at traffic lights, if they stop working, then everyone wants to move first and tries to fight. At religious places also, people push each other to move forward. While parking, purchasing tickets at social events, a few people disturb the atmosphere. In these circumstances, police and security force only can control people. Security of the right and cool people and to control wrong people make it necessary to have police and security force in a nation.

Chapter 26
Law

Million Wings feels that law is common sense. Law helps to find solution by human ways. Million Wings feels that everyone doesn't do mistake is not of same level or seriousness. So punishment should be given according to crime.

Every nation has their own law, which is made on the basis of citizens. Most people live comfortably, may do small mistakes. But national and international law is made for those who do serious crime which becomes equal for all. Million Wings feels that just because of a few serious criminals, every common man also has to undergo each and every law and rule. It's true that everyone tries to break rules on getting a chance. It's human nature too. Million Wings feels that when humans are taking rights of animals, then they are unable to do anything. When human is using natural resources for his purpose, they couldn't say anything. When human is roaming here and there in the universe without any permission, then also it's all right. But when a human tries to overtake others' rights and freedom, then obviously others will also not sit quietly. Today children, females, others are also becoming aware and want law and security for their rights and self-respect, and it's right too. Million Wings feels that if a human is unable to follow idealism, then he should atleast follow humanism, and this is the future.

Million Wings feels that there is human law everywhere, every second. Study the law which is useful in daily life as a subject, as the law of any

283

nation will not take lack of knowledge as innocence. There is the same law for flaws that happened because of lack of knowledge. Million Wings feels that most people get to know the law only when some problem occurs with them. A devious person doesn't accept his fault easily, instead coming out of that by finding deficiencies in the law and using those deficiencies to come out of it.

Million Wings feels that a few people use law against each other as a weapon. These people apply penal code sections on each other and entangle each other. Million Wings feels that punishment of serious crimes, like killing an innocent, making someone handicapped, rape, should be even more dangerous than death. This type of crime can be clearly seen by everyone, so no need to give much more time to criminal to clarify his point of view, as criminals should be clear that they will only get serious punishment whenever they are caught.

Million Wings feels that best way to escape from law is to support law. It sometimes feels likethe law is not right regarding a related issue, or we want to change the rule than do this with law and rule. Million Wings feel that every issue in life has so many possibilities, feelings, intentions, and thinking that no permanent and best law can be made. That's why from time to time, amendments in rules and law are done. Million Wings feels that while the intention of a person is not to harm anyone, then everything is allright at personal level. But we have to be right according to human courts too. Human law sees and consider human work firstly and then intention. It's true that once something is done, it can't be changed, but intention can be changed.

Million Wings feels that law in a country is made for protection and security of everyone's rights in the society and nation. Law never stops anyone from doing work but protects and secures rights of people related with that work. While our work is not to betray anyone, then we are right. Million Wings feels that whoever is right according to the present law, he will be taken as right. The rules which are already mentioned in law, issues, and matters are considered according to those only, the human rules and laws which are already present. A person has to answer on the basis of that only. If he is unable to answer, then he is guilty. But if still person thinks that he is right then he has to prove himself right, on the basis of which amendment of rule can also be done.

Million Wings feels that with time, the vision of humans is becoming wider, more genuine and impartial; this is the reason behind amendment of rules and laws. But till the law is changed, then the same rule and law should be followed which is already fixed. Million Wings feels that a few people try to find weakness in the law and take advantage of that. Then what's wrong in this? They are more intelligent and clever and devious than law. To use a weakness of law for personal benefit is human nature and it's important to control these people, and management of human law should think and discuss more widely and fast to make the law stronger.

Million Wings feels that the highest justice also considers compromise of two parties as best. The longest, biggest fights or matters are resolved in seconds if both parties compromise. Million Wings feels that it's better to try to resolve the fights and issues with the help of relatives and friends before reaching police and courts. One who agrees first is not weak; instead he is best. Million Wings feels that sometimes misunderstandings and doubts rise so much that they are resolved only with the help of police and administration and courts. To fight for self-respect and pride is a right of human beings. Million Wings feels that money is just a need or support in comparison to death of innocents or in handicapped situation; the biggest thing is self-respect. It's necessary to understand the self-care which a human can fight for himself is best; no one else can fight in the same way. Today, a lawyer fights for his client with his colleagues and, on the basis of evidence, tries to get justice for his client.

Million Wings feels that there is a difference between normal and special cases. The issues which are related with every human and which require only general knowledge can be understood by any lawyer, who can fight for those cases. But for the issues which are related to special science, there should be special lawyer, special judge, and special courts, e.g. medical issues, related with human life, which are not easily understandable by common person, simple lawyer, simple judge or these may be half understood then these will be more problematic.

Million Wings feels that the medical field is one side and the rest of the world is on one side. It's an important science which wants to provide health and fitness to life to make people comfortable and happy, and a doctor always wants that everyone should become all right through them. That's why Million Wings feels that diseases and treatment related to them are better understood by specialists and specialists can handle related issues and matters more rightly.

Million Wings feels that special medical courts will be the future's courts. Million Wings feels that mostly differences between humans arise because of misunderstandings. Both persons think that they are right and both are unable to make the other understand or both fail to understand and often issues reach physical harms. Million Wings feels that who is right depends on justice working strategy of that time, that who is more near to it.

If any person on basis of his faith, misunderstanding, or less knowledge tries to prove another wrong, the person will not become wrong. In life, every issue/matter has so many possibilities that if we think or discuss on them, centuries may pass.

Million Wings feels that it's not human nature to accept one's mistake. Infact to save oneself and escape is a priority, is natural tendency. Humans accept their mistakes when they don't have any other way to escape. National and international courts make rules by considering thinking differences and fights.

Do amendments in laws so that everyone will get a more secure and managed future and more justified atmosphere. Every decision brings a better atmosphere in society. Life moves towards more civilized and balanced living. Million Wings feels that even being more wrong, doing big mistakes, humans first try to find ways to escape.

Million Wings feel that courts should be a medium through which both sides can get a chance to question and answer each other to solve the matter/problem/issue. As every person can fight better for himself, then anyone else can make others understand personal conditions and activities in the best way. Administration is needed when misunderstanding reaches the level that both sides don't even want to talk to each other or one starts misbehaving. Courts should provide secure a chance for both sides to talk and should give justified decision according to law on the basis of information got from their debate. There will be faster and more right decisions in these types of courts, as when both sides talk face to face, then truth can't remain hidden for a longtime. Million Wings feels that lawyers of both sides entangle the case on basis of possibilities. Because of this, it takes years to get a decision of the case.

Million Wings feels that to clear misunderstandings, both sides have to listen to arguments of each other. Mediator may be any friend, relative, or some intelligent person. Lawyers and courts are the last choice to get justice on human level. Million Wings feels that police, administration, or law provides emergency or primary security. Later on, it's just answering section through papers and all. Till decision, a person can move to one court, then second, and then third for justice. By solving matter/issue with the help of friends or relatives, a person can escape from the long, expensive, and tense procedure of court. But in today's era, no one is weak. Everyone is aware, intelligent, understands rights of law, and knows to fight for his pride and innocence, and this is the best gift of civilization.

Million Wings feels that it's a responsibility of law and administration to control riots and fights in society, nation, and world. The police and security force has power and rights. If they are unable to control unlawful events in society, then how is it possible for common man to control those?

Even after having so many rights, administration feels itself forlorn, then who else will maintain peace in society? Million Wings feels that people have full rights to complain to administration in civilized way regarding their needs and problems. If needed, they can do a strike also but no one has the right to harm government or public property or to disturb working schedule of other departments. Every department knows weakness and problems of their own department and to make government aware of their demands, strike may be needed or done. But if they disturb work of other departments or daily schedule of common people, their own side gets weakness. On disturbing other departments, they also oppose. It's also possible that leaving the primary issue, both departments can start fighting with each other on unnecessary secondary issues, and a new issue may arise. When a department blocks the way, then work of transport department also stops. Life and work of common people also is disturbed. People start becoming annoyed, and instead of supporting strikers, they feel nothing for them and move on, on their way. Because of one department, all may be bothered.

Million Wings feels that every department has to fulfil needs and demands of their department on their own. Other departments and common people have nothing to do with that. Everyone has to handle and operate their own department. Million Wings feels that strike by jamming of roads, railways, etc. is not needed, as just common people are affected by this. If related department or administration is not giving attention then do jam work of employees or heads of the same departments. It should be difficult for them to come out of their offices, not for common people or other departments. If still no one is paying attention or answering their demands, then employees should strike by resting at their own homes, not on roads. Million Wings feels that people are getting tortured in dust and sand on roads and railway tracks and start fighting with each other, and high authorities are sitting comfortably in their offices and persons are discussing comfortably. Million Wings feels that employees of a department should also strike in peaceful and comfortable manner without harming public or government property. Strike infront of offices of high authorities or sit comfortably at home by leaving office work. Police force is also unnecessary, wasting their time and power. If the police force will get out of these issues, then only can they concentrate on serious and important issues related to the society and nation.

Million Wings feels that when a citizen of a nation starts understanding the law and government of the country, his age is about 30–40 years. Before that, he is entangled with his studies, enjoyment, and children. Million Wings feels that need and change of society and nation are better felt by the age of 35–40 years. Before that, people take administration as power, glamour, and pride and are devoted to clearing the examination of IPS/IAS. To feel the possibility and seriousness of administration and intentions of doing everything allright is the right ability. Million Wings feels that the right age for IAS/ICS examination is between 30 and 40 years.

Law of the nation is for citizens of the nation and there is law on every step. Million Wings feels that there are government acts in every field of life, which give surety of protection and security of social life. But all these laws are mostly known and understood when person is entangled in some problem. Law is not a special category; neither should it be special business.

Law should be known in daily life so that people shouldn't even know that they are living life in so-arranged manner.

Law should be felt so easy and comfortable that law for them should not be any burden but it should be felt so attractive and enjoyable that every person should wait for new changes with interest and should understand.

Million Wings feels, what's the use of making law with so much hard work and experience of life, if it is just to keep in books? Law is to increase happiness, and using law only in confusing times feels like a person had not done anything else in life other than breaking rules, regulations, and laws. And later on, it feels like law is used to entangle each other rather than pulling out of problems. Million Wings feels that law related to daily life should be an important part of education in schools and colleges and should be taught in a comfortable manner by means of examples, with the means of mass media. New changes of law (e.g. regarding marriage, traffic, entertainment, families, parents) should be delivered to citizens in arranged and attractive manner.

Some corrupt or bad personality may use weakness of law as a weapon on innocent people. So, if a kind and true-willed person also uses the same strategy to teach them a lesson, it's not wrong. It's exactly right and logical. If non-genuine people use this power as weakness of law for their benefit, then it's totally right for a genuine person to use this strategy; it's patriotism.

Million Wings feels that great laws are naturally common activities of human. It's important to publish these in bold and attractive manner at public places, where these are easily visible, e.g. in police station on fights or using miswords, the case will be registered under which section? On breakage of hospital, what would be the penalty and punishment? It should be paid for, if doing misbehaviour at a public place. It's the responsibility of government to deliver law in interesting manner to the public with the help of mass media, TV, movies, digital media so that it should not look strange or burden citizens in daily life. If someone is right according to common sense but seems not to be right according to law, still he can escape from serious law results. It's true and right too.

Chapter 27

Health

Health means to manage ourselves. Million Wings feels that health means self-dependence, in other words, independence. Health doesn't only mean healthy or not diseased; infact health means to take care of ourselves and to be able to do our own work. If person is independent for basic/main needs of life, then he is healthy. He may be physically or mentally sick or tense. Million Wings feels the best stage of being healthy is being totally healthful and happy physically and mentally.

Million Wings feels that everyone has to develop oneself in such a way that one remains healthy and doesn't get sick. Million Wings feels that no one wants to be sick knowingly. Everyone wants to enjoy and wants to remain away from problems, tensions, burdens, diseases too and think and to do this is right and logical too. Million Wings feels that everyone has a right to live more and more healthily in life. No one can stop/alter natural hazards or diseases but can apply barriers or reduce diseases which occur because of human factors. Million Wings feels that cause behind the disease may be any, i.e. natural or man-made, but we can try to manage those diseases. At national and international level, there are various branches for various diseases which can be treated, or comfort can be provided. That is, a person can be independent by getting proper treatment. Million Wings feels that there are various treatments available at national and international level. Get the disease treated by authentic treatment. In serious and dilemma diseases, take the advice of two to three specialists. Contact the specialist concerned, surgeon, and investigator. Disease can be located soon if there will be good coordination between patient and doctor. Patient has to deliver the right and best knowledge as per their knowledge, and the doctor has to do his best as per experience, knowledge, and investigation to treat patient.

Million Wings feels that healthy person needs a balanced diet, good amount of rest in his daily busy and working schedule. Food is not to eat first and then to digest it; instead it fulfils many needs of the body. For development and doing daily work, humans need energy, which we get from food.

Million Wings feels, eat food as per your work, as extra food is deposited in the body and causes obesity. If food is imbalanced, the body weakens, and if eaten in excess, it causes obesity and diseases. The body gets energy andstrength from building blocks (protein, fats, carbohydrates), and all this we got from food (wheat, pulses, grains, egg, and milk). The body becomes beautiful by micronutrients (vitamins and minerals) which we get from fruits and vegetables. The body is purified by water. If a person wants energy, then he has to eat building blocks. If person wants to look beautiful too, then he should eat micronutrients too. Million Wings feels that every human wants to be strong along with beautiful, for which he needs all the nutrition, building blocks, micronutrients, and water in right amounts. Whatever will be eaten will definitely affect body and mind. Whatever will enter our body, may it be natural or synthetic, chemical particles will do work according to their action, may it be beneficial or lethal. Today, humans have collected enough knowledge with the help of science and technology about available food (solid and liquid), regarding the need for it according to age and schedule. Every person should collect minimum required knowledge of balanced diet according to schedule and need so that we can eat food according to likes and in right amount and remain healthy so we can enjoy life fully, to maximum extent.

Million Wings feels that the mind and body become fresh by sleeping. Day is to work and night is to sleep. Infants should sleep for 12–14 hours, children should sleep for 8–10 hours, and elders should sleep for 8–6 hours. Atleast in night every natural constituent gives signal towards rest and is helpful in doing so. When it starts darkening, it's the start of night, and when light starts suppressing darkness, this means day starts growing. Million Wings feels that from 11 p.m. to 5 a.m., it's the naturally best time to sleep. Humans always want to extract maximum benefits from everything. So a person has to choose best beneficial time to sleep also. That is sleep by atleast 11p.m. and wake up maximum by 8 a.m.

Person can remain awake for seven days and two nights maximum in a week, for work and enjoyment etc., and then try to catch up on his rest and sleep within a week. By taking minimum required rest, person can remain healthy, fit, and fresh. Million Wings feels that in a year, a person can be awake a maximum of three months. Reason may be professional, personal, or compulsion but try to fulfil demand of rest and sleep by body in one week, one month, or maximum in one year.

Million Wings feels that for general fitness it's enough to have good and balanced diet, sleep, and working schedule. Exercise is required when a person wants extra flexibility, strength, and stamina. Million Wings feels that physical demands of the body are the same according to passion or profession. Everyday, a person has to work in almost the same way and body becomes habituated to that schedule and work. That's why it doesn't need to do extra exercise in daily routine. If a human wants flexibility, then he can do a bit of exercise also, e.g. walking, physical exercise so that hands, legs, feet, arms, neck, wrists remain flexible, and if it requires sudden dance or walk etc., then it will remain easy. If a person wants to gain physical strength, then he should do heavy physical exercise. In these types of exercise, food should contain extra nutrition, specially proteins, and doing exercise against weight is helpful in physical growth. If a person wants to increase strength, then he should do repetitive exercise, e.g. running, jogging, swimming. Monthly exercise can be increased slowly in a planned way and can be done 4–5 days a week so that the body can get healthy benefits for muscles also.

Million Wings feels that for exercise (running, jogging, etc.) the best place is a park / joggers' park, as here a person feels good and can do exercise for a long time because of the atmosphere of exercise all around. The biggest disadvantage of doing exercise alone at home is an individual getting bored, and exercise can be continued for a few days only, not for a long time. Real enjoyment of doing physical exercise is with friends in gym. Million Wings feels that according to professional or physical demand, a person can continue exercise for a long time. Persons whose hobby, passion is playing or whose profession is playing can continue exercise for a longtime and can take advantage of that.

When a person gets sick and it becomes important to exercise, then it's not possible to exercise and it becomes compulsion too. Million Wings feels that exercise can be enjoyed while health is maintained and these are those exercises which help in fighting against disease also.

Million Wings feels that in reality yoga is used to exercise various parts of the body. The body becomes more flexible. Million Wings feels that dance and sports are such an entertainment which gives enjoyment along with health. If a person is passionate for sports and dance is their profession too, then it's a double benefit. Million Wings feels that making a child passionate for dance and sports is the secret of their physical and mental fitness. Million Wings feel that exercise means to utilize our power and bodies ourselves. There is no use for that exercise which vibrates humans; that exercise is beneficial only when a human himself moves the machine. Million Wings feels that to do exercise only those machines are useful which have atleast some part of strength and power.

Million Wings feels that obesity is an enemy of both humans' beauty and health. There is not one single use of obesity; infact it gives birth to one after another disease and makes the life of a human hell. Everyone's weight can be easily controlled according to age and height, and a person has to maintain weight 10 per cent above or below required value. Those people who take proper meals morning, afternoon, and evening or night-time mostly don't get obese as mostly these people who want to become slim by leaving outfood at one time usually eat more at another time and become more obese instead of getting slimmer.

Million Wings feels that by eating food at the right time, a person usually eats that amount of food he really requires. Million Wings feels that obesity is a reason for many diseases. A person has to eat food according to his requirement and not eat more foods and then do exercise to digest that food. Obesity doesn't occur by eating at the right time or can be in less. God has made food for every organism/creature so that it can grow/develop and can get energy and strength, and God made a strategy to avoid its misuse. It's natural to become sick by eating less and even by overeating a person can get disease and will die. Eating according to need is health. Balanced diet is health and happiness and long life.

Million Wings feels that food which is less tasty maintains person's slimness and food which is tastier causes obesity. A person can't eat tasteless food for a longtime and can't resist getting tasty food for himself for a longtime. It's a reality of obesity. Obesity due to diseases can be corrected by medicines. But obesity due to overeating can be corrected fast by exercise. By doing exercise, a person becomes strong along with becoming slim. But medicines used to reduce weight or to become slim can cause weakness in a person. Exercise done after doing jogging for 15 minutes helps in reducing weight. So to reduce weight, a minimum 30–45 minutes of exercise is a must.

Million Wings feels that no one can stop natural diseases. But those diseases which occur only because of own mistakes can be definitely controlled and should be controlled, e.g. road accidents, use of high dose of drugs and illegal things. In road accidents, mostly small injuries can occur but sometimes cause serious hazards to life also. While you are on the road, it's important to take note of important rules, as road accidents can change life in seconds. Thousands and lakhs of lives change to deaths because of road accidents. Sometimes life becomes worse than death. Serious injury of brain or backbone can make a person permanently handicapped, which neither allow a person to live normally nor allow the person to die. Million Wings feels that safety is priority on roads. Afterwards there can be enjoyment or other commitments. It's not right to drive after consuming drugs or when a person feels sleepy, as while person is in a drowsy state, he is unable to make even small decisions, which can increase possibility of major accidents. Yes, it's enjoyable to drive fast, but if it's necessary to handle the vehicle urgently, it may cause a problem and accident may occur even while trying to control the vehicle.

Million Wings feels that losing life in a road accident feels like just wastage of life. Often people escape striking each other but stop and start fighting and it feels like big stupidity. On roads if persons are saved from accident, then it's better to move on their way rather than fighting as traffic rules can't be taught while moving on roads. Instead only quarrels can occur, as on the spot, instead of clearing things, people start misbehaving, using miswords. Because of this, no solution can be gained; instead only fights increase.

Million Wings feels that on roads everyone feels that they are right and this can be decided only with the help of CCTV cameras on roads. Who is right and to what extent and who is wrong to what extent? Million Wings feels that there should be cameras in every accident-prone area so that mistakes can be judged in road accidents, so that more right decisions can be made and can be managed in future.

Million Wings feels that persons who drive after having used any drug should not be spared as, not only for themselves, they can be dangerous for other innocent people too. Mistake may be of anyone in road accident, but innocent persons are also harmed. If anyone misbehaves again and again on the road, then it's better to inform traffic police instead of fighting or arguing with them, and move oneself from there. In road accidents, if you feel you can, then do help. But firstly make video, take a few clips of the incident and then help them. Give information to the nearest hospital, police department, security and social organizations. Million Wings feels that moving on your own side is the best safety rule.

Million Wings feels that yes, drugs give enjoyment to the body but if used within limits. But consuming alcohol, tobacco, etc. more than capacity makes a person sick. Because of use of these things, liver and lungs can get so damaged that it may cause tension and worry in daily life schedule. It becomes tough for the person to live comfortably and to treat it requires help of people and finance and the person feels irritated while doing so. In treatment, a doctor can try to cure disease and provide comfort but the body can't be regenerated as ever before. When a person is using drugs for a longtime, then the person falls sick and it also becomes tough to treat fully and this too can happen in progress slowly.

Million Wings feels that a use of drug before the age of 16 to 18 years won't allow the body to develop fully. Because of this body is entangled with many diseases. If forcefulness is done to the body before its full development, then it will be damaged, then it can't be corrected. And if the body is damaged/sick before 18 years, then how can a person fully enjoy that moment which he will able to do after the age 18? If persons will remain fit, then only can theyenjoy life. Otherwise they will miss that enjoyment which they are going to enjoy later on in life, and hope and strength will be destroyed. Alcohol and tobacco should be taken in an amount that will give enjoyment, not give more sorrow and pain. So wait till the age of 18 years to consume alcohol and tobacco. And if you want to consume it, then get full information of safety limits; that's how long and in what doseit will not damage the body, and use in that way only.

Million Wings feels that drugs should not be used as inebriants. Drugs are invented and used to set humans free from diseases. To banish problems/diseases, humans invented drugs. But a few people use drugs for enjoyment or show people the wrong way to live happily. Doing this is totally wrong; use of drugs just for fun and enjoyment should be banned. Government, administration, police department should take strict steps for them, and stopping this by giving serious punishment is very important. A person can be treated by giving medical aid when he falls sick by use of inebriant. Those who want to come out of use of inebriants should be helped and motivated to leave it. Beating addiction becomes easy with the help of ownones and doctor. One can surely come out of any sort of addiction, may it be taken in more amounts, may it be taken for a long time. It just requires willpower to beat addiction.

Million Wings feels that awareness regarding health management should be given at social level also so that knowledge and understanding of people should increase regarding important issues of health. So instead of getting sick, they remain healthy by taking precautions and by being aware. There should be awareness program in the country as per need. Needy and intelligent people with positive attitude should surely get benefits from that.

Million Wings feels that if there is a faithful relationship between doctor and patient, then treatment can be done in a fast and good way. Only registered doctors should be certified for treatment. Doctors who are fake or fooling people, without any degree, on the basis of their own thinking should not be tolerated, as the thinking of sick/ill persons becomes so that they can be fooled by fake promises and people get stuck in those fake promises and waste their time, money, and health.

Allopathic/Ayurvedic treatments are certified therapies and these are taught in good education systems, and registered and certified degree is given to them. It's a right of patients to ask about the degrees of doctors anytime. It's very beneficial if a patient will give the complete and right information of his disease. When doctor and patient meet with full trust and responsibility with each other, then it becomes easy to manage disease. Sometimes it happens that disease can't be fully treated but some comfort can be given. It's in the doctor's hands to treat every disease. Some diseases can be treated in early stages, but on getting late, they take such serious form that it becomes difficult to control them. If a patient is not satisfied with one doctor, then he can get advice from another doctor. If still patient feels unsatisfied, then it's advisable for him to get an opinion from a higher institute of the state/nation. Certified and registered doctors never want to harm patients knowingly. Most of the time, diseases suddenly take a serious form. Not all diseases can be controlled, even on giving the right treatment at the right time. Complication in treatment can occur even at higher institutes at national and international level. Patients choose doctors according to comfort and capacity, and the doctor tries his best according to his knowledge, capacity, and experience to treat disease.

Million Wings feels that a person should get treatment of disease from a specialist doctor, and the doctor should also treat patients of own field only. For surgery, choose experienced and specialist doctor.

Million Wings feels that a doctor should deliver all available information related to disease and treatment to a patient and let the patient decide himself which treatment he wants to adopt. The doctor should not decide for the patient and instead should help him to choose his treatment according to his condition and capability. A doctor can take a risk for a patient only if the patient agrees to take the risk, as sometimes diseases become complicated during treatment. Because of this, there may be tension and arguments that take place between doctor and patient. A doctor has to give full information regarding related dangers and complications, and if the patient understands and agrees to take the risk for treatment, then only should the doctor take the risk to do work; otherwise advise him to get advice from another doctor or institute. A few emergency diseases or emergency complications may arise by which diseases may worsen. Sometimes it may be very dangerous, e.g. serious allergy from some medicine, shaken and weak mentality of patient, losing balance and becoming more serious, heart attack because of intolerance of disease or sudden complication of disease. In these conditions, patient may die even on getting full treatment. In these conditions, the atmosphere may worsen and become unsatisfactory, and a patient starts blaming and fighting with the doctor.

Million Wings feels that doctors don't want to kill patient knowingly. If a patient doesn't get well, then it's first meaning is not that it's the doctor's fault or mistake; instead, the first reason is taken as seriousness of disease. In these conditions, if the atmosphere worsens, then doctor and patient should firstly inform police instead of fighting with each other and let police manage and send patient body for post-mortem so that the real cause of death should be clarified.

Million Wings feels that Ayurveda is the oldest treatment therapy. All other treatments are derived from Ayurveda. For centuries till now, Ayurvedic treatment has been used to treat diseases. Allopathy, which is also derived from Ayurveda, is developed according to modernization and with the help of technology and research, new chemicals, machines, and helps in treatment of diseases. Allopathy treatment works faster and in emergency conditions.

Million Wings feels that worldwide, allopathy works on the basis of clearer and research-based issues. In emergency conditions, allopathy works fastest, and all other therapies act slowly and act well on long-acting diseases. Million Wings feels that if an allopathic doctor says no to curing a disease, then a person can try other -pathy also. Nothing's wrong in doing so as a ray of hope gives moral support to life. Million Wings feels that allopathic doctors advise for operation or advise only to give comfort, not to cure fully, then most of the time they are right. Allopathy mostly gives explanations on the basis of practical explanations which are certified.

Million Wings feels that every human wants authentication and proof of everything. In the same way, treatment should be started. Science and technology take steps in better direction only. There may be slight differences in different hospitals or differences of expenditure, but the main line of treatment is same. If a disease keeps on growing even after medical aid and expenditure is also more and possibility of life is less, then let the disease grow naturally, and taking care of the patient is not wrong. If the condition of the patient worsens even after having the best treatment, then it's right to stop treatment and give only that treatment which will provide comfort to patient.

Million Wings feels that treatment is to treat person from sick to normal. Sometimes sudden adverse effects of medicine can occur, which are natural. In these conditions, to correct/handle the problems is the urgent work strategy, not to blame disease, treatment, doctor, or relatives at the time. Million Wings feels that no one wants to harm patient or worsen disease knowingly; instead it can happen even after lots of efforts. It's a truth of efforts.

Million Wings feels that if we compare all professions, a profession only related to treatment is related to life. And it has to be seen as not just an emotional point of view; instead it's important and must be seen through the point of view of a doctor/specialist also. Disease and treatment is special science and education. It should be observed and inspected by special courts and lawyers who have rights and full information of treatment. In life, all issues can be settled by exchange of money, but if misunderstanding related to death of a patient arises between doctor and relatives of the patient, then it's very hard to make them understand and it becomes a causeof lifelong annoyance and persons can't recompense life. That's why treatment should not just be compared by emotional views only and a doctor should not be judged only on the basis of emotions. Instead, a decision should be made under guidance of special lawyers in special medical courts. In emergency conditions, a patient's condition is very serious, so a doctor has to make very fast decisions. In these situations, a doctor has to handle apatient and try to save him, and along with this, he has to handle common people related to the patient and needs to let them know about possible complications and expenditure also. This situation is very complicated for the doctor, as the patient is sick and relatives are confused and those people who came along with the patient are not responsible as per law. And money is also not there on time. In these situations, if adoctor treats a patient without the will of the relatives, then in every way, the doctor is more responsible. Relatives waste precious time in discussions. In emergency conditions, relatives of a patient should give full consent/permission and trust to the doctor to do the best as per requirements, as in an emergency, the biggest energy and courage of a doctor is the trust of the patient's relatives. The doctor should also try to let the patient and his relatives know about the disease and treatment in easy and few words so that they can decide fast.

Million Wings feels that it's very urgent to start treatment in emergency conditions. As the time passes, the condition of a patient starts worsening and possibility of saving his life decreases. A doctor should start atleast very important treatment in emergency to save patient's life. As if life of patient is saved, then only further treatment is possible. That's why every patient should atleast allow to do urgently required treatment so that doctor can try well and confidently to save patient heartily. Once patient is handled, than there will be enough time to discuss about further treatment. In emergency conditions, it's intelligence to start immediately required treatment as treatment can be stopped anytime. But the right decision is to start immediate required treatment on time. When a patient reaches the specialist doctor, then the patient should agree, allow, and motivate doctor to do the best treatment according to need.

Million Wings feels that diseases which are unable to be cured or can just be controlled but if the root cause can't be treated or half treatment is available in present time, then treat the disease as per available treatment as by doing so, doctor and patient both get time and in future, better treatment may be available with the help of research. The better the today, the more the hope of a better tomorrow.

Million Wings feels that diseases are such enemies which require both medicines and dietary management. Germs and microbes of diseases are so small that it's impossible to catch and kill them; neither can disease be cured by fighting with and beating ourselves. Diseases can be treated by treatment and medicines. A patient has to be courageous and bear up himself, and he needs the support of his own ones. Million Wings feels that in sickness, a patient has to contact and discuss with the concerned doctor and get treated. But if the disease is not curable and the patient becomes forlorn, then adopt best available ways and treatment of being independent.

Million Wings feels that government should provide/insure free treatment of natural and human diseases which are serious and emergency. There should be relief services in the society and nation in all health-related conditions. If citizen feels safe and secure regarding free emergency health service, then surely he will live in a happy, plausible and tension-free atmosphere. Million Wings feels that emergency is health and if citizen feels secure regarding life-taking emergency like heart attack, serious accident, then a big tension of citizens will be banished. Government and administration of country has to ensure/provide treatment for a few life-taking events in private and government hospitals which require immediate treatment.

Million Wings feels that seven actions and reactions of the body should not be controlled. Sneeze, vomit, urine, potty, fat, belch, hiccough are those actions of the body which eliminate poisonous and harmful substances from the body. These actions have no fixed time. Whenever a person feels any of the above, he should respond immediately. If the action/reaction is more than normal, then concentrate on food and diet. Million Wings feels that if a person is unable to utilize best time (11 p.m. to 5 a.m.) for sleep, then it's allright but in 24 hours get proper sleep (6 to 8 hours), even maybe in daytime.

Million Wings feels that human can use anytime to take proper rest (sleep) but the best benefit can be taken between 11 p.m. to 5 a.m. It's that time which nature is providing to everyone to sleep. Million Wings feels that night can be converted to day. If it is so, then use day as night to take rest and refresh body and mind.

Million Wings feels that a person lives his life freely but when it's about forlornness or the death of a near and dear one, obviously he becomes tense and sad by thinking the same again and again. Everyone becomes sad by thinking about death. It's not because he will die but he thinks what his family would do without him. Because of this thought, he becomes busy in earning more and more money and the person becomes stuck in this circle. Today he does hardwork day and night and spends money for future security. Today's happiness decreases or dies because of tomorrow's happiness. If a person is set free from tensions of death, forlornness, serious diseases, and tense time than his today and tomorrow both will be filled with happiness.

Million Wings feels that a person can make urgent resources with the help of different insurance policies. With the help of health insurance, education insurance, death insurance, and life insurance of family members, the future can be made more secure. These security insurance can be made active with just negligible amount of money. Tough times related with disease, forlornness, and death can be made easy with the help of insurance policies. With the help of insurance policies, a person can set himself free from doing more work day and night to earn more money. By working for 6–8 hours, an average person can earn enough money which he can use freely for daily needs, dreams and desires of family. Government should make sure about insurance policy for tough times only, not to get benefits by this strategy. If a person spends the earned money on healthy food, living standard, safety, and enjoyment of family, then obviously, chances of falling sick may decrease or vanish. Everyone will live more healthy and happy. And this is the motto of every human being. Live for the future in such a way that today will also be filled with happiness. A beautiful future will make today beautiful. If today is happy and plausible, then there are more chances of healthy and beautiful future. But if today is tense and unhealthy, then we never know if the future comes or not. Million Wings feels that today filled with health and enjoyment will provide the same future too. Live today in such a way that the future will also become beautiful and plan the future in such a way that there will be an atmosphere of happiness all around. It's right management, it's right policy, it's happiness.

Million Wings feels that being healthy, a person can feel every happiness. A sick person will live a tense life. But if a person is healthy, then he can well manage even in tough times. An individual should try his best to maintain his health and the health of near and dear ones. Healthy persons can concentrate more on every use of life. But if a person is unhealthy or forlorn, then obviously he will feel sad and broken and he is unable to concentrate on other matters. Everyone should do one's best efforts to maintain one's health and the health of near and dear ones. Contact doctor immediately on any kind of suspicion or disease. All other works are secondary or can be managed somehow. Priority is health and the rest of work can be managed on secondary parts. Priorities should not compromise health in any condition. Arrange things according to own capability near and dear ones' health. Logical treatment is to maintain health.

Million Wings feels that along with maintaining own or near and dear ones' health, while working for their disease and problem, if an individual is somehow managing time for own dreams and desires, it's not wrong. Availing of minimum required services and treatment is logical management. If someone is seriously sick at home, along with taking care of him, if a person is managing his own dreams, it's right, logical. If individual is availing of service and treatment by himself or with the help of business strategy and he is managing time for it, by doing so he is doing right. To be sad in someone's sorrow that person himself falling sick is not right. Neither is it necessary nor it is compulsion as worldliness. Managing work for ourselves is not wrong. In long-term diseases (chronic diseases), being with your near and dear ones and managing minimum happiness and enjoyment of oneself is right, is logical, is happiness.

Million Wings feels that there is a very easy way to escape from common diseases: washing hands properly before eating. Microorganisms causing diseases can spread in atmosphere by sneezing or coughing.

Million Wings feels that every individual wants the best time, opportunities, things, and partner for himself and will always desire same. Humans are using the best things from the whole universe for their best in the best way and will keep using these also. Today is better than yesterday and tomorrow will be better than today. It's right and a truth of humans. Million Wings feels that life can change in seconds. Humans become forlorn infront of natural problems and hazards. Natural powers like storms, winds, tsunami, lava, rain, summer, winter, lightning can destroy humans in seconds. Natural allergies and diseases can make human life hell in seconds. To save and control these natural problems and hazards, humans have to do common efforts with the help of science and technology. Otherwise, natural powers can arise from anywhere and become active and can take serious form and can destroy whole human life in seconds. If the whole human species can work together, then they can surely find some way. The whole human species has lots of brains, lots of plans. If all minds can get together, then surely the universe can be understood faster and more easily.

Million Wings feels that to maintain health, a human lives for his happiness, has to live for his betterment and enjoyment. But he needn't do anything forcefully or tensely, has to eat and drink well. Eat that amount of food which can be easily digested. Sleep as per requirement busy.

Meditation is total clearance and coordination of body and mind. Meditation is clear coordinated spirituality. Being definite is not being right or wrong. Neither is it related with disease or health. Instead it means being fully clear and agree to themselves, whatever they think, whatever they do.

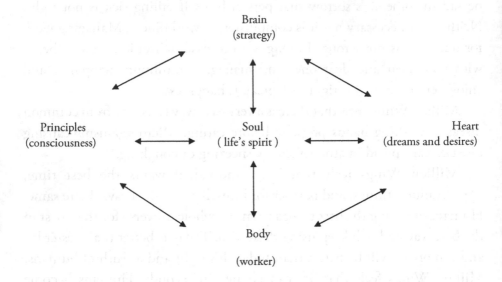

Meditation
A clear and doubtless state of self

Meditation is being right for ourselves, being clear according to ourselves. The form of meditation is cleared for ourselves. Every second, every day we do meditation only. Every action which relaxes us and gives peace of mind is meditation. In the state of meditation, whatever persons do, do tension free and with will or we do everything to take ourselves into a state of meditation. Meditation is not a thoughtless situation. Meditation is a doubtless condition of body, heart, and mind, and when a person is clear and coordinated according to himself, then a person feels motivated and filled with positive power. Chances of happiness, satisfaction increase in every work and working strategy.

Million Wings feels that a doubtless situation of ourselves is meditation; this means a person should not have any doubt or puzzlement as per his mind, heart, and soul. Every individual knows about himself, who he is. What is his desire? What type of thinking has he? Whatever is the level of his physical health and whatever type of person he is, he knows himself very well. Now firstly we have to make sure whether the person is in a state of meditation or not. It's very easy to confirm so. Mostly people are so busy in their lives that they are unable to understand/clarify their intention, curiosities, desires, work, work strategies, happiness, doubts, etc. Million Wings feels that self-analysis is the best way to know ourselves. By self-analysis, a person will get to know about his real doubts, deficiencies, problems. Mostly people do self-analysis everytime while doing work etc. and live their life.

Million Wings feels that every person does self-analysis and meditation on a daily basis, but if they will do self-analysis in total cut-off relaxation, then their meditation will get clear direction and motivation. Most people do self-analysis while doing work or being busy somewhere else, i.e. ongoing self-analysis. This ongoing self-analysis is logical and right.

Million Wings feels that in busy life schedule, an individual is unable to think much on every issue of life, i.e. unable to do complete self-analysis. This happens because the surrounding atmosphere diverts the mind and because of this, the individual is unable to think more possibilities. Million Wings feels that if the mind is least diverted and no distraction or confusion is there, then obviously he can think better and widely regarding his conditions and can make better decisions and can choose better work strategies and can achieve a state of meditation faster. Million Wings feels that has made a comfortable way and technology of self-presence, by which an individual can get total relaxation and self-analysis.

Million Wings feels that if individual has done self-analysis in a beautiful and comfortable way, then he can recognize himself fast and the possibility of happiness will suddenly increase. Million Wings feels that by self-analysis, a person will get to know whether he is in a state of meditation or not. If he is in a state of meditation, then he is happy and should live freely, has to live as life is showing the way. If a person feels that there is any doubt, tension, curiosity in any of directions, then the person will achieve meditation state soon by understanding that clearly and settling the concerned matter; clarity and satisfaction in all directions is meditation. Million Wings has made an easy way of self-analysis so that a human can understand himself easily. For self-analysis, it's important that he should stop doing work, whatever he is doing. Be in a maximally comfortable position as you can decrease gravity to maximum extent to which it can be decreased. The more our body is near to zero, the more it will be comfortable. Take our minds away from live signals of the world just by closing our eyes. We are cutoff from the whole world. By closing our eyes, it hardly matters that where we are at home, at the office, in a park, in a jungle, at the mountains, in a hermitage, on the road, or in an open or closed area. It hardly matters what colour and type of clothes a person is wearing. A person should wear clothes according to his likes and comfort. Comfort means fewer problems while sitting, standing, walking, and the body should get more comfort. The less the surrounding noise/disturbance, the better it is so that there will be less live signals to disturb us least. A person should cover his ears or a disturbing voice should convert to a melodious voice, like melodious relaxing music.

Like this, the body will be in a complete comfortable position and the mind will cut off from disturbing social signals and will start thinking and observing about own four directions. Analyzing each and every situation and condition of heart, mind, and soul is self-analysis. Like this, a person will investigate coordination between his mind, heart, and soul and will search for, locate, and eliminate doubts, problems, tensions, and curiosities according to their level. These are the issues on which the person needs to think, discuss and will try to clarify them and this is the direction towards meditation. If a person is tense, is physically unfit or because of unhealthy physical state, then he has to know, understand and will have to gain healthy state. This is meditation. If a person gets to know about his dreams and desires, then he has to collect information and reserves to fulfil them, and this is meditation. If a person is having problems in making a strategy to fulfil his dreams and desires, then he has to contact experienced specialist and should make strategy to achieve them; this is meditation. If person is confused by self-consciousness, then he should contact prominent far-sighted people and should overcome these situations; this is meditation.

Self-analysis is the first guidance for meditation. Life is meditation. Those who achieve a state of meditation become tension free. All this is meditation. Sitting peacefully is part of self-analysis, and by this, a person gets the right direction towards meditation. Whatever a person doesthe whole day is meditation. If a person is clear for himself and every person lives life in a coordinated way, then that's the state of meditation. If person has no doubt, problem, confusion, then what's the need of doing meditation separately? Whatever he is doing is meditation for him. Every person can do self-analysis easily. Million Wings feels that self-analysis is very beneficial and a comfortable process for every human being. A person who is happy will get comfort and one who is unhappy will get ways to achieve their happiness.

Million Wings feels that to understand ourselves by self-analysis is to achieve wings of happiness. By self-analysis, a person will get to know about his doubts, confusions, curiosities, dreams, and desires and then clearly determine his dreams and then it's easy to work in the right way and right direction which is called meditation. The process of self-analysis is not meditation; instead the main logic is to check whether meditation is moving well or whether it needs clear directions or power is required. A person wants to be self-satisfied and have a coordinated life free from tensions, by which the sky of life looks wider and more beautiful. In a state of meditation, a person feels a graceful freedom. In reality, self-analysis is meditation by which an individual gets to know about his desires, interests, and dreams and starts understanding real problems and starts working them out. A goal of a human's life is his own dreams and desires. Through this, a person gets the real meaning of his life and by clear once of this, he gets direction for his work and working strategy.

Million Wings feels that forcible concentration can't be raised; neither can anyone compel another to do so. Concentration arises from interest, concentration arises from need, concentration arises from demand, concentration arises from curiosity, concentration arises from responsibility, concentration arises naturally. Actual concentration is natural concentration which arises by itself in a person. One can't raise artificial concentration in another by any way/thinking. It's not so that it's difficult, impossible to raise concentration in individual. But concentration can only arise if the person himself has interest or curiosity for the same work. Only then can he concentrate on that thing/work/project feeling.

Million Wings feels that either concentration arises by itself or a right guidance can raise concentration by awareness about personal benefit and happiness. Concentration is that power secret which can help in fulfilling dreams and desires faster. Concentration is positive attitude. Concentration is shortest, fastest and an easy way to achieve happiness. Concentration is perfection, concentration is capability, concentration can convert impossible to possible, concentration is speciality, concentration is craziness which fills personal happiness with power, speed, and success.

Chapter 28

Relaxation

Million Wings feels that the real meaning of rest is to take mind, body, and soul in workless position; that is, to take ourselves in position towards zero work done. Million Wings feels that sleep is the best way to rest. Sleep is that action in which the body merges in a situation towards maximum gravity. Together mind and heart do minimum work, and soul is always in action. Sleep is state of maximum possible complete rest. Complete rest gives maximum energy and comfort to person.

Million Wings has created a relaxation technique which can be done anytime, anywhere by all. The technique is called total cut-off relaxation technique. It leads to conscious relaxation. Million Wings feels that just a little relaxation and being with self enlighten our inner powers. Self-analysis is an excellent, more intelligent way of finding solutions for our happiness. The main fundamental is to relax body, heart, and mind. First step is to cut off body loads by putting it in a relaxed state. The body becomes relaxed only if not in action, and that can be created by positioning the whole body in the gravitational attractions. If our body will be totally in line with gravity, all the muscles will be in inactive and neutral position. One should opt for a maximally comfortable position with support whatever it may be, e.g. lying on the ground or a relaxing chair. Second step is to cut off from the visuals, and a simple step is to close eyes, maybe with dark cloth for better effect. Third step is to cut off noises from surroundings by means of plugging ears, maybe with cotton or by listening to instrumental relaxation musicof your choice with ear phones. Million Wings feels that music is a better way to cut off noise because it will help not only blocking outside noises but at the same time help in relaxing the heart and mind. One should preferably use music if possible because it's not easily possible to cut off noises from surroundings. Once all three steps are done, just try to sleep. Total cut-off technique is actually an all-time wonderful method to relax and at the same time is a personal secret test whether we are in a state of meditation or not. If we are in state of meditation, i.e. state of fully coordinated self with world, we will move towards sleep. And if some thought, maybe good or bad, is disturbing us, that is where our happiness lies. And one must try to find out practical satisfactory solutions to that issue or concern.

When a person tries to divert his mind to get comfortable and take rest, then in reality they are diverting their mind's thoughts by which they surely get relaxed for sometime. But complete rest is when a human's mind is doubtless and in a clear situation; that is a state of meditation. This is truth and will remain true. A person phase can feel complete rest with the help of the strategy and way of total cut-off relaxation and start understanding himself more. Self-analysis in this condition is more effective. In total cut-off relaxation, a person is just involved in himself and can get complete comfort, or by self-analysis, a person can get to know about the authentic person in meditation. With the help of total cut-off relaxation, a person is able to achieve/feel both rest and self-analysis in a better way.

Million Wings feels that for peace of mind and soul and to fix mediator situation, a person can use many ways. For complete rest of body, every part of body should merge maximum towards the gravity of the earth. Merging every muscle towards direction of gravity is rest for the body. Relaxation of thoughts means good coordination of feelings of mind and heart. Million Wings feels that a person who is in a situation of meditation will take quality sleep as a signal of the state of meditation, a work which makes/fixes coordination between four powers (heart, mind, body, and soul) action of meditation. By meditation, a human goes into a state of meditation where he can feel/enjoy beautiful and satisfying sleep. Melodious music also gives comfort to the mind. Those actions which help to cutoff signals of awakening situation give comfort.

Million Wings feels that meditation is doing work to achieve doubtless and satisfying situation of mind and soul. Taking rest is not meditation. Infact if a person is in a state of meditation, then he feels comfortable. The greater the state of meditation, the earlier he gets comfort. Total cut-off relaxation is not doing meditation; instead it is an effective way for comfort and self-analysis. Self-analysis is to understand ourselves more clearly, which gives the best moral support and right direction to search for personal dreams and desires.

Million Wings feels that a person surely gets a bit of peace and power by half/incomplete way of rest. Even incomplete rest is better than not taking rest. Whatever, however person is relaxing, refreshing himself, all is good, all is right. But it's also true that complete relaxation is got from quality sleep and there is no alternative for this. Everyone should sleep to take rest. Sleep is the best rest/relaxation. If all four powers of a person are well coordinated, then the person can sleep anywhere. Million Wings feels that average sleep of 8 hours refreshes the human mind and body both. Infants should sleep for 10–14 hours, then naturally their minds sharpen and remain balanced.

Million Wings feels that sleep is the best way to take rest. A person has to take work to increase the quality of his sleep. Persons should take rest for 8 hours. Million Wings feels that day is to work and night to sleep. Time between 11p.m. and 5a.m. is best to sleep as it allows us naturally to sleep where a person can get quality sleep. Mind and body are refreshed completely by taking sleep of approximately 8 hours. Rest is a must for development, health, and long life. Rest provides strength and rest provides a new start. Million Wings feels that a person should concentrate on quality sleep, and if he fails to adopt a comfortable way of sleep, even then he will get full relaxation. A meditative state can provide complete quality sleep. Living by heart is meditation. The security of self-respect is meditation. Meditation is comfort and everything which relaxesa person is meditation. Meditation is clear coordination of ourselves. This is that melodious song (lullaby), which can give deep sleep. That is meditation state is that adorable state which can provide the best sleep. Quality sleep is complete relaxation, and complete relaxation is that freshness, that power, that health which is a vast helper to get adoration fast and in a better way.

☷ ☷ ☷

Chapter 29

Spirituality

Spirituality is communication of soul with soul, a way to merge with the Creator in seconds. A person can look at the whole universe from one place only. By spirituality, a person can be present everywhere at every second. To understand the universe clearly and rightly is to understand God. Spirituality is a special type of concentration by which a person can get to know about his power. With the power of soul, a person can attach to the whole universe in seconds. By physical presence at one place, a person can connect to the whole universe, can feel, can see the whole universe and can understand, can make coordination with the whole, with every creature of nature.

Million Wings feels that by spirituality, a person can adjoin every single particle of nature. With the help of spirituality, a person can understand about the real mind, intention, soul, brain of any creature easily. When a human can see, listen, understand the whole world, then his mind, heart, and soul will become free from doubts, confusion, misunderstandings. Then he automatically becomes satisfied and peaceful, and a spiritual person understands universe and then he understands God also. To understand the secret of the universe is to understand God. Without understanding the universe, a person will never understand God. Rightly understanding the logical motto of the life of every living and nonliving creature is to understand the greatness of God. By understanding the secret of nature, a human will love it, respect it, and then can't stop himself from loving the creator of nature, i.e., God.

Million Wings feels that spirituality is to rightly understand logic and principle of life and the universe. By spirituality, a person gains power to differ from every small particle of the body. By understanding life and creatures, humans get happiness and enjoyment. By spirituality, a person will get to know about logical meaning of life and then it becomes easier, more comfortable, and clearer to live life. Spirituality is not to get away from life, but it's about coming closer to life. Being fully civilized is the first step towards spirituality. By spirituality, life gets balanced guidance. Spirituality is not to get away from sex, anger, affection, ego; instead it's to satisfy them with the best guidance. Spirituality is not to disown life; instead it's the way to live life more logically and happily. Humans can get God by living in this world. Spirituality is not to move to jungles/mountains by leaving the world. Humans can understand God by living life in the same world. Spirituality is not living alone. Spirituality is not about avoiding social sorrows. Spirituality is not just one way to get God. Spirituality is to control one's soul completely. Spirituality is to adjoin ourselves with the whole world. By spirituality, a person can roam the whole world. In reality, spirituality is not to get God. Instead it's to understand God, and to understand God, a person has to understand the secret of life. The one who gets to know/understand the logical motto and principle of life starts moving one's life on the way of redemption. A person who gets to understand the secret of redemption becomes eligible to achieve redemption. Spirituality adjoins a person with the power of soul, by which humans adjoin with the whole universe through soul. It becomes easier to understand the whole universe better with the help of the power of soul.

Million Wings feels that one can't merge with God during life; infact by moving towards the secret of redemption though one's work and principles, a person can feel the presence of God all around him and try to collect his capability to merge permanently in God. The secret of redemption is same for everyone, may a person be living a common life or uncommon (special) life. To live life is to achieve quality for redemption. Lifespan may be short or long, may be right or wrong but moving towards the secret of redemption is the only principle to achieve redemption. All creatures of the universe try to make themselves capable of redemption in their lifespan and creature can merge with God only after death. During lifespan, person can't get out from universe and move to God. But capable creatures always feel the presence of God near to them and merge permanently in God after death.

Spirituality is control on soul. No particular position of body is required for spirituality, neither is it a particular word that needs to be said again and again. For spirituality, a person needn't move to a special place, neither is there a need of giving up life. No need to give up basic qualities of sex, anger, affection, greed, ego, neither is it necessary to wear any particular clothes or makea particular form. For spirituality, an individual needs to concentrate on every small part of the body at one point. When the individual feels the soul (operating heartbeats) with full concentration, then he takes it in weightless form. A person doesn't feel the need of the body. A person can be invisible by merging all five contents of body with nature. Feelings of heart, mind, and innerself mix with the soul and enjoy the huge universe and nature by being invisible. Emotional soul power of an individual makes relations with the whole universe, can clearly and authentically see, listen, and feel feelings, emotions, action, reaction of all organisms in the universe. An individual has full control of his soul power. A person can roam anywhere in the universe. Whenever he feels, he can again adjoin the five basic natural particles and can take the form of the body. Spirituality is to gain the power of soul, which is the best way to see the creation of God (universe and nature). To understand the logic and principles of the universe and life is to understand God.

Spirituality is the superpower of full control of ourselves. It's not necessary that a soul can also understood or merge with God. To merge with God, spirituality is must. To feel/understand the presence of God, it's necessary to understand every smallest particle, creature/organism and coordination between them. But souls can't merge with him, being alive. To make ourselves capable of redemption by living life is the logical goal of life. God decides redemption of individual as per his intention of living life. It's true.

Chapter 30

Society, nation, and world

If there will be no one, then who will see/feel our feelings, if there is no one, then how will a person feel pleasant? Who will listen and see whatever human will say and do respectively? If there will be no people than human will be alone. If there will be no difference in thoughts, then how will newness arise? If there will be no people, then there will be no issues, and if there is nothing to do, then how will a person spend his time? Million Wings feels that it's much better to be with humans than with no one. There is no meaning of thinking to move to jungles, mountains alone in search of happiness. Life is to live with people. Today, the human is more civilized than other species, organisms, creatures on earth and this is the main difference between humans and other species. Today, the human is the most powerful not because he is the biggest, most clever, or strongest of all creatures. But the real reason behind this is that all human units together live collectively in an arranged manner and increasing quality and capability of every generation with the help of an education system. That is, telling/sharing their experiences to the next generation by means of education. Humans understand the secrets of life and nature with the help of science and technology, and all humans are moving towards civilization. The meaning of civilization is to respect all creatures. Firstly, humans have to respect humans; then only can humans respect other creatures and try to improve relations with them.

Million Wings feels that the first unit of arranged life is family. There may be any species in universe, everyone has their own family. But managed and arranged coordination of life is a very lovely and happy rule of family, nation, and world. Million Wings feels that the world is because of coordination of different species, and the human is guiding everyone. Now a human has to fulfil his own happiness too and has to take others also towards happiness. This means if a human himself will remain happy, then only can he guide others. The arranged world is made by humans only and humans have to take them to highest level of civilization.

This world is a working area for humans, and there is everything available in this world to fulfil every dream. A human just has to find his ways and has to get his happiness. Million Wings feels, what has to be done to make world happy? Let's see. Who is he who can make the world happy? How is the world made? The world is made up of continents, and continents are made up of countries. Countries are made up of states; states are made up of districts. Districts are made up of cities, towns, and villages. Cities, towns, and villages are made up of societies. Societies are made up of families, and families are made up of humans, i.e. every individual. If everyone will be happy, then everyone in the world will be happy. Million Wings wants the happiness of everyone living in the world and works for that. Happiness of humans is related with issue of humans, and the issue of humans will be resolved only if human will get solution according to their capacity, nature, and desires. Then only can humans live happily.

Society is an atmosphere where we all humans have to live and have to make coordination so that there will be happiness and success in life. Everyone has own priorities, capacities, and desires, and everyone wants to live life according to oneself and one tries also. If a person doesn't have good coordination with society, then surely he has to face many problems. In these situations, persons have to change according to society or live in the same society unwillingly or live tension free as per their own will.

Million Wings feels that if a person wants to live happily than he has to make positive and plausible coordination with society. Otherwise our own or others' mentality has to change or the atmosphere should be changed or both have to be changed. An individual should be clear that he can shift anywhere leaving one place. But there will also be a society. Society is the least atmosphere from whicha human can extract his happiness. Society is the source of happiness; without society, every person is like that garden which has no flowers.

Million Wings feels that either we have to make everyone's thinking according to ourselves or we have to search for, meet the people whose mentality matches with us. Million Wings feels that if we are unable to change thinking of others or unable to switch to a new place, which often happens, then we needn't be sad. Every person has a right to live according to himself, but the only thing is he shouldn't force or betray anyone. There are many people in society of the same mentality, whatever that may be, and alike people are nearby only. We just need to find them, and just in a few days, we will get friends of our choice and nature within the same society, same surroundings. For this we need to meet more and more people in society, need to talk to each other. And while talking, we will meet many people who think like us, who have same intention and desires as us. We can live happily and can enjoy every moment with friends in the same society. Million Wings feels that we can get friends of our choice soon. We just need to search, express ourselves, meet and talk to each other, and then we needn't search for our happiness; it will come by itself.

Every type of people lives in society. Everyone has their own thinking, circumstances, and priorities. Million Wings feels that there may be different colours, forms of people worldwide. But everyone has feelings, emotions, soul, and self-respect, which have the same importance. Million Wings feels that happiness and freedom of every individual is attached with peaceful and secure surroundings and society. It's easy for everyone to movearound, if society is peaceful. If atmosphere is plausible and wide, then individuals can enjoy freely. If atmosphere is serious, terrorism, riots, etc. are going on, then everyone will be afraid of moving out from home. If atmosphere of society is not good, then obviously the life of citizens will also be worse, and if social atmosphere is good, then obviously the life of people will be filled with happiness. It's possible that the atmosphere might be a good and plausible life. But it's very difficult if riots and war in society persist and still personal life is cool, and person is enjoying outside. Million Wings feel that surrounding atmosphere always affects the personal life of an individual; maybe there is not much role of his personal life in society. Everyone should try their best to make plausible atmosphere in society, as society is because of people. Million Wings feels that the first responsibility is of government and administration of country to maintain peace and a secure atmosphere in society. But if citizens themselves are fighting with each other, then it's easy for outsiders, terrorists, corrupt people to take advantage of this. Million Wings feels that it's easy to control outsiders but if citizens are fighting with each other, then obviously it's difficult to beat and control them. Society is because of us, society is because of you. Concentrate on social issues, give your opinion on social issues, and if possible, do take steps regarding issues. Social issues affect the life of every individual in society, e.g. thriving of terrorists, social security of children and girls, adulteration of medicine and sweets, etc. Personal and familiar issues of everyone are personal and secret. In these issues, no one should interfere till the other demands help or while the self-respect of person is not harmed. Every citizen should concentrate on social issues, as by doing so we are creating plausible, free, and secure surroundings for ourselves.

Million Wings feels, join with organizations who are doing good work for society and nation. Help as per capacity and will. Million Wings feels the first meaning of social service is occupational/professional service. Individuals needn't do social service differently. Instead they have to do their own profession and business rightly and neither is it compulsion for every citizen to do social service. The smallest unit of society is family; that is, society starts from family. This means if a person is providing good service to his family that means he is serving society. Helping those who are living alone is another thing. Million Wings feels that help should be done within capacity; you needn't help in such a way that you yourself are harmed or get sorrow or tension in return. Giving food to another baby by snatching food of own baby is not help. It's not respectful to leave own sick parents as they're in pain and helping someone else's parents. There is no meaning of social service if an individual is busy in serving the nation and own family earns to meet them; by doing so, the condition of family (parents, children, partner) will be same as those who have no family and then they will also seek/hope for some another social worker to help them. It's enough to help others for a few hours in a week, two days in a month, and one month in a year. Help others only if you are capable of fulfilling basic needs of your family. If an individual himself moves out to help others for social service, and behind, his family has to ask help for food, security from others, then what's the use of this social service? Either person has to insure minimum fulfilment of needs of his family or has to not make a family so that he can serve the nation tension free. Only those whose dreams and desiresare to serve the nation and want to spend life in serving nation can do so, and this is their happiness. Not everyone can do social service.

Million Wings feels that happiness in society can be maintained if all departments are doing their work properly. If any of the departmentsare not doing their work properly and responsibly, then the general public has a face problem. Every department like health, education, electricity, irrigation, security, transport, farming, industrial, entertaining, and media all are working for citizens of country. Million Wings feels that no department is less or more important; infact every department is necessary and important. Employees of every department should do their work responsibly and with capability; this is the first social service working strategy of every government, and private department should be easy so that services and products should reach people in comfortable ways. It's service of department.

Million Wings feels that there is dissatisfaction and annoyance in every professional department regarding an issue, e.g. regarding pay or recruitments, service and rights. Often employees of different departments do strikes for their demands and rights and nothing's bad in this. Every department has the right to express their anger to government regarding their needs, and nothing's wrong in this. Million Wings feels that every department or employees can do strikes for their demands and rights but no one has a right to harm government, public or private property, neither to disturb the working schedule of other departments or the daily schedule of common man. It's often seen, people of one department obstruct/stop transport and this creates trouble for the general public. And sometimes both departments have quarrel between them and start fighting on a secondary issue, leaving the primary and important issue. Police and road departments often have quarrels and fights with all. General public also doesn't bother much about demands and, seeing road blocked, move to work through some other ways, and instead of supporting them, they show their anger and annoyance and get a busy schedule.

Million Wings feels that it's the responsibility of every department to take care of their own department. It's true that every department is working for betterment and to provide facility to general public. But general public obviously wants service, facilities, and products from other departments and businesses but has nothing to do with their pay, demands, needs. Everyone is so busy in their own lives that it seems to be very difficult or impossible for them to come out of their work and tension.

Million Wings feels that common people/general public collect together only if there is a very serious social issue which creates trouble/problem for everyone. Every department itself has to think about their own problems/issues, not the general public. Every citizen needs service and products to fulfil their need and comfort. If there is any problem/issue in any department, then they should talk to higher authority of their department or government and administration and not to disturb working schedule of other departments or general public. It's true that all departments are working for general public but mostly general public or other departments are not responsible for dissatisfaction and problems of employees of department; infact, employees of their own department, high authority, policies, rules and regulations of government are responsible. Then what's the use of disturbing the general public or other departments? If government, leader, or high authority of department are not listening or understanding them, then instead of blocking trains or roads, they should block their offices and their working schedule and compel them to listen to them. Employees of department should move to their homes and take rest instead of moving to roads in chilly and warm weather and being disturbed. Chosen leader of every department has to take issues/problems/demands to government and has to find satisfactory solution by coordinating with them. It's the right step of an arranged and civilized world towards happiness and success. Million Wings feels that to remember those great personalities who have done something for society, nation, and world is a real tribute to them. Great persons live for others or lived for others. To do this is not any compulsion or need for them. But to do this is their heartfelt will, dream, and desire. Great persons have not done this to get name and fame or to earn money. But this is their first choice and desire. These are those persons because of whom the nation and world get positive attitude, service, and lifestyle gets a beautiful and beneficial direction by which people get happiness in their life. It's not necessary to move to rallies or gatherings. Just remember those to give them tribute. Great personalities never get annoyed as they didn't expect anything. People may not be remembering them but are living life according to their rules, policies, and direction. And it's right too. Maybe it's difficult for every person to remember great personalities. But everyone is able to have enjoyment and live happily because of the guidance of one or another great personality, and this is the right tribute. A motto of great personalities is not that common people remember, but their main motto is to merge their guidance and principles in such a way that even people are also unaware when they have adopted their principles and are enjoying happy living. Great personalities make the lives of everyone enjoyable and happy.

Fighting for the self's rights and the community must be in a maximum of pleasant ways. One should involve people in light, easy, and happy moods. Make strategy in such a way that the jobs and responsibilities for others should beof people's capacity, comfort range, and interest. The best way to fight is dialogues, delivery of concerned issues, and physical violence must be the last resort by default. To win any fight, one should maintain reasonable health or at least survival till victory. Be sincere, not necessarily serious at large. Issues may be of any gravity but action should be in pleasant ways.

Million Wings feels that persons have to adjust their daily schedule in such a way to help the forlorn, helpless, powerless, orphaned, etc. without disturbing their own lives and others should also get some help. Distribute your old clothes and things to the needy equally; if you want to give one, then give that to sick or unhealthy persons, then to infants or small children, then to aged persons, then to females, then to young males, and in the end to animals. Million Wings feels that firstly, as priority, humans have to help humans and try to decrease their problems and sorrows, and along with this, if they can think about other creatures/species on earth, then it's a much better civilization.

Million Wings feels that people who are living below minimum living standard in society are the first responsibility of government and administration, to raise their standard. Providing facilities to the needy is not the main policy; infact providing them ways/things to be independent is logical management. Providing food to the needy once can fill their hunger of one time but permanent problem can be permanently resolved by providing job/work opportunities. People should not choose easy process of begging; infact everyone should earn their living by doing work, and government has to motivate them to do work. Non-government organizations and general public should also help according to their capacity and capability. It's more right to help others after achieving personal logical level. Million Wings feels that it's not important that only financial help is important help. Instead, motivation, guidance, and prayers for individual also provide moral support, which humans can do at any place, any condition, at any time. Million Wings feels that individuals should help others freely, maybe with things, with intelligence, or by praying heartily. It's right, it's logical, it's good.

Million Wings feels that all important things necessary for living are available in the world which are kept in arranged way in all the four directions. If we look according to nature, then it's kept rightly at proper place and we humans have divided nature to countries according to our ways. And because of this, natural things are also divided into countries: crude oil in one country, metal in some other country, farming-favourable atmosphere in one country, and natural beauty in some other country. Like this, natural resourcesare divided into various countries. In short there is no single country which can independently fulfil all requirements of daily life. Now if one country needs crude oil from one country, then another needs metal from other country. Some want food and another wants something else. Like this, one country has to be dependent on another country to fulfil all daily needs of living. A few have brains and another has opportunities, a few have science and technology and another has raw material, a few have manpower and others have natural resources. Needs of all countries are fulfilled by mutual import and export. That's why the whole world can move together, so that people all over the world can live happily and comfortably.

We need international leaders. The leader must have global thinking and should work locally. The leader should have command on common issues of the country and must support global bodies on genuine international concerns. The leader should establish his own country by reasonably modifying the global norms depending on his own country's resources. In all cases, the main aim of the strategies must be overall best management in the interest of the society and citizens.

Million Wings feels that all countries of the world should make good balanced relations with each other so that humans can live united, then only will they be better than all other creatures and organisms. If all people of world will live collectively/united, then only can they guide the whole universe. If humans will live affectionately with each other, then only can they think about other organisms and creatures. If human will live united, in a friendly way, then only can they fight against organisms/creatures and enemies rising against them. Today there are so many organisms which can control a whole human on getting a chance. There are so many creatures who keep on attacking humans. There are so many organisms and creatures which are so small and capable which can attack humans and make them sick and can spread fast and can destroy humans permanently. Humans have understood that a small change of nature can permanently destroy life in few seconds. Water bodies and animals can disturb human life in seconds. Today, humans need to come out of all their mutual fights and have to think and invent good and effective things for themselves so that humans can escape from their enemies. To control them is to save ourselves. Every human has to live according to his will and happiness, has to provide facilities and products to each other so that human life can move in easy and comfortable ways. If humans will keep on fighting with each other, then the hope/possibility of goodness of nation, society, and world will die which is here because of the life of humans. Million Wings feels that today humans are well managed but still need to be more civilized. Civilization was started by humans and only humans can take it to the highest level. Every country on earth has to understand that while they live in cooperative ways with each other, till then life will be easy, comfortable and happy. The day they started fighting and get separated from each other is the same day the power of humansstarted decreasing, and other organisms and creatures will start dominating earth. Today, humans are able to understand nature after living thousands of years and trying to understand more. All other organisms and creatures are still uncivilized. Now humans are able to guide all of nature and creatures, and humans will able to do so if human will remain powerful and if they live united. And to live together, they should behave in civilized and coordinated ways.

Million Wings feels that if anything is common in the family, society, and world, it's relations and emotion: may a human be living in any part of world, he has parents, siblings, partners, friends. Maybe a human is living in any nation or society but has his own feelings, emotions, and dreams.

Every person moves through every phase of life. Society is made by combination of children, teenagers, youngsters, and old people.

Role of children (10–12 years) in society is like the future's atmosphere. Children will develop same nature and thinking, react in same way the type of atmosphere they will get from society and will handle society, nation, and family in same way familiar and social atmosphere have great effects on thinking, direction, and working strategy of life. To give plausible, free, secure, positive, and arranged atmosphere to children is social responsibility. To make a child a responsible and good citizen is the equivalent of making good society. If the atmosphere of society is good, the mentality and attitude of a child will automatically develop well. If the atmosphere of society is insecure, tense, and disturbed, obviously a child will be afraid of all this. Million Wings feels that if the surrounding atmosphere is good, then society will automatically develop plausible atmosphere. The future of the whole society will automatically shine if children will get a positive, free, and secure atmosphere. Children are innocent, helpless, equal for all, ingenuous, and everyone in society should behave in friendly and respectful ways with them so that they can learn and understand behaviour skill every moment at every way to make a beautiful future. Children are equal for all (12–18 years), very soft and sensitive. In this age, girls and boys meet new people with full hope and zest. In this age, girls and boys feel the natural inner physical and emotional feeling of male and female towards each other.

In this age, teenagers try to understand all ongoing customs and right and wrong, and understand and accept that. It's not possible to understand all the benefit and harm of anything or action, as being teenaged is the first step toward self-dependence and not a combination of experience and far-sightedness. There are many people with wrong intentions who thought to betray teenage girls and boys and take extraadvantage of their dreams, desires, and curiosities, entangle/involve them in antisocial activities like fights, drugs, jackpot, sex for personal benefits. Million Wings feels that if teenagers/youngsters are taught well about life, then it will be so easy to banish wrong people's will, wrong intentions from society. To be alert for these people is safety and strength too. Guide and educate children in such a way that they can protect themselves from those people who have wrong intentions and desires. Million Wings feels that to reduce freedom of children and restrict them is not their safety. Infact, secure atmosphere and personal alertness is a much better way. To provide security to citizens is the responsibility of government and administration, and any criminal should not be able to escape. The secret of the future is to provide them security, managed education, and social alertness.

Million Wings feels that youngsters (18–60 years) are a strength of society. Million Wings feels that every person of any age with strong, logical thinking is a youngster. Youngsters live a happy and positive life. They fully enjoy life along with success. The thinking of youngsters becomes wide, open, and balanced in every direction. Youngsters have many qualities and they work hard to make them shine. Youngsters are a strength of society who have power to change the world. Youngsters want to make positive thinking and attitude management. Youngsters are proud of society. They are friends and defenders of children, teenagers, and old persons and take care of them. Youngsters want to make an atmosphere of love, friendship, and happiness all around.

Youngsters know well to use their strengths for personal, familiar, social, or the nation's pride. Youngsters have a combination of zeal and sincerity (consciousness); they have the capacity to bring positive change in society. Youngsters have sense and zeal to teach a lesson to antisocial elements. Youngsters need the right chance and guidance to fulfil their dreams and desires. Youngsters know well how to take the society and nation to the highest level of success. Youngsters just need the right guidance and advice and management. Youngsters want to enjoy life freely and peacefully. The atmosphere of society becomes powerful and strong with youngsters. There is happiness and zeal all around where youngsters want to do something for the society, nation, and world. Youngsters want to be famous in the world. Youngsters want to shock the world by their capabilities and qualities. Youngsters have full capacity and strength to guide the society, nation, and world. Youngsters can do everything which is helpful in providing happiness to the world. Youngsters can win any field, may it be education, music, sports, government, science and technology, entertainment, etc. Youngsters are combinations of many qualities. If the power of youngsters moves in positive directions, then they can make the world move towards happiness and success very fast. Youngsters can vanish antisocial activities in seconds. Youngsters can teach a lesson to corrupt and antisocial elements who misguide youngsters. Youngsters have that power which can take the whole universe towards happiness. Million Wings feels that society should see youngsters as sensible along with grateful. Youngsters have atleast that much intelligence that they can understand antisocial activities. Youngsters can't entangle in their words, but havethe power to answer them. Positive future and guidance is with youngsters. Youngsters are physically, mentally, and socially so sound that they can make the atmosphere of the society, nation, and world filled with balanced freedom and happiness. Million Wings feels that old person (above 60 years) can suggest to the society and nation on different issues to make it more happy. Senior citizens contributed for their family and society as per their capabilities and qualities and havethe experience of long life too. They got to understand realities of life by moving through phases of happiness and sorrows. This experience of their life becomes suggestions and guidance for children, teenagers, and youngsters which helpa new generation to fulfil their dreams and desires in better ways. Feelings of belongingness and care area need of old persons. Old persons give unmatchable contribution in bringing up of children, give effective suggestions in confused and problematic situations; their suggestions matter a lot. It becomes easy to get success, if their experience stands along with thinking in life and related profession.

Million Wings feels that a logical way of life for the whole universe is to pass experience, research, strategies to the next generation. Every step of every person should be towards betterment, not only for family, society, state, or nation but it should be beneficial for the whole world, which will live united in affectionate and more civilized ways. Freedom and happiness of every person living worldwide is attached with peaceful and secure atmosphere of society. It's normal that personal life of individual may be disturbed but peace in society is still maintained. But it's not possible that there is disturbance in society and individual enjoyment is there too. There will be happiness all around every individual if social atmosphere is good. But if the atmosphere of society is disturbed and torturing, then no one can feel secure and comfortable. Million Wings feels that everyone should concentrate on social issues of society. Persons may interfere in each other's personal life but have to suggest and inspect according to own capacity and capability on those social issues which have the same effect in the life of every citizen. Million Wings feels that every individual should take minimum required steps on each and every antisocial activity/issue happening anywhere worldwide so that everyone in the world can enjoy everything like sweetness and power, civilization and principles. After all, society is because of humans and humans are because of us (you and me). Million Wings feels that family should be as big as can be easily handled and taken care of easily and in reach. The first responsibility of taking care and making children capable is of those individuals who have given birth. A human should give birth to only that number of children whom she can bring up easily. That is, the bigger the family, the more the responsibilities will be. Million Wings feels that a couple should have atleast two children and their difference should not be more than two to three years, as two children are moral support of each other and if they are in the same age of life, they can understand each other's thinking and feelings well.

Million Wings feels that if family will be small, population will be controlled automatically. Resources required for living will not run short if usage is equivalent to requirement. But if population is more, then chances of hunger, sickness, and insecure life will increase. As population will increase worldwide, then it will not be possible to fulfil demand for food, clothes, water, comfort, employment. There are more chances of diseases, theft, trouble. If it's a responsibility of government to provide basic needs of good quality at cheap price, then government of a country can decrease or stop facilities of those who have more than two children. And this is right too. If it's responsibility of government to provide medical help to citizens in any natural or human hazards, then government has a right to allow only those couples to give birth to a child who has full possibility of a healthy life. A mother should not give birth to a child who hasa possibility of serious disease or handicap. If people want to use technology to check whether a foetus is a boy or girl, then government of the country should make sure that every couple should have one girl and one boy baby. Then it's right with the help of science and technology if congenital disease or weakness can be known before birth, then the possibility of more healthy children will be there. It's also a responsibility of government and administration.

Million Wings feels that either yield of resource should be increased or population should be controlled so that yield and usage will be equalized. If speed of reproduction of children is more than required resource, then it will be difficult to survive. Million Wings feels that a couple should give birth to only that number of children whom they can bring up comfortably, and population should be that many which the universe can control easily, as if there will be space in the universe, then only will there be space in the family. Resources can be purchased only if they are available in society, inspite of having a big amount of money. And it will be population of family and country which need to be controlled. People generally make different organizations on the basis of religion, race, etc. Nothing wrong in doing so, as mostly these organizations are developed for managed presentation of needs, working strategy, responsibility and right. Million Wings feels that motto of new organization is to do work according own managed way and not to divide society on small issues. If people think to ask for their rights or things differently, it's right; even then, respect and mutual coordination should be maintained. Do management for society, nation, or world, don't divide it, as management can be done upto any level but the last level of division is to live alone.

Reservation should not be done on the basis of religion, race, etc. but it should be done on basis of real level of living, and the real meaning of reservation is to provide facilities and chance to those people who are living below poverty line so that they can get help in doing work, not to increase status or to reach targets.

One department must fight for their rights, and at the same time, they should request other public departments to support. They should also involve and invite common people/citizens. Supporting other departments of social interest is rewarding for whole society at large.

Million Wings feels that it's important to participate actively in social issues. If there is some familiar issue or fights, then let them solve themselves specially while they don't ask for help or suggestion. But this should also be done according to own will and capacity, till the level it seems to be right; otherwise everything done is right. Million Wings feels that a person can atleast interfere in a social issue which directly affects an individual's life; otherwise there are a few people whose dream is to make society secure and happy. Million Wings feels that to help one's family by one's capacity is also logical help. If an individual can't fight himself but helps the families of those who want to do something for society and nation, it's also a great help. Government and administration should ask for contribution of renowned/popular personalities for social awareness on social misbeliefs and disturbing obstructions in society. Million Wings feels that to talk on every social issue is solution of every social issue. Any issue, may it be personal or social, good or bad, national or international, everything can be resolved by talking. Argument doesn't mean to prove ourselves right. Instead it means to agree another person with our point of view. To agree is to change. Million Wings feels that change arises by argument on views, and fights give birth to tense atmosphere. It's normal to have difference in points of view but regular talk in managed way, questioning and answering on issue resolves every issue. Arguments don't stop betterment but make it better. Million Wings feels that the main motto of arguments bringing up deficiencies, weaknesses, and problems of related issue, and along with that, giving better suggestions on related issue is better. Arguments doesn't mean to entangle issue; neither does it mean to prove ourselves right. Instead it means to agree another with us and make him ours forever. Million Wings feels that starting an open, wide, optimistic, and balanced talk in society in a plausible and arranged way and so that atmosphere of society can be made more better, plausible, and proud.

Million Wings feels that human has to get together/unite in more arranged and balanced way to fight against natural hazards andother creatures for security. Humans have to do new discoveries and research to find out secret of life so that the world can be made better and civilized. Million Wings feels that the best way to help all creatures of the world is to pass experience, strategy, research to next generation. Every step of every person of every country should be so effective that not only his family, society, state, or country but the whole world should start connecting.

Million Wings feels that humans can act forcibly with another creature or organism, but humans can't act forcibly with humans for a long time. Every creature of the universe is fighting for self-respect, security, and his power and it's right too. Human also wants so. The one who has power can collect more resources. The more the resources, the more powerful the creature will be. It's a rule of nature: creatures of different species can easily kill each other. But organisms of the same species can't tolerate forcefulness for a long time, infact demanding equal rights. It's true that humans also fight to be powerful and want to collect more resources to be powerful. Mutual agreements are done to make own country more independent and powerful. Every country makes own strategies to be powerful or to win against other country through war and want to show their power.

Million Wings feels that today every person wants to be more forward than each other by suppressing, by fighting, by winning against others, but everyone needs to understand that if human species are united, then only are they powerful. If we are united, that's why our needs are fulfilled. If we are united, then only is there new hope. If we are united, then there is a future. If we are united, then only are we happy. If we are united, then only can we enjoy. If all countries will unite, then only will they be most powerful. Each and every country of the world, instead of fighting with each other, should make coordination to fulfil each other's needs. Countries should give stress on mutual agreements. Mutual relations should be made with a more and more friendly and calm way. To increase education, business, technology, tourism, and human lifestyle. Everyone should unite together at world level to maintain peace. It's needed to tackle forcefully those people and countries which are not trusted in fighting and disturbing peace and increasing terrorism. The countries which are more capable, powerful, independent in themselves should try to join the world with feelings of friendship; this is real benevolence of humans. Million Wings feels that teaching and force are also necessary for every country to maintain peace and to control problematic situations and to stop forcefulness by other countries like terrorism and to teach a lesson to another. Million Wings feels that police and army are needed for internal and external security of country so that corrupt elements and enemies can be controlled if needed.

Every region of the world manages its lifestyle as per their natural atmosphere and resources, for example: condition of soil and water, climates(hot or cold, humid), hills, deserts, plains, sea. The living style depends upon the availability of food and drinking water.

At international level, the countries should exchange their natural resource mutual benefits in friendly ways rather than in forcible captures.

Cultures and beliefs differ from one country to another country. Language changes. Even the meaning of the same word changes. Even good actions and behaviours in one area may be taken as bad behaviour in other areas. Same postures and styles in one place may carry different meanings and signals to others in different states. Two boys sitting together are taken as good friends in some places but may be taken as gay at some other. Kiss means kissing on cheeks by someone but may be mistaken as lip kiss by some other parts. Mother tongue is a secret language at places of other languages. One should be a little aware of facts beforehand while going from one country to another.

Million Wings feels that a secret of human happiness and mutual friendship is to tie the whole world with one thread. Today, mutual coordination of all countries is increasing worldwide. An amazing achievement of science and technology is to connect whole world. Today, the whole world is connected by Internet, media transmission, phone. It's very easy for everyone to talk, to meet each other. Today, with the help of science and technology, new transport is available by which persons can easily travel from one corner of the world very fast and easily. People move to different countries for mutual benefit. All these are indications of humans moving towards civilization. Million Wings feels that moving forward with mutual agreements and coordination is a step toward better and happy future.

Million Wings feels that the whole world should have one official language. Language should be that which has the least letters and is easy to understand. If already any language is popular in the world, then fix it as authenticated language (e.g. English language). Million Wings feels that the main motto of language is to deliver our message to another person. And if there will be one official language, then it will be very easy for people to deliver and understand each other's message and feelings. There will be huge saving of time, money, and brains which are utilized in conversion and study to learn different national and international languages. The whole world will tie one knot. Children's burden will reduce to 66 per cent. Every person should leave emotional ego and should join to one international language, so that persons can move anywhere in the world atleast he will able to talk freely, express himself, and understand other persons. Million Wings feels that the world is joining with one another for mutual comfort and easiness and to do this is right, and logical too. Every individual wants more comfort and the least tension in life. Worldwide, if any society, country, state, or person is doing a work which is beneficial for the whole of humankind, then obviously everyone will definitely adopt that and it's right too. If living standard of any country is giving comfort to citizens of another country, then nothing's wrong in adopting that. Today, people love each other's culture and adopt that; nothing's wrong in doing so. A person will do this if he likes; this gives comfort and is beneficial. Million Wings feels that this mentality of humans is awesome, that they adopt everything. May people be of any caste, religion, society is doing so, and to do this is a right of every human.

Million Wings feels that humans have to leave those personal feelings, emotions, things which give pain and have to adopt those social, international things, thinking standard of living which gives comfort and is beneficial for humans. By doing so, coordination and friendship will increase worldwide, and along with this, the logical motto of research, invention, living standard, and thinking of life will also be fulfilled. Million Wings feels that every human should take advantage of every strategy which is beneficial for the world. If a human wants to adopt them, let him adopt every thought/thing to which he agrees easily. Socially beneficial and comfortable things, thoughts, and service easily cross barriers/boundaries of caste, religion, society, and nation. It's truth. Million Wings feels that all humans and nature choose more comfortable, capable, and quality things in life. It's that future too. Million Wings feels that persons want to achieve every new thing, work, or thought which is more beneficial, comfortable and provides happiness to humans.

Million Wings feels that humans need to understand priority/importance of plausible coordination with each other. Humans may united torture other species for their benefits but can't tolerate coercion of each other. Every human lives for his self-respect, dreams and desires, and power, and it's right too. Humans have to live in coordinated ways with each other. Humans make strategy to defeat physical power by brains and brain power. If one person refuses to give genuine rights and respect, then the future will itself grab that. It's true, it's future. Idealism makes plausible coordination by providing all rights to every human in comfortable and respectful ways and power of personal and public population maintains own rights and respect. Million Wings feels that persons should leave thoughts of coercion on basis that first ever weakest person is powerful by thoughts; the day is not far when every human will live with social and administrated security in society with full rights and respect. Every human will himself do protection of his rights, and responsibilities will be fulfilled automatically. In future there will be balance of rights, not responsibilities. This is that balance which completely matches with human nature. Balance of the future is not so far now. Million Wings feels that every creature is attached to another creature because of one or another reason. Every life surely has some importance, may that be any creature. The universe moves with natural coordination of all creatures, may that coordination be good or bad.

Million Wings feels that restrictions are applied to happiness of all people just because of faults of a few people getting familiar and social freedom. Along with social rights, they have their personal right too. A few people take extra advantage, e.g. if there is freedom to drink alcohol occasionally, then they start consuming it on a regular basis. They drive rashly on getting vehicle (car, bike); on getting more money, they spend it in a wrong way, e.g. drugs. On getting permission for night parties, they are lost in drugs and sex. If someone in a family is in the police department, then they show attitude and coercion with others. Million Wings feels that just because of very few people, parents don't give freedom to their own child. They are afraid that even their children will misuse their freedom, and chances of getting personal harm and losing self-respect increase. Million Wings feels, why should freedom, enjoyment, comfort, trust of everyone be restricted just because of a few people? Let those people enjoy who are utilizing and enjoying freedom in the best way. Those persons should not be spared who don't care for minimum fixed boundaries/limitations, tackle them seriously and let those enjoying their freedom who are using it rightly.

Why do we not have international bodies which can take a solid stand against common odds? Why cannot a global body of peace raise firm and strict voice and take solid actions against killing of innocent people by certain groups? Why do the international bodies not work on common odds created by unbalanced human beings against the common people? Global peace needs backup of strict rules and powerful actions against clearly inhuman activities, by the collective global body.

When we all know that corrupt leaders divide the people into various groups on the basis of caste, religions, race, etc., then why are the people still falling into same traps every time? Why are people being divided further and further and letting themselves down to corrupt masterminds?

The terrorists (killing innocent people) should be given a genuine chance to express themselves, and if they keep on doing such inhuman activities (destroying peace and human resources), they should be given strong reply in the same manner, pain for pain when politeness gives no gain. Terrorists and negative people disturb the peace of the nation by creating issues on one or another thing. Million Wings feels that reason may be any but to kill innocents is not tolerable; it's totally wrong, it's non-civilization, Million Wings feels that if terrorist or negative people really has some great issue, then they have to put their written side infront of the world and government, and security force should give a motivation to start a talk on issue without any fear. If those issues which terrorists use to fight are personal, then why do they take lives of other innocent people? If enmity is between a few people or organizations, then what is the fault of the general public? And if the issues of terrorists are social, then they should make common people part of that. Everyone should get together on social issues. Make sure about desire and agreement of all and find new ways to get justice and make sure that innocent people should not die. Million Wings feels that administration, government, police force, and security force have not only to teach a lesson to terrorists or violent people but they also have to take care of feelings, self-respect, and life of common people, and terrorists, violent and cowardly people, thought themselves brave by taking advantage of this and executing their wrong and bad thoughts. Nothing is bad/wrong to find an issue; neither does anyone stop this. But no one has right to kill innocent people. Million Wings feels that today media and organizations working on human rights are here. Every person has a right and opportunity to put his point of view infront of the world. If issues are strong and powerful, then everyone will surely understand and support us. Common people may be unable to guide but can collectively make better decisions. Million Wings feels that killing common people is not the solution of any issue; infact it is the cause of more anger and annoyance for terrorists and violent people. Million Wings feels that few intentions and work are those for which there should be strong and powerful action, and negative people dare to do that, e.g. rape, killing innocents, fleecing, betrayal, making someone handicapped, expanding use of drugs. People should be well aware and clear about punishment/penalty of these crimes, that there is no apology for these crimes, there will be only punishment for these crimes. The more serious the crime, the more serious the punishment will be. Government and administration have to keep genuine fear on non-genuine activities and they have to prove it from time to time. It's the best way to prove to people with disgusting thinking. Serious punishment and fear is necessary for mental and physical well-being.

If there is solid proof against terrorists or criminals, there should be serious punishment as they get caught. It should be clear to criminals and terrorists that they are going to get a worse punishment even than death whenever they get caught by humanism. If weapons can be used to kill innocent people for personal benefits and happiness, then those weapons can be surely used for protection of innocent people and it's right too. Million Wings feels that bad people don't bother about emotions and feelings of common people, and to fulfiltheir demand, they misbehave with them. Million Wings feels that it needs power to stop them and they can be given a chance to reform. Maybe they can improve.

Million Wings feels that if bad and corrupt people change in the right direction, then it's very beneficial for society and is a thing to be praised. If a person changes his direction towards goodness from badness, then that person can guide in better ways. Million Wings feels that a few chances, help, and initiative should be given to bad and corrupt people to change themselves, maybe realize/feel that goodness has more comfort and easiness than badness and come to know that lifesaver is much greater than life taker.

Fights often occur in society because of misunderstanding in religions, races, countries; because of misunderstanding, often the innocent have to suffer from violence and fights etc. Because of this, other people related to them also become annoyed and angry and start killing innocent people around them. Now the second group gets annoyed and starts fighting and killing family members and friends of group one, and like this, many innocentsare affected by this and are entangled with each other, which leads to serious enmities. Just because of misunderstanding between two, many people fightwith each other for years. Misunderstandings are so much raised that no one tries to solve them. Everyone keeps on moving behind each other, and above all, a few people don't let people out from these issues by relating these feelings of self-respect of religion, caste, race, nation for their personal benefits.

Million Wings feels that the world tries to resolve most issues with positive and friendly attitude in starting. Million Wings feels that one who gives a start to peace and friendly behaviour is the right religion, right caste, right race, right nation, and he is the right human. Million Wings feels that those terrorists who kill innocent people, if they are caught red-handed, may the reason be any, should be killed at the sametime and it's right, may theybe of any religion, caste, nation and may they be doing this in any part of the world.

Million Wings feels that if any person wants to do anything, he may be trying to get or search for his happiness by fighting or moving against his family or society. But the person is attached to social issues to such an extent that while society is not changed to higher level or society is not moving along, the person can't live comfortably and daily happiness can't be achieved for longer time. Firstly one person feels to bring change and he tries to bring change at social level also, as a person can't live happily alone, he has to live in society only. Million Wings feels that change definitely comes in life but it definitely takes time to prove it and be validated by society. People government and administration take years to understand. The lives of those who start something new are spent in problems and obstruction. But slowly, slowly they provide comfort to more or less millions of people.

Million Wings feels that society needs to think with a positive and plausible way regarding every change so that society can be made better as early as possible. Government and administration should try to apply that change at social level. It's logical management of power.

Million Wings feels that mostly personal happiness is related with society. Much personal happiness can be fulfilled only if society, nation, or government will accept and administrate it. Million Wings feels that even the strategies, policies, or thoughts made by common sense for social benefit take a very long time to understand and formulate. It's true that the world is changing but not at that pace at which it can change. Million Wings feels that to bring change at social, national, or international level, we should freely use mass media (TV, movies, newspapers, books, etc.) so that more people will come to know about issues, matters, thinking in less time. And more quickly, better rules and principles can be formulated. Personal tries are OK for personal issues but social changes are a must for social issues; it's a secret of happiness, it's true.

There should be displayed name, time period, and contact number of high authority of all public works (e.g. dwelling, bridge, building, sewerage, roads, etc.) so that citizens have a chance and right to question the related authority.

Creatures made by God are the best emotional creation. Today, everything can be made with science and technology. To save humans from diseases, many parts of organs can be made with technology. But still natural organs are best. So by keeping this in mind, if human will donate his parts after death, then many needy humans can hope for betterment. Many needy humans can hope for better lives. As the body of a human will mix in soil only, only the soul reaches God. Redemption is got by soul, water, air, fire, and light. Million Wings feels that every individual should donate his eyes and other organs which can be donated after death. The body is not harmed by doing so, neither does it harm self-respect of humans.

Social customs also don't get obstructed/affected. It's true, it's right. Till now, even blood can't be made; humans donate blood for each other and save lives. Everyone should donate blood; it doesn't cause any weakness or harm. Infact, concentration of blood is regenerated in one day and composition (particles) becomes the same in three months, as before. Now the question is, what is the minimum responsibility of family, society, nation, or world when a child is born? When does a child start understanding? Million Wings feels that there is age of body but no age of mind. The body startsbecoming younger by age of 16 years but no one knows when the mind becomes mature. Million Wings feels that body becomes younger by 16, so minimum time of 16 years should be given to brain to develop. When the body develops, the mind should also develop. Development of body is natural but it's the responsibility of family, society, nation, and world to develop the mind and brain. What is the real meaning of development of brain and mind? What is the meaning of being mature? Being mature means a child can make social decision by himself. That is, he can understand at least minimum required social matters of daily life, e.g. behaviour skill, personal security, and ability to understand about drugs, sex, romantic relations, etc. The family, society, and nation have to manage education in such a way that along with physical development, a child should develop mentally also and should able to understand logical and necessary feelings and emotions of society so that he can make every decision independently for personal security and benefits. It's the future, it's the biggest social management and happiness.

A pregnant woman has maximum concentration on her child. No one should misbehave physically or mentally with a pregnant lady. Protecting a pregnant woman is one of the best ways to make God happy. In the world, if there is any person who has a right to say anything, that person is mother. It's also true that whoever is heartily attached with each other may take care of each other with lots of love. But a mother's love is not replaceable; it's natural feelings of belongingness even before birth. It's unbreakable and priceless prayers. A child may be right or wrong but it's the mother who always stands along with child and gives her best to save her child. Million Wings feels that feeling like affection can't be just human feeling. It's definitely a part of some magical power of God. It's true, it's right.

Yes, it's difficult to change society but not impossible. A voice arisen for change may not affect you directly but definitely influences you in one or another way. Do say that whatever you feel, it's not necessary to fight. We want change, not violence; maybe we can't fight or react as stubbornly, but our thoughts can be delivered peacefully also. If thought is powerful and effective, definitely it will bring change in every direction, may it be at small scale, maybe large scale, maybe earlier, maybe later. Small changes are the start of big change. Change is a souvenir of need. Change becomes powerful by strategy. Strength is also collected and increased by strategy. Strength affects by strategy only, at the right place. Expert strategy gives speed, success, and right direction to change. First use brain powerfully and, if needed, only then use physical power. It will be stupidity to disturb peace and power for those things which can be done peacefully.

If you're determined to bring social reforms, sense the system. One can get success only if majority of the administrators or at least the highest authority is genuine and attentive. When the whole system is corrupt, then the only hope is either total powerful revolt or harmonious awareness of the mass. Plan in such a way that you can survive to witness the change for which you put your life.

Social changes happens to humans in a natural or planned ways. Million Wings feels that most of the social changes are done by innocent and people who suffered and do not think much about the outcome of their actions, but just fight against the corrupt world for the benefits of human life. Million wings feels that this natural way of human changes will always keep on happening from time to time but now we all should unite and must do the needful and must plan changes in the society, the nation, and the world.

Million Wings feels that alertness is the strongest weapon of society. Social awareness is the biggest power. Alertness is security, awareness is the answer. Now all the corrupt, terrorists, religious gurus will not escape as now there is no need of any guidance, as now people are alert, aware, and united and they themselves act as powerful weapons against enemies. People are now understanding clever thoughts of corrupt people. Now they will not enrol in their games and talks. People are becoming united. Now people will not allow anyone to play with their emotions and feelings and they themselves will think and understand better about religions, caste, and society. It's right, it's logical. Let's be aware and alert our family, society, nation, world so that any criminal, terrorist, religious guru will not dare to disturb the peace of society and create trouble or violence in society.

Million Wings feels that the people who enjoy helping others are needed by needy people. People who are helping others with good intentions and affection should understand that they are not just needed for one or two days; infact they are always required every day, month, year. Million Wings feels that this social helpfulness should help in such a way that even they themselves should also get time for rest so that they can live healthily and can help people for a much longer time. If they themselves will remain healthy, then only they can help people in much better ways, with more power and more comfortably. It's better to help others for a few days without rest and fall sick for longer time. Million Wings feels that the people whose dream and desire is to help people, and whose profession is also the same, should work an average eight hours, rest for eight hours, eight hours for family and personal time. A person whose profession is something else but wants to help people should help people for an average of two hours. Million Wings feels that every profession or business is a way of social work/ help. Doing one's work responsibly is necessary for everyone. But delivering products and service in a friendly and skilful way is the real meaning of social work. For profession or business, a person gets money in return. But if a person does his job calmly and in caring ways, there is no replacement for that goodness and respect. Persons can't give extra money for that but they surely feel happy. That is, doing professional work calmly, affectionately, and peacefully is real social service.

The whole world is a friend.

Chapter 31

National and international economy

Million Wings feels that the sole aim of the economic system of any country is actually the happiness of citizens. The most important point of economic status of the country is the independence and satisfactory status of the people of the country.

The currency rates and its ups and downs are related only to the purpose of import-export. The logical ethics of the government is to provide basic facilities and to fulfil basic needs of the people.

The foremost requirement is to provide food, water, sanitation, health, and education in the country, and this is the minimum economy of the country. All the raw material or product which can be arranged and prepared within the country should not be imported from other countries. Whatever is left after fulfilling the requirement of our own country's people, the rest can be exported to other parts of the world. Only those raw materials or products which are really valuable demands of people, which are not available or running short in our country should be imported. Million Wings feels that purchase of costly product by the people will not help in raising the country's economy. Utilizing costly products of foreign brands will raise the economy of foreign country, not of our own country. Economy never means to increase the value of currency only, but the actual and right meaning is to make available the basic living to every citizen, may it be of cheap rates on world scale.

341

Gross domestic product (GDP) is the standard of economy of any country and is a comparative parameter worldwide. Million Wings feels that it is more important to understand that the people of the country should get basic products and services and on cheap rates rather than to concentrate only on the value of currency as compared to other countries. It is most important to understand that if the citizens are happy, it means economic management is at its best. But if the people are not getting basic necessities at reasonable prices, then the economy is the worst even if the value of the national currency goes to the highest level as compared to global standard. Million Wings feels that if our citizens are happy and our currency has high value in the global market, that means our economy management is the ideal one.

Million Wings feels that economic management is the happiness for our country's people, not for foreigners' happiness. Economic management is related with each and every area. The simple rule is to export the products and services which are extra in our country and must be given to the country which pays more or similarly. We should import only those things which are our basic requirement and must purchase from the country that gives us cheap rates. If the country cannot manufacture some product on its own at less expenditure, then import of the same product at cheaper rates is the reasonable, right approach rather than self-manufacturing. It's really true that even if the capacity of the person to afford is very high, still he tries to purchase things at minimum possible rates and will be happy to purchase things on as low prices as possible. Million Wings feels that whatever is available in our country at cheaper rates, there must not be any need of purchasing the same things of foreigner brands at high prices.

Every country has rich and poor people. If rich people want to purchase costly things, others must visit another country and purchase things as per import policies of the country. The government should try to manufacture products within the country from range of cheap to highly standardized quality and scale so that every citizen can purchase it as per paying capacities. The product and service must be as per our people's requirement desire and demands, not as per foreign countries. The things which are beyond the paying capacity of average citizens of the country must not be promoted as standard product through fascinating ads on mass media. The products and services of our country must be projected in a useful way in media that the citizens of the country develop faith and feel proud to use them on priority basis. It is more useful, logical to use things of our own country at low prices as compared to purchasing the same things of foreign brand at higher rates. It's 100 per cent sure that by purchasing our own products, a lot of money can be saved, and that saved money can either be utilized for some other useful purpose or one needn't have to work hard to earn that extra money.

The economy of the country is not dependent on one sector but related to all sectors. If any one area is weak, then the other department will cover it.

Million Wings feels that independence is the main factor of power of the country, not only the economic status of the nation. The economic status is computer scale within the nation. Any country can sell one or combination of products, manpower, or brains to other countries. The government should sell their important products to them who value them and need them and give good returns; after that, sell to those countries who demand/need them and give a very low price. We should not sell our best quality to the countries which are economically stronger than our country, giving low price especially when the people of that country don't like to use them. We should provide them only those things which they demand on their own and value, e.g. skilled specialist brains and products. Similarly we should sell our products/services to the countries having weaker economic status than us so that they use them happily and respectfully.

Million Wings feels that one nation can't manufacture everything on their own. The rich-and-poor scenario will always remain there while the world exists. The basic fundamental of economic management will also remain the same, and that means the government and administration should always formulate and fix trade policies as per the utility, need, and value of concerned products and services. Anything which is running short in our own country must be utilized by citizens in very useful ways or they should try for easy and equally effective alternative ways to cover that deficiency. The government should make the people aware about the basic factors deciding economic trade management. The people must know how to use various available resources within the country. For example, if petrol/diesel is running short and is being imported from other countries, then the people should not have any right to waste it unnecessarily. If the people will do that, then nobody can stop its price inflation. If food, cloth, and milk production is more than the need, then it's better to export it to a needy country rather than its undue wastage. The people must understand that they are the ultimate consumer of all/any product and service available anywhere in the world. Million Wings feels that if the people use oil, milk, and food in a proper way, then there will not be any reduction in their happiness at all. There will not be any increase in happiness of their party if they will leave the home lights on or there may not be any problem with their parties or enjoyment if they switch off lights and fans at their home before leaving for parties.

The economic management of the country is dependent on government, administration, and the citizen. If we analyze it, the government has major responsibility. It is the government who has to inform people about the economic issues, problems, restrictions of management. It's the government who has to analyze the different sectors and areas running in the country and to formulate the various trade policies within the country so that a harmonious coordination and balance must prevail. It is the prime responsibility of the government to make policies with great care so that the nation becomes economically sound and strong and the people will feel happy and friendly atmosphere. Inspite of maximum possible logical management of economic issues, if a few antisocial elements disturb the peace of the nation, they must be handled with strictness by the government. Million Wings feels that if we want to bring some better change, then it's not necessary to be unduly serious and adamant. The good change can be done with happy mood, politeness, and harmonious strategies too. The government should be strict only if the citizens don't care even about minimum required responsibilities.

Million Wings feels that the biggest obstacle in the happiness of people is undue worry about future security, death, disease, old age, handicap, etc. The life insurance policies have a big role in the economy of the country. Future security can be ensured though banks and insurance departments. If the people will be free from insecurities related with natural hazards and diseases, then the people will not be so tense and busy day and night to earn so much money for future security. Through banks and life insurance policies, the citizen can easily avail of future security benefits for the whole family on life expenditure and the government funds will also keep on increasing. The people will get a high level of mental peace because people need to work for daily living standards only.

Million Wings feels that by reducing the education system to minimum necessary logical subjects, then almost 60 per cent finances and manpower can be saved. Otherthan basic school education, the rest of the education must be based on professional utility. Professional courses must have observation, assistance, and independent phase of learning. The theory and practical teaching must run parallel to same energy, brains, and time, and to achieve maximum benefits at earliest.

Million Wings feels that tourism can give high/large economical support to a country. Tourism will increase relationship among countries, along with entertainment and amusement. The government should support tourism at the maximum.

Million Wings feels that the foreign investor within the country must invest money in equal rates as they invest in their own country because only those countries can think of investing or expanding trade who are economically stronger than the consumer nation. The investor must get the same rates of benefit as they are getting in their own country, not more than that. Million Wings feels that the biggest advantage to any of the investors is to get more consumers for their products, not the chances of making unduly more money. The people will sell only those things which they have in ample supply and the people will buy only those things which they need and are running short. The minimum cost of any product depends upon the feasible utility of the same product; that simply means that one should sell the product or service at those rates above which the product or service are going to be wasted. Million Wings feels that trade the money will not come from the things which are available in huge quantity but money comes basically from the utility/need of the product or service by the people.

Million Wings feels that every person earns money by his hardwork, maybe earning less money or more whether he has followed all the government instructions or he has taken advantage of loopholes in government policies but definitely he has done hardwork. Whether he has used more brain or more hands or maybe both, hardwork would be definitely there. Money is always earned by hardwork by the common man. Black money never means that the money is always earned by cheating, but most of the times the money which is earned by the people by hardwork is not shown to government fully. Black money actually means any money the details of which are not provided to the government. Million Wings feels that people always try to save their money, may it be called black or white. Every human has the first tendency to save his money whether it's black or white because a person feels that his hardwork is involved in earning money, whether right money or wrong. Money is a big resource which can bring alot of facilities and luxuries, so everyone wants to secure it safely. Million Wings feels that whatever money is shown and explained to government is a logical way according to law, is white, wrong ways. And the money which is earned by proper norms and regulation as per law but not shown to government is labelled as black money. The government should concentrate on real practical aspect of the human mind rather than theoretical aspects only and must amend its rules and regulations at the indication of better understanding of rules and policies. People credit their so-called black money to a world bank and utilize their money in the foreign countries only. Our country's money known as black money goes to world banks. Who are using that money to give loans worldwide and earn interest over it?

Million Wings feels that if a world as per as black money account worldwide, then why cannot our own country open a so-called confidential bank in our own country? The country's money will remain in our own county while it can be tactfully and safely utilized in our own country's benefit and the depositor can also get full benefits within the country. Million Wings feels that money is money, and money should not be labelled as white or black. There should not be income tax system in the country. There should not be such rules and regulations while classifying money as white and black. People keep their money in worldbanks rather than our national bank, but if the same money remains in our own country, the government can get huge benefits from differences on interest from loans, which can be utilized for the country's development. The policies should be liberal and easy. Anybody can earn as much money as they want, can keep it in national banks without any fear of right or wrong. The people should show all the money and proposed sources as per their own choice. The people should have liberal power and safety to submit or utilize money as per their need without any questions. By such ways, the whole amount of money will remain within the economy of the country. People will be happy, the country will be happy. Million Wings feels that as long as the trade or relationship between two people is harmonious, no one will have any objection to each other. It is very important to understand that no one allows someone to grab his money by any means, so by default, if no one is filing any complaint against anyone, it means money is earned by logical ways and everything is right, whatever amount may be unvalued. And if someone complains against someone for cheating etc., only then should the government ask for proof/explanation from the concerned parties. The government should give full encouragement, protection, support, and insurance to people so that they can raise complaints against the cheaters. Million Wings feels that there must be one highest selling price of any product or service within the country. No one should be allowed to sell above that (tips). Most of the times the reason for fight is not the money, but actually it is cheating related with money.

Million Wings feels that we should not stop money, rather we should stop cheating. And the only way is to make rules more liberal and, at the sametime, encourage people to fight for their right to save their money. This is the only logical way of economic management. Government must encourage people to complain against corrupt people by giving them fast justice. By such action, the country's money will remain within the country and both the people and government will be happy too. Money will grow and corruption will come to an end.

Million Wings feels that the main reason behind increase of corruption is that people want to fulfil their dreams with the world's best projected standard of quality by the government, by the people. Developed countries will definitely have a little better quality of products as compared to developing and poor countries, and obviously those products from rich countries will be available at high cost to poor nations. The media mostly project developed countries' products as if they are the utmost standard of that range of products and services and try to develop a psychological quality impression of such products to the world and pressurize people to buy those products on social and ego issues. Every person has to choose and buy those products only to show their standard, sometimes even against their will. A person works day and night to afford those costly things for himself and his family. Many times the hard work cannot be sufficient to raise the required money, then the people start making money by alternative corrupt ways. Some people do with a legal manner and some by illegal means.

Everyone knows that people can easily get reasonable good-quality product within their own country on half prices compared to foreign brands. Somebody in the family is usually interested in high-profile costly brands of a foreign nation and which may be somewhat beyond their personal capacities too. There are many things which are not available in our own country but belong to other rich countries. And to avail those benefits, more money is needed, e.g. tourism, legal nightlife, higher education. If a person wants to enjoy these things, he needs to earn a lot of money. Million Wings feels that the world has made costly things as a standard of quality living and every person is drifting towards that to achieve that showing off. Everyone wants to get high status as decided by the society and world. So everyone wants to earn as much money as possible to fulfil his dreams as per worldwide standards. In the interest of grabbing more money, everyone works hard and sometimes people start using undue tricks and cheat with other people. Million Wings feels that people want to achieve their dreams at the earliest with the highest standard; that leads to various corrupt ways to collect money. This is the sole reason of corruption, because of more and more facilities, for a longer time.

Million Wings feels that government and administration should concentrate on their efforts on basic reasons behind corruption. It is necessary to present the products and services of their own country in a very attractive and useful way, along with raising their quality and performance. The better presentation will attract people to buy indigenous products and services. If the people will get good products and services in their own country at low prices, then they need not earn more money. If dreams and desires are achieved with less money, then there will not be any requirement for earning more money with corrupt ways. The people are not worried about only day-to-day living but mainly tense because of future safety and security against diseases, handicap, child education and marriage and old age, etc. Every individual nowadays needs a future security to be happy.

Perhaps everything is justified. What else will the person do? Today's world has made people think about future safety and security to such an extent that every person is busy in making a future and forgets to live the present. The people are under double burden. They have to live today with a high standard and also have to secure the future to maximum extent. That means every person needs to earn money today only for both present and future. In such cases, either the person will be busy day and night to earn money or he will indulge in corrupt practices to collect money.

Million Wings feels that the government and administration are responsible for giving protection to its citizens in case of emergencies, natural hazards, diseases, and situations, along with providing them the basic living. The government should make policies so that people will be more interested in the present rather than preoccupied with future security and safety. Million Wings feels that the policies should be in such a way that there should be no space for corruption for making money. The government should leave no chance for people to take advantage of policies. The government should fix prices of products and services either based on their manufacturing and transportation cost or atleast should be pocket friendly to citizens. The rules and regulations must be straightforward and in simple language so that people can easily understand well. Corruption should be reduced to zero level by the people. People should be assured of action, safety, and justice by the government in a specified short period, against corruption, so that people get encouragement to complain against corrupt people without fear. The government must ensure accountability of each and every department of the nation and that will be the first and most effective step against corruption.

Million Wings feels that government funds must be unitized in a proper and effective way to serve the nation. The government should utilize the already established buildings, products, and services rather than to create the same things again and again. The government should not waste money by unnecessarily constructing new things, rather must use money to give better facilities at the already established structures within the country. That will save alot of money, and that money can be unitized for some other area and purpose of service to people.

Million Wings feels that it is much better if so-called black money remains in our country and it's easy to do so. Money is money, whether it is black or white. Money can bring alot of facilities in the country. The citizen earns money in the country premiers, whether he gives full details to government or not. Just think, if the whole of the money will remain safe in the national banks only, it is far better than to bank it outside the country. By allowing all the people of the country to credit their accounts with all types of money, atleast the national treasure will remain fully loaded. Million Wings feels that to convert black money into white money is the first step to bring black money back to own country and winning the confidence of people regarding safety of their money. It is important to understand that black money actually means money collected from anti-human activities, not the genuine money concealed from the government. Money is money, not black or white. The people of the country should get liberal and safe opportunities to keep their money in the nation's banks with full safety and security. The people can keep any amount they want in the banks and can also utilize as much amounts as they want to keep as per their interest. The people should have liberal options to submit any documented range of occupational sources for the concerned money. If some opposite party complains against someone for cheating/fraud, the government should welcome them and must punish them strictly once they are found guilty. The people should keep records and proof for their income with themselves and must show them only in case of legal response. The people should give 10 per cent of their income as only one tax to the government for the country's development and the people should have full power to ask for details of national fund usage. The government should encourage the people in such a way that their personal, professional management will itself lead to development of the country. One action will serve all purposesand all people will be happy at the same time. The most important point is that the country's currency should remain with the country, rather than going out of country, and the second important goal is not to harass or defame our country people, rather to encourage them gracefully with a friendly manner so that they feel secure and protected in keeping their earnings in the national banks and use their money at their will and enjoy.

Million Wings feels that instead of collecting more tax from a single citizen, government should make policy to collect small amount from all the citizens and that will surely lead to better economic strength. The natural treasury will always remain full. The economic rules and regulations must be like that; every individual, maybe earning less or more, should feel comfortable and happy to pay taxes to government. The people save their taxes by many legal loopholes when they are supposed to pay high taxes and the government will remain at a loss overall. The policy should be such that even with small taxes, the national treasury will be at its peak rather than remain empty for want of collection of high taxes. The common people always want to fulfil their basic needs on a priority basis and, in the same way, government to manage that only, because the luxury is a hobby, and for that, the people will have to pay any high amount.

Million Wings feels that worldwide the standard of human happiness should always be people's behaviour, thinking for comparison among countries. Otherthan the money, the overall happiness and satisfaction of citizens must be the utmost comparative standard among the countries. That's the best way, that's right and important too.

Chapter 32

Religion

O n the talk of religion, people unite together. In every religion when people come together, it feels very good. Million Wings feels that usually people unite in their own religion but people from different religions usually do not accept each other but have arguments, fights with each other. The attitude of the people belonging to different religions is not good. Million Wings feels that religion has no role in the development of a country's happiness of people because we have been watching people having arguments and quarrels with each other and being separated on the issue of religion. What is the need of religion, if it gives only pain to whole world? The guru made religion to enlighten humanity toward goodness, but the humans are now busy in proving their own religion best of all rather than following the real sense of religion. Million Wings feels that there are as many teachings as there are religions. And there are as many fights as many are teachings. More religion, more teachings, more mismatches, more quarrels hence more bloodshed. Then what to do with many religions, when these are a cause of pain to humanity? What is the need of such religions which are separating humans instead of uniting them? We don't need such religion which cannot even remove the minor misunderstanding or mismatch between humans. We don't need such religion which teaches us fights rather than brotherhood. We don't want such religion which fills hearts with enmity. We don't need such religion which becomes issue of fights between people all the time. Million Wings feels that no religion is actually spreading love and friendship nowadays; rather, every religion's leaders or people are in front to prove their religion as the topmost.

Million Wings feels that the main impact of any religion is not related to personal living beliefs, but the most important purpose of any religion is to teach humans to respect, love, and care about the people of other religions. Million Wings feels that we need a religion which teaches similar living norms and regulations to the whole world. We need a religion on the name of which the whole world unites together within seconds, the only religion which makes this world one. Million Wings feels that humans and all creatures have only one religion; that is life and earth is our caste, happiness is our aim and harmonious relationship is our working strategy. This is the ultimate truth of the future's world and this will remain while life is sustained. All living beings, One religion

> One religion, same teaching
> same teaching, less contradictions
> Less arguments, less fights
> more peace, more happiness all around

Million Wings feels that the living being will exist while the universe is sustained. The life continues while a living being are there and life means religion. That means life is religion and the religion is life. Million Wings feels that the whole universe has one religion, i.e. religion of life. Life is the biggest and last religion of every creature of God. Million Wings feels that religion of life is the religion of all living beings. Life is the real religion of every human being. No religion is bigger than life. Each and everything is because of life. Life is beginning if no life means death. Life is teacher. Life is way. Life is moksha. Life is a chance to meet God. Life is everything. Life is religion. Life is the only religion of all the humans all around the world.

All creatures, one religion, and that is life.

Million Wings feels that all the religions are different, not alike. God is one but not religions. Religion actually is a collection of concepts which give knowledge and guidance to live life. The great people, gurus have tried their best with their knowledge, experience, vision, and optimistic approach to provide ways of happy life to the world. Religion is attached with humans since their birth till death. The ones who established religions were great humans, but not God. Million Wings feels that the real God must appear alike to all, when he will come on the earth. The religions are many, but God is one. Different religions have different views about God. Everyone understands that the universe is created by someone and that someone is known as God, greatest of all, most powerful, super intelligent, unbiased, ultimate planner, and visionary scientist. Different religions explain the same God in their different thinking and theories. Religion may be any, may it be Hindu, Sikh, Muslim, Christian, Buddhist, or Jain, but gives their point of view regarding all as any aspect of human life. No religion is standard of the universe, that's why there are many religions created by humans. The religion means to understand God, not to blame God. Religion in reality gives us a way or guidance to pray to the Almighty for best options and decisions in life, but not to indulge in proving ourselves the best of all. Thereligion is a moral support, the religion is a way to bring peace in life. The religion is guidance for a happy and optimistic life.

Million Wings feels that religion has even more lines of control than the LOC between countries. The LOC divides earth but religion is working to divide hearts and minds. Million Wings feels that the main aim of any religion is to unite the world, not to divide it. The religion logically works to increase the harmony among the people with great love and care, but not to fuel the fire of fights between them. The religion is to remove LOCs, not to create. The great spiritual leaders have created different religions as per the demands of time on different eras for humanity. All thought their teachings and beliefs were different from each other but their sole intention way to show all the humans the path of happy living and to achieve moksha.

Million Wings feels that one religion is a must to direct life. The one common religion is a must to understand every big or small issue of life. The one common religion is a must to give solutions to all worries and pain. One common religion is a must to guide for moksha. One common religion is a must to give benefit to the whole world. One common religion is a must to teach humans a balanced approach to live happy lives. One common religion is a must to increase the coordination and cooperation in the whole world. One common religion is a must to satisfy feelings. One common religion is a must for standard guidance for all humans.

Million Wings feels that the religions must be stable in all circumstances. The religion must concentrate on sole requirements of humans. The religion must be based on logical basic aims of life. The religion must bring happiness by removing pain. The religion must unite the people. The religion must amend its rules and regulations for better life from time to time. The religion must respect everyone's will, comment, and self-respect. The religion must give freedom to life. The religion must expand, open wide and balanced thinking. The religion must be comfortable. The religion must correct mistakes. The religion must be for all. The religion must be away from unnecessary restrictions. The religion must unite the people with friendship. The religion must guide as life moves. The religion must understand the demands of life and guide accordingly. The religion must teach us guiltless power. The religion must raise hope. The religion must prove genuine in all situations. The religion must teach how to behave with others. The religion must improve humans. The religion must win hearts. The religion must attract everyone. The religion must unite people of all races, castes, and countries. The religion must not divide people, but bring them close. The religion must bring similes all around. The religion must be comfortable. The religion must heal wounds. The religion must teach love. The religion must improve relationships. The religion must be easy to follow. The religion must be understandable. The religion must belong to all. The religion must be strong. The religion must give relief from pains. The religion must provide the way to satisfaction. The religion must teach how to live life. The religion must show the path to feel God. The religion must be beautiful. The religion spreads happiness, peace, and a logical way of life.

Million Wings feels that the people would like to accept only that religion which provides maximum comfort and easiest logical teachings of human life. Humans would like to accept that religion which understands humans' deep mentality and teaches human ways to human happiness. Humans would like to accept that religion which considers humans' deep heart desires, potential, capacities, and limits along with humans' demand of life according to era. Humans would like to accept that religion which concentrates on basic logical life strategy rather than entangle people in formalities and misbehaviour.

Million Wings feels, establish life as a religion of every creature. Every living being has one religion and that is life. Million Wings ensures that life religion is the same for all and the same teaching for all. Life religion respects every living creature of the universe. The life religion has one belief for all humans on this earth. The life religion gives minimum of the same path from birth to death so that there would be minimum misunderstanding and maximum understanding between the people. Everyone has one religion and that is life, may he/she belong to any caste, race, country. Life religion respects feeling and religion of every human in any age and phase of life. The life religion understands every individual's need, capacities, desires, and limitations. The life religion believes that the best creature will lead the universe from time to time and divert the whole universe into an optimistic direction. The life religion provides moksha through human ways of balance. Today, humans are the leaders of all creatures and living in a systematic and organized way. Million Wings feels that if human beings will themselves live a logical and happy life, only then can they show the same paths/ways to other creatures of the universe.

Humans' are the leaders and if they will unite happily, only then can they do something for other living beings on earth. Million Wings feels that the life religion is for all the living creatures of the universe, but specifically concentrates on humans on priority basis because of leaders. We'll be happy, only then can they think and keep other creatures happy. Million Wings formulated logical norms of living for every human so that their life will be easy, comfortable, and have logical direction.

Million Wings respects and believes as each and every religion is the highest standard of living for their followers but Million Wings religion of "Life" is a common lowest level of human happiness for every human being belonging to any religion of the world.

Beliefs and regulations of Million Wings Religion Of Life;

1. God is one and he is the most powerful, unbiased, best planner.
2. God has created this universe to give chance of moksha early and to every creature.

3. Every living being is already fixed with unlimited circumstances and possibilities by God.

4. The creatures get life on the basis of random selection. The soul can get anybody and life and any number of times till moksha. Random selection is not even in the hands of God, although everything is created by him. The life will take its path as it flows.

5. The living creatures will get their basic inbuilt qualities, behaviours, and feelings at the time of birth, which cannot be changed.

6. The creatures will get whatever atmosphere the parents and grandparents have created on the earth.

7. One soul can get any number of lives till moksha will be achieved. During any birth, the chances of getting moksha are equal.

8. The basic strategy of getting moksha is behaviour skill with the rest of the world.

9. The human can get married or take divorce at his/her will. Anybody can marry any number of times but only one marriage at one time. New marriage is possible only after getting divorce from the previous one. Only one male and one female can live as a husband and wife under one roof at the same time.

10. The childbearing can be done by a couple by mutual will and to bring up, earn their living (food/shelter)is minimum responsibility of mother and father.

11. Male and female are equal interms of respect, opportunity, and care.

12. Son and daughter have equal rights on parents' property. After marriage, a couple has the option to live in the husband or wife's home. The person who will leave his/her house will get advantage to get a share from their property, and that depends upon the devotion of staying. The longer the stay, the more the share. The maximum share is possible only if they have a child. The couple can decide their jobs and responsibilities as per their mutual comfort and consent.

13. Anybody (male/female) can have physical or emotional bonding, or both, with any number of males/females, but the responsibility, harmony, security, and protection resources are solely personal.

14. One can wear any type of clothes but must cover more than 90 per cent of sexual parts and at public places.
15. The aim of life is to live for our dreams.
16. To give food and shelter to his/her parents and children is the minimum responsibility on any creature. The rest of the relationship hopes can be started with self-will and desire. The humans are responsible for only those relationships which are started by them by their own will and consent, e.g. marriage and children.
17. We can pray to God in any place, any position, anytime. Wherever a person is praying to God is a religious place. God considers sincere and faithful prayers only.
18. The fight for self-respect is every creature's right. Guiltless power is the best weapon.
19. The elder person must teach the younger person, and overall optimistic approach is the best guidance.
20. All-time prayer:

Hey, God! I pray to you to bring the best situations and circumstances in my life and give me the power to choose the best out of them as per my dream sand desires of that time till I get moksha.

Million Wings feels that religion is a human's strength, his belief, his hope, and his guidance. Any religion in the world never wants to separate people, but works to unite people. Only a few leaders of all religions started moulding the religion for their personal benefit; these few leaders of religions brainwash innocent people and motivate them to fight with the rest of the world to prove themselves the best religion of all. The more the people get involved in such activities, the more benefits the corrupt religious leader will get. The common people follow them blindly with their full strength and belief and keep on fighting with others too. The innocent people indulge in religious war. The corrupt leaders will keep on enjoying benefits. The common people will remain busy in useless provocation of religious base and will not take time to think and ask religious leaders. Each and every human being on this earth must understand it very clearly that no religion of the world will advise them to fight with people to prove themselves the best. The religion will not be the winner by telling people, rather will be the best by uniting people. The people will not follow any religion by force but they will accept if they will feel the religion is easy, comfortable, and efficient in showering happiness in their life.

Million Wings feels that every religion in the world teaches humans a lesson of peace, love, and happiness. The human is born in one or another religion. Whatever is the family's religion will be his/her religion by default. Childhood and youth grows under the same religion of the family. The norms and regulations become a part of human's lifestyle and the human feels their religion is right and the best because he spends his life in those religious circumstances and beliefs. It appears right and true also.

The human will definitely respect and believe in his religion he has lived from birth, and it should be like this only. Million Wings feels that to appreciate one's own religion is good but it never means that one should disrespect other religious feelings and beliefs. To live life as per one's religious belief is every one's life, but forcing the same on others or thinking of one's own religion as the best is orthodox thinking, which is not justified.

The leaders of the religion rather than the general followers should come forward to clarify doubts/queries/misunderstandings/misbeliefs raised by other religions. The reason is very obvious, that only the top gurus and religious leaders have maximum and genuine right knowledge about their religion and they are in the best position to manage the sensitive situation of religion than the general public.

Million Wings feels that only the sincere prayer will reach God; the rest is lost into the universe. God never changes someone's circumstances but actually highlights optimistic possibilities on sincere prayer. Million Wings feels that the prayer filled with true intentions, belief is directed to God. Most of the people belonging to any religion always remember God and say prayers with full belief and sincerity, but only a few leaders of any or all religions have modified the wordings of our gurus as per their own benefits. These are a few corrupt religious leaders who misguide and misdirect the innocent people in the name of God and religion. There are a few corrupt religious leaders who make their followers orthodox of the superiority of their own religion and fill their mindsand hearts with disrespect and enmity for other religions. There are a few corrupt religious leaders who control the people and rule over the world. Million Wings feels that most of the religious leaders understand well the writings of religious gurus and spread the right message to their followers. Most of the people also obey the guidance of gurus with the best of their belief and strength. Most of the people visit holy places with full faith, enthusiasm and mannerly behaviour. Most of the people listen sincerely to the words of gurus at holy events and places. Most of the religious leaders construct religious buildings with full faith and belief so that the followers can visit them and understand the belief of holy gurus.

Million Wings feels that a few people have sole intention to extract their personal benefits from religious grounds. Such psychically corrupt, clever, and criminal people have made religion an occupational advantage. Even some people who visit holy places try to pull and push other people to enter first, sometimes misbehave or fight with others. To handle such people, we need security guards even at holy places. We need to arrange systematic organized security system at holy places. We have to announce again and again to maintain discipline at holy places. Sometimes security man has to control the people forcefully. Just think what is the need of police or security at holy places? If the people really understand their religion and their great gurus, then there is absolutely no need of forceful discipline arrangements. If the people really follow their religion with great understanding, belief, faith, and sincerely, then they should behave with other followers of atleast their own religion, with great care, love, and respect, and don't you agree? A holy place has an atmosphere of peace of mind and soul, where the prayers are delivered in a melodious, musical manner which gives immense pleasure to mind and soul.

The smallest prayer for every human being on this earth, which can be done anywhere anytime, is as follows:

Hey, Creator! Bless me with the best of circumstances and the best of decisions all the time.

Prayer is the only purpose of any or all religion.

帚 帚 帚

Chapter 33

Ententainment

Million Wings feels that every human must be guided to enjoy every moment of happiness. If there is opportunity, then he should use that opportunity fully and enjoy the moment. Million Wings feels that as life is so long, in the same way, make every moment long. Don't let happiness be small. Happiness increases happiness. Happiness gives rise to happiness. Try to enjoy every moment of happiness. Million Wings feels that whenever it's a chance of celebration, then it is the best time period. Try to manage the moment of happiness as early as possible. Long time period means that the opportunity is going to waste and happiness will be diverted. Maximum importance of today's happiness is today only as today one is most capable of celebrating. What will the future bring? Nobody is clear about it. What will the future circumstances be? No one knows it today. If circumstances are good, favourable then enjoy today fully. The more the strategy of tomorrow is clear, the more graceful happiness will be. It's true, but will situations will be the same as humans think them? It's not definite. Million Wings feels that if the future has better and favourable conditions, then it's good as then a human will get a better opportunity of happiness. But in future, mental or physical circumstances may be worrisome because of this. We will be unable to enjoy that happiness which we have put in tomorrow. This means often with the passing of time. Chances of happiness decrease instead of increasing. Million Wings feels, utilize and make true every moment of happiness fully, and get happiness and enjoy.

Million Wings feels that life doesn't take time to change. It can be something else in the next moment and can be anything else in the next moment, sometimes better, sometimes even better, sometimesa bit bad, sometimes worse, sometimes we dislike it, sometimes worse situations may arise. It's not important that only bad things are results of bad things. Sometimes there are a few unwanted causes, non-genuine reasons also for any problem or trouble. Life can be entangled in pain in seconds, for which human is not even ready or has not even thought of. A person might not be able to come out from these situations even if he wants. Million Wings feels that emergency situations like road accidents, diseases, fights, sudden mistakes, natural problems, doubtful relations, betrayal, are like unwanted guests which harm us, which raise mental and physical problems and confuse a person. Million Wings feels that if harm is clear because of a mistake of the person, it's still understandable but sometimes human suffers because of innocence and natural problems for which it's not only a human who is responsible. Sometimes he makes such mistakes which sometimes prove to be very dangerous, which the human hasn't even thought of. Now who is aware of these sudden problems? So because of this, we are bit unsure and the possibility of any problem is there which can decrease or suppress human happiness. Million Wings feels that if today there are chances, circumstances of happiness that our personal balance of cycle should be maintained. Million Wings feels, today manage and get ready for a chance of happiness, today only, and take action soon and enjoy life. The opportunities of happiness, which are got suddenly, should be enjoyed at that time. It's right, it's logical.

Million Wings feels that persons should try to enjoy present happiness to maximum extent for a long time. Million Wings feels that everyone lives his life completely, then a person should enjoy happiness to the highest extent so that every moment will become memorable, which can be enjoyed today and becomes a beautiful part of tomorrow. It's true, and make it true.

Entertainment is the world's biggest profession after food and clothes. Entertainment provides happiness and refreshes humans. Entertainment, like music, dance, tourism, festivals, supports, digital media, are capable to provide physical and mental enjoyment and refreshment.

Music is a wonderful source of entertainment. Music has limitless entertainment, music is happiness, music is meditation. Music provides plausible comfort in every situation. It is heard according to interest and heart. Being lost in music gives a wonderful feeling. Music is a sweet and beautiful way to express feelings of heart. Real music is that which provides relaxation. Music is that which gives comfort. Music is that which is sweet to hear. Music is that in which a person loses himself. Music is the name of expressing our feelings in melodious ways. Music gives happiness everywhere, every moment. Music helps to link up every caste, religion, border, colour, race.

Music doesn't have any border. Music is filled with love. Music has wonderful indoctrination. Music links up hearts. Music erases boundaries. Music is friendship. Music links up the whole universe in one thread. Music is just relaxation. Music lets our body dance. Music gives satisfaction. Music erases sorrows. Music banishes tensions. Music gives health. Music is treatment, music provides mental and physical comfort, music is a source of happiness.

Million Wings feels that every person should let himself bind with music; music of choice should be made as part of their own life. Choosing entertainment according to one's will provides relaxation in every happy and sad moment. Music is a melodious source of entertainment which can be enjoyed everywhere, every moment.

Million Wings feels that to dance is very strong and effective way to enjoy happiness, being lost gives relaxation and refreshes heart, mind, soul, and body. To dance according to interest and capacity is ultimate action of enjoyment. This wonderful chance of music and dance takes humans to the ultimate level of entertainment whenever you feel like enjoying, dancing, singing.

Million Wings feels that it's very enjoyable to have a glance of natural and artificial beauty. Tourism lets human feel natural atmosphere. Mountains, hills, flowers, sea water, air, snowfall, clouds, rain, weather, birds, greenery, etc. refreshes humans internally and externally. Human-made/constructed buildings, bridges, etc. are also very marvellous sources of entertainment.

Humans should manage time for tourism from time to time. Enjoy the opportunity of tourism at national and international level. Thinking also changes and improves by visiting new places and it's healthy too.

Always check for holidays and opening and closing timings of visiting places before going there. Travel timings of trains, buses, planes, and other travel media must be checked beforehand. Try to arrange all tickets in advance because many times, tickets are not available on the spot or take a lot of time to purchase or ofcourse are costly on the spot. Wherever you go for tourism, plan beforehand or atleast get all the information the very first day so that you can plan the best tourism experience there. Food habits and climate condition can make your packing best utilized. The mindset of people to be visited must be analysed, especially on religious views and female status.

Family and social customs and festivals fill life with energy and power. Festivals celebrated at national and international level are opportunities of happiness for every human. Humans should enjoy every festival of their choice. Festivals and functions provide beautiful opportunities to meet own ones and to enjoy. A person should not just enjoy festivals of own state or nation but should enjoy festivals of own choice of other countries too.

Festivals and functions are sources of happiness and increase togetherness. It doesn't matter that festival is of which state, which country. It's upto you. If you like that, then do celebrate, must enjoy. The meaning of festival is happiness only.

Million Wings feels, invite just that number of people at parties, functions, festivals, to whom you can attend well. The easy way of this is that other than neighbours, invite important relatives and best friends to a wedding and other functions. To attend doesn't mean to arrange costlier event. Infact it means to meet and attend to everyone with love, affection, and respect and to manage comfortable arrangement of food, stay, and living.

Million Wings feels that sports are the beautiful way of entertainment. Sports along with entertainment provides mental cleverness and physical health. To play is a powerful way of entertainment which gives happiness to heart, health to body, and business opportunity too. Million Wings feels that a person who is attached with sports remains healthier and enjoys happiness to more extent. A person whose passion and profession is related to sports will get both entertainment and health together. Million Wings feels that making sports a passion of children is really a great achievement.

Digital media are new and enjoyable ways of entertainment. Mobile, video games, movies, social network software are technical research of entertainment which are available everywhere at international level. Enjoyment doubles by giving more original form to technology. With the help of social network software, today a human is attached with the whole world. Everyone is trying to make coordination with friends, relatives living in other countries. The whole world can talk to each other with the help of mobile and Internet. Through social network software, humans can make friends of own choice, can talk to each other, and can understand well. By digital media, humans can entertain themselves whenever, wherever they want.

Million Wings feels that the natural sources of entertainment which have been the same for centuries are to meet, laugh, enjoy with family and friends. To sit and talk with family, to listen and share each other's views, eat together, and playing together are comfortable and evergreen sources of entertainment which provide happiness and moral support to every person. To meet best friends is entertainment in itself. But to enjoy other sources of entertainment doubles the enjoyment.

Million Wings feels that a person always enjoys every act, work in which person is interested. Coordination made in every work done with agreement and will fill humans' life with happiness. Million Wings feels that whatever a human wants to do should be done by heart and will, then it will be happiness all around, entertainment around, and doing this with agreement of another doubles everything. Million Wings feels that bad habits of humans give them feelings of entertainment and happiness. Bad habits have their own enjoyment, i.e. a different type of enjoyment. Million Wings feels that if a person is enjoying his bad habits within limits then they are not bad. Bad habits like taking drugs, sex, enjoyment, etc. are bad because humans are using wrong ways to fulfil them which are harmful at personal and social level. Million Wings feels that bad habits are bad when they start giving pain to others and ourselves. If a person will move in balanced ways, then these can be enjoyable; every person has less or more bad habits which are a priority of personal entertainment. Humans should enjoy bad habits in balanced way. While bad habits are not harmful to anyone, a human is right, logical. Personal harm is of human himself upto whatever limit he can do and can save. Million Wings feels that a bad habit gives enjoyment upto some extent within some limits, above which these are harmful for every person, and because of this, humans can enjoy bad habits for a short time only. Doing bad habits in unbalanced ways harm the body/health to such an extent that than bad hobbies just becomes compulsion, but don't give any enjoyment.

If bad habits don't entertain, then what's the use of those bad habits which give only temporary enjoyment and, after that, create only tension and problems for the rest of life? A human should manage/enjoy bad habits in such a way that he can enjoy them his whole life on 0 percent harm. Harm should not occur to such an extent that the human needs to be dependent on time, money, and ownones or destroys or uses his personal resources, and without resources, freedom, happiness, and entertainment it's all zero. It's true, it's right, it's logical. It's reality and it will remain reality. Let's understand deeply upto which extent and how he can enjoy bad habits.

Million Wings feels that if a human wants to enjoy freely then he can do it very comfortably. Enjoyment is not bad. Actually, humans have to make good coordination to have enjoyment. If a human wants to manage more time for himself, then he has to spend less time with others. It's not wrong to do so. If a person has to give less time to others, then give it to those who need it more and who are your responsibility also, e.g. parents, children, lifepartner. According to daily schedule, give quality time with full presence to your family, fulfil their needs. By receiving such quality time, they get their share of belongingness and happiness, and they will not become any compulsion or cause dissatisfaction.

Actually if a human needs to spare time for entertainment, then he should not try to manage family time; instead he needs to collect it from other resources, e.g. social programs, unwanted relations, or solemnity.

Million Wings feels that management increases happiness. The human heart, mind, and soul get power, satisfaction by fulfilling minimum responsibilities; they getunique comfort while having enjoyment. Somewhere mind and soul feels unhealthy and tense about enjoyment by hurting our near and dear ones. Every person should fulfil basic and necessary needs of dependent near and dear ones by himself or with the help of someone else. It's right and logical management which provides personal peace of mind, motivation, and moral support, and a person will enjoy every happiness to higher extent. It's true, it's right, it's logical.

Million Wings feels that if humans have resources, then it's not bad to use them for personal happiness and entertainment. If a human has money/good financial status and he wants to use/spend it for his passion and comfort, then what's wrong in doing this? All members of family using spare money for comfort and enjoyment after fulfilling basic needs of family is not bad. If financial status is good, then enjoy comfort and facilities to easily reachable limits. It's not any crime. It's good to take benefit of every comfort which is in reach, which a person is capable of. Million Wings feels that if a person is able to buy any comfort, then he should use it to that extent upto which it doesn't cause any personal physical harm. Alcohol can be drunk to such an extent that it doesn't cause any damage to liver. Fight to an extent till we have the power of being right. Spend money to such an extent that logical facilities should be maintained. Million Wings feels that if a human has unlimited money, still he needs a few such friends from whom he can borrow money as even unlimited money can decrease or may be destroyed easily, as most people have not only to live in present but have to live in the future also. Very few people can die before time. Everyone lives their future fully and has to use resources according to their whole lives as if death occurs before time, then the rest of the resources can be used by near and dear ones to fulfil their passion and desires; otherwise, humans will enjoy unlimited, unstoppable source of entertainment.

Million Wings feels that a human can't just have enjoymentthe whole day and if he can do so, then for how long? For how many days? If he does any harm to his health, then disease will surround him and if the person will be diseased, then he can't enjoy entertainment and if he can't enjoy it, then what is entertainment about? Million Wings feels that if a human wants enjoyment, then he should atleast maintain his capability of enjoyment. The more a person remains healthy and capable, the more he will enjoy. It's important to sleep an average of 6 to 8 hours to remain fit and healthy. It's important to take two good nutritional meals. If it's important to work, then it's also important to take rest and to take nutritional meals. If we want enjoyment, then it's urgent to earn money. If we want enjoyment, then it's important to do professional work. If we want enjoyment daily, then it's important to take care of ourselves. If we want enjoyment daily, then it's important to change according to time. Million Wings feels that enjoyment, relaxation, and comfort can be part of daily living; it's not to do in the remaining time after work, after this, after that, etc. To increase personal physical and mental capabilities, relaxation is the best logical, permanent secret. Million Wings feels that every person should enjoy not only for a day, two days, a few weeks, a month but for a whole life.

Million Wings feels that law is common sense and is here to give the right direction to life. Law is not meant to complicate issues but it's to solve and simplify matters. Law is to maintain and increase peace, not to disturb people. Law moves with life, changes with life. So rules, security, and principles can be changed, with changed rules, change of time and people. Law is not permanent but amendment can be done according to circumstances. If any law is made, then it is the same for everyone but can't be applied the same in every condition. Police should not follow the law blindly in every situation. Infact they should understand conditionsand situations and should make decisions according to that situation so that peace in society can be maintained; only this is logical. Every rule or law should be made to maintain social security, safety, justice, and balanced happiness, not to increase personal problems and tensions. At time of need, use of law as common sense is the best way to use law. It's the right law, as law can't be permanent.

Million Wings feels that people with wrong and bad intentions betray and harm others cleverly for personal benefit, and to avoid them, these actions rules are made. Common people also suffer from those formalities of rules. Just because of very few people, new amendments in rules and law are done, which increases tension for government, administration, police, and common people. Million Wings feels that rules and regulations can be made for only those things and actions which have authentic possibility to cause serious hazards. A real and logical motto of law is to catch and punish people with wrong and corrupt intentions and not to increase tensions of innocent and common people. By keeping bad intentions in mind, law should be made to get maximum effective administration so that police and security force and common people will be least disturbed and maximum lesson can taught to corrupt and criminal people.

Million Wings feels that Internet and digital media area very good source of entertainment. Science and technology have given an amazing and praiseworthy happiness to the whole world. It has connected the whole world together. Social networking software of Facebook, Whatsapp, Wechat, etc., are very fast and enjoyable forms of networking. Million Wings feels that by this technology, people attach with each other, know about each other, understand each other. Million Wings feels that if girls and boys talk through their social media apps, it's good, as it will not create any serious harm to their personal security. The more they talk to each other, the earlier they start understanding each other. Like this they easily recognize people of their own choice, with whom they feel comfortable and secure. They can further go ahead, meet other. Social media is the best and easiest way to express our feelings, a good way to improve friendship and relations. Million Wings feels that girls and boys should not share/show their personal pictures on social media. Everything else is all right.

The only way, if we want to enjoy the best of everything, is to stay connected with the whole world because every country has something in its best form, which may be available in another continent or country too, but may be average quality and quantity, e.g. natural beauty, food, adventures, enjoyment (like liquor, music, casino, sex), cultural melody, education, technology. Million Wings feelsif whole world is a friend, then it's easier to enjoy specialities of each other in a harmonious and happy mood. Let's respect and stay connected with everyone on this earth.

Chapter 34

Are bad habits really bad?

Sometimes, heart feelings become bad because the ways adopted to fulfil them are wrong. Million Wings feels that there is nothing good or bad; infact it's a comparison point of view. A good habit means happiness and bad habit means sorrow. Everything which gives us happiness is all good and our every habit which gives pain and sorrow to others is bad for them, and it's right too. While our habit is giving us happiness, it's good for us, and when it starts giving pain, it turns into a bad habit. It's true and right too. Feelings of anger, sex, affection, greed, ego are not bad and neither are they any crime. All these feelings are human nature, which has beenthe same for centuries and will remain the same while life lasts. Infact these feelings can be made more enjoyable by the right strategy and efficiency. If these feelings will not remain in humans, then what will be the source of motivation in human life?

Million Wings feels that mostly needs, dreams, desires are right only, but the ways to fulfil them might be wrong, and because of this, everything seems to be wrong. Feelings like sex, anger, greed, affection, ego, fights, drugs, betrayal, lies, mistakes, jealousy, expectations, force can't be separated from humans and are not easy to separate or destroy. If it will be so easy, then religions, holy books, saints have taught so much to humans to make/build atmosphere of idealism and civilization on this earth. Worldwide religions are also unable to pull humans from these habits, infact putting

370

humans in stages of depression and crime. Million Wings feels that there is nothing wrong, bad, shy, nor is there a crime in these feelings, dreams, and desires. Infact they can be fulfilled rightly and will give good experiences of maximum enjoyment.

Million Wings feels that sex is that desire which is attached naturally with humans which God has attached with beautiful and expressive feelings. Desire and enjoyment of sex is so high in males that they're naturally attracted towards this and it's very normal to have romantic relations. If sex is done with mutual understanding and will, then it gives feelings of comfort and enjoyment. It's not a crime to have sex with mutual coordination, will, and agreement. Sex can be done with whoever heartfelt feeling matches. Million Wings feels that will to make romantic relations in male and female is a natural feeling which is not built by God; infact God made this. It's natural attraction between male and female. Except God's love and human love, everything else is done after being thought. Love is a natural feeling on which there is no control of anyone, and in this feeling, male and female concentrate onone male or female. But feelings to meet, flirt, enjoy, be affectionate are well-thought feelings. The feeling and intentions which humans can think before doing that should be arranged in such a manner that no one can be harmed, self-respect of anyone should not get harmed, and our own desires should also be fulfilled. If a human wants to make romantic relations or physical relations or sexual relations, then he should make them away from blood relations and near relatives. Our first-degree relations are non-romantic relations. Second-degree or relations further from them are safer and more secure. The further the romantic relations are from permanent home, the more comfortable it will be.

The male/female is with whichever male/female should give complete intention to that person only. A person may make romantic relations with whatever number of person. Two males can make romantic relations with one male, but both males and both females can't tolerate each other after knowing each other; neither can they live together. To betray for fulfilment of sexual feelings makes a person wrong. Flirting by making false promises of love, marriage with any male or female is not right. Making relations by clearly and truly talking about our feelings is real happiness; nothing's wrong in this. Being clear to the related person is the best thing. Every person can have personal life; to do this is his right and also he will. When any male or female chooses another male or female for romantic, physical, or sexual relations, it's not sure the other male/female will like him/her in the same way. Humans have to make relations with mutual understanding. Every person has lots of people around him/her and not only those male/female or with any male/female whom our thinking can match. That's why the search for a person with alike thinking is a search for happiness. If one male/female refuses, then don't torture the person to accept you. Most people feel that they have to make relations with only that male or female; this thought is totally a misunderstanding. Million Wings feels that there are thousands, millions of people with alike thinking and are near to each other. It's better to find a person with the same mentality and thinking, then why change someone as per own thinking? A person doesn't have just one or two male/female around them; infact they have a whole society, nation, and world. Persons should try to find some new male/female if one refuses them, then surely and soon they will find some new partner of their choice with whom their mentality and thinking matches and they'll enjoy life fully and tension free.

Million Wings feels that sex is just physical enjoyment; a person has many options to fulfila need for sex. The most comfortable is that which is done with heart, will, and understanding of both sides. But the same will be very painful when it is done forcibly and with betrayal. Having sex just for physical satisfaction has no importance. Sex can be human nature, compulsion, responsibility, need, enjoyment, betrayal, or profession. Sex done without any feeling has no use. Million Wings feels that sex is not just presence of male and female but agreement and will of selected male and female is logical meaning and enjoyment. Sex can't be done and enjoyed with anyone but can be done with those with whom thinking matches and heart agrees (selective sex). But prostitution is much better than forcing someone or betraying someone. Government and administration should implement rules and make prostitution authenticated and secure so that a human can satisfy his feelings like sex, and crimes like rape should be banished from society.

Million Wings feels that feelings of sex should be fulfilled by the age of 16–18 years as before that sexual organs are not fully developed and doing so before time may cause harm to health. If sex can be done after understanding it rightly, then it's not any crime, nor does having sex cause any harm. Neither there is any harm to self-respect and nor any cause of harm to life. Having sex safely is a good thing. By use of a condom, a person can be saved from unwanted pregnancy and sexual diseases. Give important and urgent information related to sex to youngsters in arranged manner so that misunderstanding fear related to sex can be removed. Sex is neither a big thing nor a bad thing. It's not important to have sex; it's love only. Sex can be a beautiful part of love. Having sex gives mental and emotional satisfaction and health. Sex gives enjoyment. Sex should be done according to our capacity and will. A person should have his own resources. Have sex while taking care of money, time, and physical capacity. Don't let sex control the mind. If sex controls the mind then it becomes madness, craziness. Then sex doesn't just remain a physical act, which has no enjoyment. Have sex as per capacity with people of one's choice, clearly with mutual understanding and will, and enjoy it fully.

Million Wings feels that sex is a feeling filled with love, and while enjoying this, humans should act softly and respectfully. Reacting wildly and as a beast while having sex is totally wrong. Those males and females who have sex with mutual understanding and will are much better than those who are just crazy for sex and whose minds are controlled by sex. These kinds of people are those whose intentions are to create terror in society. They should be handled seriously. These types of people should be caught and should be punished strictly. Those who try to rape a child or anyone in society should not be spared at any cost.

Million Wings feels that teenagers and youngsters have curiosity and interest regarding sex and they become victims of porn movies. What's the use of that masturbation which can't provide complete enjoyment? Government and administration should provide information and knowledge to teenagers and youngsters through movies atleast once in a week. It's important to guide youngsters about diseases and prevention related to sexual organs, sexual relations, pregnancy.

Million Wings feels that being annoyed/angry is a natural reaction of humans. Do it whenever you feel like and upto any limit you feel like but no one should die because of your anger on the spot and neither should anyone become permanently handicapped. To show anger to the related person is good but to be annoyed with one and blame and torture other is totally wrong. A human is annoyed only when something or work happens against his will and agreement. So doing this is right only. Whenever you become annoyed with someone, just tell the related person on the spot only. Raging on that person only who is the reason behind your anger and telling him on the spot only is right, is logical. Scolding another because of someone else is cowardice or to rage on nonliving thing is also wrong to some extent. The best thing is to rage on the spot. To rage onthe spot is the best option; by this a person is able to maintain his peace of mind and satisfaction. If we keep anger in the heart, it keeps on disturbing mental peace. By doing so, rage isn't collected in the heart and neither does any misunderstanding or burden remain.

Million Wings feels that if on the spot a person rages on another, then just saying and telling the related person peace of mind wasn't disturbed. By this, things don't worsen to fights etc. Express your anger as early as possible so that frustration isn't collected inthe heart and mind. The more time we don't express our frustration or anger, the more it keeps on collecting in our mind and the result is more dangerous fights and quarrels. Often, fights, arguments, and quarrels naturally occur with own ones. There is nothing like relations will break within sometime; everything becomes normal in relations. In heartfelt relations, there may be fights to any extent but they never leave each other apart. They may fight to any extent in rage but it's totally wrong, unacceptable to kill anyone or make another permanently handicapped. One shouldn't take life or permanently handicap another just for the sake of rage of a few seconds, as after a few seconds, every person calms down. Everything will be corrected after being annoyed, but if anyone is permanently handicapped or killed, then how will it be corrected? Words can be taken back, apologies can be given for unmatchable miswords said, but it's impossible to bring back the person who died or who becomes permanently handicapped. Chances of anger the annoyed has for a lifetime increases.

Million Wings feels that greed is part of human nature. If person didn't have a feeling of greed, then for what does he collect resources? And resources are important to fulfil dreams and desires. Money is very helpful to collect important things of one's choice. So humans have greed for money. Actually money is a unit of humans' hardwork. The more dreams and desires are, the more money is needed to fulfil them. So more is the hardwork to be done. If humans want to collect more money by doing more work, then what's bad in this? Infact cruelty is to earn money by betrayal and by wrong methods.

Million Wings feels that the greater the financial status, the better it is for individuals. Even the desire of earning more money is not bad. A human should workhard, and let him earn money to any extent. Nothing's bad in this, and let him collect more comfort and facilities. Persons should workhard for an average of 8 hours (comparable money). But to thieve, betray, or maraud are wrong methods and these should not be tolerated at any cost. This is not the right way to collect money. Infact it's to fleece others of their hardwork. Easy money is that for which an individual personally needn't workhard (i.e. equivalent to its real deserved value), e.g. theft, marauding, corruption, betrayal, etc. Million Wings feels that gambling is a game to earn money, in which a person earnsor loses money with his cleverness, intelligence, possibilities on the basis of guessing, then it's his personal will. Government and administration of the nation should make safe, secure, and authenticated casinos, and playing should be once in month, when it should be played with digital card money. Whoever wants to play games of gambling should give full details of his money. Everyone can use 25 per cent of one's earned money to gamble. Details of gambling should be sent to government. To gamble is not wrong. But to gamble with money earned by theft, marauding, betrayal, etc. is surely wrong. To get property from one's share without any hardwork is not wrong but forcibly or by betrayal taking property from the share of one's brother/sister or mother/father is totally wrong.

Million Wings feels, earn to any extent, any limit, but by hard work. The logical way is to take any amount of money from anyone, but surely give the deserved value of that money. Take any level of work from anyone but surely give them value of their hardwork.

Million Wings feel that everyone should earn and save atleast that amount of money from which his food, clothes, and atleast minimum needs and facilities of life should be fulfilled. Dreams and desires come afterwards, to fulfil which human needs money, and all this seems to be right. Actually, a human isn't greedy for money but he needs more money to fulfil his dreams and desires, which seems to be right also. Passion doesn't have any limit, passion doesn't have any value.

Million Wings feels that a human earns enough money by working hard in his profession. Yes, if a person has many resources to earn money, then it's better the person should spend the rest of money in gambling or other business or opportunity after fulfilling primary needs. Government and administration should open different authenticated casinos where people who are interested can play freely and in plausible way.

Million Wings feels that affection is the main feeling which binds human relations. If there is no affection, then people will not meet other people. Million Wings feels that it's natural to have affection with own ones. Persons can be attached to another to any extent but it should not bind or restrict anyone. Affection means the will of staying with one, means taking care of each other. Affection gives a comfortable feeling. Million Wings feels, do love and care for anyoneto any extent but it should not be any compulsion or restriction for anyone. Love is good to an extent while personal freedom isn't disturbed. Binding anyone with ourselves forever in the name of affection is totally wrong, as that affection doesn't seem to be good which has lots of restrictions.

Million Wings feels that the logical meaning of affection is being affectionate with someone to such an extent that he should give full freedom and motivation to another to fulfil his dreams and desires. Love, affection that works to the extent where freedom starts decreasing the freedom of another is not affection, but it becomes suffocation and restrictions to another. Million Wings feels that every creature has his/her own life; they have to live their own ways. But parents and own ones have to help to live life. A person doesn't feel belongingness if there is no affection. Affection binds the universe, affection is belongingness; affection with own ones is strength, morale support. The real strength of relations depends upon affection. If affection is there, then only humans bring up their children and children take care of parents but more affection than required becomes boundary and compulsion. Affection doesn't mean to reduce personal freedom. By care and love, affection arises so that everyone should live with full strength to fulfil one's dreams and desires. Families have been families for centuries because of love/affection. Humans live for each other because of affections. Affection gives feelings of care and happiness.

Million Wings feels that ego can be done for everything which helps in decreasing problems and sorrows of others and helps to raise a ray of hope. A person can show ego for every thing, work, strategy which hasa possibility and hope to reduce sorrows and problems of others. Nothing is bad in bragging or showing ego about these things. Every brag which will give positive direction and which will increase confidence and moral support is respectable, is right, is logical. Million Wings feels that a person can brag about everything which he has done by himself, or bragging about maintaining natural beauty is also not wrong. Bragging and ego is for others, not for own ones. Because ownones are real cause of strength behind ego and bragging not to tolerate. Million Wings feels that to maintain bragging and ego, a person himself and his other parties, helpers, colleagues have to work regularly for brag or ego on the basis of successful results, not just on talk. And successful results can be maintained if persons will work cleverly and intelligently with fresh mind and body.

Million Wings feels that every habit which will give enjoyment to person, he should adopt that and do that. The habitsshould give pleasure to the human and should neither be harmful to anyone or should give pleasure to others also. Those habits are good. The habits which give personal happiness but harmother people will be obviously restricted by other people, but the person himself will want to do those, as who wants to be sad or in problems because of others? Obviously no one. If anyone has a problem from another, then obviously persons will react in many ways. Firstly they will try to stop them, then try to make them understand. If still the person will not understand, then obviously he will react forcibly or boycott them. Those people who are attached emotionally or are weak or are not independent, e.g. children, females, old persons, or parents, may tolerate even problematic habits of an individual. Million Wings feels that few habits are those which harm a person also along with giving him pleasure. OK, let's agree that a person does those activities which will give him pleasure, may others be harmed or benefit. OK, let's agree to this also, that a person should not bother about the world and not about his relations but everyone has to atleast bother about oneself so that one can enjoy one's bad habits.

Million Wings feels that an individual has to manage his objectives and activities in such a way that they will provide him pleasure his whole life. An individual has to think about what he needs/requires to fulfil his bad habits. If individual has all these things with him, then bad habits have their own enjoyment. To love ourselves, we need to be physically fit, have money status and togetherness of own ones. We ourselves have to manage resources for our every habit, as only we ourselves know what our happiness is. Firstly we should know about our limits and physical capacities so that we can enjoy our habits by staying with ourselves. A person can enjoy the maximum capacity of hisbody every time, again and again, as if the person will enjoy more than his capacity, then his body will be damaged soon. So when the body is not fit, then the body will not feel good or fit to enjoy. It hardly matters if the world will not stand with us, but if our health will stop supporting us, then humans will feel restricted. Then what will a person do? The years for which human wants to enjoy life he should stretch his possibilities, capacities, limitations, and security to that level and should fit his bad habits in that. Million Wings feels that expenditure of bad habits is also important. If there is money, then only can a person easily collect things to fulfil his bad habits.

Million Wings feels that if bad habits are our own, then a person should have his own money to fulfil them. Why will someone else give us money to fulfil our bad habits? Instead of giving money to us, he will use the same money to fulfil his bad habits and this is right too. To fulfil bad habits even more, money decreases, or only that person will give us money who doesn't know where we are going to spend our money or that person is also the same along with us or another person wants that we should be destroyed because of our bad habits. Million Wings feels you must earn money yourself and then use it for your bad habits. Neither is there any need to take money by telling lies, nor is there any need to return that. Earn it yourself and use it yourself. Own money can be spent anywhere, any amount of money can be spent. What has another to do with that?

Million Wings feels that firstly, individuals should separate that amount of money which is necessary for daily living, e.g. food for 2–3 times, clothes to cover body, education of children, water and electricity bills. After keeping money safe for daily necessities, utilize the rest of the money in your bad habits. Sometimes, if health worsens because of bad habits, then keep spare money for that also. By doing so, bad habits become more enjoyable. Manage today the money you earned today and make the right budget for your bad habits. Million Wings feels that security and safety are also necessary for bad habits, as government and administration keep on looking around so that government can catch the persons with bad habits and can provide security to the rest of the people. If a person wants to enjoy his bad habits, then he needs his security too. Mostly bad habits are personal life of individual. Humans want to keep them secure too, and to think and do this is right too. Personal happiness is for ourselves only, not to show to the rest of the world. If a person wants to keep any matter or thing safe and secure, then he should do that with more security and with more responsibility.

The things, matters, chances which are in front of people, it's obvious that they can misuse these. If a person will fulfil his bad habits more safely and more securely, then only he can enjoy his bad habits more. If it will be disclosed at social level, then it can't be enjoyed comfortably and securely. If people will be interrupted by someone, then the chance can't be enjoyed again and again. Personal safety is also important to enjoy bad habits. Wherever there's risk, there is enjoyment. But if risk is reduced to minimum, then it's more enjoyable and prideful. Every type of risk can be taken to fulfil a bad habit. But taking risks for anything that restricts us or makes us dependent on others or takes us towards death is nothing less than stupidity. Bad habits are enjoyable only if they can be enjoyed again and again. Persons need to be fit to enjoy them again and again. If we ourselves remain fit, then only we can enjoy them again and again. Small wounds are normal but avoid danger of serious injuries and do prepare for them so that if needed, then a person can handle himself. Nothing to be worried about or tense from injuries, but precautions and awareness and preparation are for a tension free and secure thing. Obviously, enjoyment important doubles by doing so. So a human has to collect maximum information about his bad habits and has to manage according to its good and bad effects.

Million Wings feels that after health, money, and security, a person needs related people and resources to fulfil his bad habits. Everything is available in the world for every habit and passion; only the support of experienced and confidential people is needed. Million Wings feels that coordination made by mutual understanding and will is the best moment of happiness. Trying to harm or doing forcefulness or betraying others for personal benefit is not to get anything. The enjoyment which is in mutual coordination and agreement to fulfil our demands is how the same enjoyment is possible in forcefulness, betrayal, compulsion, and when everything is ready, then look for real enjoyment. It's very important to choose the right trustworthy people and resources to fulfil our bad habits.

Million Wings feels that whatever a person wants to do in life or is already doing, the biggest strength is to have the support of trustworthy people and friends who stand beside in every situation and who resolve every problem. Friends! Do whatever you want to do, but complete information and resources are needed more and then you yourself will feel that enjoyment, plausible and awesome. These will be happy and enjoyment is doubled; it's atmosphere. Enjoy your bad habits your whole life in such a way that no one will be harmed. Infact, enjoyment will be doubled everytime; it will be more powerful and strong.

Million Wings feels that after crossing limits, even good things start giving pain, then it's natural that bad habits will surely give pain after crossing limits. Bad people work only for themselves, for their happiness and keep on crossing limits. And good people stand along with bad people who are attached with them and try to pull out their near and dear ones to come out from bad habits. Million Wings feels that bad people don't listen and understand while they don't fall sick or don't become dependent on others, infact misbehaving with their near and dear ones who take care of them, which is totally wrong, totally non-genuine. Mothers/wives/sisters/ friends of bad people try to convince them to leave bad habits like taking drugs but druggies don't understand, don't listen to them, and when they fall sick, then family members take care of them. Still, druggies behave with anger and jealousy instead of giving them love and respect. Million Wings feels that these types of people need to understand that near and dear ones take care of lung disease because of cigarette smoking etc., those diseases from which humans can escape by using those resources within limits, even after knowing all of them, because of love and affection, not because of compulsion. Remember, if they feel very bad or things become intolerable, then they will also leave, and people with bad habits have to stay alone. Then they will be absolutely right. It's the future and they will be busy in their lives. They tolerate misbehaviour because they love them; otherwise, it's not their compulsion or need to get them treated. It's affection only, because of which all seem to be very busy. Million Wings feels that either bad people should not try to cross their limits or if they do so and are entangled in serious problems, then they should accept that and should behave in the right and respectful way.

Million Wings feels that near and dear ones should help each other in which person is not directly involved, but natural problems entangle them. But the problems/diseases which the person has raised himself, he is responsible himself, e.g. liver damage because of excessive intake of alcohol, cancer, orif the person is using more drugs and falls sick, then near and dear ones take care of the person because of affection only. They don't have any compulsion or responsibility. Million Wings feels that those habits or interests can directly/clearly harm bad people, and if you are unable to change them, then just change their atmosphere. With a changed atmosphere, the mind starts diverting, and if there will not be any resources, then habits will automatically cut off.

Million Wings feels that if we enjoy within limits and safely, then our ownones also don't restrict us. Enjoy every bad habit upto that limit. While it's giving pleasure, don't let it control the mind; that is, every habit can be stretched to that limit while it gives pleasure, not any problem or tension. Friends! We just need to pull our every habit to maximum safe and plausible area. This way is the right and intelligent way to extend our happiness for a longtime, which provides us enjoyment from our habits, maybe bad or good. Enjoy.

Chapter 35

Fights

Million Wings feels that a person fights for the safety of their self-respect, then he is supposed to do right. When another tries to cross limits and does not behave genuinely, then to fight for self-respect and rights is totally right. What's wrong in this? For centuries, humans have fought for themselves and will keep on doing the same. Everyone has self-respect, everyone lives for self-respect, and obviously it's one's right and happiness too. Anyone can fight for one's self-respect. Strong issue for a fight is a prideful thing. Fighting on very small issue, making it as question of self-respect doesn't seemto be an interesting thing, e.g. while taking ticket, while parking.

Million Wings feels that before fighting, make yourself free from flaws, which can be gained easily. When a person is right, then he givesa chance to the other to accept his mistake or if he himself is wrong, then accepting his mistake. These are very simple ways to become strong. If still another didn't understand and tries to not be genuine, then it's OK to fight. Because by doing so, a person may be right or wrong, may be good or bad, but he becomes right and good. When person becomes right, then he becomes powerful. The first mistake may be of the other, may be of ourselves; to win afight, a person needs to be strong. And the greatest power is being right. Apologizing if in the wrong is equivalent to being right. Then if the other got beaten up, it's also OK if the person himself is right, then giving one or two genuine chances to the other to say sorry makes us more powerful. Million Wings feels that fights are done with spirit, not with weapons. When both heart and mind are powerful, then there is such a spirit that there is no fear to fight with anyone. The other person may be very strong, powerful, or financially strong. Issue may be any, but being faultfree or flawfree is a powerful victory. Being more right than the other is great power. Less fault means more right. If the other is more powerful or non-genuine or stubborn, then firstly inform police, administration, or media. An individual may fight for himself or get the help of government or administration on personal issues, but on social issues, it's important to inform government or administration and it's personal safety too.

Million Wings feels that fights are done on the spot only; afterwards it's just talks to resolve the issue or matter. Firstly confirm the proof of your innocence on the spot and then teach a lesson to the other. If a person is more right or is less wrong than the other, then he has more flawless power. And to telland prove truth to society, nation, world, government, and administration, click a few pictures and make video on the spot so that there will be sure proof of being right. To fight, collect personal flawless power.

Million Wings feels that fights should be done on the related issue only. Then everything is OK, as when the issue moves on otherside then the main issue of the fight, then the mind is diverted towards that issue, the issue which is responsible for the fight. And if we try to clarify the same issue, then obviously it will be more in our favour; the other person intentionally tries to divert our mind towards some issue other than the issue which is responsible for the fight, infact puttingoff that talk or thing for which we are responsible. For example, another person has misbehaved with us and we have used an abusive word then he focuses onand highlights the word which we have spoken and ignores his own misbehaviour and tries to find our flaw and tries to increase our fight. Remember that by using abusive words, instead of being right, we move towards false. Those people whose work is just to fight will try to find reasons for fights. Don't fight with these stubborn and cowardly people. People like them infact fight with innocent people, family members, colleagues, or people busy with social work, and entangle them, harm them, and think of themselves as very powerful, as common people, intelligent people, and good people first fulfil their familiar, social, and professional responsibility as priority and they don't have extra time to waste on stupid things. When common people take anything seriously, then they know better how to handle big criminals. Million Wings feels that it's better to boycott people who don't have any stand, any principle than to fight with them. Or the right way is to teach them a lesson with the help of police, government, and administration. There is no use in fighting, arguing with those who don't have any principles.

Million Wings feels that if anyone drunk, fights with us and even if gets thrashed by us, then also it's OK. Addiction to drugs might be one's personal happiness and as for that drug which gives happiness to him, he himself is responsible for every mistake which happens unconsciously because of the drug. If someone misbehaves being sozzled then he himself is responsible for that. Individuals may drink, take drugs just for enjoyment, but if someone gives 'being sozzled' as an excuse for his misbehaviour then it's totally illogical, intolerable. Who is beaten up being sozzled is totally genuine, as if an individual can forget his limits being sozzled, then it's logical that he will forget the thrashing too. Being sozzled is personal will, not natural compulsion. Near and dear ones of druggies should understand this thing. If a sozzled person is not responsible, then obviously a person who is fully conscious is surely not responsible. Making a mistake while being sozzled is surely wrong, but thrashing a sozzled person to such an extent that he will die or become handicapped is also not right.

Million Wings feels that on the spot during a fight, always stay among your own ones. If your own ones are right, then combine to give answers to the others, and even if your ownones are wrong, then try your best to save them, and if you are unaware about the situation of who is wrong or right and by how much, then also support your ownones. Support your ownones on the spot; afterwards you may scold them and make them understand. Saving your own ones is one thing and punishing them for being wrong is another thing. Saving your own ones from enemies is the need of the time, on the spot, then you can punish them afterwards. Million Wings feels that sometimes it's difficult to understand each other on the spot as everyone is arguing by talking regarding their own points of view and isn't listening to others or keeps on fighting by stretching talks. Even an intelligent and unentangled person can't control himself on the spot, and agreement converts to physical thrashing and fights. The only way to control fights on the spot is to separate the two who are fighting. Taking them away from each other's vision is even more effective.

Million Wings feels that profession issues should be fought or decided in professional ways only, not to interfere or comment on personal life. If we comment on or obstruct the personal life of someone in a professional matter, then we start being wrong and increase the flawless stage of another person. Million Wings feels that abusive words are always non-genuine which aren't concerned with the issues or matters related to fights. Infact, such words canwork as oil on fire in issues of fights. The side of the one who starts using abusive words is weakened though he may be right on the main issue, e.g. someone collided with our car and we start using abusive words then obviously his feeling of saying sorry starts to be reduced and it hurts his self-respect too, and because of this, quarrels increase. If someone broke our car unknowingly and in return we break his car, it seems to be right. But instead of getting the harm of the car, if we start using abusive words for him, his mother, his sister, it's totally illogical. Is there any match between our car and respect of his mother or sister? Million Wings feels that you shouldn't weaken your side by using abusive words.

Million Wings feels that there is a difference between quarrels of males and females. Females usually fight with words and easily forgive each other. Being annoyed everytime they start repeating old things, they soon maintain their coordination and affectionate feelings. Mutual fights of females should be left to females only. Females can handle each other better. Generally, males convert their arguments to physical strikes. Once they fight with someone, generally they don't continue normal life with them. Generally, females want that males should stand along with them and speak for their self-respect, but they don't want them to start physical fights and get harmed. Females should try to calm males in their fights and not speak in between. But if fights take the form of life or death, then everything is genuine.

Million Wings feels that thrashing each other's children in a mutual quarrel of adults or elders is totally wrong. Seriously injuring or killing a child is a sin which can't be tolerated at any cost. Million Wings feels that if we want to take revenge from one who betrayed us or misbehaved priorly, it's not wrong. Million Wings feels that solid proof is required to take revenge, as level, issue, and seriousness should be the same to take revenge. Taking revenge is a way to get peace of mind and personal satisfaction, and it's right, logical, true too. But yes, if we ensure that there is no misunderstanding on either side before taking revenge, then we are absolutely right and clear and our flawless power increases. Million Wings feels that to choose an equal level and way to take revenge is logically right. To take life for abusive words is wrong. In a matter of money, thrashing the other and telling the truth to his mother/sister/daughter/lover is right. Taking life for life is only right when someone has done it knowingly and not genuinely. Million Wings feels that if someone feels sorry and ask for forgiveness, he/she can be forgiven only if his way/style/tinge feels like sorry. If his matter/issue is so serious and we are unable to free him from revenge/forgiveness, thenatleast the level of the mistake can be decreased. Extracting logical meaning of the punishment in revenge is the right decision. Mistakes can be made by anyone. But if someone realizes it heartily and also says sorry, then he/she can be forgiven.

Repeating same mistakes again and again decreasesthe endurance power, tolerating power. Million Wings feels that whilethe person is logically alive, then everything can be corrected. Punishment of serious mistakes is given and it's right too. Sparing/forgiving the one who has made a serious mistake knowingly or unknowingly is greatness of other person. Million Wings feels that whilethe person is alive, every mistake, flaw can be corrected but it's important that sorry should be felt at heart.

Million Wings feels that there are different ways to fight with own ones and the rest of world. There may bea mutual fight with ownones but being together when someone else try to fight increases power and moral support and is beneficial too. One with whom we are attached may have lots of complaints, reproach with each other but never let each other alone; when someone hurts our self-respect or feelings, then we should always tell that to the related person, may the matter seem to be small or big. Don't let the things reside in the heart, talk on the spot, ask for and talk about reason. Million Wings feels that matters go wrong because of misunderstanding only. It's true that our ownones guess that we have some tension, problem, complaint but it's not important that they will get to know the right reason.

So it's better to talk clearly to each other while examining each other. Try to talk within twenty-four hours; infact one can talk to ownones any number of times.

Million Wings feels that most fights are of words, but many times, power also needs to be used. Power needs to be used when the other person attacks in life-taking manner or behaves in corrupt and stubborn manner. These types of people need to be handled powerfully and it is really important to do so. Million Wings feels that anyone can be taught a lesson by using power, and their thinking can also be put on track but it's also true that only goodness can make anyone our own forever. Million Wings feels that thinking is the biggest power, and physical power, money power, status, living standard come afterwards. If anyone is supposed to oppose forces or betray, then he works as an ant in the ear of an elephant. No one can be judged just by looking at him. It's impossible to judge physical and social power in the first time as it's not necessary that other will attack on the spot. Restriction on the spot gives cleverness and strength for tomorrow. Million Wings feels that being right as priority is the biggest victory of an individual. The one who has made a serious mistake first, only that individual is answerable. The matter stops at that who had made its non-genuine start.

If a mistake occurs because of good people, then bad people get a strong chance to use their non-genuineness. Good people often accept their mistake and ask for forgiveness. But sometimes bad people become more non-genuine. In greed for personal benefit, bad people start misusing the personal lives of good people at social level and do stupid acts like blackmailing etc. Million Wings feels that good or bad people may makea mistake but by feeling sorry and asking for forgiveness, they become flawless and once they become flawless, they again start becoming right and powerful. If still another person misbehaves after asking forgiveness, then the person becomes responsible for flaw. And again the person who is flawless attacks back is again not wrong. He is right and clear at his place.

Chapter 36

Drugs

Million Wings feels that usage of drugs in lives of humans is just a source of entertainment. Drugs create such feelings in the body which are combinations of good and bad thoughts. Many types of natural and chemical drugs are used worldwide. Alcohol and tobacco are world-famous and the oldest drugs used for entertainment. Humans also start using medicinal drugs for entertainment.

Million Wings feels that a drug may be any but it's not better than using no drugs. But still if a person wants to use drugs then he should use that one which causes the least damage to the body. Even if we see then we got to know that there is no drug which is safe, secure to use. But still a few drugs are less dangerous as compared to each other, e.g. alcohol, opioids, opium, bhuki, codeine, cannabis (marijuana, hashish). But a few drugs are very dangerous, e.g. heroin, cocaine, smack, methamphetamines (crank, Ecstasy), phencyclidine. Along with dangerous they are costly too. That is, one who sells these drugs earns a lot and makes others sick, thieves, etc. Using two or more than two drugs together is very dangerous to do. A drug may be any but using in smaller amounts and rarely is less dangerous. It's real enjoyment and safety too. Million Wings feels that using medicines as drugs in the body is totally wrong. Medicines are made to treat diseases of humans. Medicines should be used to save life, not to take life. Using medicines as drugs should not be tolerated at any cost. Drugs like alcohol, tobacco, codeine give pleasure to humans. These have been used for centuries and humans are well aware about drugs' good and bad effects. An intelligent person uses these drugs insuch a way that these drugs can be used to take pleasure, enjoyment but it should not cause any harm or painful effect. Doing this is really a great thinking and strategy. It's right, it's logical.

Million Wings feels that drugs give pleasure to that limit where a human has control on himself. Dose of drug is the most important thing to use any drug. Every person should use drugs in such a way that he should only get pleasure and benefit, not personal harm. Every drug has a proper enjoyable dose till which person can use the drug freely and can enjoy. A person will just be entangled and dependent on a drug if the person will use the drug more than a certain dose. A human can enjoy it only if he has atleast that much sense that he can enjoy every feeling of enjoyment and he should remember the same. Million Wings feels that enjoying use of a drug is also a very capable quality. Getting unconscious, falling down somewhere and misbehaving with people after using is just like obstructing happiness. If person is unable to enjoy the world enjoyment after using drug, then what's the use of having the drug?

Million Wings feels that there is no use in taking drugs but surely have enjoyable limits till which limits humans can use drugs and enjoy maximally. The biggest challenge for the society is to restrict themselves to pleasurable doses of any chemical, and on the top of that, every chemical has the bad character which overpowers an individual's brain and willpower. Humans are still poor in front of chemicals and weaker than the weakest enemy. Every individual must understand alcohol is still better than drugs. Alcohol can be taken one peg daily (60ml) and at one time average two to four pegs (i.e. 120 to 240ml) once in a week. Alcohol should be consumed slowly with some eatables. Consuming more alcohol than the recommended limit can cause personal harm. Alcohol is that chemical which causes many types of harm in the brain. Starting and low dose of alcohol gives free and light feeling by setting one free from restrictions and tensions, by which the person feels it easy to express his small desires and feelings and the person feels happy and enjoys the moment. There is a feeling of heat and power in the body. But an average more than four pegs disturbs the limits of enjoyment as more than this dose disturbs coordination of mind and body, and a person loses control of himself. Body and mind both become flabby.

If person consumes more alcohol and drives any machine, it's like giving an invitation to dangerous tragedies. With less consumption of alcohol, both the body and mind become romantic, and enjoyment of romance, love, sex increase. But every person should understand this thing very clearly, that romance will rule the mind but body will not support that. If both the heart and body will support that, only romance can be enjoyed. More amounts of alcohol damage the liver of a person. The more the amount (and for a long time the person will consume alcohol), the earlier the liver will get damage. Diseases like liver cirrhosis becomethe reason for sorrow and pain. In these circumstances, drinking alcohol doesn't just remain enjoyment but becomes a compulsion which just harms the person with every passing moment. Peace of mind, health, money, tears, everything flows like water.

Million Wings feels that it's not necessary to drink alcohol but if a person consumes alcohol rarely and in the right amount, then nothing is even wrong. Maximum 60ml peg is OK, is genuine, beneficial, enjoyable, intelligent. Consuming alcohol in the right amount may be a benefit for health, and humans can enjoy alcohol for a lifetime. Alcohol should not be consumed at social place. Alcohol should be consumed at personal place, pub, or bar. Drinking and driving is totally wrong, as possibility of accident increases chances of full injury and, even more, death. Million Wings feels that drugs should be used after physical development, as drugs have those chemicals which harms important organs like liver, kidney, heart, reproductive organs, lungs before their full development. If a person will damage his body organs before their full development, then no medicine, no power, no treatment can correct that damage. So using drugs in childhood or teenage is just harmful.

Million Wings feels that tobacco is a drug which is chewed or used for smoking. Tobacco acts to activate mind. A few people use tobacco as style. Tobacco contains nicotine, which pulls humans towards itself and makes persons addicted. For centuries, humans have used tobacco in chewable and smoking form. Tobacco gives enjoyment, tobacco gives style, but along with this, tobacco gives such a suffocated breath for which even whole atmosphere feels like less. For centuries, humans have used tobacco to such an extent that today we get to know that tobacco doesn't give much pleasure. Tobacco plays very dangerous games with humans very cleverly. Tobacco contains approximately4,000 dangerous agents, which cause very dangerous problems to children. Nicotine is one of them which gives little pleasure to a person and make a person addicted, attracting humans towards itself and doesn't let humansleave tobacco. And 4,000 agents combined damage human health. Using tobacco in the right amount is intelligence; using tobacco with the help of filter is less dangerous. Hookah is the least dangerous. A cigarette can take a long time to exit from body. The less the time cigarette is smoked, the less it will harm. Now it's clear that tobacco can cause oral and lung cancer. There is possibility of serious heart and lung disease. COPD is such a disease caused by tobacco in which person feels lack of oxygen even in open air. Just understand that person has to forcibly take breaths in smoke and if a person gets the chance to come out of that, then on other side also there is just smoke.

Million Wings feels that drugs can be enjoyed within limits only for a longer time; otherwise when it will start to reverse counting is difficult to judge. If there is any serious problem in family because of some drugs, obviously the risk is for us also. We should understand that signal. If anyone in the family suffers from cancer or COPD, then tobacco can bring same to us also. Million Wings feels that in starting, a human's body is fit and it moves according to humans only. But when it is damaged because of drugs then a person has to move as per his physique/body. That is, a person is unable to enjoy or speedup life. Smoking should be done in a smoking zone or in the open only, as at social places, smoke has negative effect on other people too.

Million Wings feels that natural drugs (e.g. morphine and cocaine, marijuana, cannabis, LBD, cyclidine) their different parts give different types of pleasure to humans. These drugs slowly, slowly make humans so much dependent that even light physical work is difficult to do. Sudden use of drug in excessive amount is proved as life taking. Million Wings feels that a drug should be natural, may it be any, and it should be used to such an extent that it doesn't harm physical health and humans can enjoy it fully.

Million Wings feels that using medicine as drug is totally wrong and against civilization. These drugs are used to inject through veins also.

Because of this, serious diseases like AIDS, hepatitis make life very painful, which should be stopped strictly by government and administration. Government and administration should take serious and effective steps to stop use of medicine as drug.

Million Wings feels that a human should have control of himself. If anyone stops individuals from taking a drug then they use them by hidden ways secretly, and if we agree to use drug, then they use that in excess amount.

Million Wings feels that strictly, a person should keep within limits. Otherwise it's human nature to misuse every freedom. A person should have freedom on issues to use drugs but it should be along with strict limits so that both persons can be saved from both social and personal harm. Million Wings feels that people who want to enjoy drugs for a long time, have full control on the dose of drug, not let the drug control them. Personal limit for every drug is up to that level where human has full control on himself, as above that, even a powerful, great, clever person becomes worthless and is unable to do any work.

Million Wings feels that a person may be addicted to drugs because of any reason, e.g. entertainment, status, or to get rid of tensions, but in any situation happiness should not decrease because of drugs. Government and administration of the country should clear dose and frequency of drug and who tries to cross that should be handled strictly. Million Wings feels that after a limited dose, drugs start ruling the mind to such an extent that a human loses control of himself. Using a drug above the limit increases greed to take the drug, because of which desires arrive in the heart but the body can't support. Commonly people consume alcohol while doing romance, sex, etc. so that they can get more pleasure. But consuming alcohol more than four pegs doesn't let persons to do sex. If an individual wants to enjoy sex, then he should take a maximum of four pegs.

Million Wings feels that a person takes alcohol, tobacco, and other drugs for his entertainment. People are experimenting for science and research. People are using chemicals like idiots and entangle themselves in physical, mental, and social problems. People may use the same drug by following them, but use that amount only which should not harm them; that's why most people don't suffer and enjoy life. Those people who take drugs just by their own estimate are just like experimental animals from whose experiments other people get to know about the right dose of drug. The life of these types of people becomes hell, but because of them, other people get to know about the right dose of drug and use it in same amount and enjoy life by escaping from problems. Million Wings feels that an intelligent person learns from mistakes, weakness, problems of other persons and uses drugs in the right amount and takes real pleasure. Million Wings feels that right information about drugs is collected by effects on common people. This information should not be stored in books; infact it should be delivered to people in a very effective manner so that common people don't do any stupidity and don't get harmed by drugs, by taking dose by themselves. Infact, common people should also use available information.

Today all information which is collected regarding problem serious harms regarding alcohol, tobacco, morphine, cocaine is because of wrong acts, using in wrong ways, using a wrong dose. The right dose can't be calculated by machines. It is cleared when people use it. The right dose and serious symptoms is got by problem to common people. Science and research is done by doing experiments on common people and then waiting to get the right information and then drugs can be used in the right manner and amount to get maximum pleasure. Million Wings feels that usually people take drugs to reduce tensions and problems or just for showing off or just for enjoyment and are often entangled in them. Enemies of a person try to pull him in drugs to humanism to such an extent that he should become dependent and sick so that those enemies can have enjoyment. Enemies of nation and those who are personally jealous make people habituated to drugs, from which they get two benefits. Firstly they destroy the young power and mind by showing them the wrong path so that neither are they capable to fight nor can they can think about anything other than drugs. And secondly they earn money by selling drugs. Either youngsters destroy their own money or use theft to collect money for drugs and push innocent youngsters in ocean of drugs and steal their beautiful dreams and enjoy their own life by destroying life of common and innocent people.

Million Wings feels that today humans have so much information about drugs that they know well that which drug will give pleasure to which extent and repetition after which it will become the cause of disrespect, problems, tensions, and diseases. Using drugs more without thinking even after having so much information is just stupidity. If a drug is new, then also we can understand that dose and repetition is unknown. If a drug is new, then also before using it ourselves, let it be tried by some other stupid persons. Why use it ourselves and die by taking drugs? Instead let others try that first.

Take a lesson from others who are dying because of drugs. Million Wings feels that drug may be any but firstly know about its repetition and dose upto which it can give pleasure and then use that. If you want, then confirm the right dose and repetition from government or drug seller or any other related department about different drugs. Drugs can be changed. Today something else and tomorrow it can be any new drug. But it doesn't matter which drug it is. What matters is knowledge about the right dose and repetition.

Million Wings feels that a few persons use a lot of drugs but still they are saved. They are physically fit, so they can escape from serious problems and diseases for less or more time, but it doesn't mean that they are 100 per cent safe in the future also. Government administration and scientists make and put new drugs infront of people even if they don't have100 per cent solution for every serious disease caused by the drug when individualsare entangled in some serious problem become of the drug, then everyone wants to escape. People give drugs but no one (government, people, scientists)has sure solutions and resources to correct the hazards. It's right, it's true.

Million Wings feels that every person who wants to use a drug should fix a permanent circle for himself as per his health, time, and resources, not according to others. After collecting full information about effects of the drug, then only do experiments on himself.

Humans use drugs for enjoyment and fun. Drugs give many types of mental and physical pleasure to humans. Sometimes person gets tense on small natural things and a few times he is stuck in serious problems and pain and he loses his self-confidence and thinks that taking drugs, alcohol, etc. is the only way out from tension. Most people don't want to be dependent on drugs; neither do they want to be habitual of that but inreality they don't have clear information about drugs. In media, movies, advertisements, drugs are shown as pleasure and as status symbol. But no one provides right dose, repetition, serious health hazards, treatment, etc. Innocent people get stuck in these habits without knowing clearly. Treatment for health hazards because of drugs is much costlier than drugs themselves. Those people who sell drugs should do the health insurance of people to whom they sell drugs so that if a person falls sick because of some drug, then he should get free treatment which is in lakhs but physical and mental lacks have to be tolerated by the person himself.

Million Wings feels that people start taking drugs because of one or another reason, but drugs keep on entangling individuals. Drugs gives pleasure and enjoyment to a person, because of which he takes that again and again and after sometime that becomes compulsion and dependency, which don't have any enjoyment but are used just to fulfil physical dependency and slowly person moves towards death. The drug may be any; each drug use to entangle individual in such a way that on one hand, a person wants to take the drug, and on the other hand, it stealsthe health, money, relations, and dreams of the individual.

Million Wings feels that a human's happiness is he wants to pull out innocent own people from circle of drugs. Those who are lost in drugs are someone's own ones also. They may have started taking a drug because of any reason and they may also want to come out from that drug. The drug may have entangled them in such a way that they are unable to come out from that dangerous ocean. It's very important to pull back the person from that drug which has started ruling the individual's mind and soul. Ownones need love and care to come out of drugs, and to pull them out from drugs, medical and doctor's help and support are required. Today, a person can beat addiction to every drug.

Million Wings feels that a great strategy of beating addiction can be followed only if the person himself feels so. If the person himself wants to leave a drug, then no power of the world will be able to stop him. The individual may have been addicted for a long period of time, by any quantity of drug, but if he has strong willpower to leave the drug, then he can easily do it with the help of doctors. But if the person himself is not willing, then no power of the world can stop him from using the drug. Million Wings feels that near and dear ones should first raise a feeling of dedication in the addicted mind and that can leave drug easily and successfully. Person can beat addiction easily with the help of medicines. To correct mental habits, individuals need love, support, family, friends, and relations. With the help of doctors and own ones, a person can easily come out from this habit into a beautiful life again.

Million Wings feels that drug should be taken by mind and let the heart enjoy it. Never let drugs rule the mind. When drugs start ruling the brain, then the heart becomes versatile, the mind stops working, and the body becomes worthless; that is, the person becomes unbalanced and useless. Million Wings feels that when feeling of the heart cannot be fulfilled by mind and body, then how come personal happiness can be obtained, e.g. self-expression, dance, romance, sex etc.? Use drugs to such an extent till desires bloom, the mind is tension free and controlled, and the body is able to support in every condition. Then only it's a real pleasure of using drugs. Otherwise drugs don't have any other role other than moving from one sorrow to other.

Chapter 37
Who are bad people?

Million Wings feels that being good or bad is personal comparison point of view, but being a troublemaker is souvenir of being corrupt.

Million Wings feels that most wrong people are not wrong to that extent that they seem to be, or to the extent they are made to be, but at heart they are good and soft and don't easily harm anyone. Actually they are misguided or perverse. They are tense because of some pain and sorrow, stuck in some natural tensions and misunderstand or are entangled in sorrowful thinking and reserved nature, or victims of betrayal. Mainly the reason behind people who are bad or who misbehave is some genuine care or some misunderstanding, but bad people also have some feelings and a few principles. If others will try to understand them, they will also find them right and they can be easily made our own by love and respect.

Million Wings feels that just a few, very few people are bad, who are really bad, who are real troublemakers. They bother people on every little cause, fight unnecessarily, and misbehave without any reason. Bad people generally misbehave with bad people only. But troublemakers, corrupt people have no rules and principles, who misbehave and force innocent people to do certain things just for personal happiness. Their main aim is to harm the hardwork, respect, and knowledge of common people and to make trouble somehow in their lives. These people have no control of themselves as they are mentally sick. They should be or need to be controlled by power only as they cannot be made to understand; instead just need to control them. Complain to police on primary basis regarding these people and let government use their power for them.

Million Wings feels that everyone likes good people, as they don't harm anyone intentionally and always want and do benevolence for the society/ world. No one has any problem or any complaint regarding these people, as good people don't fight. Instead they keep on tolerating and maintaining peace in society, but the whole world remains tense because of bad people, as they start fights, forcibly do things with others, harm others, are stubborn and betraying people. If bad people think that they don't have any fault, then it's for sure that good people absolutely have any fault. If person misbehave with one who had misbehaved with that person, it seems to be right to some extent but it doesn't mean that he will start misbehaving with other people too. Million Wings feels that good people should get more respect, right, and security and try to understand bad people and their conditions and compulsions and behave in friendly manner and give them a chance and help them to be good. Million Wings feels that the main aim of people who are rascals, troublemakers, non-genuine, stubborn, corrupt, betrayers and terrorists is to give pain and problems and harm others; they should be handled strictly and with power. It's important to teach them a lesson. Praise and respect good people. Million Wings feels that good people should get safety and security and give genuine chance to bad people to improve. But don't give freedom to bad people in any condition, at any cost to misbehave or apply force on innocent and good people. Respect of civilization is to take care of logical boundaries of human life. Million Wings feels that troublemakers, stubborn, corrupt people have to be handled collectively by government, administration, security forces, and common people, especially the youngsters. Youngsters have to banish terrorists and corrupt people with power and intelligence.

Million Wings feels that rascal and stupid people are mentally sick. They are just moving in their own rhythm in the wrong direction and they think that whatever they are doing is right and it's true. These types of people are very few in number. They become tortured from every small and huge misunderstanding to such an extent that they take the whole world as their enemy and they start taking revenge from every common person at social level of their enmity and misunderstandings. These people's mental balance is so disturbed that they enjoy harming, betraying, killing others. These people create disturbances in society and interfere in social peace and security. Million Wings feels that mainly it's the responsibility of government and administration how they will have to handle or stop to spread terrorism in society, nation, world.

Million Wings feels that non-genuine people, misbehavers betray, act forcibly with common people. It's not because they are powerful and intelligent. Infact, it's because common people have many other and more important work in life other than all this. But rascal people have just one work and that is to create disturbance in the life of others but the main work of common people is to do professional hardwork, take care of family, etc.

Million Wings feels that if common people get free from their general work, then they can teach a lesson well to corrupt people and the misunderstanding of these people can be banished in just seconds.

Everyone has self-respect. One may not be strong physically but has power for security of self-respect.

Million Wings feels that corrupt people survive because of tolerance power and forgiveness of good people, as if good people suffer by serious harm of respect or life of own ones, then their tolerance power, idealism, forgiveness, and goodness also vanish with that and then nothing else matters to those people except teaching a lesson and taking revenge from corrupt people, with free mind, power, and intelligence. Being right has great power when it takes its form, then it has power to turn power of troublemakers into ash. Million Wings feels that awareness is the best way to take revenge or to teach a lesson to trouble creators. Common people need to understand that if they want to take a risk for peace and life, then they should take a risk against the corrupt, trouble creators, terrorists instead of using it against in the name of religion, caste, race, as people suddenly join in the name of religion or caste and become powerful. In the same way, torture of terrorists and trouble creators can be destroyed in seconds. Police and administration also stand among common people.

There aren't separate worlds of good and bad people. Good and bad people live together in society, related to each other by some relations. Good people leave good impact on all, may it be their own ones or some other people, but bad people always leave their negative impression on others. Ownones tolerate and then try to make them understand but others don't tolerate and answer equivalently or even more to their response. Million Wings feels that anyone good is that person who is favourable and beneficial for someone and bad is that person who is against and harmful. Who is good and who is bad depends on one's thinking. Someone can be good for one and bad for another. Million Wings feels that it's not about good or bad people but it's about mutual coordination between good and bad people. Million Wings feels that bad is that person who tortures others, misbehaves, acts against the will of others just for his personal benefit. Mostly people are not bad; it's just a different mentality, because of which people are unable to coordinate with each other.

A few people are those whose nature, mentality, thinking, intention is to harm, bother, fight, kill other innocent people unnecessarily just for personal benefit. Million Wings feels that these are those people who are mentally too sick. These people createa tense and unhealthy atmosphere in society. These people create terror in society and personally feel and enjoy happiness, power, and intelligence. Now the question is whether these people are born with these intentionsand nature or do they become like this while living life? Million Wings feels that only very few people are really trouble creators whose aim is to fulfil their non-genuine and nonsense desires and intentions. It's totally wrong to misbehave or torture innocent people misbehaving with innocent people because of someone else's mistake. Million Wings feels that mostly when a mistake is not clear, infact on the basis of a guess, misunderstandings take place. Mostly a matter is not as serious as the dangerous turn it takes. Infact, entanglements more because of misunderstandings and issues take the form of enmity. Small misunderstandings can't be clarified, as at a place sometimes arguments and anger increase to such a level that it doesn't remain a matter of being right and wrong. Infact it is converted to a matter of power. If anyone fights on personal issues, it doesn't matter for other people in society, but when personal issues are pulledinto social issues and a name of religion, country and party is given to an issue then it createsa tenseand trouble atmosphere in society. Common and innocent people keep on fighting with each other and devilish people enjoy the personal benefit from that issue.

Million Wings feels that clever troublemaking people know that if people will keep on fighting with each other, then only they can be saved and enjoy their life. They know that if common people will unite, then their minds, brains, and power will increase to such an extent that it will be difficult for troublemakers to take even a breath. For centuries, troublemaking people entangle people in the name of religion, caste, customs of society, self-respect of country, policies to such an emotional extent so cleverly that common people start fighting with each other like idiots.

A few leaders, a few terrorists, a few troublemakers, a few saints have misled society, nation and world. These bad people make common people fight whenever they want and enjoy it. These people play with feelings of innocent people and misguide them in the name of religion, God, boundaries. These people decrease power of common people by dividing them for political power, property, financial power and other personal benefits. They don't let people join and if people able to gather than entangle them in stupid, illogical talk and don't let them to come on right issues and decisions. Millions of good and intelligent people don't linkup and are scattered. So they are unable to build their power and troublemaking people, being much fewer in number, remain knitted together and become powerful and fool people or scare them differently and takeadvantage of that. It's true.

Million Wings feels that now people are able to understand intentions of these corrupt people, and day by day they are becoming aware. Million Wings feels that people need to understand that no religion says or tells them to fight with each other, then why do people fight with each other in the name of religion? No God wants to develop superstitions. Then why do people become religious followers without understanding their betrayal? Every religion teaches to live affectionately and help others in every problem. When people have this knowledge, then why do they start fighting by forgetting everything? Leaders' duty is to join, link up people, then do why people listen to their silly talks which provoke people to fight? Million Wings feels that a few religious followers, leaders, and a few of those who misguide, emotionally blackmail people and use them against each other in the name of religion, caste, and borders took advantage of this.

Million Wings feels that few people are really trouble creators who have nothing other than destruction and fights. These people who have intentions against humanism, against life should be controlled powerfully, and it's of utmost importance to teach them a lesson. Mainly police, military, administration is needed for this type of people. Those who didn't understand anything with love need to make them understand with power.

Million Wings feels that mostly people are not bad; maybeno one taught or guided them affectionately. No one helped them in the right manner to fulfil their needs and desires, or someone misbehaved or forcibly acted against them and they started behaving in the same manner with others. Million Wings feels that there are so many such things in society whose desires and feelings are not wrong; infact the way used to fulfil them might be wrong and on the basis of this, a human is said to be wrong. It's necessary to consider rightly and correct them.

Chapter 38

Unbalanced life

Million Wings feels that every person has their own lifestyle and it's right too. A few have some desire and a few have some other dreams. A few give attention to everything and a few just think about one thing. A few remain busy day and night and a few don't want to do anything. A few are busy in taking care of family and a few are very careless. A few are busy in serving society and a few are busy in fulfilling their dreams and desires and needs. Everything is right, everything is logical. All are right at their place. If everyone will be alike, then what will be enjoyment in meeting different people? This difference is life.

Million Wings feels that everything is important for life. Everyone has personal feeling, everyone has own relations, everyone has their own needs, dreams, and desires. Everyone has self-respect. This is exactly true, that everything is important for everyone but this is even truer, that personal dreams and desires are more important than everything else. Whatever a human is doing or wants to do with his will and desire is most important for him. Maybe it will not seem to be very important for other family members, the society, or the world. If a person is very busy in just one field, it may be madness or stupidity for others but it is a dream for him.

Million Wings feels that whatever a human is doing, that is balance for him, may it not be balance for others. Personal inability is that when person is using carelessness in fulfilling his minimum needs. Taking sleep

403

of minimum of eight hours, if not possible at night, then to sleep/rest in day is personal balance, may it not be balance for the world. Eating necessary diet for the body is balance, may it be eaten at anytime, may it be unbalanced for the world. Million Wings feels that whatever a human is doing without harming others is all balanced, may it seem to be unbalanced for people. While a person is fulfilling their minimum needs, then whatever the human is doing without harming others is all balanced, may it seem to be unbalanced for people. While a person is fulfilling his minimum needs, then whatever he is doing is all balanced, may it seem to be unbalanced for others. While a person is fulfilling his promise, then everything is right, may it seem to be unbalanced for others. While a person is collecting his resources by himself, then everything is balanced, may it seem to be unbalanced for others. While a person is using every invention in its limits, then he is living a balanced life, may it seem to be unbalanced for others. If a human is entangled in natural problem or disease, this is also balance, may it seem to be unbalanced to all. If a human feels himself healthy, may he sleep or not, may he eat properly or not, even this is also balance, may it seem to be an unbalanced life to all. When a human does anything and is happy with himself, then that is balance, only it may seem to be unbalanced to others.

Actually an unbalanced life means it's missing mutual coordination. A person comes to take a meal when all others are sleeping; another person is doing work at that time when a near and dear one needs him. A person is going to sleep when it's time to wakeup for others. A person is spending money in enjoyment when it's needed to give loan or has to return borrowed money. Million Wings feels that according to society, a person is unbalanced when he is not even fulfilling his minimum responsibilities or when he doesn't completely fit into ideals according to the time. Everyone wants happiness and satisfaction of their share, and above that, whatever human is doing is all right. Providing satisfactory arrangement/management to related near and dear ones and then fulfilling related needs of each other in satisfactory ways is being balanced for each other, may a person be doing whatever after that.

Million Wings feels that hearty feeling and emotions of a person are the most important personal treasure and then comes his body and the rest of the things come afterwards. Personal property is everyone's own desire and balance. On both personal properties, a human keeps maximum right of himself. With whoever he may want to share, in whatever way is his personal will, agreement and freedom. A person doesn't want to give full right of his personal property to anyone else. It's true, it's right, and it's logical too.

Million Wings feels that it depends on every person whether he gives the full right to his personal property to someone, not that it becomes anyone's right by birth. It is personal will and agreement how many persons he/she wants to share his/her personal properties and up to what extent. In worldly relations, there is no natural right that a person has full rights to the feelings, body, or time of others according to himself. Million Wings feels that worldly relations are just made to fulfil needs of each other and the main motto or agreement of which is to fulfil each other's need. Relations are those which are made by heart. Only in heartfelt relations does a person give his personal properties with full quality and will. A person wants to share himself with those with whom he feels comfortable, loved, and secure. He can share himself with whatever number of loved ones; it's his personal need, desire, and nature. He may meet with one for a longtime and another for less time. Million Wings feels that a person can share both his properties only with those whom he likes, not with those who like him or demand time from him. Any right can't be taken forcibly on one's personal properties. Infact, a few relations care and affection is very precious for another. It's more important that he is getting property of his share in the form of quality time. A person needn't interfere in his complete personal life and property and will increase doubt, oppose other partner. It's very important for another person to understand that letting the person spend/share his/her time and feeling and body with those whom he/she wants to share and maintaining own love and care is the only secret to gain both the properties of a person. It's a truth of relations and it will remain the same. It's right too.

Million Wings feels that if a person is spending more time for his passion, then it's all right. But for regular/daily enjoyment, if a person is playing with his personal health, it can give enjoyment for sometime, but in the long term, to do this seems to be difficult. A human has full right to fulfil his passion and to enjoy that, but the person is unable to do all this by personally harming himself, even if he wants. Million Wings feels that persons who become lost or busy in themselves, involved in their own rhythm, their near and dear ones try to make them understand emotionally and try to teach them idealism. They are right at their place, as they are worried for the person's health. Million Wings feels that most people understand and buy the arguments and logic given by near and dear ones and they try to manage it in a balanced way or happily or as compulsion. Sometimes they ignore talks of others and remain busy in themselves or revolt against the world and get lost in themselves. Million Wings feels that it's worthless to powerfully pull back people to understand or to compel them. Infact it's necessary to understand the passion and desires of these people and help them to fulfil these in managed ways and motivate them to live a balanced life.

Million Wings feels that sometimesa person is busy on just one side and he wants to spend his maximum time in that only. To do this is his personal happiness. That's why he remains busy in himself. To do this is not wrong. Everything is all right.

Million Wings feel that the main motto of the life of every person is to live and fulfil their own dreams and desires, the rest of the things to maintain moral support of each other. Million Wings feels that a person will do work only as per his dreams and desires. It's true. But in between, he needs physical and mental rest and comfort. Million Wings feels that to spend time with near and dear ones, family, and friends and to sleep refreshes humans. The company of near and dear ones and sleeping for six to eight hours provides plausible energy so that a human can fulfil his dreams and desires in the right manner. Million Wings feels that everyone should try to fulfil his main dreams as early as possible so that person should achieve a satisfactory level and can move towards balanced life from unbalanced life happily.

Million Wings feels that it's impossible to pull back worldly passion and desires. But support to do work in better, easy, and managed ways will give more time and affection from ownones. If someone is busy in his life and doesn't have any responsibility, then the right thing is to let him be busy in his life. But if he is not giving any attention to his responsibility or he doesn't feel them, then nothing can be done forcibly with him. In these conditions, support, guide, and help him to fulfil his dreams and desires and passion as early as possible so that person can take the next step to fulfil dreams and desires and he can save more time, which he can easily spend with his family and friends. This technique will turn towards plausible balance life cycle from determined desires and life circle. It's the right/successful technique/ strategy to get and to help in getting personal quality time and balance. Million Wings feels that it's not to stop specific desire; infact helping and guiding to fulfil that desire as early as possible gives motivation towards a balanced life. If a human is able to fulfil dreams, desires, and passions fast or early, he will give attention to other important things. It's true. It's right, it's balanced happiness.

Million Wings feels that every human has to make personal balance according to his good and bad habits, dreams and desires, money and relations, life strategy of average people in society; the world helps to build basic balance. But a person has to pull it a bit above or below to make personally beneficial coordination. He has to fix such a level that he will get maximum benefit and least harm from his dream, desire, behaviour, and nature. Every human should make the personal best arrangement for his happiness. So that he can enjoy maximally, comfortably, tension free for a longtime his health, money, relations, time. Just find out today the balance of personal enjoyment.

Million Wings feels that carelessness is human nature. Every human should leave and should enjoy today and will think about tomorrow, and nothing's wrong in doing and thinking so, as if a person is not happy today, what's the advantage of tomorrow's happiness? If a human can't enjoy today even after having the opportunity, then it's not understandable how he can enjoy tomorrow's possibilities of happiness. Life may take a serious turn which a person could not even think of. It's all is unsure and secret but today is in a human's hands, which he should live and can be corrected.

Million Wings feels that if any sudden new and natural problems arise in a human's life, then what's his fault? Persons can work for those things which can be thought of and understood according to worldliness, but no one can do anything for natural problems and restrictions. If a person is in any problem, he won't be relieved from that problem, and to think this is absolutely right. But once the person overtakes the problem or circumstance, then he again turns towards his priorities, dreams, desires.

A human wants to resolve his problems and tensions because they become obstructions to his dream and desires. Once the problem and obstruction are relieved to an extent, then he can live his life by choice, then again he starts doing carelessness. It's true and will always remain true.

Million Wings feels that it's not compulsion that humans will live a balanced life. Infact it's a dream. The whole society and world hope for balanced behaviour from every person, may he himself be living an unbalanced life. Often, every person likes himself and his own things and then that way he does those things; sometimes even the person himself realizes that he is living an unbalanced life according to others and even according to himself. But still there are a few habits and passions which cannot be controlled. Even after understanding and knowing lacks, the mind goes towards that direction only which the mind wants. Nothing's wrong in doing and thinking so. If a person will not think according to his mind, then whatelse he will do? Million Wings feels that habits and passions of persons are not any compulsion; infact these are happiness. If these can be fulfilled in the right manner, then no one will object to that and the person himself will also feel happier. Actually most people are living unbalanced lives and society is a balance of unbalanced people. If one will become unbalanced, then others will balance that by being balanced. It's true, it's right.

Unbalanced life is actual life of humans and to balance it more is a long and permanent way of happiness for ourselves and society too. Million Wings feels that everyone should fulfil his passion and desires in such a way that happiness will increase in his own familiar and social life, not problems. Arrange and manage our own good or bad habits.

Chapter 39

Astrology

Astrology is the fastest and widest study of the world which tells about good or bad conditions/things to happen in nature or human life after studying effects of the whole universe and tells ways to escape, reduce, or banish possibility of sorrowful acts.

The main base of this study is to guess about effects of the whole universe on all organisms and creatures and to make suggestions according to that.

Actually the logical motto of this study is to save/escape organisms from harmful problems. Million Wings feels that astrology is a group/collection that guesses about future effects, which don't have authenticated proof or are unable to be proven. This study is basically scientific technology which uses sayings instead of instruments. Million Wings feels that great persons have made this study according to their thinking by using their vast knowledge and far-sightedness so that natural effects can be judged before and direct the whole universe towards happiness. Great persons tried to give mental satisfaction with the help of astrology. Intentions of right/great person is to provide comfort and happiness to the whole human species; till today right and true great persons work to take steps in the right direction for the whole human species. But these kinds of saints are really few. Million Wings feels that a real/true saint is one who can heartily feel others' pain and who rises above sex, anger, affection, greed, ego and tries to help calmly to escape from the power of the universe and its effects. A true saint is one who is the same by heart and by action, who can be loved more and more after knowing. Dreams, desire, and motto of a true saint is to provide positive direction to the universe, and doing this is his happiness.

Million Wings feels that few liars or false saints use astrology just for personal benefits. They know that astrology is organized from guessing effect of universe on each other, for which a human doesn't get any proof. The thing for which no proof is needed, anyone can misuse it and can astonish people. Treacherous saints took advantage of this and bluffed innocent and tense people for personal benefit. Treacherous saints keep on entangling innocent people and keep on taking personal benefits from them. Million Wings feels that prediction gives more negative effects, and instead of thinking positively or taking the same in a positive way, people doubt, feel insecure, and take tension from everything happening around. People visit saints in hopes to get comfort and happiness in life but instead of being happy, they return tenseand sad. Mostly saints make suggestions on the basis of guesses, as per own feeling. If they accomplish by chance, then they become famous, and if the thing they said went wrong, then by finding faults, deficiencies they prove the innocent person responsible for failure. These types of fake saints have many ways/choices to play with feelings of innocent people, which they use very wisely, and people keep on being entangled in their talks. Astrology can be used to treat mental sickness or in natural way, for which they take full credit. But if a person didn't get the benefit or problems increase, for this they already have many pre-planned ways to tackle wisely, e.g.:

> direction of sun was not right
> water should be kept in clay utensil, not in metal utensil
> right time was between light and dark
> thread was less
> wheat should be kept instead of rice
> food should be eaten one minute after reading holy saying
> not effective during menstrual cycle

any another planet was more effective
holy saying should be done regularly for ten days
why was the cloth of red colours not kept?
half water should be drunk, half should be kept.

Million Wings feels that thinking/mentality can win or be defeated by mentality only. True saints help persons to escape from mental illness, problems by correcting their mentality, and fake saints use the mentality of people to entangle them instead of solving their problems. The problem which was not there arises with themselves and then they solve that so that they can earn their living by astonishing people. Fake saints want that people should move to them and then help the universe by their recommendation.

Million Wings feels that when people themselves can pray directly to God, then what's the need of fake saints as mediators? A few times the tension and problems which are inexpressible disturb mental balance, and they are the real cause of tensions and problems. Persons are unable to understand that what to do and what not to do. In these conditions, the mind and heart of a person become so sensitive that on getting a little hope, they start moving towards that direction. A few fake people take advantage of this sensitive situation of people and took full advantage of these conditions. Fake saints show fake rays of hope to tense people and then collect their living by fooling innocent people. A few fake saints know very well that it's easy to entangle people in fake mental conditions. But it's very difficult and takes lot of time and needs hardwork to pull them out from the same. Entering the circle of fake saints is equivalent to entering squared planning; it's very difficult to come out from this. A few fake saints entangle people very cleverly and it's like dissolving poison in their life for a lifetime and sometimes it becomes impossible to clear that poison. These fake saints don't allow people to become united. They know that if family members will talk to each other then they can easily understand clever actions of the fake saint and their business will be stopped. Usually these fake people tells that alternative/solution which has to be done by hiding from each other, e.g.:

No one should get to know about this, you have to go alone under the tree, add this welfare ash in his food without his knowledge.

Elder people should not have even doubts about this, eat this fruit when everyone is sleeping.

Keep this welfare thing under his pillow, without letting him know. Keep it in mind that no one will see you while doing so.

These fake saints will tell about those things only which often happen, e.g.:

> If any family member will give anything to the child to eat, don't let him eat.
>
> Your husband/wife will say something to your mother/sister.
>
> There will be financial loss this week.
>
> Ill-fated if milk will boil
>
> This thing should be kept in cloth by 1 a.m. at night.
>
> Spread this rice/wheat in their house.
>
> Keep this thread in your hand for whole week, you should be just quiet if he/she says anything to you.

Million Wings feels that a horoscope is an estimate about mental and physical locations and effects of planets. Horoscope is collection of estimates of mental and physical conditions of a person which tells us about the physical and mental behaviour of a person but doesn't give any authentication. At time of arranged marriage, if horoscopes doesn't match, then it hardly matters to not marry them, but if girl and boy have good mutual understanding and love and care for each other then it hardly matters if horoscopes doesn't match. Match horoscope to past life till now. If it matches, then accept that horoscope, but if it doesn't match, then it doesn't have any meaning. Astrology study is incomplete as this study is based on study of just planets and nature doesn't have just planets but many, numerous things are there in the universe, which have their impact on humans. Right and authentication prediction of future of human can be collected on the basis of nonliving creature and things on human life.

Million Wings feels that the past and present of human life are the horoscope of humans. The future is real and that horoscope always makes a person seem perfect, more intelligent, plausible, and elegant. A person's work and working strategies give clear and right prediction or estimate of the person's future. If the past was not good but the present is improved and is better than the past, then the future will be better. If the past was good but the present is worse than the past, then there are more chances of worse future. If past was good and the present is better, then there are more chances of better future too. All these are just possibilities and are applied the same on everyone. Million Wings feels that along with circumstances and working strategies of a person, it's the intention of the person which has more impact on horoscope.

If logical prior nature is positive, then moral support and encouragement will be maintained in each and every circumstance of life. Million Wings feels that before making relations with any person, try to know the past and present of that person and then try to know his intentions by knowing circumstances and working strategies of the person, and changes which he brings in himself till now are a real authentication for that person. It's the authenticated and easy horoscope of the future.

Million Wings feels that astrology is horoscope of natural effect on life. Logical future is to understand intentions and priorities of person from his life. As than may any type of circumstance can arise in the future. The future's decisions depend on his personal behaviour and working strategy. To understand behaviour skill of a person, e.g. positive or negative thinking, active or passive body, soft or strict nature, hardworker, comfortable activities, emotional or careless style, plausible or tense nature, is to understand his future. It's the best horoscope. It's logical, it's true too. Persons needn't go to any astrologer or saint to know all this; infact it's important to talk and to meet each other and by this, persons can easily get to know about right intentions, capacities and nature of each other. Assurance of future happiness is to meet with alike people more and more.

Million Wings feels that the universe has some effect on everyone, everything at the same place. So if we see impact of only stars and planets, it's not everything. To recommend mutual coordination of two people, their inbuilt character also matters, which plays a major role recommending their nature. A person's own ways of life give maximum impact on everything, other than anything else. It's true, it's right. Million Wings feels that females are more sensitive than males so they are easily entangled in the talks of fake saints.

Million Wings feels that everything, creature, organism is attached to each other by one or another logic and everything/creature has less or more effect on each other, may it be living or nonliving, stars, planets, moon, surely affect each other, surely affect earth and life on it. A few things are fixed/permanent, which are guidance signals, and a few things change their direction, position, speed. Because of this, these effects also change at different places at different times. These planets of the universe also show their different effects on nature and humans. When a human is born, these effects definitely participate in building of nature, mentality, and behaviour. Everything will always show these effects on each other. Since birth till death, humans will affect nature and nature will affect humans. As the universe changes, its effects also change. Humans took action-reaction as per build-up effect from birth. Astrology tries to know a creature's development in which circumstance he was born. Both still and movable things give their effects while birth and its effects on life fixes action-reaction. Humans develop as per effect of planets at birth, and as per basis of this, human future action-reaction can be judged but it's hard to get conclusion; it will be clarified with time only.

Million Wings feels that astrology is a science, a great science which is trying to know about mutual relations of the whole universe and its effects on each other. Million Wings feels that effects of planets change with every moment, every place, and to know about so many different things is very difficult. A human doesn't stay still at one place. He always keeps on moving from one place to another. Still planets or things have the same effect at one place but a human can't stay still at one place as he has to move to different places, in different directions for different work. So along with change, effect of still things/planets, effect of movable planets or things also change and show their impact, i.e. impact changes every moment. Whenever still movable impact unite, everytime they give new impact. A human also changes his direction, place, speed everytime, so movable human and movable planets everytime give new and different impact on each other. If a human will think about it deeply, then he can just imagine, and be unable to do anything else. Even after arranging the every moment changing impact than also human will get to know after doing his work whether the guess was right or wrong. If after thinking and understanding so much, a real result is got only after doing work, then what's use of this? Million Wings feels that every human has to fulfil his dreams and desires after knowing and understanding the real practical experience of the human species till now and has to move life according to their result. It's real strategy; only this is in human hands.

Million Wings feels that a speciality of astrology is to understand changing effects of stars on small and movable creatures more deeply and with more authentication. By knowing about effects of stars and planets at time of birth, behaviour and nature of person can be judged or guessed but it's not possible to know every situation of life, as it's not only stars and planets which have impact on human life but there are many other things and action reactions which also have important impact on human life, not only the impact of the universe on every moment of life also gives its impact on the whole universe and each other's life.

Million Wings feels that astrology is not to know about human future of human life; infact it can determine nature, behaviour, and build-up of human. Few predictions by behaviour and action-reaction of future circumstance can be done. In future, astrology will take full form of science and technology. In future, humans will love to move on authenticated ways rather than guess. Million Wings feels that astrology is one form of technology behind which technology is moving, and one day, science and astrology will merge in each other. Science is a true friend of astrology and divulges fake saints. It's right.

Million Wings feels the future is filled with vast possibilities and the future is that which moves forward everyone, is that which can't be caught. Humans can't combine and understand uncountable, unlimited possibilities altogether, and this is the true cause of not understanding completely and will remain always. The present and future can be secured by positive hopes. But the future can't be captured with full authentication. Humans should try to know and understand the future, but in reality, knowing the future is present. Whatever we can think is the possibility of future. Only the future can prove whether it's right or wrong as we have to live, and to live is the real future.

Million Wings feels that whatever a person comes to know is the present and whatever is not-known today is the future. A person has to live in the present for the future, and the future can be guessed/predicted, can't be authenticated.

Million Wings feels that if anything can tell the future, then that is the past of the universe, or that matter of the present on the basis of which the future is predicted, or curiosity of humans and thinking filled with far-sightedness. Million Wings feels that the future which is known today is basically present knowledge but not the future. Present knowledge guesses about the future and makes the present as part of the future. The future is basically the next moment which is yet to come, and possibilities and imaginations are the present only. A human should not try to know the future; instead he should try to make the future more secure and better by learning from conditions/circumstances and actions. He should try to move towards the future to live his dreams and desires with more secure hopes. It's education, it's guidance. If complete knowledge of every organ can be got from astrology, then planning can be done to know about his disease and to make him healthy. Every person can choose the most beneficial place and time to live in. Every small particle of the universe can be arranged at the right place with the help of astrology; it will be easy to do new research on nature. Million Wings feels that astrology can predict about natural happenings in human life. Mostly every person himself can predict about his many future conditions and can understand related causes.

Only natural happenings about which a human doesn't know anything may be known and understood with the help of astrology. With the help of science and technology, humans have researched DNA which fixes mental and physical growth of humans. Million Wings feels that something is here which fix DNA and maybe that is a mutual impact of the universe. With the help of astrology, DNA can be kept healthy and happiness can be naturally converted.

Million Wings feels that it's easy to know and understand physical problems, as everyone can see them but those problems which are related to mentality/mind that can be felt by the diseased/sick only. This mentality should be felt first and then need to treated in same way. Million Wings feels that one form of physiological treatment is *Tantra-Mantra*, which is for basically psychological disease, doubts, tensions, problems that can be banished. Sympathetic magic banishes problems/sorrows related with psychology, basically banishing a condition of sensitive mentally suggesting ways as phonologist so that person can be made happy; mental condition can be made better by releasing from stage of unnecessary doubts. Million Wings feels that Tantra-Mantra, which doesn't harm anyone or which is used for betterment of others, is really right sympathetic magic. In sympathetic magic, if anyone is asked to do something for another organism/creature to banish his problems, then the organism gets benefits from that, e.g. providing food to hungry people, providing food to insects, arranging water for birds, chapati to cow, donation to poor. This sympathetic magic will not harm anyone to recover physical condition of one. It's really a right art. But a few fake saints say that they can pullout your sorrow and can put it on someone else or give them happiness by harming others. To do and think this is not sympathetic magic; infact it's conspiracy, which is totally wrong.

Million Wings feels that sympathetic magic was originated to provide happiness and peace at mental level. But the strategy of this sympathetic magic was never used to harm another. There are many fake saints who misuse this magic and are doing conspiracy behind the name of sympathetic magic. These cruel people enrol innocent people psychologically and make them afraid and disturb their peace by arising fear, misconception, false notion, and negative attitude. These types of cruel saints are the main cause of wants to give happiness to one person by enrolling others in conspiracy strategies of magic or black magic. Million Wings feels that magic itself can't do anything, but most people harm themselves being afraid or tense and cruel saints took advantage of these weaknesses of people.

Million Wings feels that ghost, shadow, soul are misconceptions, false notions, and fear of human psychology which is converted to imaginary feeling. In reality these feelings may have personal imaginary form but don't have social or real form. Million Wings feels that those organisms/creatures which don't have any physical or emotional similarity with humans don't matter for humans. But if any invisible power wants to give pain or discomfort to any person or the whole universe to clear its existence, it's a security problem. If any person is feeling so, then he should tell many people about that, as if the whole human species is together/united, then they can handle any pain of the universe easily and can easily defeat any problem. Science and technology is knowing the universe with full clarity and authentication.

Million Wings feels that tension or problems related to psychology can be revealed to some extent in a satisfactory way. Million Wings feels that sympathetic magic which works to release tension of one with creating trouble for anyone else is very beneficial, is exactly right. No one has any problem to use that alternative which provides happiness to one without harming others, e.g. worship, applying black dot to save ourselves from the evil eye. Doing this is personal satisfaction, peace, and happiness, nothing else.

Million Wings feels that the universe can be small but there is no limitation of human imagination/mind. Any thought can arise and break anytime, anywhere, of any level. Mentality can jolted to provide peace, happiness, satisfaction; any psychic treatment can be used. Million Wings feels that plausible psychiatric treatment works only for personal satisfaction, which might have any form but the basis is to correct psychology with the help of psychology only. But to obstruct anyone physically or mentally to defeat the disease of one is totally wrong. Any cruel saint that tries to pull a person in any physical or mental misconception, or false notion of any disease will not be spared at any cost, will not be tolerated. To put one person in tension or disease to correct another disease is a totally wrong and cruel mentality which will not be tolerated by any person at any cost, infact will try to teach a lesson to the same person. It's true, it's future. These kinds of cruel people should be taken strictly by government so that innocent people can be saved from cruel, dramatic saints. Million Wings feels that true saints are those who will help people to overcome pain, sorrow calmly, without expecting anything inreturn.

Million Wings feels that whenever any problems arise, then try to solve those firstly and on basis of available knowledge and solution. If still it can't be solved or is far from thoughts of worldliness, then only think about invisible effects, and an alternative solution should also be that which will not harm others; only this is right and true too.

Million Wings feels that the natural thing or fate or form on which there is no personal control can't be obstruction or bad luck for anyone, e.g.

sneezing. To sneeze is not any obstruction or bad luck for anyother. Yes, it's surely beneficial for the one who sneezed. If accidentally any creature or organism gets in the way of humans then also it's not any bad luck or problem infact, it's due to innocence or non-civilization of that organism. Only the human has systematically arranged the whole earth according to himself but still other organisms on earth are uncivilized and not arranged. Howcan cats, cows, dogs, etc. come to know to move on which road from where to cross?

Million Wings feels that astrology can be guessed rightly only after collecting right information of every moment, every place, star, planet and the rest of universe at the time of birth and during life. Direction of sun, stars, moon, planets, and the rest of universe at the time of birth are responsible for the build-up of a human, and as they change their position, according to that the human's nature and behaviour also change. Any impact on life is not the same, neither will it remain the same, nor has it remained the same. Every moment impact of still and movable universe changes in combination. Impact of every moment of movable and still universe need to be known with each change to comment clearly and authentically.

Chapter 40

Science and technology

Life is becoming comfortable because of science and technology which provides life easily and in bulk, e.g. travels, communications, food and water, clothes, houses health, and protection. The science which is decreasing problems of humans, entertaining humans, and connecting the whole world is most welcomed. Giving motivation and positive direction to science and technology for betterment of life is for the compatible universe. Science gives authentication and clearance to far-sighted thinking and curiosities of humans. Inreality, humans' mind and thinking is best. Humans move forward and science is following humans. If there is no curiosity in humans' minds, then how will science grow? Dream and desire of doing something new in life, doing something better is the life of science. Firstly human thinks, then makes it, then checks its capability and quality and then tries to make it better. This is what has been happening for centuries, and this will keep on happening while life exists. Science is that way or medium by which humans can get comfort and facilities; with the help of science, the human is trying to understand universe.

Searching for the secret of life, nature, and the universe in series is science and technology. The main logical motto of science and technology is to make life better, beautiful, and plausible.

Million Wings feels that science is working to decrease problems/sorrow with every passing day. Today, thousands of organisms which cause diseases are investigated with the help of science, and microorganisms can be seen. By understanding their behaviour, disease can be obstructed by finding medicines, and many other treatments are possible with the help of science and technology. Humans have made many machine and instruments by which diseases and problems can be treated to greater extent. Increasing science and technology for safety, security, betterment and happiness of life and living is socially beneficial working skill.

Million Wings feels that humans are understanding the universe with the help of science and technology. Clear and authenticated information on planets, stars, sun far away in the universe can be collected. Natural hazards are judged before they harm so that better safety measure can be taken. Serious/dangerous climate/weather like wind, rain, typhoon can be judged prior to their occurrence with the help of science and technology. Natural and human effects on the universe are known to us. With the help of science and technology, humans are able to manage and prevent many natural hazards in life. Million Wings feels that science is trying to make a better present and future. In almost every field of life, science and technology is used. Facilities and comfort in life are got from science and technology. Air-conditioning machine, transport (e.g. cars, trains, airplanes), telephone and Internet facility, invention of light, invention of fire, etc. are possible because of science and technology. Humans have made science, and science is making humans more powerful and intelligent.

Million Wings feels that the biggest achievement of science and technology is the special ways of connecting the whole world. Telephone to talk, connecting the whole world by the same way through Internet, fast and comfortable transport by which humans can travel comfortably anywhere in the world. Invention of electricity, invention of wheel, fire, telephone, transport, etc. made the world even more beautiful. Million Wings feels that science and technology will provide better thinking and living in the future. Million Wings feels that there are many entertaining resources available to humanswith the help of science and technology. Use of science and technology for digitalmedia, games, music, travelling the ocean, sky, mountains is beneficial and comfortable. By this there is no need of capturing and training animals for entertainment.

Million Wings feels that everyone should try to attach with minimum technology according to time. Fulfilling basic requirement is the real meaning of working skill. Million Wings feels that if someone is trying hard to know God, then that is human only, and trying hard to collect proof of authenticity with the help of science and technology is the best channel to clearly open the secrets of life, the world. It's even true that thinking and understanding is firstly responsible for every invention nowadays, which is a very powerful and amazing weapon of humans.

Invention—Million Wings feels that invention is the future. Inventing new things is moving towards the future. Talking invention is better direction, is civilized future. The main motto of invention is to make human life better, more comfortable and easy. Humans are doing one after another betterment with the help of science and technology. Million Wings feels that when any need arises in a human's life, then he tries to find its solution. As he got a solution, than he tries to find its solution. As he got the solution, then he tries to make it better. It's the truth of invention and it's right. Invention can be improved by using that, then problems and deficiencies arise and then science works to improve it. As life changes, new and better changes are done. And this is called invention. Invention is only possible if humans will use, investigate, test the usage of new inventions, and calculate the things, and calculation is only possible if human will study deeply every aspect of related things and discover new things. If working strategy, working way, policies of daily life of every department and field are kept in record as proof, then it will be easy and science speeds on to new discoveries. Relating everything to life will move invention in the right direction. Million Wings feels that the life of every person is very important for the whole world. Sometimes it's good for others, sometimes dangerous. But every human lives for his happiness. If we see every human separately in the right way, then he is guidance for the whole society, nation, world. The life of every creature is a lesson for the whole human species. The life of every human leaves more or less impact on others' lives. The life of every human is discovery in itself. A human may be weak, forlorn, right or wrong, happy or sad, but naturally or as humanity, he is not less than guidance for others. The life of every human is also invention for himself. Whatever comes in a human's mind, he doesthe same, slowly, slowly; when the human realizes that his invention is harming him and nature, then he stops it or tries to make it better.

Then what's wrong in doing so? It's right. Invention is done for growth and development of the whole human species, and later on, it's beneficial or harming effects are known. Use of new invention by all humans gives reviews about beneficial or harmful effects of the new product or service. Otherthan scientists, common people also need to tell and see which product, thing, service, technology is beneficial and which is not right. Actually every scientific research invention wants to move the whole universe in a positive direction.

Million Wings feels that for their own benefit, humans started using science and technology up to any extent. It's human nature, it's true. By understanding the reproductive mechanism through medical science, humans defeated many diseases but the same positive inventions are used against nature and civilization by humans for their personal benefit. To do this is wrong. Maybe it's also one way to understand life. Humans have started using power of reproduction in artificial production of animals, organisms, or creatures so that he can use them as food. Reproducing an organism/creature just for food when it has emotional similarity with humans is wrong. It's against rules of civilization and nature. Humans need to produce food directly from soil, water, fire, air, and light with the help of science and technology so that feelings of any similar organism/creature can't be hurt. Million Wings feels that medicines/drugs are made to treat diseases and to get relief so that the whole human species and other creatures will get comfortable and plausible life. But human is using these medicines as drugs and converting healthy life to unhealthy and sorrowful. Medicines are used to save humans from diseases, not invented to use them as entertaining things and to move our life towards diseases. Million Wings feels that humans have made explosive substances, with the help of science and technology, which are used by humans to kill each other. A science which is used against life and the universe is not a logical civilized invention. Humans are moving forward, leaving behind all animals, not to become the most dangerous animal; instead, the real motto of human life is to move the whole universe towards civilization along with him.

Million Wings feels that science and technology should be used to fill human life with happiness. Nothing's bad in using telephone, Internet, digital media, games, and entertainment. Using science and technology more towards the right direction is really awesome. According to time, a person should most attach with minimum technology. Doing this is very right. Use of technology should be restricted to that level above which it has negative effects instead of positive effects.

Million Wings feels that with the change of needs/requirements, science and technology is also making new inventions, and it's right too. Making everything more capable is the right science. Collecting resources of power in more comfortable ways is the main goal. Getting maximum benefits from nature by least disturbing nature is the best science. Regarding every corner of the universe and getting complete information about that is science. Clearly and authentically understanding every situation and natural effect happening in humans' life is science. Raising false notionsand misconceptions by reality is science.

Knowing the secret of the universe is science. Invention is science; needs give birth to invention. Science and technology will clarify ways of life while life exists. The human brain is the best. Science and technology is a beautiful way to fulfil his needs and desires. Million Wings feels that if someone is trying to know/understand the secret of God, he is human only, and with the help of science and technology, the human is clearing, comparing, and attaching the secret of the universe in an authenticated way. Million Wings feels that humans who are using microorganisms/organisms/creatures which cause diseases or kill humans are proof of well-thought-out beastliness. Inventions of science and technology are done to banish or decrease sorrows from the universe but a few humans are using these inventions in negative ways to entangle and confuse people in disease and sorrow for personal benefit. Whoever is using science and technology in negative ways to kill or cause disease at any cost should be seen seriously. Million Wings feels that if any technology or invention starts to be used in negative ways, it should be stopped immediately and, along with that, remove deficiencies and negative effects and convert it to beneficial direction as logical invention. Rascalsand idiots who are using science and technology to disturb the lives of common people or misguide them should be treated harshly. Scientists need to invent, research effective ways to stop misuse of inventions.

Million Wings feels that every invention is done for common people to accept the new invention and use it. Common people are more in number, have more brain, are right also and wrong/dangerous also. Use invention as per own will and then after sometime, positive and negative effects of an invention come forward. Commonpeople give direction to new inventions. If common people are getting the benefit, then the invention is capable. Attaching invention with just social benefit is the logical meaning of invention. Making life and the universe prosperous is invention, is technology.

Million Wings feels that science and technology are to get those needs, requirements, comfort of humans which are right as per natural rules and expectations. Those inventions of a human for which he himself has given wrong directions to use science and technology, education and information to fulfil them are wrong. Science and technology should be used to remove/reduce those natural or human sorrows, by which basic logical actions of the whole universe should not get hurt/harmed. Use of science and technology in the wrong direction is a symbol of beastliness and takes humans away, in the opposite direction, from redemption. The human is using his vast knowledge about the universe for fulfilling a few illogical desires and intentions which are totally useless. Machines are used to investigate and to treat diseases, e.g. USG machineswhich people now want to use for sex determination. We needn't destroy the machines but it's necessary to change thinking at social level. If girls and boys should be given equal importance in society, then use of science and technology in non-social ways should be decreased. Not only knowing about disease/problems of reproductive organs, but people also want to use this for sex determination. People want to misuse medicines as drugs. Humans want to use disease as weapon. Those who want to take the universe towards the right direction need to be strict so that bell in the temple should give sweet and melodious music, not noise pollution. Use power to teach a lesson to nonsense thinking and intention of rascals and idiotsand, along with that, give permanent form/solution to that thinking and intention.

Million Wings feels that media, television should stop by default by 11 p.m. to 5 a.m. so that everyone should have to sleep. Only important news channel or important international sports event can be broadcast. Everyone keeps on watching TV if it is switched on. If TV is off by default, then everyone will enjoy quality sleep. Sleeping by 11 p.m. to 5 a.m. keeps humans more healthy, wise, beautiful, and happy. Million Wings feels that humans have to sleep atleast five nights in a week. It's a basis of the country towards success and happiness if citizens are healthy, beautiful, intelligent. Million Wings feels that many inventions of science and technology suddenly fill human life with happiness. But long-term effect on humansand atmosphere is also important to know. If person has any question or doubt about new inventions which are providing comfort, entertainment, and benefits, then he should express it freely. Let your suggestions, curiosities, doubts, questions reach government and administration and science and technology so that only benefits can be taken and none will be entangled in any danger. The invention whose beneficial effects are proved according to time, with complete information available, can be used to get more and more benefits. New inventions may be electronics, food, power resources, may be any, but use them rightly, as per safety measure, and according to limitations so that we can save ourselves from personal harms, especially from serious and dangerous diseases.

Million Wings feels that all aspects of products and services which have arisen from science and technology are known in future after its use. If humans feel any danger, problem, or negative effects of any invention while using it, then humans should keep it infront of everyone. Not only scientists but common man should also give direction to life. The faster the human will give the right direction to inventions of science, the earlier and with the least harm the human will make life better. Million Wings feels that every human should give suggestion to government and administration about every new scientific technology and invention. You may never know how beneficial your suggestion can be for the whole universe. Million Wings feels that today humans are doing new inventions for more betterment of life but only the future will tell whether these are beneficial or harmful in long-term use and these need to be studied thoroughly on life of every human to know about effect of invention on them and their experience, and explanations need to be taken in managed way. It's the right way to increase understanding.

Million Wings feels that for centuries, the human has been making changes in his life for betterment and doing this is right. A human wants everything to be good. Even new inventions working for betterment and to get more comfort also show their harmful effects with time. Future tells about harms, tensions, problems, and negative use of inventions and then by correcting them in search of better life. Humans move forwards. It's a truth of life. It's positive direction, which will take the universe to highest level.

Chapter 41

Nature

Nature and universe are decorated by coordination of creature and nature. Every organism is a living organism which has life. Every organism which has soul has life. Every organism which has soul, has life, is living which grows by itself, which has feeling, which can give birth to organism/creature similar to itself. In nature, every organism/creature, may it be living or nonliving, is mainly made of basic elements. It's made from nature and got mixed in nature. Everything in which soul resides becomes living and the rest becomes nature. Insects, animals, birds, humans, plants, trees all are living. Water, air, fire, soil, light are parts of nature. Million Wings feels that every organism/creature, may it be living or nonliving, is directly or indirectly related to each other.

Nature is a working area, the birthplace of every organism/creature. Nature is most powerful. It can disturb the universe in a fraction of a second. When air, water, fire, planets become balanced, they change the form of the whole universe. If there is a most powerful thing in the universe, then that is nature only. Million Wings feels that in starting, everything was at its place in nature. But slowly, slowly, the curiosity of humans has started disturbing nature. Because of this, the balance of nature is surely affected. Somewhere forests are destroyed, somewhere mountains are blocked, somewhere water is decreased, somewhere earth is dug deep. For centuries, nature has been changed, and change is changing in search of balance.

Needs, curiosity of better life, search and research of humans are not the only causes of change in nature, but many more natural causes are here. Humans are doing change on earth, but earth is just a small part of the universe. OK, it's acceptable that humans are changing earth but who is changing the whole universe? On earth, organisms/creatures and nature are evolving but who is evolving earth? Who has hung it among planets, moon, stars, and air and how? Who has designed and planned and made this universe and nature and how? What is all this? Who has that much of brain? How is it planned? Power, balance, and management are chosen by whom? Million Wings feels that the universe is science and a great scientist has made this. That best scientist is God. How great God is who has planned this whole universe, it's impossible to even guess. God has made everything very logical and based on principles. Everything is directly or indirectly related to each other. There is nothing useless in this universe. Everything has one or another purpose. The whole universe is moving in search of balance; every living and nonliving thing wants to make its own balance and this search keeps on moving the whole universe.

Million Wings feels that nature is helpful in growth and development of life, gives basic building material and provides favourable conditions to life. Everything originates from nature and mixes in nature.

Plants and trees convert carbondioxide (CO_2) to oxygen (O_2); that is, purify impurities released by our breath and again provide pure air to us. Million Wings feels that every person should grow atleast one tree for purification of their lungs, maybe at anytime, but do plant.

Million Wings feels that humans should use wisely the natural resources of energy which are available in nature. But if still natural resources are decreasing or vanishing, then nothing's wrong in this, as according to time, different new resources of energy should be searched for and these will be the main secret of the future. Million Wings feels that a human needs to know and understand about how to use natural resources in better way. He has to do this at social level, so that the power of natural resources can't be wasted and humans can use them for a longer time. It may be possible that to get new natural resources, water supply and light supply can be stopped/interrupted for a few hours. Just think how difficult it will be to live without these resources. Million Wings feels that while humans are not getting new resources, humans should use old natural resources wisely instead of washing them. It will be right, it will be logical. Million Wings feels that by using caution signals, natural resources can be saved from misuse. It's human natural, it's true, it's right.

Million Wings feels that in the universe there is nature in different forms. A human may move anywhere in the universe but nature will always remain with him; it will never let humans alone. Nature is the best friend of life. Million Wings feels that nature is a scientific series which is moving at its own pace. There is coordination in the speed of nature and its creatures and life is coordinated. Nature and life definitely affect each other. Creatures have to understand secrets of the universe collectively and have to solve this puzzle of nature and life clearly and in authenticated way. It's the main need of the universe, it's a right of God. It's redemption of the whole universe.

茶 茶 茶

Chapter 42

Humans and Animals

The universe is life. The meaning of life in the universe is having personal development, emotions, and power of reproduction. Numerous creatures/species live here. Numerous plants, tree, insects, birds, and animals are here. Everything which has life is a creature. The universe has millions of creatures/organisms. A human is also an animal which comes forward and livesa managed life. Today, humans guide every creature in the universe; teaching and understanding the next generation is logical reason. The human is just living his life; infact he is also transferring his experience to the next generation so that life can be made better.

Million Wings feels that all organisms and creatures are made for each other; everyone has some relation with each other because of some motto. For centuries, organisms have had mutual coordination. Organisms contain feelings from friendship to enmity. Every organism and creature lives for food, comfort, reproduction, power, and self-respect. Needs, dreams, and desires keep on moving life. Every organism/creature coordinates with other organism/creature for mutual need, dream, and desire. Humans also coordinate with organisms for personal benefit. Humans are more powerful and managed than other organisms/creatures. A human has collected resources for his safety and security. Understanding the whole universe and nature with the help of science and technology is not possible because of the reason that human is the most powerful, but it's because he is living unitedand is delivering knowledge to the next generation through education system. Unity and education of human is his biggest power, success, and cleverness. Million Wings feels if today humans are living together with unity and in coordinated way, then only he is able to win all the creatures in the universe. Otherwise, anytime any animal can kill a human if humans will live separately. Collectively, humans are raising science and technology. The human is getting more intelligent, learning from life, and is moving forward on earth and in the universe. The human is using all other animals/species/creatures for his personal benefit. Collectively, united humans are winning all other creatures/organisms. The animals which become coordinated with each other, humans make good relations with those animals. But the animals who attack humans, humansteach a lesson to those animals. Humans have good coordination with cow, buffalo, elephant, goat, dog, birds, ox, etc. because of mutual benefit from each other. Humans use a few creatures/organisms for food.

Million Wings feels that to live with animals for mutual benefits is a good thing. In every condition, both should atleast have minimum advantage and respect from each other. It's easy for humans to use animals for personal benefit but it's very difficult for other organisms to control humans. That's why only humans need to think and understand to how to react or behave with other organisms. It's a rule of nature that whoever is more powerful and intelligent wants to collect resources for living with his power and intelligence. Today, the human is the most powerful and intelligent on earth, so he wants to use nature and organisms for his personal benefit and is using them also.

Million Wings feels that today humans are living organized and regulated lives but still they are not fully civilized. Civilization doesn't mean to be educated or to have comfort in life but it means to behave affectionately and respectfully with all creatures. It's all right to make relations with other organisms/creatures for own benefit but other organisms/creatures should also get minimum benefit from the relations, e.g. food, shelter, treatment, rest, company of own species, respect, and if possible, love and affection. Don't keep any animal alone/single at home. Minimum two animals of same species or race should be kept so that they can talk to each other and feels belongingness. It's not right to bringup just one, just for the purpose of entertainment; it's totally wrong. Today with the help of technology, every creature can be made and can be given its original form (shape and size). Civilization is to capture animals in zoo or national parks. Capturing any animal from natural jungle or place just for entertainment is totally wrong.

Million Wings feels that reproducing animals just to kill and eat (food) is against civilization. Hunting and using natural animal for food is still better. Animals which have same feelings and emotions as humans can be killed/hunted and eaten only if nothing else is available as food. Today, a human is civilized and if he is able to get food in a managed/arranged way from any animal without harming that organism/creature, there is nothing wrong in doing so. Nothing's like non-civilization in this. Nothing's bad in collecting from cow, goat, buffalo, camel the milk which is produced naturally, but their children should be provided favourable food. To eat egg in which life doesn't develop is not wrong; infact it's beneficial for health.

Million Wings feels that it's not bad to use animals as transport but it's important to take care of their capacity and comfort. Working for six to eight hours daily is good. Putting more weight than capacity is wrong facility of food. Security, medicine should be provided when required. Using machine vehicles for transport is a better way.

Million Wings feels that humans should know/learn ways and facts to talk to animals. It's important to know language of other animals to understand their feelings. With the help of science and technology, humans can research on talks of animals with each other and human will understand their signals by this and will be able to talk to them. By mutual talk between animals and human, they will develop more, in better mutual understanding, mutual coordination will increase, and it will be more supportive and more satisfying experience. It may be proved very useful to learn language of animals.

Million Wings feels that killing animals for clothes and decoration is not civilization. There are many organisms/creature which are away from human reach. In natural water, air, soil, there are thousands and millions of organisms/creatures which may not even be visible to humans. But all those are very essential for growth and development of nature. Every organism/creature may that be in water, soil, earth, air, universe has their own importance; they surely have some motto. To give direction to life is a logical principle of every organism and life. The microorganisms which are humans' friends fulfil humans' need and inreturn they also get benefit from humans. So both the sides get benefits from each other. But those microorganisms which are harming need to be recognized and defeated; for example, a few microorganisms cause many serious diseases to humans and today humans are trying to defeat or kill these through research of new medicines and chemicals, with the help of science and technology. Million Wings feels that it's good if naturally organisms/creatures kill and eat other organisms/creatures which are destructive or dangerous, e.g. lizards eat insects, mosquitoes, a few insects which harm crops are eaten by other insects. Million Wings feels that it's totally opposite to civilization to reproduce organisms forcibly just for food. Reproducing and bringing up creatures like hens, goats, fish, pigs, cows, buffaloes, lambs, birds just to kill and eat is totally wrong and against civilization. Killing natural organisms, in natural conditions, in natural way to eat is not against civilization. Million Wings feels that even if the human compares himself with animals, he is also not wrong if he wants to react with other animals as an animal. Human has to capture natural organism/creature and natural power to eat them. Today, a human is living an arranged life, human has power, intelligence, and resources but he is using skills in more wrong ways even than animals. Today, humans capture organisms forcibly by natural or artificial ways, reproducing them to eat them. This formula/process is against civilization and taking human away from redemption. Million Wings feels that every organism/creature with which human doesn't feel comfortable can react in anyway with that organism/creature, as there are no emotional similarities so that is dead according to humans. Plants are organisms which have no emotional similarity with humans so humans grow, cut, and eat them for food. Then that's not wrong. Million Wings feels that for complete civilization, humans need to get food directly from water, air, fire, soil and light, without killing any animal. Million Wings feels that a human just does not live an arranged/managed life but he needs to be completely civilized to know the secrets of the universe, nature. Solving the puzzles of the universe will give redemption to the whole universe.

Chapter 43

Future world

Million Wings feels that the future is the name of more betterment. The world is becoming better day by day. From living till thinking, everything is improving. Intention of humans is to make life better. The present is better than the past, and wants to make the future better than the present, moving towards betterment and will keep on moving. It's true, it's right, it's logical.

Life is same from the beginning. Every creature in this universe is passing through the life cycle of birth, food, learning, sex, reproduction, profession, entertainment, and death. Everyone has same cycle of feelings, e.g. love, care, anger, fight, jealousy, power, friendship, ego, revenge, romance, respect. And the driving force is always the dreams and desires of the creature. The great kings of all the continents and countries to present day, every creature is also living through the same cycles and this will continue in future while life remains. Presentations and technology will keep on changing and the rest, everything will remain the same. The only thing that is becoming clear day by day is understanding of the Creator's universe and life.

Million Wings feels that in future also relations and feelings will remain the same. Affection and care will remain as they are. It's true that a human wants more freedom but it's also true that the human always needs love, care, affection of someone and he himself also loves, cares for, and affectionately loves someone. In future, relations may have fewer responsibilities but love, care, and affection will remain the same in hearts. In future, a child (egg and sperm) may be produced by any machine but affection filled with belongingness in parents' heart will always remain the same. Every family member may live separately but belongingness for by-birth relations will never be over. Parents, children, husband-wife may be living at different places or government-organized arrangements, but the feeling of belongingness will always remain the same.

Million Wings feels that the world may want freedom and rights but never wants to end mutual affection and care; the world wants that freedom which can bind up relations. The future is moving towards freedom. But the base will be affection, love, care, friendship. The future may have wide and free thinking. But a mother will always pray for her child, a sister, a lover; a wife will always love and care for her brother, lover, parents, always want security and safety of their children. A brother/close friend will always stand beside in enjoyable and problematic situations. Food, clothes, living desires, dreams, profession may be of any type. Relations and feelings of life will always remain filled with love and care forever. The day love and care will be zero, that day there will be the last day of the universe. That will be end of life, it's true.

Million Wings feels that humans will keep on improving everything in future. Better facilities, more favourable conditions, better qualities, better use of everything are goals of the future. With the help of science and technology, new fields of power and energy are used. With the help of five natural resources, new inventions/things/matter/substancesare used to get energy. Humans want to gain more benefit by least affecting nature, finding new secrets of nature everyday. The more a human will understand nature, the more he will be near to God and redemption. Trying to make science and technology more natural, in future, a human will invent those things which he is unable to understand today.

The future form of marriage and family will be a combination of complete freedom, social-professional arrangement, and science and technology. A human is running from marriage as he feels obstructions in his freedom by doing so. Girls and boys need freedom and time to fulfil these dreams and desires which they had to spend in giving birth and bringing up children.

Marriage feels like social restrictions, where a person has to live with one girl or boy lifelong and it's problematic to make numerous romantic relations or these are not allowed to be made. Time is consumed in taking care of elders and doing daily housework. In future, human will restrict marriage to birth part. All problems and responsibilities related to marriage will be removed.

Million Wings feels that society will become a professional family, as everyone lives in family and fulfils their minimum responsibilities the same way; every work of family will take professional form. Every need of society will be fulfilled in professional form. Food department, department of artificial pelvis for infant, department of children, teenager department, old age department will be handled by humans only with the help of machines; it will be default compulsion for every human by government and administration to have two children. If a human will be born, then only these departments will work. If human will not be born, then who will work for familiar or social departments?

Today people are working in their own families at different places. Then these people will work at social level in professional way. Boy will donate their sperm and girls will donate their ovum to artificial pelvic department to develop child. Best sperm from boy's sperm will be chosenand best ovum from the girl's own will be chosen and then by artificial fertilization, a child will be developed in an artificial ovary. In society, girl and boy have to choose atleast their husband and wife respectfully by their choice, whose sperm and egg they want to develop their child. From every marriage in society, atleast one girl and one boy will be given birth so that there will be equal ratio of girls and boys. Those girls/boys whose egg/sperm have serious disease will not be allowed/permitted to give birth to baby like this; society will be balanced combination of technology and humanism.

Million Wings feels that humans will only save only those which are either small or are impossible to make. A child should be given birth, as till now there are no better machines than humans, neither it can be. Humans may secure him from all four sides but inside it will be the same natural human.

Million Wings feels that God is the best scientist and this whole world is moving on the basis of science and technology. Everything in the world is understanding or may not. The things/work/matter which humans have understood seems to be science and technology. But things which humans can't understand or in which a human is entangled or about which things are missing, that seems to be magic. Million Wings feels that in future science and technology will find out the reality and attentions of those things which seems to be magic today and that will also become science and technology, and like this, science will slowly, slowly understand the technology of this best creation. Million Wings feels that humans will start making food directly from soil, water, air, light, and heat, for which creatures needn't be killed and humans will start understanding civilization.

Million Wings feels that humans may be dependent on machines to any extent but feelings and emotions will always be there. Minimum requirements of life will also remain the same. One other truth is humans can't make better machines than themselves. A human is that machine which has capacity and quality to do every work by any way. Million Wings feels that a human is trying to do everything from the future's sense, knowledge, experience, capacity, and quality so that he can collectextra, more and more facilities from nature in more favourable and secure ways. As a human moves forward in future, then he realizes the painful and dangerous effects of inventions done in part and then to correct them, the human tries to find a new way fast for better life. It's a motivation of life. It's a hope of logical direction of life. Million Wings feels that change comes with time and will keep on changing ways, and process will also change. But needs, dreams, and desires will remain the same, will grow as they are.

Research is the mainstay of understanding life. Every life is an experiment and research for generations. Every creature should give their true views of personal experiences of life as far as possible so that true research comes forward. Every human should try maximally to participate in one or another form of research studies in which they feel comfortable. Research methods should be simple, relevant, respectful, easy ways so that everyone can happily join. Research should always be in positive direction so that our resources (time, money, brains, manpower, energy, etc.) should be utilised in a maximum of fruitful ways. So before choosing any topic of research, one should collect maximum information already available at that point in time on the subject and must thoroughly discuss the issue with specialists and relevant persons before enrolling.

Million Wings feels that the future is to get logical life. The future is to get redemption. The future is to get God. The future is to understand nature/universe. The future is to understand every natural creature. The future is to move towards civilizations. The future is a search of balanced life. The future is to achieve happiness in better and exclusive way. The future is hope of everything which is need, dream, and desire of humans. The future is opportunity for humans. The future is one more chance. The future is that hope which has the ability to fulfil every dream. The future is hope. The future is curiosity, the future is right.

Chapter 44

Freedom

Freedom means to do the same whatever heart says and to keep on doing what we like. Freedom is the right to live life as per our own will. Freedom is that kind of happiness which everyone wants to enjoy. Freedom is a beautiful way to live and everyone needs it. Everyone wants more and more freedom. Everyone likes and loves to live freely. This thought is right and logical too. Actually freedom means personal comfort; actually personal comfort means maximum freedom to live and minimum responsibility to fulfil. Freedom means to live maximum life the way we want. Everyone needs freedom equally. Freedom is a right of every individual, family, society, world and all want/need freedom.

Million Wings feels that a logical meaning of freedom is personal happiness and satisfaction. The more the freedom, the more plausible life. The more the rights, the more will be freedom. The fewer the responsibilities, the less will be restriction and the more will be freedom. The more the freedom, the more will be possibilities of happiness. This means to increase happiness, freedom needs to increase. Million Wings feels, let's increase human happiness upto that level above which there should be only sorrow/ grief, and decrease responsibilities to that limit below which life should not be possible. Expanding the area below rights and responsibilities to highest level is expansion of happiness. Maximum right means doing everything with mutual understanding and agreement and fewer responsibilities means fulfilling promises done with parents and those done by own will and agreement (e.g. upbringing of children). Freedom means to avoid or to throw off our unnecessary, useless, and non-essential personal and social restrictions. Freedom means to make life easy and comfortable. Freedom means to eat food according to will, wear clothes according to will, fulfil education, profession, and marriage. Freedom means to freely express our feeling.

If everyone wants freedom, then who will manage family and society? Do only youngsters want freedom? Do parents and grandparents have to live in restrictions? Everyone wants freedom but the question is, what kind of freedom? How much of freedom? Does all scatter by giving freedom?

Million Wings feels that if humans don't get freedom, then they will feel as bounded, feeling grieved, disappointed, disheartened, will do fights. Freedom will do revolts. And if they get freedom, then they do things out of limits, misuse, decimate themselves and others. If someone resists them, then they do revolts and start fighting. Now what shall family and society do? If they give freedom, then there's tension/problem. If they don't give freedom, they seem to be wicked. Disadvantage on both sides. The one who gets freedom does everything as per their own way and their ownones try to pull them up from every problem. Now what's the fault of ownones? They give freedom too and become wicked too. Elders give freedoms to the younger for their happiness and restrict them for their protection and in end for their benevolence, they start decreasing their freedom. They are doing right and what else shall they do then? Either one should enjoy freedom in secure and plausible way or they shouldn't get more freedom. It's exactly right that if we enjoy freedom with secure ways, then no one will restrict us and there will be a free plausible atmosphere and coordination on both sides. It's correct, it's right, and all want this.

Million Wings feels that freedom means to make life more comfortable as per will, not to have unnecessary fights with families or to get apart from them. The countries where freedom has broken family and they're living alone are suffering from mental disorders. Everyone in family, grandparents, parents, children, siblings havethe right to have freedom. Everyone should have equal freedom. Then how come it will be possible that all can get freedom? Freedom should be like that, that everyone should live freely and their mutual understanding and coordination should also be maintained, i.e. balance of maximum should be maintained in such a way that everyone should live as per their choice, being attached with one another.

Million Wings feels that one who is free-willed never wants, neither allows to their freedom to be decrease. Freedom can just be increased but can't be decreased. It's also true that there is no upper limit of freedom. There should be balanced freedom, graceful freedom, which means to cut off unnecessary restriction and to live freely with own dreams, desires, will, and goal and to fulfil those responsibilities which are necessary, i.e. a graceful and balanced freedom. We need freedom but balanced freedom. Freedom should be for all and all that at freedom should have good coordination so that no one can object to each other. Everyone should live their life as per their own ways. Balanced freedom means balance between personal freedom and restrictions. Balanced freedom means balanced personal rights and duties. Balanced freedom means balancedbetween personal life and other lives. Balanced freedom shall increase happiness, not problems. A freedom which everyone desires. A freedom which gives equal motivation and ways. A freedom which can maintain balance. Million Wings feels that balanced freedom is for everyone, i.e. grandparents to grandchildren. Everyperson in the worldhas a right of having balanced freedom, which has a five numbers path for everyone to live life according to will and dream.

Million Wings feels that freedom is not about being alone but freedom is togetherness, to unite with ownones. If son wants freedom, then freedom should be for daughter too. If father has freedom, then mother should also have equal right. Grandfather has right to live freely; grandmother can also do everything as per her will. If grandson wants to live freely, granddaughter also wants to fulfil her dreams and desires according to will. Grandparents to grandchildren all want and need to live freely. Freedom should not be for one but everyone should have equal rights. This is healthy thinking.

Million Wings feels that a logical principle of balanced freedom is whatever a person does should be done with mutual understanding and will of others too. It's right, it's true, it's that secret which can fill life with lots and lots of happiness. Million Wings' main aim is to reach out, to make others understand, to let all enjoy the world, every country, every society, every family, and every human so that there should be numerous, unlimited ways for every human to get happiness. Every human should get millions of wings of happiness so that they can live as per heart, will, dream, desires, hope in the sky of life and enjoy the life fully.

Let's understand freedom deeply, the meaning of balanced freedom. Million Wings feels that logical principle of balanced freedom is whatever a person does should be done with mutual understanding and will of others too. It's right. It's true. It's that secret which can fill life with lots and lots of happiness. Million Wings' main aim is to reach out, to make others understand, to let all enjoy the world, every country, every society, every family and every human.

1. Live by heart, and let others live according to their will, not putting unnecessary restrictions on each other.
2. One has to express one's feelings freely, not make others silent and forcibly put restrictions on each other.
3. Choose education and profession according to their will and desires, not pull them forcibly in other subjects and profession.
4. Come out of home, look and try to understand the world, and enjoy, not be lost in the world and be apart from ownones forever.
5. The principle should be same for male and female and not to capture female and let males roam about.
6. Enjoy freely and do not cross each other's limits.
7. Use the best of comfort resources and opportunities and do not misuse these.
8. Enjoy positive thinking, plausible and healthy, our own good and bad habits, not to increase social problems or against humanism.
9. Laugh, meet, increase the atmosphere of being friends, not to behave forcefully with others.
10. Let the children choose education, profession, partner according to their will, interest, thinking and choice, not choose forcibly against them, against their will.
11. Children also have to get the partner of choice, not to fight with family and get apart.
12. Wear comfortable clothes of own choice but don't show private parts.

13. Improve and prosper in life, not to interfere and intense others' lives.
14. Enjoy maximally our each and every right, along with fulfilling minimum required responsibilities.

Responsibilities of every person having superb, marvellous, graceful thinking in youngster

Million Wings feels that youngstersare the main force and a youngster is the founder of balanced freedom. Youngsters can freely enjoy life in balanced way and can give direction to the whole world. Also wherever a youngster is, there isa positive and plausible atmosphere. Change is plausible, where a youngster is. Freedom is there where a youngster is. There can't be forcefulness and unnecessary crime, where a youngster is. There will be enjoyment where a youngster is. Million Wings feels that youngsters are the grace and elegance of Million Wings. If a youngster is pleasurable, acceptable, delightful, then the nation will surely get lots of success. Million Wings feels that it is usually sad about youngsters that they are spirited and energetic but do not have sincerity. Consciousness doesn't listen and understand serious and easy issues but knows only how to fight. Their main aim is enjoyment only. They are just busy there and can't make the right decision. Then it's impossible for them to take their rights and make good decisions regarding social peace and success. Youngsters are busy in their minor fights, then how can they make neighbour and world atmosphere tension free? Youngsters use the whole of their power and energy to handle tough and rowdy people. They can fight against social dons and terrorists? What kind of future will youngsters give to the world when their own future sinks in drugs? Patience is less in youngsters. Only fights weapons are not in it to handle and carry world. But discussions are also needed as first priority. A youngster doesn't have much knowledge and experience of life, so he can't right profitable decision different feel at social level.

Energetic and responsible, we are youngsters.

Million Wings is not fully agreed with these kinds of trends of thinking of the world; it's not like the elder and old persons are saying everything wrong. But on other side, the truth is this also, that if youngsters will get the right guidance and direction, then not only society or nation, but they have power to change the whole world. Today, youngsters are managed, educated, and are doing well in every field, understanding life deeply. A youngster is getting experienced in almost every social and professional field. Youngsters of 18–40 years belong to the energetic/spirited contingent, and youngsters of 40–60 years belong to the conscious contingent, are specialized in their field. If we see carefully, then youngsters are of both soft and warm types, which have power to make life successful and happiness in plausible ways.

So, young friends, let's change the thinking of the world regarding us. A youngster has capacity to make a comfortable and beautiful atmosphere around the world, where no one can be afraid of anything and take care of each other. Every member of family, society, the world can roam around freely and securely without only fear. A world/society has there some necessary social principles, and everyone should follow them with heart and understanding. All will respond and react in respectful way. Having without of youngsters no one can able to force, misbehave, or spread terror.

If someone dares to react this way, then he should be ready for what he will get in response, in return. One should feel (grandparents to grandchildren) secure, safe, and morally supported, having support of youngster and can enjoy their life fully. So that everyone in society should live freely according to their own ways, that no one has objection to each other's personal life or creates problems in each other's life. Only personal youngsters can bring, can make a beautiful atmosphere by their effort.

Million Wings feels that it's not necessary to have power and leadership to bring better change in the world. But being busy in our own life, own place while enjoying it can be done. Every nation, every state, every society, every family, every place, everywhere has active youngsters. Every youngster is like a melodious and powerful wave, in which they themselves and everyone swing with joy. When worldwide these waves of happiness combine/unite, the whole universe will swing in a melodious wave of music where everyone can swing, dance, sing in happiness. Every youngster is like a bullet and when these bullets unite and move in one direction, then that will be powerful wave. Youngsters can easily overcome/defeat enemies of humanism. Friends! Life is to enjoy. Let's bind the world with freedom. That balanced freedom which can bring happiness and freedom to everyone's life.

That balanced freedom which has love, care, and friendship. That balance in which everyone should live by heart. Balanced freedom filled which has capacity to make true dreams and desires. Friends! Let's together to make a beautiful society and world, where everyone can happiness and success. It's the biggest dream, biggest need of tomorrow, of future i.e. balanced freedom.

Million Wings feels that modernity is a feeling to bring betterment and innovation, mental level and comfort. Modernity is newness, recentness of life. Modernity is better life. Modernity to make worlds everything better andmore comfortable. Modernity is the future. Thinking and things all demand change with time. As a human lives life, he gets to know about the weaknesses/problems of old things and thinking. A human wants those things to improve in more comfortable and suitable ways. Needs and demands arise with time. Human keeps on searching for new things, makes new things, judges new things. The thinking/things which have some deficiencies the human wants to abolish them and tries to make them better and the things which are already good, the human tries to make them more comfortable and improve the quality. Freedom is also one of the thinking of modern life, in which everyone has a right and opportunity to live life according to his own will and way and he can get more happiness. To think this is right.

Million Wings feels that the meaning of modernity is not just about clothes, food, or comfort, but to have open, wide, optimistic, and balanced change and development in every field of life is freedom, is modernity. To fulfila logical life is the first happiness of a human and then to have quality is success and happiness, and in the end to live with passion is will, success, and happiness. Youngsters have to make the meaning of logical modernity understood to the world. To make youngsters and elders understand the right meaning, use of modern technique, things is a must and motivate and encourage elders to use them. So that children, youngsters, eldersand others should spread their thinking. So that everyone should enjoy freedom and happiness at social level. Modernity is a change towards better life, better future, better happiness. Million Wings feels that every thing or thinking which moves humans towards better comfort and positive direction is modernity.

Million Wings feels that females also have same rights and freedom to enjoy life as males. Million Wings feels that girl and boy don't want to suppress each other's freedom but need equal opportunities, motivation, help, security, self-respect, and rights. If girls and boys will get the same atmosphere, then it will be only about qualities and capabilities. One will be more ahead who has more interest, willpower, and capabilities. It's freedom, to provide equal opportunities.

Million Wings agrees to provide equal freedom, rights, and facilities to males and females. Females should understand that they have to conflict for freedom. They only need to suppress stubborn males, not all the males. Females' motto is to get freedom for themselves, not to decrease freedom of males. Females want the same freedom as males, so why agitate against freedom of males? Instead females have to arise to get the same freedom. Million Wings feels that males have not at all problems with freedom of females; instead they don't want to decrease their freedom. Most males also favour, support females for their rights. Females need to surprise the stubborn males and get freedom, not humiliate every male. If females do this with every male, then obviously nice males will also support them for theirself-respect. Girls and boys who have some principles have to get the support of those who have some principles. As to being together is enjoyment. If one will keep on suppressing/humiliating each other, then both will remain alone. Million Wings feels that it is more easy and comfortable to increase freedom than to decrease. Males are enjoying more freedom so it's difficult for them to step back. This means not to decrease freedom of all males but to increase freedom of females. Million Wings feels that males love, care for, and respect females related to them, so they want to give them more comfort and security, e.g. a father to his daughter, brother to his sister, husband to his wife, lover to his love, son to his mother, so he makes few rules and limits and sometimes these rules and limits become restriction, limitations, demarcation for females. Million Wings feels that female and male have difference of pregnancy of nine months and to feed baby for six months. A female can't enjoy outer freedom for these fifteen months, that's why she gets stage of best relations and life. If mother is here, then life is here. Life is here, so redemption is here, so ultimate happiness is here.

Million Wings feels that males have to give respect, opportunities, security in such a way that they are able to do things with maximum independence and can do self-protection. They can understand good and bad things themselves and can make their own decisions and can enjoy plausible atmosphere with full freedom. Females should have strong belief that if they need, then their near and dear ones, government, police security will help them. Females need to diminish, decrease misbehaviour and unnecessary restrictions of males, not decrease their genuine freedom. Females have to get their freedom, not insult males.

Million Wings feels that males have benefits from freedom of females. Firstly, responsibilities of their security decrease. If girls get education, then they can think about their future, then boys have not to worry much about their future. If girls want to do outdoor work, then she can earn her living herself and boys needn't worry much about her requirements. If girls can move outside, then she can able to do some of her work herself and obviously responsibilities of boys will decrease. If girls rightly understand the good or bad, genuine or non-genuine, sensible and senseless things, then obviously she can make better and safe personal decisions then fear for their security will decrease. If a girl will search for a life partner of her choice, then only canboys be able to marry the girl of his own choice. If a girl can roam freely in society, obviously then only can a boy roam with a girl freely anywhere in the world. If a girl will rightly understand the feelings/emotions like love affairs, flirting, care, affection, sex, and enjoy this, then only can boys fully enjoy these emotions. Million Wings feels that firstly if a girl will feel happy then only will she be able to make males happy. Million Wings feels that girls and boys combined/together have to increase/give rights or respect of equal freedom. Girls and boys have to move together, not suppress each other.

Million Wings feels that finding girl alone, a few idiots and corrupt people try to dosome non-genuine, unlawful act. It's true besides having strict law and rules, still sometimes it's unable to protect from these kinds of acts at that time, especially in places far away from public places where there is less interference of police and public. Million Wings feels that females should not go to these places alone, from where even a voice calling for help can't be heard. Females should know and be aware of new styles of protection so that they can ensure their security and protection more.

Million Wings feels that a person has to do whatever the heart says, dress up as you want, eat food which you like, do things you feel like, talk to one whom you like, study according to interest, choose the profession according to will, live your passion; that is, do things which you like, which give relaxation, which give happiness. Million Wings feels that mostly small/little things are known to be as per will, then what's wrong in it? To stop ourselves and our own ones to act as per will just by thinking what people will say is totally wrong, against happiness, is restriction, is forcefulness. Million Wings feels that one will assume the things whatever is their own intentions and nature. It's right, one will keep on saying that thing which is right according to him, may that fit common sense or not.

Million Wings feels that it's not like that whatever people says will be wrong only. But it's true that a few things which people say are right also. Ones who are people/others to us, we are also others/people to them. People withstand and people stand against. People guide people, sometimes with positive attitude and sometimes with negative attitude. Million Wings feels that society changes because of them who live by heart. These kinds of people are either carefree or unfazed whatever people may say but they do as their heart says, but by doing arguments or revolts. Million Wings feels that one should be clear to oneself. If we are clear and agree with ourselves, then think that the world is because of you only.

Million Wings feels that society has its own decorum and people live according to that. If someone changes decorum, then most people object to that. Million Wings feels that the right thing is to think according to the whole of the world. Million Wings feels that people say whatever they feel, will say obese to obese, dwarf to dwarf, tall to tall, fair to fair that means they'll say the same as natural things appear to them. Everyone can make their own views from their talks according to their experience, thinking and nature and will react according to that.

Million Wings feels that it's one's personal thinking whatever they say. They are right, it's not necessary the people who are good will motivate us, give us happiness, encourage us. But the ones who unnecessarily restrict, use wrong words, misbehave, those irritate us, irk us, make the atmosphere disturbed and suffocated. Actually if a human is clear, agreed, and sure at mental level, then collect the positive attitude by talks with these kinds of people and enjoy life. Do the same as they feel but with more improvement and security.

Being right or wrong is a personal point of view; one will have positive and others may have negative attitude about something. Everyone has their own process of being right or wrong. Why worry about that? Whatever feels right to us is right. That's happiness. It's difficult for a person to bring that change in the world which is objectionable at familiar and social level, but not impossible. Million Wings feels that the change which is more comfortable, beneficial, secure, caring, affectionate, beautiful, hopeful can feel good to everyone and everyone will accept that with little effort.

Million Wings feels that people wants to change each other according to their thinking as everyone likes their own thinking. Million Wings feels that everyone is right at their place, whatever they think, but it's not necessary that which match balanced thinking too. Everyone is right at their place. One has open thinking and another has narrow thinking, then how they have plausible mutual relations? Both may have narrow thinking or both should have broad thinking, then the coordination can be managed. But who is more right can be decided if there is impartial, open, and balanced thinking, which can be based on reality and for rightness. Million Wings feels that whenever a tension or grief enters our life, irritates us, then firstly we need to think that it should not be because of our own narrow thinking, as these problems can be resolved in seconds.

Million Wings feels that persons themselves want to get those changes which are related with human nature and will, but may not able to begin. It's good to spend time in another society and atmosphere for sometime but permanent change is possible; if it's better or fine, then earlier. Either people choose the place according to their choice or guide family, friends, relatives about the benefit of new, better, and comfortable thinking and convince them to understand and accept that change. Permanent change can be possible by clearance and convincing by fight and forcefulness. It's powerful. Million Wings feels, do everything/anything but by secure way. Victory is to fulfil desires more securely.

Million Wings feels that only we know about our happiness and we will act according to that. But thinking of a few people may create tensions or problems. We will live as we want but our dreams and desires should not be our weakness so that idiots and the corrupt can misuse that and hurt our self-respect and emotions. Million Wings feels that while we are fulfilling our social limitations and fit in common sense, then we can do everything, whatever we want to do. Then anyone may say anything. If we are fulfilling logical respect and possibilities, then just for other people we needn't restrict each other, needn't be restricted just because of fear of relatives and society. Instead we need to motivate each other to live more securely and in managed ways.

Million Wings feels that a person himself has to take the first step to fulfil his needs, dreams and desires. Happiness is our own dreams and so firstly we ourselves have to do effort to fulfil those dreams. A person himself has to find ways for satisfaction. If we do effort, take a step, then people themselves start joining and help and guide us. No one can help others, one can't take a step forward. If firstly the person himself will raise his voice against personal exploitation, then only will othersable to support him. Firstly we ourselves have to raise a step for our freedom. It's true, it's right, it's correct. A stentorian voice against familiar and professional exploitation is a beginning for freedom.

Million Wings feels that may it be personal dreams or may need relief from personal extortion, in every case firstly we ourselves have to take a strong step as only then other people, friends, relatives, or organizations can help easily. Another can do something only if a human himself first shows courage.

Million Wings feels that change for betterment can be done in plausible way too. It's not necessary to do revolt to change the world for betterment, but change can be brought by plausible, peaceful, and friendly way too. May work be easy or difficult, it's not necessary to do that by a serious way only. Instead efforts can be tried by plausible and devotional way too and that way may give equal or better result (be sincere but not serious). It's useful to give stress on real feeling, emotion, and explanation on logical basis. Million Wings feels that it's easy to ensure corrupt and stupid people can't harm people of own family, society, and nation. It's necessary to make our own ones understand, maybe by love or force. Million Wings feels that thinking of person increases, widens and becomes plausible if they come out of own family and meet and converse with people of society, nation. Million Wings feels that if persons meet each other, then he can be free from his limited and restricted thinking and it's a strong step towards personal happiness. It's education, it's personal development, it's true, it's a secret of happiness. Million Wings feels that when people talk, say, making understand or complaining at loud voice, then the first meaning of this is to say on point stressfully and jealousydoesn't always mean enmity. Million Wings feels that another has to listen if issues are strong. Million Wings feels that strong and powerful weapon to bring change in society is exchange of views of thinking level to make it more open, wide, optimistic, and balanced and to give new direction to society. Satisfactory questions can bring change. Clearly describing all things can bring change. To link everything rightly can bring change. Question and answer is change. Arising curiosity is change.

Million Wings feels that there should be more open possibilities of open, wide, optimistic, and balanced views in society. Everyone should get the right motivation, guidance, and opportunities. To fulfil these dreams there should be fewer restrictions and limitations but if someone is crying then it should not be tolerated at any cost instead it needs to handle them powerfully. Million Wings feels that everyone should live their life more freely but if trying to cross minimum decided social boundaries then, and he can't be spared, will get punishment according to humanism. Million Wings feels that the main motto of punishment is to erase wickedness, not human.

Million Wings feels that to fight or beat is not change but it's to teach a lesson or defeat another. It's true, power is needed for wicked people but there are very few corrupt people in society. But the limited and restricted thinking can be a challenge for change. In these circumstances, change can't be brought forcefully or by fighting and beating but permanent change can be brought by talking, exchanging views, making them understand, and making them agree. Million Wings feels that everyone is already so stuck and busy in their own lives and don't want to be stuck anymore. Those considerations which can break their tough knots and can give social satisfaction, benefits, and comfort, they will surely adopt that. Change can be brought by plausible way. It needs devotion, needn't be more serious. To increase thoughts of social benefit and comfort in society is real happiness for all. Arguments don't mean only to prove ourselves but they mean to make others agree with us. Real change is to make others agree with us. Million Wings feels then change comes/arises by arguments on different views and fights only increase tensions. It's normal to have differences in views but continuous question and answer in managed way will resolve these differences.

Criticism doesn't stop change but brings better change. Million Wings feels that the main aim of criticism is to tell, to give better suggestions along with telling faults, problems, and deficiencies. Arguments don't meant to knot issues but it's to prove ourselves right and make others agreeand making him own forever. Million Wings feels that positive, open, and balanced point of view should be increased by means of plausible and arranged talk in society so that there should be better, more powerful and plausible atmosphere in the society, world.

Chapter 45

Hope

Million Wings feels, love your dreams, love yourself, respect your dreams, respect yourself. Be courageous for your dreams. Do efforts for yourself. Efforts and tries are the beginning of success. Keep on trying something to fulfil your dreams, get knowledge about that, find ways, find methods. Don't accept defeat without doing efforts. There is satisfaction if we fail even after trying our best. There will be no regret in these conditions. Give the power of efforts to your dreams and they will surely start being fulfilled. Don't let yourself and your dreams alone, remain attached. Keep on doing till you can. If we try, then something will surely happen. If something will happen, then surely some new ways will arise, will raise, will get right directions from a few mistakes. If we will do the right efforts in the right direction then surely our needs, dreams, and desires will be fulfilled. If old dreams will be fulfilled, only then new dreams will arise and like this, every dream and desire will come true and humans will enjoy every happiness one by one. This is life, this is energy, this is happiness, this is redemption.

Whatever a human wants to do, he should do and surely the human will get some benefits and experience from his efforts. If one gets success then surely his needs, dreams, and desires will be fulfilled, and happiness will be all around. If he fails, then he will come to know about weakness and deficiencies and can make better decisions in future. He will not only think about one dream, but he will give attention to other dreams too. Failures force him to find some new better ways. One can feel sad and worried for sometime because of failure but it can't stay infront of strong will and desires for a long time. One has to judge, has to learn, has to make new strategies from one's mistakes and deficiencies, and then again has to take steps towards his dreams and desires with full power and capabilities and will surely get success in one's mission. Strong desires and will are life of efforts.

Million Wings feels that the aim of every human is his desires. One's dreams and desires are power and motivation of human life. Everyone lives for one's dreams and desires. Dreams may be of any type. Dreams are not good or bad, right or wrong, big or small, but our dreams are personal happiness and personal happiness is the main aim of life. Dreams and desires change according to time and it's right too. Nothing's wrong in that. As age, thinking, and situation change, in the same way desires and dreams also change and became better. A few small and big changes of dreams become part of the future's permanent dreams. Actually the dreams and desires which come to mind that time to time became motivation, goal, aim, and happiness of that time and along with this are preparation of the future's dreams. After fulfilling one dream, a human wants to fulfil his next dream, so what's wrong in this? After that the person is busy and makes efforts to fulfilthe next dream. Life moves on with the help of dreams and desires only. It's true, it's motivation, it's hope. Happiness is all about fulfilling every dream one after another. Sometimes even after much more efforts, we are unable to fulfil our dreams or fail to fulfil dreams, then so what? If a human can't get success then he becomes tense and feelings of failure disturb him, it's natural. A person firstly has to see, think that the hardwork, effort, direction, and guidance has gone in the way he wants. If the person has tried his best, but still he fails, then he is not responsible for failure. Unsuccessful plan and dreams of person never go in vain; instead it's foundation for fulfilment of future's better and more powerful dream. That's why even today's failure brings lots of experience which helps in fulfilling future's dream. Today's dreams and efforts are part of preparation of tomorrow's success. When person is sad, tense because of today's failure even that's also helpful in improving thinking.

Million Wings feels that failure is also a kind of success, a success which is giving surety for tomorrow's success. Every work takes some minimum process time to be successful. Often a few mistakes occur while working. Something unexpected often happens while working. But yes, process time of every work can be reduced. But every work has minimum process time, may that be any work. Million Wings feels that a few mistakes often occur while starting new work specially in the beginning, which can be reduced but can't be decreased to zero. By taking advice from experienced person, we can surely get help in getting success by more accurate ways.

Million Wings feels that one can easily understand the base of success by thinking according to world, society. Everyone has his own dream, may that be already happening in the world and maybe one's dream can be new. Which he is doing first time, no one has listened to that till date. Million Wings feels that if a person's dream is that about which full knowledge of pro and cons, advantage and disadvantage, etc. is available, then the person has to collect full knowledge about work and working process so that the time, money, mind, resources should not be wasted on repeating same mistakes. Intelligence is in learning from others' mistakes. It's even right to do, because failure is not a lesson for only that person but also gives positive guidance to the whole world too. Failures, mistakes, deficiencies are making human success better, more comfortable, effective resources, and thinking from centuries and it will continue. It's a truth of success and will remain so. Mistakes are tomorrow's hope. Deficiencies are tomorrow's hope; failure is tomorrow's ray of hope. Keep on moving with this ray of hope and will surely get more happiness and success, today, tomorrow, and always.

Million Wings feels that if one is not getting the response he want, not able to express himself, then he should increase his resting (sleeping) time; that may be bit beneficial.

Million Wings feels that sometimes a person is stuck in some ambiguity. Ambiguity means to be stuck in some other work or mind is stuck in some thought or feeling and he is not getting any way out. What to do and what to not? A person gets into depression, miserableness, dispiritedness. Every human feels stuck in ambiguity at one time or another, sometimes escaping from one ambiguity and becoming stuck in another. The human may feel forlorn and powerless, maybe person is not able to express himself to anyone.

Actually the main tension and greed is that which can't be shared, or feels difficult to express.

Million Wings feels that person needn't worry or be tensed, as there must be some way out in nature. For every ambiguity in nature, there is a hidden solution for every problem. A person just needs to realize, feel, and use the universe's nature and other creature has capability, has secret to eliminate, to get rid of every tension and problem is human just need to find that in his surroundings. So let's come and try to pull out the human from ambiguity. Nothing is right or wrong. Things which are unprofitable are wrong. Bring right or wrong is just comparison point of view. Whatever are one's dreams and desires, do efforts for those only. Then what is wrong in this? So while doing efforts a person may be stuck in problems, tension, failures, so what's wrong in it? Maybe stuck in ambiguity, so what? Again find a new way to come out. If person is stuck in ambiguity because of himself, than to find way out, he has to see that is it due to his personal tension, narrow thinking, or misunderstanding, as this problem can be resolved in seconds. The world will look alike as we think about it. It's not necessary that another will think the same as us or can say that what we want or think the same as the rest of world or others are thinking that there can be ambiguity because of difference in views. Million Wings feels that it's everyone's right to think according to themselves, but it's important to know how far or near he is to open, wide, optimistic, and balanced thinking. Every person is right at his place but it's difficult to decide who is more right or more wrong.

Million Wings feels that to know and understand all humans, use a more practical and balanced point of view according to humans. There are numerous views in world. Narrow to broad thinking is there in the world.

Million Wings feels that personal thinking and views matter, are important. If another also thinks the same, than there will be good coordination. Otherwise, differentiation will exist. It doesn't matter whether a person has wide or narrow thinking, but what matters is plausible coordination between two. If there is difference in the thinking of the two, then the person with narrow thinking suffers more, as this thinking became the reason for pain and grief as person with open and wide thinking feels restricted. Million Wings feels that it's difficult, tough to restrict the open and wide thinking; instead it's more logical to spread open wide thinking. In future, thinking will be open and wide not narrow and restricted. It's more comfortable to increase freedom instead of living with restricted and limited thinking. The person with narrow and limited thinking is stuck more in ambiguity instead of person with open and wide thinking.

As person with open and wide thinking lives tension free and easy-going. Million Wings feels that if a person changes his thinking, then the world can change for him. If thinking is open and wide then life will seem to be more open and wide. A person has to free himself from his narrow and limited thinking. As this kind of thinking can give nothing else than pain & grief. As open, wide, optimistic and positive thinking keeps on improving our life day by day and frees us from unnecessary tension, doubts, and worries. By which human can understand and manage his feeling in a better way. By which life will became more beautiful. Open thinking opens ways for happiness. Humans need to understand that it's also important to balance our thinking along with open, wide, optimistic thinking. Million Wings feels that our life will be more beautiful comfortable and enjoyable if we leave unnecessary social restriction and responsibilities. Let's come and free ourselves from feeling of weakness, failure, and move forward with positive attitude. Everyone in society needs to concentrate on important issues, on which are be related to happiness on big scale not those issues which increase restrictions, tension, or distance or difference in relation. Friend! Now we have to think about life with new and practical way.

We need to discuss clear and describe every issue with absolute practical, social, impartial, comfortable, assured, and more emotion way. We all should have same opportunities and freedom so that we can know about more possibilities and choose the most suitable. Million Wings feels that a person needn't change his dreams and desires and needn't blame himself; instead he has to widen his thoughts and rules. So that there is more open, wide and balanced and then mutual understanding will start improving by which one can easily escape from ambiguity. If ambiguity is due to some mistake or lie, then confess to the related person, it's the easy way to come out from ambiguity. If related person is elder and intelligent, then tell him clearly the whole matter and reasons behind that and listen to him. If the other is younger, innocent or less intelligent than express yourself in managed way and try your best to handle the other person. Give time to that person to understand and forgive and wait for the right time. That will be his personal decision to what to do and then act and react according to that decision. Million Wings feels that if intention is to clear and settle the things then everything will be allright soon. If ambiguity is due to some third person(like blackmailing misunderstanding) then talk to confidential person or elder as early as possible; everything, anything can be done with unity. Million Wings feels that there is no one alone in this world. There must be some friends or relatives, or atleast law and government are there for everyone or social working organizations or media will surely provide some help. Always remember that there must be someone to help.

The person in ambiguity in which he is stuck is the world's biggest issue for him and even it's right too. It's important to come out of ambiguity than the rest of the work. Million Wings feels that the issue which is in mind 24 hours, and disturbs us isthe most important, may that be small or complicated. Everyone's personal issues are their priority and their solutions are their need. While a person is not free and satisfied from his issue and ambiguities, he will keep on thinking about that only, will be stuck in that only. He will not be able to concentrate on another issue and things and to help him in coming out of these ambiguities is a step towards happiness.

Million Wings feels that sometimes a person stuck on some ambiguity and wants to come out from that. But personal, familiar, social or professional problem lowered the strength of a person. The person feels sad and went under feelings of hatred and loneliness, which are serious problems or tries to express his sorrow or problem by one or another way. Million Wings feels that firstly, the person himself has to take a step to come out of ambiguity. He himself has to ask for help, has to find people with same thinking, same mentality, courage/guts of being independent is the secret to come out of any ambiguity, may person be rich or poor, maybe alone or with friends, maybe a girl or boy, educated or uneducated, villager or modern, younger or elder. If he himself tries/wants, then only he can enjoy personal happiness and freedom. We can make our own ones understand by respect and love. But if they don't understand or agree, then also don't be on knees. Keep on working hard to fulfil your dreams and desires and grab your happiness may be it need to do revolt also.

Million Wings feels that person always confuses in ambiguity of relation. A few are by-birth relations parents, siblings, and a few are made by ourselves, by our own will e.g. life partners, children. Humans' dreams and desires of life keep on changing, before marriage, after marriage, after having kids. A human tries to fulfil his dreams and desires and life keeps on moving. Million Wings feels that the dreams which become passion, the desires which become interests, and the will become aim of life that takes much of his time (e.g. social worker, love, bad habits). If their dreams, will, desires become their permanent aim, passion, interest afterwards also remain the same, then priority of marriage and children change and responsibility of only parents remains. Permanent relations don't demand just time but also demand quality time and the person who is busy with some passion or aim is always remain busy with his dream and desires. Permanent relation demands/needs time, not only the company, and being busy with themselves only.

Million Wings feels that the person who develops these kind of dreams after marriage and kids, for them it's hard to handle life. A person remains busy with his dreams or tries to know that but permanent relation like lifepartner and kids also demand time. In these conditions, either family or person himself or both feels bounded along with being loved. This ambiguity really makes person sad and stuck. Million Wings feels that in these circumstances after marriage a person may leave all other relations other than by-birth relations and relations of heart and can utilize that saved time for himself. To give quality time to our near and loving ones is like relations and entertainment or you can say that everyone needs a break and change, the best way of which is to spend time with loved ones.

Million Wings feels that approximately 8 hours rest, 8 hours work, 8 hours to spend with your loved ones, near and dear ones and can use for their dreams. Human can't work day and night for all the time. He has to manage some time for his rest and entertainment, as human will be bored by doing same work all the time as mind also needs change and rest for sometime atleast.

Million Wings feels that a person is entrapped in truth and lies of relations. Normally every person gives more time and compromises more in starting of every relations and work. So that he can understand more and more. There is nothing wrong in doing so; infact it's right. Sometimes a person lies in starting. A person grabs happiness with the help of small or big lies. Maintain coordination in relations; this sequence keeps on increasing. Million Wings feel that while intentions are good, it hardly matterswhether person is telling the truth or is lying but it's necessary to maintain the coordination if a person lies in any circumstance or situations, then he is doing so just for happiness and benevolence of all. Balance and trust is maintained while coordination of lie will be maintained. It's easy for a person to make balance and coordination of lie in starting but if it's elongated then it seems to be difficult to carry that and person feels stuck in ambiguity. Person feels it difficult to balance and compromise with their work and time. This happiness often, as it's difficult for person to cutshort his responsibilities and work for a long time. Because of this, coordination of the balance and adjustment disturbs.

Million Wings feels that person is tangled in intense dilemma in these conditions. It's not only hard but seems impossible too, do accept the truth. Demand of relations remainsthe same. Other person also has the same hope which was earlier and their lies also start coming forward. Million Wings feels that to come out of lie and move towards truth is not easy. Tension of hurting them along with losing them worries our mind.

It's easy for a person in starting to make a balance of lie. But when a lie is stretched to some limit, then it's difficult to stretch a lie and the person feels very confused and there is responsibility of taking care of the other person too. The main cause which obstructs person to move towards truth from lie is fear of self-depression and a feeling of shame. Million Wings feels that if the intention of the person is to make permanent relations, till then it hardly matters whether the person has spoken truth or has lied. But person should try to move towards truth from lie as early as possible.

Million Wings feels that firstly, a person needs to be good and to be true can be the next step. Whenever a person feels to move towards truth by overcoming lie then he should surely try his best to overcome that, as only truthfulness can give calmness and peace of mind in permanent relations. As lie can give temporary happiness and truth can provide tension-free permanent happiness. When a person tries to move towards a balance of truth from balance of lie by same strategy the way he planned for lie. Use the same strategy to link up truth and opt such a way that other person should not get hurt and then truth will merge with lie in a very planned way, and happiness given by lie will convert into happiness of truth. If a person has made temporary relations on basis of lie and the other is attached by heart and carries on relations then it will be a more confusing and problematic situation as this situation along with lie becomes betrayal also. In these situations, it's good to break that relationship as early as possible to save ourselves. Now it depends on other person, whether he goes under depression or feels to take revenge. The best way to avoid these circumstances is to break a relationship respectfully so that the person himself can also be saved. Always remember if person alone is unable to give answers of betrayal then he can join hands with someone else to answer and to do this is right and logical. Million Wings feels that to betray anyone for personal benefit on first basis is totally wrong, illogical.

Another confusion is that when one is attached with love and affection and wants to attach in permanent relations and person is confused regarding relations. Million Wings feels that if another also feels the same by his presentation then it's right, logical. A person should spend some minimum time of 6–12 months to clear this confusion before making any permanent relation, as an individual can't carry on flirting, lies, or betrayal for a long time. If the intention is to attach by love and affection, then relations will be same today, tomorrow, and always. Atleast there will be no change in nature of affection and care, may person manage less time or may priorities change. Million Wings feels that person can make any type of relations, maybe of flirting, affection, friendship, love, or marriage. Nothing is wrong in making any relations. But remember that person is only answerable for that thing which he has promised about. The thing which he has not promised, neither has he any responsibility for that nor has he any liability for the same. Million Wings feels, just be clear to the related person regarding every promise. You needn't explain to whole world.

Million Wings feels that whilethe person is alive and is able to manage himself, then everything can be corrected. The biggest sorrow is death of someone who is close to us, which can't be replaced by anything else in the world, neither can it be fulfilled. The second sorrow is that tension which a person can't share with anyone or can't express to anyone or a disease which is incurable. Another sorrow is betrayal. All other sorrows are of lower level. While a human is alive and independent, then everything can be managed. Million Wings feels that making the right and best decision according to knowledge and thinking is humans' working process. But if still it fails, then a person should not worry or be sad. A person can just try his best in every condition and situation, then results may be good or bad. Why worry about good or bad results? Infact make the best decision in that condition also as per knowledge and thinking and let this sequence go on. It's right, it's logical, it's the future. Humans should firstly have to look at true intentions and efforts of each other, other than results or we can say not only results.

Million Wings feels that desires and habits of person are said to be wrong or become wrong when the ways of fulfilling them are wrong. Habits like sex, drugs, fights are not wrong. But giving right conclusion to them at right place, right time in right way is logical. When elders directly say no to these things without any discussion to the younger, then curiosity arises in them. Even being in boundaries and restrictions, they use wrong ways and do the same for which they are restricted and entangled in problems. If these things are told or taught to children and understood at social level by elders, friends, teachers, and other great personalities, then all the natural and human dreams and desires can be enjoyed fully.

Million Wings feels that hope resides in possibilities and possibilities are around us. Whatever seems to be more right in problematic situations, a person has to opt for that only, and everyone picks the best of possibilities according to their own thinking and planning and epitomized happiness of life. Sometimes a person fumbles, worries, is tense or afraid in a difficult time. That's why he wasn't able to understand what to do and what not. There are many possibilities around him, but he is unable to recognize them.

When a person himself feels depressed, helpless, forlorn, powerless, then he got disappointed and he is unable to look for possibilities filled with hope. Hope is somewhere around us only. If we think calmly, then a ray of hope is easily seen. Thinking calmly and with relaxed mind and then looking for possibilities all around us gives some positive light of hope and then working according to that strategy helps to come out from any/every problem. God firstly looks at intention (good/bad) of person and then working strategy or work done. Prayer done with devotion is accepted by God and God in return provides possibilities filled with hope. The more the prayer done with devotion, the earlier and clearer possibilities of hope a person will get. Million Wings feels that before losing hope fully, a person should once pray devotedly and think calmly and surely some hope will arise from already present possibilities and show path and give energy to life.

Million Wings feels that the mistake which is felt by ourselves should be accepted heartily and covenanting to do the work in a better way or not to repeat the same is flawless power. Million Wings feels that profit and loss are part of life. Loss is loss, loss of personal hardwork and obviously it is painful. Everything of the world which can be regained is less bothersome than those things which can't be regained (e.g. life). Less loss is better than more loss, temporary loss is better than permanent loss. Million Wings feels that it's OK if a few fruits of the tree are destroyed and the tree is all right, as fruits can be regained. If a person is all right, then he can regain everything again. Million Wings feels, don't do any natural loss if there is loss as per worldliness.

To think negatively is not wrong while it's giving positive direction to life. Every aspect has positive and negative sides, has possibilities. Positive thinking gives energy, increases desire, helps in getting success. Negative thinking alerts us, helps in getting better strategies and capacities, decreases problems. Million Wings feels that there is success if we think positiveand if there is alertness along with positive thinking, then it's better to get success. Listen carefully to talks or sayings of people who have negative thinking, as we can be alert from their talks and can fulfil our dreams with fewer problems. A person with negative attitude may not do anything by themselves in life, but their negative attitude, point of view, and experience are really helpful to other people.

Million Wings feels that negative thinking is not any obstruction in fulfilling dreams and desires; infact it helps in fulfilling them more securely. Million Wings feels that for greater betterment of work, it's better to know about negative effects and sides of work so that it can be managed in better ways and provides more security to success. People with negative thoughts have equal importance as people with positive thoughts. Important is what we think, what we do, what we extract from negative thoughts of a person with negative thinking, not his thinking. Million Wings feels that to move on in life and to fulfil dreams and desires, it's devotion which matters. It's not about good or bad dreams, but devotion to fulfil them matters. It's not sure that positive thinking will give success only and negative will harm self-confidence. When an individual has to fulfil his dreams and desires then negative and positive attitude don't contraindicate each other; infact both are helpful in their own way. Positive attitudes give energy and power and negative attitudes alert us. The best tries according to person to fulfil his dreams and desires and to achieve happiness is logical power energy. Positive and negative attitude are those aspects of life which increase self-confidence and provide benefit in every circumstance.

Million Wings feels that people with negative thoughts themselves remain there or get destroyed. Listen to talks of negative people in such a way that you can get personal benefit from that. Talks of negative people are like that sugarcane from which a person can extract sweet juice and throw the rest of the waste. Prayer with devotion is very powerful. A person prays to God and God provides possibilities filled with hope. Million Wings feels that every individual has different circumstances. If a person closely look at circumstances, they may appear some but if person sees every circumstance in detail, then they are different and it will show the right direction, e.g. if person see just part of a picture then it will not be clear whether the red colour is blood or flower. The colour of two picturesmay be the same but it's not necessary that all colours together will make the same painting, i.e. circumstance can be one for two individuals but life of every individual is different. If our one circumstance matches with painful circumstance of other, then negative thoughts may be born in the mind. But hope of happiness arises by looking at all circumstances together.

A person judges about circumstances according to his own circumstances and experience and everything is all right. But an individual clearly comes to know about the possibility of all guesses after knowing the circumstances properly. A person may think, understand, guess anything but along with that, try to know the real circumstances as early as possible. By doing so, a person will make a fast and successful decision and the person will get personal satisfaction and peace of mind.

Million Wings feels that persons are motivated by lives of each other. Circumstances and working strategy of each other makes personswiser.

If a person is tense or confused, then he has to read and understand true facts related to myths based on human life. Surely there will be a way out. Someone's life can make others' lives beautiful and better. Experience of individual gives motivation, guidance, and self-confidence to others. Million Wings feels that most issues regarding which person is tense are either happening with someone else also or have already happened. A person becomes more capable and wise by learning from experience and strategies of other people. A person's life acts as motivation, confidence and hope for life. Whenever a person feels alone and loses hope, then he can read biographies of personalities; he will surely feel confident and tensions and problems will start wiping off.

If a person is worried and loses self-confidence because of non-genuine, arrogant nature or mannerless behaviour of some other person, institute, organization, then he should not even think of committing suicide; infact individual should tell the reality to the whole world. It's better to fight and die than waste life (to die) committing suicide so that only the sinner/ guilty should suffer, not innocent, and other weak persons should also get motivation, ray of hope. It's better to fight against crime, raise voice, bring change in society than to commit suicide. It's the right decision.

Million Wings feels that to cure one's disease, it's the patient himself who has to take care of himself and own ones have to help him. If a person is sick, he has to handle it calmly and carefully as disease is not that enemy which can be shot but can be cured by keeping ourselves calm and by taking care of ourselves. The more the patient will do forcefulness with himself, the more it will worsen and will harm. Million Wings feels that to cure disease is like making a child fall asleep who can sleep only calmly, not by making him afraid of beating him; instead he starts crying on doing so. Million Wings feels that health doesn't mean 100 per cent all right or 100 per cent free from disease; instead taking care of ourselves means health. Independence physically and mentally is being healthy. Logical meaning of health is that he is able to handle himself.

Million Wings feels that a human may be wrong, corrupt but always wants that others should make him understand in soft ways. It's a ray of hope, hope to do everything right. When a near or dear one does something wrong, then everyone scolds him for their well-being only. To do this is not wrong; neither is any wrong thing there. It's necessary to understand that when elders or brother/sister scold us, then their real motive is not to fight or scold; infact they want to make us understand and want their benevolence. Elders scold also, understand that the younger don't make mistakes knowingly or intentionally; infact it happens by innocence. Elders should also need to understand intensions and circumstances and, according to that, have to make them understand. While talking to them, they should give them a genuine chance to explain their things. If a sinner has surety that his/her near and dear one will understand him/her and will make a decision according to his/her circumstances, then he/she tries to improve himself/herself with a great hope.

Million Wings feels that the present surely has some way for the future's dream. It may not be any clear way but surely has some small opportunities or ways. The present is derived from the past and this present is raw material for the future too. Try to make true our future's desires from today's available ways. The future's need may be whatsoever; everything is available in the present, which can be combined to make new things, services, products. Million Wings feels that analyzing the present from every aspect, it will surely have something for every desire of the future.

Million Wings feels that humans' feelings and respect are more important than his/her body. A person may have multiple physical relations but emotional affection makes relationsdeeper and more permanent. Million Wings feels that problem, tension, failure is surely planning something good, beautiful happiness and better direction for future. It's true.

Million Wings feels that God has already kept the solution of every problem in nature and this universe. If a person is entangled in some problem or tension and he is not getting any satisfactory answers in this system of worldliness, then he will surely get some solution from nature and the universe. A human needs to understand his problems by connecting them to nature; the person will surely find some plausible solution. Solution of every problem related to human life is hidden in plausible ways in management of oceans, stars, moon, sun, life of another species, fragrance of flowers, development of plants and trees. Ofcourse the best machine so far is the human himself. Understanding the human body is understanding management.

Million Wings feels that every human has to give a start to his dreams and desires by himself; only then all the ways open by themselves. God surely helps those who have true intentions and strong commitment. It's that truth which a person feels a lot of times. God is that hope which can't be destroyed by any enemy, worst situation, sorrow, or restriction. The real work of God is hope, which is the biggest power to adjoin with happiness of heart. True tries and personal confidence is liked by God and that gives wings of happiness to hope. It's true, it's happiness, it's secret.